TRANSFORMING CALIFORNIA

*Published in cooperation with
the Center for American Places,
Sante Fe, New Mexico, and
Harrisonburg, Virginia*

Stephanie S. Pincetl

TRANSFORMING CALIFORNIA

A Political History of Land Use and Development

The Johns Hopkins University Press Baltimore & London

© 1999 The Johns Hopkins University Press
All rights reserved. Published 1999
Printed in the United States of America on
acid-free paper

9 8 7 6 5 4 3 2 1

The Johns Hopkins University Press
2715 North Charles Street
Baltimore, Maryland 21218-4363
www.press.jhu.edu

Library of Congress Cataloging-in-Publication
Data will be found at the end of this book.
A catalog record for this book is available from
the British Library.

ISBN 0-8018-6110-1

Contents

Preface and Acknowledgments

THIS BOOK is about California's land and the historical evolution of the political institutions that have regulated its use and development. Land in California has particular significance because of its extraordinary beauty, richness, and diversity. But California is not the only state where land has played a uniquely significant role; American history and evolution has been shaped by land issues.

The early settlers came to a continent that was already inhabited, but colonists treated it as though it was theirs to take. American democracy arose out of the desire for even greater freedom than the British crown was able to offer, and its institutions and ideology were shaped by the experience of the possibility of free land and expansion forever westward. Jeffersonian democracy was founded on the belief in independent, rural, yeoman farmers with a great deal of local autonomy and control over a decentralized state structure. Such a system, where states would govern themselves and the federal government would act to protect individuals' rights and property, demanded an active citizenry involved in governance decisions that affected their locality, their places. It was possible only where land was freely abundant and unencumbered, where free men could own land in their own names. In this manner, land and its availability has had a profound influence on America's political identity and institutions.

California became a state only in 1850, at a time when much of the rest of the country had already been explored and was in the process of becoming settled. Its unusual concentration of land ownership belied Jeffersonian agrarianism and set up a dynamic tension between the ideology of democracy, based on a large number of independent farmers, and the reality of huge latifundios that rapidly passed into the hands of sophisticated corporate-type farmers and land syndicates. This book explores the political history of land use in California and the complex nexus of land, democracy, and citizenship.

Today Jeffersonian democracy no longer corresponds to the political, economic, and social reality of the nation, yet its ideological vestiges remain. Combined with Progressivism—a strong political reform movement at the turn of the twentieth century which was based on many of the ideas of liberalism regarding the role of the individual and of the state—Jeffersonian ideals have continued to inform politics. These ideals fundamentally contradict late twentieth-century life and have led to the political gridlock and cynicism that prevail today. One has only to look at the processes of land-use planning to see the dysfunctionality of current political institutions. Land-use planning is the jealously guarded prerogative of local governments, competing fiercely for any revenue-generating activity, willing to sacrifice well-paid jobs for sales tax revenues and to give tremendous incentives with little regard to regional transportation, housing, health, school facilities, open space, jobs, the environment, or other greater concerns. This ability to make local decisions is ferociously defended in the name of democracy, democratic accountability, and local independence. Yet each locality forms part of a geographic and political web that constrains the effect of local decisions—whether the decisions concern pollution that is generated all around or the building of new, larger roads the next city over that will dump traffic. Many other dysfunctionalities exist, which this book will explore and explain.

I have been driven to write this book as a native of California who has observed the tremendous changes in the landscapes that have occurred in a relatively short period of time. I am also a lover of cities, of public spaces where people come together as social beings to see and be seen; California's patterns of urbanization are quite the opposite of such cities. Instead, Californians are isolated from one another, and our public spaces are now malls. The state's sociological composition has also changed dramatically since my youth, becoming far more ethnically diverse in terms of numbers. California is now a place where hundreds of languages are spoken, where many different cultures contribute to making it one of the most interesting and dynamic parts of the nation. Yet the predominant feeling seems to be one of alienation: alienation from others, from politics, from involvement in our democracy. For me, this book has been an attempt to understand these phenomena and to formulate a vision for a renewal of our democratic spirit and process. We do not sufficiently appreciate the potential that exists among us to create vibrant and nurturing places to live in this wondrous state called California.

It is a cliché to say that a book is not written solely by the author but is the product of the efforts and input of the community surrounding that person. Nonetheless, that is certainly the case in this work. My parents have played a large role in the formation of my values and political orientation. Their confidence in my abilities and their material help and constant encouragement over the past several years have been important in sustaining my writing. My graduate studies in anthropology at the University of California, Davis, where I was exposed to rigorous critical thinking contributed to the approach I have taken in addressing issues of land use. Earning my Ph.D. degree in the Graduate School of Architecture and Urban Planning at the University of California, Los Angeles, exposed me to some of the sharpest minds in planning of the time. I am grateful to all those with whom I worked during that period.

Living in Los Angeles itself has been a tremendously valuable learning process, and for that experience and his unwavering confidence, loyalty, and continuous support, I thank Jonathan Katz, my husband. A Ciriacy-Wantrup Fellowship from the University of California, Berkeley, was the critical factor in providing me the time to write the manuscript, and I thank those who made it possible. Thanks too to Carmen Concepción for her friendship during that period and afterward. Dick Walker was extremely helpful, providing me with institutional shelter and reading and commenting on the manuscript in a detailed way. John Walton was also a meticulous reader and pushed me to better elaborate my ideas. Jeff Lustig's comments contributed to a stronger conclusion, and his enthusiasm for the project was uplifting. Thank you, too, to the anonymous reviewers whose comments I incorporated to the best of my ability; the errors, omissions, and inconsistencies remain my own. My editorial consultant, Colleen Daly, forced me to be more precise, to articulate and bring to the fore the underlying ideas that had prompted the writing of the book. One could not wish for a more competent, tough, and wonderful human being to work with. Without Victor Reiner's patient assistance, this manuscript would have never been formatted correctly; my thanks to him. Finally, I have to thank Basil and Sophie, who have lived with this project for several years of their still young lives, looking forward to its completion, and to the book party.

Introduction

CALIFORNIA: Just the name conjures up visions—wealth, escape, creative futures, El Dorado, Hollywood, the Sierra Nevada mountains, Big Sur, the Pacific Ocean, San Francisco, the Golden Gate Bridge, Disneyland, the redwoods, and maybe Death Valley. California's landscapes, its land uses, its physicality are intimately bound up in its mythology. Yet little attention has been given to how and why the state's landscapes have changed in the ways they have and what these changes imply for its future. This book attempts to capture the transformation of California land over time and to explain the changes by looking at the state's political structures. Theda Skocpol remarks in *Protecting Soldiers and Mothers* that it is important to take seriously processes of state formation and patterns of political organization, and to notice how these intersect in varied ways with economic and social transformations. What government does and how it does it has significant effects on society and its physical infrastructure, on people, urbanization, and nature. Skocpol goes on to observe that Americans typically write and speak as though the United States were just a collection of self-reliant individuals and local or occupational communities, tied together by a competitive marketplace and an impersonal Constitution. But Americans, and Californians, have a very particular set of governing institutions that need to be examined if we are to understand current circumstances.[1]

It is my contention that California's political paralysis, environmental degradation, and economic inequality are due, in large part, to the structure of the state's systems of governance from local city halls to Sacramento. By examining the evolution of these systems historically and through the lens of land use, I aim to elucidate how and why contemporary California finds itself polarized along race and class lines, following a path of continued environmental degradation, and gripped by cynicism about government. In so doing, I hope to reveal why public participation and democratic self-governance have declined precipitously and why most of the state's population is alienated from its own democratic institutions. I focus on issues of land use and natural resource management because of the importance of a sense of place in the social movements that have proliferated in California. These include movements for the preservation of the redwoods and the Sierra Nevada mountains, for local growth control, for property tax relief, for retention of public access to the state's coastline, for small farms, and for the livability of inner cities that have endured over time. Place embodies contradiction and paradox, but it is an experience common to all and one that evokes strong sentiments.[2] It is the context in which people carry on their daily lives or assume the role of tourists. Place has powerful symbolic importance, and how it is constructed strongly affects people's quality of life and daily interactions. Disparities between older inner cities and new suburbs are part of the experience of place and are a result of land-use policies, regulations, and hidden subsidies. The rapid disappearance of indigenous fauna and flora in southern California is likewise a result of land-use policies, and that disappearance affects what place is like, as well as the relationship between humans and nature. The development of huge water conveyance systems in the state, transforming entire watersheds and ecological zones, is a significant factor in making and changing places—allowing irrigated agriculture to develop and cities to grow, while foreclosing other kinds of land use. But the overall direction of these changes and developments with regard to place rarely reaches significant public debate despite the direct impact on people's daily lives. This book examines why this has come about.

Places are generally regulated by local government—land uses are determined by locally elected and appointed officials—and so should be a reflection of public wants and desires, and their destinies should be decided through public dialogue and discussion. But as we shall see, institutional reforms, based on a liberal (in the classic sense of the term) ideology of government put in place at the turn of the twentieth century by the Progressive reform movement, have made democratic participation increasingly difficult over time—and place. Although I attribute many of today's political institutions and approaches to governance to the reforms introduced during the Progressive era, this is admittedly a simplification. Yet it is my hope that readers will understand how the particular political ideology—concerning the role of the individual in society, the role of government, and the relationship between society, the economy, and the state—that arose during this period has in its essence endured and is still manifest in the structure of our governing institutions today.

The book does not claim to be comprehensive; rather, it illustrates California's evolution over time through several topics—forest management, wildlife and fisheries, urban development, agriculture, and water use. These areas, which have proven among the most contentious historically, are also among the most significant in terms of land-use transformations in the state. I delve into the early history of the state simply to provide context, not to contribute original historiography, because without such background, it is more difficult to understand the present. For example, the legacy of the huge Spanish land grants has had enduring effects on the development of agriculture in the state and on patterns of urbanization as well. Without understanding this unique historical situation, combined with the patterns of land disposal of the federal government, it is hard to comprehend the patterns of settlement, the form of agriculture, and the forces of development in the state. My aim is to give the reader a synthetic and broad understanding of California's evolution through the political history of land use.

The book follows a historical timeline, beginning with the Gilded Age at the end of the nineteenth century and ending with the election of Governor Pete Wilson to his second term in the mid-1990s. There are several main themes: agriculture, water use, timber management, and urban land development in San Francisco and Los Angeles. I try to show how developments in each of these subject areas are but pieces of a whole cloth, woven from a shared ideology of the role of government and the place of business development. Similarly, I connect California to the national context, since federal government activities influenced state-level programs and policies.

Chapters 1, 2, and 3 provide the historical and theoretical foundation for understanding California politics in the contemporary period. They provide the warp and weft of the complex tapestry of the state's development and contain a great deal of detail necessary to the unfolding of the subsequent chapters.

Chapter 1 explains the legacy of the Spanish land grants, federal land-disposal policies, the beginnings of land concentration, and the emergence of land conglomerates that spanned the city and the countryside. The patterns of large-scale land ownership and corporate involvement were well established by the end of the nineteenth century. At the same time, the state's politics and social relations were deeply influenced by its immigrants and its position as a Spanish borderland.

Admitted to the Union in 1850, California attracted some of the nation's finest scientific minds, people curious to explore and understand the natural marvels of the new state. The rise of natural science studies, combined with Darwinism and the ideology of modernity, provided a fertile set of ideas for this scientific and entrepreneurial elite to test. They settled in the San Francisco Bay area and formed the core of what would become one of the nation's most visible and influential environmental organizations—the Sierra Club. In the early twentieth century they lent their strength to the Progressive movement.

In the late nineteenth century, there were movements for the preservation of the redwoods and the Sierra Nevada mountains, for the break-up of large landholdings, for the repatriation of Chinese workers, and, most prominently, for the end of the perceived stranglehold of the railroads on the state's political parties. Cities, especially San Francisco, were seen as corrupt (dominated by unions), inefficient, dirty, and poorly run. There was fear of the growing labor movement. Social movements, anti-Chinese sentiment, outrage at the extent of political corruption, and desire for a modern and efficient city and government all came together to form the Progressive movement.

In chapter 2 I address the complex factors that created the powerful Progressive movement for political reform, its political ideology, and the reforms that Progressives put in place. The election of Theodore Roosevelt in 1904 brought Progressive reform to the federal government. At the same time Progressive reforms were reinventing local government across the country. California followed a similar pattern. Progressive reforms were first adopted at the local level; then, in 1910, Hiram Johnson was elected Progressive governor of the state, charged with breaking the political power of the railroads and removing political party influence from state government. Most of today's well-known and accepted political institutions—the recall, the referendum, the initiative, special districts, and appointed boards and commissions—were put in place during the Progressive era. I examine these in some detail and explain how they were conceived and whom they were intended to assist. I examine the reasons for the deeply antipolitical stance of the Progressives and the perverse results of weakening party politics in government. This was a period of tremendous urban expansion, especially in southern California. Land speculation often played an important role in the process of land development, and those very same speculators helped mold Progressive politics. Progressive-era reforms were born from the needs of this expansionary period.

Chapter 3 treats the success of the land-owning elites in consolidating their assets during the years between the two world wars. They established rural dominance of the state through reapportionment, in alliance with urban chambers of commerce. The Depression caused tremendous immigrations into the state, which led to the formation of a rural and urban proletariat. With an economic downturn, issues of race again became heated, and Mexicans were deported from Los Angeles by the trainload. Attempts to better manage the state's resources through appointed boards and commis-

sions—which oversaw timber, fish and wildlife, agriculture, and conservation—demonstrated how the very structure of those commissions put into
power those with the strongest financial interest in regulation and resulted
in mixed allegiances and stalemate. This was the era of *business associationalism,* an approach first developed by Herbert Hoover. Alan Wolfe has described this as the "franchise state," wherein the frontier between the public
and private sectors becomes uncertain, with a substantial delegation of
public authority displaced from the state to quasi-private bodies, such as
boards and commissions, or special districts. Participation in the franchise
state requires a degree of political mobilization and economic clout generally out of reach of the ordinary citizen. Business associationalism, putting the state's police power (its authority to enact and enforce legislation)
at the service of powerful economic interests, was a natural outgrowth of
Progressivism and a significant step in removing decision-making institutions of the state from public accountability.

Post–World War II expansion is the topic of chapter 4, which examines
the effects of federal urban and land policy on California's land development. The chapter shows how the proliferation of special districts, appointed boards and commissions, and nonpartisan local politics further
contributed to wasteful land-use patterns and exacerbated regional inequalities, especially between cities and suburbs. Land conversion and infrastructure construction proceeded at a rapid clip. The aerospace industry
was growing, employing thousands of workers in the Los Angeles area. Bay
area cities were growing, federal highway funds were supplementing already ambitious California road-building efforts, trees were being felled, agricultural lands were being converted to suburban housing, large-scale agribusiness was flourishing, and universities and schools were being built. This
was a time of open horizons and no limits, artfully steered by Democratic
governor Pat Brown. But people were concerned about the uncoordinated
nature of this growth surge and the transformation of their once familiar
landscapes into something quite different. There was political and personal
frustration with the pace of development, and visions were set forth of a
possible alternative path for growth that would produce less waste and
would be more equitable. California Tomorrow, one of the most important
organizations proposing alternatives during the 1960s and 1970s, espoused
regional and environmental planning—an idea bolstered by the growing
environmental movement and indirectly nourished by the counterculture
and anti–Vietnam War protests. There were proposals for developing an environmental bill of rights, banning cars with internal-combustion engines,
prohibiting the clear-cutting of redwoods, and establishing regional governments with political power. Some proposals even made the floor of the legis-

lature, only to be voted down. Meanwhile, the state undertook to build the State Water Project, bringing more water to the Central Valley agribusiness corporations and assuring the continued urban expansion of southern California. Pressure continued for the reform of timber-harvesting practices.

One of the longest lasting changes of the 1960s, though, was reapportionment. This reestablished population-based senatorial representation, weakening the historic rural control over the legislature. With greater urban representation, environmental legislation was passed, the most significant of which was the California Environmental Quality Act. Nevertheless, the fundamental power structure remained in place, and visions of alternative paths for growth languished. The transformations, however, continued, making the visions ever harder to reach and fueling discontent at the grassroots level.

Chapter 5 is devoted to the tumultuous 1970s and the governorship of Democrat Jerry Brown. The early years of the decade ushered in a hope that old structures of power could be transcended; new ideas were introduced from the environmental movement, such as "small is beautiful" and the "era of limits," the latter in response to the energy crisis. It was a period when government-as-usual was challenged, as creative ideas of the counterculture, such as frugality and self-reliance, were fused with the paring down of government. The civil rights movement inspired a new approach, embracing the diversity of California's population and increasing minority representation in state government positions. Despite this heady start under Jerry Brown's leadership, what prevailed of these ideas was a strong antigovernment sentiment, represented by the property tax movement and culminating in the passage of Proposition 13, which drastically rolled back property taxes and ultimately provided a windfall for large-scale property owners.

This period helped determine the state's future direction, starting as it did with strong idealism, only to usher in conservative, antigovernment, business-led Republican rule. In this chapter I explain how government institutions failed to respond to genuine public concern about high rates of taxation and the problems created by the previous period of tremendous growth that led to highly inflated property values. Jerry Brown's inability to translate the rhetoric of responsiveness and accountability into genuine change opened the door for even greater skepticism and cynicism about government. It was not that Brown alone could have enacted the profound changes needed to revitalize democracy in the state, as a turn to the right was a nationwide phenomenon of the time. But he had symbolized an alternative vision in which people counted and in which, together, they could resolve some of the mounting problems. He had held out hope and fostered tremendous goodwill that was ultimately wasted and transformed into even greater alienation.

Chapter 5 also examines the events of the late 1970s and early 1980s that led to the demise of the provisions of the 1902 Newlands Reclamation Act that required owners of more than 160 acres of farmland who received federally subsidized water to sell their excess lands after ten years at pre-water prices or else pay the full cost of the water. The act applied to hundreds of thousands of acres in the Central Valley receiving water from the Central Valley Project. This was a major victory for large-scale farming corporations, allowing them to continue to receive publicly subsidized irrigation water.

Timber policy was also highly contentious during the Jerry Brown administration. Timber harvesting, especially of redwoods, was of great concern to the environmental community, which successfully pressed for legislation to create Redwood National Park. The Brown administration was in the middle of this environmental protection struggle and played an important role. I examine timber politics during this period and the perverse legacy of the Progressives' boards and commissions, showing how the appointment of representatives of the very interests to be regulated leads to stalemate and confrontation.

Urban politics in these years was no less frustrating, as all attempts to forge alternatives to the status quo failed in the face of intense and unrelenting opposition from development interests and local governments dependent on land development for their fiscal health. Over time, with the passage of Proposition 13, this situation has only become more dire.

Chapter 6 takes the reader through the 1980s and early 1990s. Polarization among interests, income levels, and racial groups only intensified, and land transformation continued unabated. City and county governments are now poorer and citizens more alienated, and land development is the primary means to increase local revenues. Faced with environmental degradation and continued environmentalist pressure, Republican governor Pete Wilson came up with ingenious methods to satisfy environmental concerns on paper, while he continued to sustain the "growth machine" in practice, developing methods to bypass or circumvent public participation and democratic process.[3]

The capstone of the century of transformation of the state through land development was the passage of the 1992 Central Valley Project Improvement Act, the culmination of years of struggle over water and land in the Central Valley. In response to several years of serious drought, tremendous environmental degradation in the Sacramento Delta from overpumping, and pressure from southern California water agencies and development interests in alliance with mainstream environmental groups, Congress voted to allow a certain percentage of federally subsidized water to be sold on the market by those holding the water allotments—mainly large-scale corporate farms. This new approach to water—clearly commodifying it—means that there will eventually be a profound transformation of the agricultural economy of the state in favor of urban development. Houses and factories use less water than agriculture and are highly profitable. Large agribusiness corporations can now more easily transform their landholdings into houses, and California's continued urbanization is assured. At the same time, precious little is being done about the increasingly precarious economic position of many of the state's residents and the fragile condition of the environment—water, air, fauna, and flora. Uncontrolled growth and continued urbanization along the same patterns will not improve these deteriorating environmental conditions or create conditions of democratic governance and accountability. The state's well-being has been reduced to the single issue of creating a good business climate, based on trickle-down economic theory. This does not make for a coherent society where people feel they are meaningful participants in political dialogue and decision making, nor will it necessarily lead to increased economic well-being overall. I hope that this book—a sort of political archeology—points to the structural reasons for the contemporary situation of political gridlock in Sacramento as well as in many California cities and can lead to a reevaluation of the perverse legacy of the Progressive-era reforms that are still providing the structures of governance.

In chapter 7, the conclusion, I explore the question of democracy in the state—the problems that have evolved over the twentieth century and some possible avenues for reinvigorating its legitimacy. Because the sphere of democratic decision making has been reduced, we now have a politics that "places outside its sphere of concern the really important choices—the choices that most powerfully affect the quality of people's lives, the order of their communities, and the way they are ruled."[4] Without a fundamental reassessment of our institutions of governance and a revitalization of the role of citizenship, the commonweal will continue to erode, and California will move into the twenty-first century ever more fragmented and polarized, with no vision of a common future. It is only in the political arena that humans choose and build their collective life in a democracy together. When politics is curtailed, then so is democracy. It is the task of this book to show the connection between the system of governance and the state's course of development, to demonstrate the present urgent need to create new political institutions to foster conditions for public debate about the state's future course.

The approach of this book is integrative and detailed, weaving together events and developments that have usually been treated separately. Some of the story that follows will undoubtedly be already familiar to readers. But it is my hope that this more synthetic approach to California's political history of land use will provide readers with a clearer understanding of the structuring forces.

TRANSFORMING CALIFORNIA

1 · THE FORMATIVE YEARS

California in the Gilded Age

CALIFORNIA WAS ADMITTED to the Union in 1850. It had already achieved mythic status with the 1849 gold rush. As a state, this land on the far western shore, with a climate and a diversity of natural resources that no other American state could match, quickly developed the patterns of land use that we now take for granted and that profoundly shaped its future. California became a state on the eve of many great changes in the nation: rural-urban migration, urban growth and the establishment of industrial cities, the rise of the corporation, and the closing of the frontier that had prompted the romantic movement. All these changes affected the state's evolution, echoing in the minds of its inhabitants and policymakers and influencing their choices and decisions. But the defining feature of the new state was its patterns of land ownership and concomitant relation to nature.

Resource development began much later in California than in the East and proceeded more quickly. California experienced "an exaggerated re-enactment of the drama of settlement and land use that had begun on the Atlantic seaboard two centuries earlier. This time the set was grander in scale, and the actors moved with . . . chaotic speed . . . but the script was familiar: overwhelm the previous occupants."[1] Already, under Spanish and then Mexican rule, subtle but large-scale changes in the natural conditions of the land had begun to take place, such as the replacement of native bunch grasses with hardier Mediterranean annuals. Livestock raising for the hide and tallow trade predominated, affecting hydrology and soils, and landholdings were immense. Much of the native population had succumbed quickly to European diseases or had fled to remote areas. Before European contact, California had sustained more than 300,000 Indians, "perhaps 13 percent of the entire continent's native population," representing six of native North America's seven major language groups. The state's extraordinary natural fertility welcomed increasing numbers of immigrant tribes.[2]

The 1846 Mexican-American War brought Alta California within the political boundaries of the United States and opened it up to settlement and subjugation. The era of the frontier in the United States was essentially over by the time settlers began to pour into the state. The "right of manifest destiny to spread over this whole continent"—as Rep. Robert C. Winthrop memorably phrased the arrogance of the period—had been fulfilled. The gold rush left well-known legacies: Hydraulic mining involved enormous destruction of wildlife, the reckless diversion of ever increasing amounts of water, the depletion of the soil, and the build-up of huge tailings. There was indiscriminate logging as well as the consolidation of land and water ownership and control. As Kevin Starr put it, "American California arose out of an enormous materialism . . . unalleviated by conscious ideals." Visions of wealth, of a bounteous future in a magnificent state, resulted in transformations brought about by both plunder and hard work. Exploitation characterized both urban and rural life, along with human hope and the pursuit of happiness.[3]

Between 1848 and 1865, 15,000 Indians were killed by the U.S. Cavalry in California. Mexican claims to land—huge ranches awarded by first the Spanish, then the Mexican governments—though often formally sustained by the courts, frequently passed intact into the hands of settlers. Mexican ranchers did not adapt to the capitalist imperatives that quickly came to dominate the state, nor were they equipped to deal with the increasing numbers of squatters and the disputes over land title. The 1860 census revealed great concentration of ownership of agricultural land, built on the foundation of the existing large land grants—a pattern that has continued to this day.[4]

More than 300,000 people rushed to California between 1848 and 1860. By 1870 California was among the ten most urbanized states in the country; by 1900 it was also the leading agricultural state in the arid West, thanks to its felicitous natural attributes as well as the entrepreneurial skills of the settlers. This rapid pace of growth brought with it the expectation of enrichment through rapid exploitation that was so characteristic of the West; it also led to disagreements over the consequences of growth. A budding scientific community and an educated, wealthy elite organized in opposition to the developing land-use patterns almost as soon as they were etched on the land. Concern about the preservation of nature and the patterns of urbanization developed along with the economic growth of the state—the conscious ideals referred to by Starr. Influential individuals, prominent scientists, and women's groups began pressing the federal government and the state for accurate scientific surveys, for protection of nature, and for regulation of private land use and development.

A basic theme in the unfolding of this story is the ever present tension between idealistic visions for the state's future—based on science and romanticism, planning and coordination—and capitalist development. Those who combined science and romanticism to create a vision of a bountiful future put forward ambitious proposals for the preservation and management of California's environment. Their proposals would have left us quite a different landscape: vast forests of virgin redwoods, a pristine Lake Tahoe, an intact Sierra Nevada ("the Range of Light," as John Muir called it), coordinated regionwide urban land development with significant park systems. Many of these early proposals for preservation and urban land-use planning are still with us, although their scope has been slowly chipped away over time in response to changing circumstances. But they have provided the stuff of visions about California, the dream of what could have been and of what still might be, and the motivation for political movements. The forces of economic development that prevailed provided the state with its wealth and allure. This book explores the visionary proposals, which have had the resilience of a cat with nine lives, and the far more powerful forces of development that have systematically defeated them time and time again.

California entered the nation just as the entire country was becoming a full-fledged industrial economy. The late nineteenth and early twentieth centuries were a period of great economic, political, and social change brought about by industrialization and the changing nature of the economy, which was characterized by laissez-faire capitalism and growth in the scale of enterprises. American governmental structures had been created for and during an agrarian mode of production and were predicated on a decentralized and small-scale society. California necessarily developed its systems of governance on those same principles, even though its economy was organized from the beginning along modern industrial lines.

Rapid economic change had far-reaching consequences that a pre-industrial state structure was ill-equipped to contend with. The disjuncture between the industrial economy and the nation's institutions of governance was the source of many of the tensions in the Gilded Age of the late nineteenth century and gave rise to movements for political reform, the most transformative of which was the Progressive movement.

Forces for Change: California's National Context

Beginning in the 1850s, the country's transition from a pre-industrial to an industrial economy and society was shaped by two parallel and mutually reinforcing factors. One was the system of land disposal for the nation's public domain. This is perhaps surprising, but the country's land base was immense and the population small—much land remained unsettled. The other was the rise of large-scale, complex industrial enterprises. This issue will be further developed in chapter 2, as it is of particular importance in understanding the rise of the Progressive reform movement. But it is important to realize that industrialization and its accompanying profound social change was taking place while the country was still being settled, its lands still being dispersed, and its rural landscapes being transformed—all while its cities and industries were growing. Understanding the simultaneity of these developments can help us see the connection, the interdependence between urban and rural, so well elaborated in William Cronon's discussion of Chicago. This coincident evolution also reveals the allocation of resources in the American population and helps explain how political institutions responded through policymaking.

Samuel Hays describes this period as one when the forces of industrialization, urbanization, and immigration were profoundly altering the lives of every single American: producing fundamental redistributions of wealth, power, and status, and creating differences based on geography and ethnicity. Industrialization led to concentration of control in the production and distribution of goods and services, extremes in wealth and poverty, declining farm income, child and female labor, and unsafe and unsanitary working and living conditions.[5]

Federal Land-disposal Policies

For the development of California and much of the West, federal land-disposal policies proved formative, largely determining patterns of land and natural resource ownership, exploitation, and settlement. They had far-reaching consequences for natural resource management, urban form, and the national distribution of wealth.

Initially, land-disposal programs were created to encourage westward expansion from the original colonies and to promote economic growth. Justified by a rhetoric of facilitating the settlement of small farmers across the nation, the rules for land distribution were predicated on the nation's revenue needs. The task of getting people onto the land was handed over to land-development companies. These companies were able to take advantage of the terms for land acquisition developed by the government, which required relatively large land purchases. The companies subdivided the lands, creating town centers and advertising land and community for sale to settlers.[6] This approach was particularly successful on the lands closer to the original colonies, but as settlers moved farther west, vastly different conditions pre-

vailed—such as aridity and distance from markets—that proved challenging and soon forced changes in land-disposal policies.

One particularly significant land-disposal policy was created to encourage the railroads to build a transcontinental line that would facilitate settlement and hence the nation's economic development. The Pacific Railway
Acts of 1862 and 1864 authorized the construction of a central transcontinental railroad and awarded rights of way and ten alternate sections (a
section is 340 acres) per mile of public domain on both sides. This policy effectively transferred millions of acres of the public domain to the railroads
to assist them in linking the two coasts. In California alone, the railroads
had received 11,458,212 acres by 1880—approximately 16 percent of the
entire land area owned by the federal government in the state.[7] Other land-
disposal policies allowed entrepreneurs to claim significant timber lands and
mineral lands (see table 1).

Land Disposal in California

By 1862 federal land-disposal policies had not created a nation of farmers,
because land prices were too high. Working classes in the East demanded
that the disposal laws be reformed so that individuals and families could afford land, and could homestead in the West. The Homestead Law was passed
in 1862 in response to this political pressure, but it was too little too late—
much of the best land had already been taken. The act provided for entries of
160 acres at a relatively low price. In the relatively humid East, 160 acres
was a viable farmstead, but on the lands west of the 100th meridian, 160
acres in arid country was an entirely different matter, one that would involve tricky questions of irrigation.

In California, in addition to low rainfall, there were also pre-existing
Spanish and Mexican land grants that gave those early settlers immense
tracts of land for cattle ranches. When the territory of California changed
hands, the land grants remained intact and were honored by U.S. courts.
Nearly 9 million acres of the state's most accessible lands were in Spanish
and Mexican land grants, which averaged nearly 15,000 acres per grant.
This meant that 9 million acres of the most desirable land in California
could not be homesteaded by the new settlers. Many of these large land
grants passed virtually intact into the hands of Anglos over a short period of
time, partly because of changing economic conditions in the state and
partly because of the difficulty of proving ownership on the part of the
grantees. The Spanish patterns on the land were thus preserved, even as the
land passed to new Anglo owners. These large ownerships endured nearly

Table 1. *Land Disposal Laws in the United States*

1796 Land Act   Provided for rectangular survey and public auction sales of public lands starting at $2 per acre, payable in 1 year, minimum purchase 640 acres.

1800 Harrison Land Act   Retained minimum price of $2 per acre, but lowered minimum purchase to 320 acres with 4-year credit possible.

1804 Land Act   Lowered minimum cash payment to $1.64 per acre, minimum sale of 160 acres on credit.

1807 Intrusion Act   Authorized penalties for unregistered squatters.

1820 Land Act   Abolished credit system, reduced minimum price to $1.25 per acre, set minimum purchase at 80 acres with cash payment required.

1830 Pre-emption Act   Authorized settlers who had cultivated land on public domain in 1829 to enter as many as 160 acres for $1.25 per acre for cash.

1841 Distribution Pre-emption Act   Authorized settlers to stake claims on most surveyed lands and to purchase up to 160 acres at a minimum price of $1.25 per acre, cash.

1850 Swamp Land Act   Authorized donation to the states of swamp and overflowed portions of public lands.

1852   Illinois Central Railroad received 2 million acres granted by federal government to encourage railroad building.

1854 Graduation Act (repealed 1862) Authorized all unsold lands on market for 10 years or more to be sold at $1 per acre; lands on market for 15 years or more, at 75 cents per acre; lands on market for 30 years or more, at 12 cents per acre.

1862 Homestead Act   Offered any citizen or intending citizen, head of family over 21 years of age, 160 acres of surveyed public domain after 5 years of continuous residence and payment of registration fee ranging from $26 to $34; land could also be acquired after 6 months of residence for $1.25 per acre.

1866 Southern Homestead Act (repealed in 1872)   Provided free 160 acres in 5 southwestern states to freed slaves.

1873 Timber Culture Act (repealed in 1891)   Authorized any person who kept 40 acres of timber land in good condition to acquire title to 160 acres thereof.

1873 Coal Lands Act   Provided for sale of federally owned coal lands to individuals (up to 160 acres) or associations (320 acres) at $10–$20 per acre.

1877 Desert Land Act   Authorized individuals to acquire up to 640 acres at 25 cents per acre, provided land was irrigated within 3 years.

1878 Timber and Stone Act (repealed in 1891)   Applicable to California, Oregon, Washington, and Nevada at first; provided for sale of timber and stone lands unfit for cultivation at $2.50 per acre, with limit of 160 acres.

1884   Estimate of all public lands granted to railroads, 155,504,994 acres: Union Pacific, 20 million; Santa Fe, 17 million; Central & Southern Pacific, 24 million; Northern Pacific, 44 million.

to the present day—nineteen of the original Spanish land grants, containing 728,139 acres, were still intact in 1950. This pre-existing pattern, combined with American land-disposal laws, meant that much of the best agricultural land in the state was monopolized very early.

The Timber Culture Act, Desert Land Act, and Timber and Stone Act, all passed between 1873 and 1878, furthered land consolidation by favoring capitalized investors. The choicest redwood timberland in the north coast, sugar pine forests of the Sierra, and dry lands of the upper San Joaquin Valley fell into the hands of large-scale exploiters.[8]

As the San Francisco *Chronicle* put it:

> There never has been a State on the continent in which the land laws were so well devised for monopoly and so directly against settlement and production, in which titles were as much clouded, and where it has been as difficult as here for men of small means to obtain a clear title, at a reasonable cost, to a homestead and farm; nor a State or country on the globe where monopolists and land sharks have found it as easy as in this of ours to secure their thousands and tens of thousands of acres for little or nothing.[9]

Land Consolidation

In its 1870–71 report, the state Board of Agriculture revealed that in 11 California counties, 100 individuals owned 5,465,206 acres, an average of 54,642 acres per person. In its report for 1873 and 1874, the state Board of Equalization noted that there were 122 farms or ranches in California larger than 20,000 acres, 158 ranging from 10,000 to 20,000 acres, 236 between 5,000 and 10,000 acres, and 104 of 4,000 to 5,000 acres. In short, 2,298 individuals or companies owned parcels of 1,000 acres or more.

By the late nineteenth century resentment of this extreme land consolidation was reaching the boiling point, and labor unions and others clamored for change. The nation was in revolt against monopoly power—land monopoly in California, industrial monopolies in the rest of the nation. This fertile terrain of discontent was captured by Henry George's *Our Land and Land Policy*, written to expose the situation in California. He wrote that "land grabbers have had it pretty much their own way in California—they have molded the policy of the General Government; have dictated the legislation of the State; have run the land offices and used the Courts. . . . Millions of acres in California have been monopolized by a handful of men."[10] George's remedy was to introduce a new system of taxation based on a single land tax. Based on his belief that land was the true source of value and economic well-being, he advocated that land be made common property. "The equal right of all men to the use of land is as clear as their equal right to breathe the air—it is a right proclaimed by the fact of their existence."[11] But in lieu of confiscating land, the wealth produced by labor could be confiscated by taxes. This called for a reformed system of taxation that would essentially abolish all taxes except those on land.[12] The question of monopoly in industry was eventually addressed by Congress, but the issue of land monopoly in California, while evoking passion and outrage, remained unresolved and provided fuel for reform movements throughout the twentieth century.

Other federal land laws gave lands directly to the states for disposal. These laws too were exploited by clever investors in California, creating a concentration of land ownership that spanned urban and rural areas. This concentration was in direct contradiction to the ideology of land disposal espoused by the federal government, which lauded small farmers as the backbone of American democracy. Yet in actual practice, the federal government favored income for its coffers over settlement by its citizens. It structured land sales on that basis, establishing patterns of ownership that still prevail. For example, in 1870 about three-quarters of the standing timber was publicly owned, yet by 1912–13 the Bureau of Corporations found that four-fifths was privately owned. Of the 88.6 million acres investigated by the bureau, 60 percent was owned by 1,851 companies, the 3 largest of which owned 11 percent of the country's timber.[13] Land companies and individual speculators acquired millions of acres using federal land-disposal laws.

It is worth noting that the ideology of democracy in America grew from rural roots. The Constitution and the land-disposal laws were written when the country was largely rural, and there is still a subtle but pervasive influence that gives our notions of democracy an inherent rural referent, which can impede our thinking about how democracy can work in a complex, highly urban, interdependent society. Rather, we continue to use nostalgic vocabulary and scales, such as "community" and "neighborhood," without addressing the discrepancy between the values implicit in those terms and our current reality. Of course, communities and neighborhoods still exist, but the ways in which they are constituted are far more complicated than in our agrarian past. To make democracy work today, we need to update our understanding of how we live together. This tension between a nostalgic view of democracy, based on the independent yeoman, and today's multicultural complex society is a major theme in California's evolution. The California landscape was not peopled by small farmers, but the ideology of yeomanry remained. This has been an important part of the political terrain and a factor in the competing visions of how the state should develop.

The Urban-Rural Land Connection

In addition to consolidation of land ownership, the identity of the owners affected the transformation of the California landscape. Some large farms were owned by individuals, but others were owned by farming corporations financed by absentee investors from Los Angeles, San Francisco, and beyond. These absentee investors had the wealth necessary to apply sophisticated mining technology in gold mining, driving out the smaller miners; to farm large acreages; to finance expensive agricultural land reclamation in such areas as the Sacramento Delta and parts of the Sacramento Valley that were subject to flooding; to develop irrigation systems; and to begin to invest in urban growth. They developed complicated land syndicates whose overlapping and interlocking directorates involved insurance companies, bankers, lawyers, and investors.

California was uniquely suited to the corporate farm because of the size of holdings and the requirements for start-up capital. The corporate model rapidly came to dominate agriculture in the state, setting the trends for cropping systems, labor relations, water development, and rural land use. Large-scale ownership by powerful urban syndicates formed a powerful economic and political force in the state.

Early Water Politics

Control of water in this semi-arid state was another important aspect of the state's political and economic growth and land development. Rainfall and water resources are unevenly distributed in California, and they do not always coincide with either the most desirable agricultural lands or areas of urbanization. For agriculture and cities to develop, for land to grow in value and yield higher returns, water had to be harnessed and conveyed, often hundreds of miles.

As Donald Pisani explains, "water law evolved slowly in both California and the West, constructed piece by piece, like a quilt, rather than from whole cloth. Individual court cases and statutes were piled layer on layer, not welded together like links in a chain. . . . Water law was more a reflection of unsettled, often chaotic frontier conditions than the product of legal precedents, dicta, or the philosophical assumptions of particular jurists."[14]

Thus water law in California developed largely as a result of lawsuits. In 1881 the California Supreme Court, unable to elaborate California-based water law, instead attempted to meld two long-standing water rights traditions into what it called the "California Doctrine." The first tradition was that of *prior appropriation,* or "first in time, first in right." The second was

Major rivers and waterways in California

MAP BY KEITH PULTZ

that of *riparian rights,* which prevailed in the East. The concept of riparian rights allowed streambank owners to use a stream for any number of purposes but prohibited the alteration of its course, the substantial reduction of its volume, or its pollution. Under the California Doctrine, both traditional water rights systems were legitimized. Not surprisingly, this approach did little to solve conflicting water claims.

On another front, the legislature addressed the problem of water development in the state by passing the Wright Act in 1887, creating special districts. The Wright Act gave agricultural communities the power to form local irrigation districts by taking water, land, and existing riparian rights by means of condemnation. The law required fifty landowners—or a majority in the area—to petition the state to form a district and to hold an election. Two-thirds of the voters living in the area had to approve. Once approved, the elected officers of the district were given broad authority to take land by eminent domain to build an irrigation canal. They could make contracts to build works and tax property in the district or sell bonds to pay for them.

Irrigation districts proved popular and multiplied across the landscape, so that in just a few years special districts found themselves competing with each other for water. Because the special districts could be established at will, often water systems were fragmented and disjointed because there was no coordination among districts. For example, by 1894 there were six irrigation districts in the Tulare Basin alone, comprising 500 miles of main canals and irrigating 800,000 acres of agricultural land.[15] The Wright Act was not an efficient answer to California's water development. It led to wasteful water practices and bankruptcies, and overbonding led to the amendment of the act in 1897 to give the large landowners a veto over district policies.

In effect, irrigation districts were a substitute for state leadership in the area of water development. Rather than taking on the admittedly large, expensive, and potentially contentious task of establishing a long-term, coordinated plan of irrigation development for the state, the legislature preferred to delegate irrigation infrastructure development to the locals by enabling them to establish special districts. This approach is fairly typical of the American system of regulation: set up the structure at the state or federal level, and hand over the responsibility for carrying out the legislation to the local level, with no financial (and often no legal) support.

As a result of the California Doctrine and the failure of the Wright Act, California passed into the twentieth century with a confused body of water law and a decentralized and uncoordinated system of water development, with plenty of potential for disagreement and for the reinforcement of economic power. The further development and allocation of water continued to provoke serious tensions in the state, compounded by the markedly unequal distribution of rainfall, its seasonality, and its unpredictability. As Mark Twain put it: in the West whiskey is for drinking, water is for fighting.

The Importance of Nature

California's remarkable natural resources have played a significant role in shaping the state's politics and political controversies ever since statehood. The early and illustrious scientific elite that came to California was fascinated by its spectacular natural attributes, most especially by the majestic Sierra Nevada and the north coast redwoods. The late nineteenth century was also a time of great intellectual ferment in the natural sciences. Genetics, botany, soil science, geology, and evolution were emerging as important fields of research, and California offered a particularly rich laboratory for testing and developing new scientific theories. Inevitably the scientists, joined by writers and poets inspired by transcendentalism and romanticism, were faced with the often detrimental environmental effects of rapid economic development. So very early in the state's history there arose movements for the preservation of natural resources. For example, as early as 1852 Mr. Crabb of San Joaquin County introduced a resolution in the state Assembly to make redwood timber the common property of the citizens of California. Although that lofty proposal died on the Assembly floor, pressure from preservationists resulted in 1864 in the granting of Yosemite Valley and the Mariposa Big Trees Grove as state park lands from the federal lands, creating some of the first state parks in the nation.

The philosophy of the nature preservation movement was based on a complex mix of interest in natural science, belief in progress, and a romantic view of nature as repository of spiritual values. Nature was to be studied for what it could teach humankind about evolution (which was confounded with progress) and also to be revered as a place of beauty that could heal the stresses and strains of urban life. Unspoiled nature could bring serenity and wisdom to people.[16]

John Muir was perhaps the best known of these early scientists. His view of nature was a product of the combination of natural science and Romanticism. Coming to Yosemite in 1868, Muir found his spiritual and intellectual home. He preached the interdependence of nature (echoing Thoreau): "When we try to pick out anything by itself, we find it hitched to everything else in the universe."[17] His passion for the mountains, and his eloquence on their behalf, made him a leader in the fight to defend the Sierra Nevada and in the ultimate designation of Yosemite Valley as a national park. For these

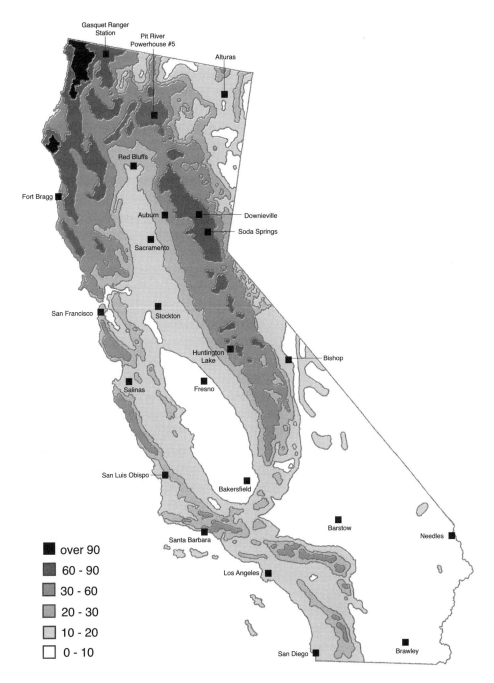

Gasquet Ranger
Station

Pit River
Powerhouse #5

Alturas

Red Bluffs

Fort Bragg

Auburn — Downieville

Soda Springs

Sacramento

San Francisco

Stockton

Huntington
Lake

Bishop

Salinas

Fresno

San Luis Obispo

Bakersfield

Barstow

Needles

Santa Barbara

Los Angeles

San Diego

Brawley

over 90

60 - 90

30 - 60

20 - 30

10 - 20

0 - 10

Rainfall distribution in California

and other efforts, he was recruited to become the first president of the Sierra Club (1892), which was part explorers' group, part advocate for the mountain range.

Managing Forest Resources

As a result of the growing movement for preservation of the state's natural resources, and in response to the increasingly obvious devastation caused by mining, agriculture, and timber harvesting, Californians engaged in a heated debate over the question of the management of the state's forest resource. Poor timber-harvesting techniques were ruining previously abundant fisheries, and there was already concern about the effects of current rates of timber harvesting on future timber supplies. City building and railroad construction had consumed more than 9 billion feet of California lumber between 1870 and 1900, and "perhaps an equal amount was unreported."[18] H. N. Bolander, a prominent botanist, wrote in 1874: "It is my firm conviction that if the redwoods are destroyed, and they necessarily will be if not protected by wise action of our government, California will become a desert."[19]

In the 1880s the governor formed a commission to investigate the destruction of forests along Lake Bigler, now known as Lake Tahoe. The Bigler Commission, as it was called, was the result of a resolution introduced by Assemblyman Coleman in 1883 which stated that it was the state's duty to preserve natural scenery for the health, pleasure, and recreation of both state residents and tourists. The resolution deplored the denudation of forests along the shores of Lake Bigler. The commission's report contributed to the creation of a Board of Forestry in 1885. The board was the first of its kind in the nation.

Lake Tahoe's stunning scenery had made it a prized tourist resort, and soon conflict had erupted among business interests, tourism, the logging industry, and preservationists. The Bigler Commission recommended that Congress acquire land owned by the railroad in the northwest part of the basin (land-grant properties that had been given the railroad by the federal government to encourage its construction) in exchange for lands selected by the Southern Pacific outside the basin that would be of equal value. The Commission recommended that the mountain land still remaining in the federal domain (which had not been already acquired through land-disposal laws) be given to the state for recreation.[20] Although these recommendations died, they established a lasting vision for the Tahoe Basin. In 1889 a group in Tulare County, led by the editor and publisher of the local newspaper, proposed to permanently save an area including the entire western slope of the Sierra, from the present boundary of Yosemite National Park to the southern end of the forest in Kern County. This was one of the first proposals in California to preserve entire watersheds—but not the last.[21]

The first Board of Forestry was headed by Abbot Kinney, an entrepreneur influenced by Henry George. Kinney was a citrus grower and real estate developer (he built Venice in Los Angeles). Under his leadership, the board sought accurate information and statistics about timber resources in the state and published literature concerning timber laws and preservation. Kinney, like others across the nation, also was influenced by George Perkins Marsh's *Man and Nature*, published in 1864, an encompassing survey of the human destruction of forests over time and the consequences of that destruction on stream flows, vegetation, and the long-term viability of agriculture. In Kinney's words, "the Pine tree sings in the Sierra a song that is echoed in the rich rustle of grain on the distant plain. Let us not forget that though so far apart, the interests of the plain are entwined with those of the mountain, and without forests we may also be without farms."[22]

Forestry itself was undergoing transformation with the rise of the science of silviculture, or scientific forest management. First developed in Germany, this was a new approach to forests in the United States. Carl Schurz, U.S. secretary of the interior in the 1870s, had been trained in Germany and brought back with him the new science of forest management. He was a proponent of the preservation of remaining federally owned timbered areas in special government-managed reserves. In 1879 Schurz called "special attention to the destruction of both coastal and Sierra redwoods, noting that the need for the preservation of these 'noblest and oldest' of trees had attracted the attention of leading men in science."[23] He recommended that the coastal redwoods and giant sequoia groves be protected in forest reservations. The recently formed American Association for the Advancement of Science (AAAS) had formed a committee in 1873 to impress on Congress and the states the urgency of timber protection. The AAAS emphasized the necessity for federal intervention in reserving forest lands, pointing to the rapid exhaustion of timber on public lands and the need to develop measures to ensure a continuous future timber supply.

Kinney's efforts, combined with Schurz's influence, contributed to the 1891 congressional repeal of the Timber Culture Act of 1873 (see table 1) and the passage of an obscure rider that authorized the president to remove land from the public domain to preserve forests. During the next ten years, over 47 million acres of forest reserves were created. President Benjamin Harrison established the Sierra Forest Reserve in 1893. This was an area of more than 4 million acres, including territory between Yosemite National Park and what became Sequoia National Park. In December 1892 he established the San Gabriel Timberland Reserve, the first preserved mountain range in southern California, to be followed by the set-aside of all the major mountain ranges in the southern part of the state. In 1899 President McKinley set aside 136,335 acres for a forest reserve at Lake Tahoe—an idea that had been presented by the Bigler Commission and taken up by the newly formed Sierra Club. The California nature preservation movement was indeed a powerful presence at the turn of the century.

The creation of a California Board of Forestry was significant because it established the precedent of a state interest in private forest management. Yet the board (like all state boards) had internal contradictions, composed as it was of businessmen engaged in timber and related industries, who had been appointed by the governor. The board's mission was to represent the state's interest (the public interest in sustainable private forest management), while at the same time representing and defending timber interests. It could not, therefore, take the lead in devising forest practice for private property without risking the wrath of industry interests, even though its mandate was to ensure that private timber owners employed sound timber practices. Instead, the board had to engage in a delicate balancing act.

In 1901 the Sierra Club, pursuing its preservationist agenda, organized a coalition of civic leaders, university scientists, and women's clubs that convinced the state legislature to establish Big Basin State Park, a redwood preserve in the Santa Cruz area. Such a measure was beyond the capability of the Board of Forestry, which could only establish rules arrived at by industry consensus. Tensions inevitably arose between preservationists and the board because of its internal structure that would always, ultimately, favor industry interests.

Concern about Fisheries

California was renowned for the abundance and variety of its fisheries, and fisheries management was an area of early state involvement. Salmon, sturgeon, trout, and a wide variety of native freshwater fish thrived in rivers and estuaries. In the years immediately preceding statehood, it was possible to pitchfork 50-pound salmon out of the Yuba and Bear Rivers (tributaries to the Sacramento) in unlimited quantities; Native American populations had found ample subsistence in these resources. The coast provided abundant shellfish, too—mussels, clams, oysters, abalone, and snails. The shells, discarded by Native Americans, composed large middens (mounds) that are found all around the Bay area today.

The giant Sacramento Delta, over 533 square miles in area, is formed by the confluence of the Cosumnes, Mokelumne, Sacramento, and San Joaquin Rivers. It is a vast expanse of freshwater marsh, teeming with life. In the West, it is second in size only to the Columbia River Delta in the Northwest. Tides extended as far upstream as the mouth of the Feather River, north of the city of Sacramento. Each river that fed into the Sacramento from the Sierra Nevada was home to its own genetically unique population of salmon. In the 1880s California became one of the nation's leading fishery states. The nineteenth-century fishing industry was most active in the Sacramento–San Joaquin watershed. As rail service improved in the Sacramento Valley, the industry lured fishing boats and immigrant fishers, and a salmon-canning industry began.

By 1873 the salmon-producing potential of the Yuba, Feather, and American Rivers had been seriously damaged by mining silt on the upstream spawning beds, the consequence of gold mining in the Sierra Nevada. This occurred in other Sierran tributaries of the Sacramento and the San Joaquin, as well as on the Klamath and Trinity Rivers along the coast. Damming and diversion of water flow for hydraulic mining, irrigation, and water supplies; farmland and range erosion; soil runoff due to lumbering and deforestation; overfishing and stream pollution from sawmills and other

Salmon fleet, Fisherman's Wharf, San Francisco, unknown date. (Photograph by A. M. Fairfield for Fish and Game Commission; courtesy of California State Archives, Office of the Secretary of State, Sacramento)

sources: all these added to the environmental insults and rapidly damaged the once abundant spring run of salmon in California. This anadromous (migratory) fish resource had been managed safely for millennia by Native Americans through ritual regulation of fishing activities. Native Americans had fished intensively during a limited seasonal interval, controlling fishing practices and takes to ensure future salmon runs.[24] By the 1870s commercial salmon fishing was concentrated in the lower reaches of the Sacramento.

Poor logging practices, especially in the northwest part of the state, home of the coastal redwoods and several important rivers, had already led to noticeable fish depletion by 1870. Parallel with concern over the state's forest resources, scientists sounded the alarm over the condition of the state's fisheries. A California Fish Commission was established in 1870. Unlike the Forestry Board, it was vested with certain powers: it could impose regulations governing the fishing season and prohibit pollution. However, as it sought to prevent stream pollution and obstructions caused by logging, mining, and agriculture, the commission quickly encountered the organized enmity of these economic interests, a state of affairs that lasted throughout the commission's lifetime.

By 1874 nearly every stream on the Sonoma-Mendocino stretch of coast had become a thoroughfare for redwood logs rather than for salmon. Timber and slash blocked the way to ascending fish, and deforested hillsides exposed spawning beds for salmon and trout and were vulnerable to drought and flooding. Disastrous floods had become so frequent in that part of the state that in 1886 the California surveyor general recommended to the governor that all state timber lands be withdrawn from sale in order to prevent further damage to public watersheds.[25] The Fish Commission, supported by the legislature, embarked on a program to force individuals or corporations to install fish ladders where irrigation and other uses were hampering fish passages; it instituted legal suits and hired a prosecutor; it required fishermen to secure licenses with fees to pay for the prosecution of violators. But by 1875 mining had already ruined one-half of the waterways in which salmon had once spawned, and the Native Americans who remained and relied on fishing for food found themselves in increasing conflict with miners and timber harvesters.

Portuguese, Chinese, and Italian immigrants dominated the commercial fishing industry up and down the state in the early years, each ethnic group developing its own fishing niche. The Chinese, for example, were shrimp and abalone fishers in the San Francisco Bay and in San Diego. As the fisheries declined, the Chinese became a target for blame, accused of fishing out all of the juvenile fish. In San Diego, for example, shortages of fresh market fish in

Quinnat salmon taken at Bryan's Rest on Eel River,
Humboldt County, unknown date. (Photograph by
S. Campbell for Fish and Game Commission; courtesy of
California State Archives, Office of the Secretary of State,
Sacramento)

the late 1880s led a local newspaper to demand that the state get rid of the
foreigners—the Chinese. Closing down the Chinese fisheries became a key
element of the state's fishery program at the end of the century, even
though patrol agents of the Fish Commission reported no small fish among
the shrimp drying at the dock and stated that they believed there was no violation of the law.[26]

The Fish Commission, which later became part of the Department of
Fish and Game, was one of the first agencies in state government to deal
with natural resource management. Although some of its popular success
was due to its anti-Chinese fishing laws, it was clearly seen as an important
agency by the legislature during the late nineteenth century. Legislation in
1878 had given the state Board of Fish Commissioners responsibility for protecting terrestrial game animals, as well as fish, and in 1895 the board obtained the power to hire game wardens. Laws added to the Penal Code
through the 1880s prohibited the pollution of rivers and required operators
of irrigation ditches to maintain fishways, fish ladders, and fish screens.[27]

The state Board of Fish Commissioners represented the application of budding scientific expertise in state programs—part of a national trend toward incorporating planning and objective technical knowledge into bureaucratic management, whether government or business. The Fish Commission emphasized the use of experts, functional specialization, and coordination. By 1891 it had created three separate divisions: one that enforced regulations, one that gathered fees, and one that oversaw applied research at state hatcheries. In 1897 the commission's power was enhanced by the state Supreme Court in *People v. Truckee Lumber Company*. This ruling upheld the state's right to force water-using industries to account for injuries they inflicted on fisheries. Only late in the Progressive period of the early twentieth century did other natural resource boards and commissions develop as extensive a program and administration.[28]

Although the commission had significant powers, it had a small budget and few wardens, and quite powerful interests to regulate. Despite its strength on paper, the commission was unable to prevent the continued dramatic decline of fisheries in the state. Harvests of raw fish peaked between 1880 and 1884, after which river fisheries declined precipitously, from a combination of overfishing and environmental degradation of the rivers caused by mining, timber, agriculture, and water diversion.[29]

Although the number of fish had dwindled drastically, the fishing industry in California continued to grow over the next few decades, pitting the Fish Commission against other special-interest commissions and groups, such as the Board of Forestry and the timber industry. In addition, it too developed an internal tension between protecting the economic interests of the fishing industry (from which its members were drawn) and the conservation needs of the resource—sometimes requiring a shutdown of the industry to protect the fishery. This tension continued through the next century.

The Railroad

Railroad construction was an integral part of the nation's, and California's, economic development. The rail lines brought California into the economic life of the nation by facilitating both trade and travel. The railroad companies were also among the largest corporate beneficiaries of federal land policy in the period 1860–80. In California they received about 16 percent of the public domain, much of which seemed of little value at the time, especially in the desert areas. But the patents also included some of the finest lands in the San Joaquin Valley, as well as valuable timber and oil properties. This put the railroad companies in a position to participate actively in the determination of land settlement and development by their choice of trajectories for their lines and by their own land-disposal decisions.

In California in 1880 the Southern Pacific Railroad employed 6,799 people, making it easily the state's largest employer. Its 9 million acres of landholdings made it also the state's largest landowner. Moreover, it was seen to have a virtual monopoly of California's transportation systems. The railroad was politically active, contributing to campaigns, influencing nominating conventions, and subsidizing much of the California press. The public perception was that the railroad nearly controlled party nominations, and hence state politics—from locally elected officials to the state legislature. At this time, local elections were still partisan, and candidates ran as Democrats, Republicans, or members of other parties. Candidates were nominated by party caucuses that would get together to agree on their platforms and select candidates for elective office. The railroad was adept at influencing those processes through its generous contributions. It cared little whether the candidate was Democrat, Republican, or other, as long as he accepted the railroad's general point of view.

The economic and political power of the railroad symbolized the profound economic changes that were occurring at the turn of the century, affecting people's daily lives and occupations. The railroad represented the consolidation of corporate power and monopoly—a menace to the principles of individual enterprise and the free market. Its power was embodied in the tremendous, overpowering physicality of the train itself, belching smoke, shaking the earth, shattering the ear, cutting swaths across landscapes and cities. An obvious agent of transformation, the railroad served to unite disparate anti-monopoly interests and provoked attempts to supervise and regulate its operation. In 1876 the state legislature formed an advisory commission on the railroad, which had the authority to set maximum rates and prevent unjust discrimination. But the railroad had a complex and interdependent relationship with the state because its own economic interests were often congruent with the state's own economic health. The railroad's promotion of the state and its investment in infrastructure contributed to overall economic prosperity. Railroad companies acquired considerable expertise in fostering economic development, and the state's economic success in turn boosted the railroads' profits.[30] In the end, the railroad commission did little to challenge the rates set by the railroad.[31] Not only was the railroad the largest employer and one of the largest landowners, it also virtually controlled shipping (the Central Pacific and affiliate lines controlled more than 80 percent of California rail traffic) and was deeply implicated in politics. The railroad also represented modernity, in the form of the new business enterprise—complex, professionalized, centrally coordinated, capable of developing and managing powerful technologies through its "octopus"-like corporate organization. It is not surprising that as political discontent and economic frustration continued to rise, the railroad became a common scapegoat for statewide problems.

Political Reform

In addition to widespread antagonism to the power of the railroad, the late nineteenth century saw a growing backlash against immigrant workers, mostly the Chinese. Once the transcontinental rail line had been built, the thousands of laborers the railroad had imported into the country to build the line—mostly Chinese and some Mexican—were released into the economy. Since the time of the gold rush, immigration from China had steadily continued, until by 1889 there were more than 75,000 Chinese in the state. The Chinese immigrants made up nearly one-tenth of the state's population and represented nearly three-quarters of Chinese immigrants in the United States. The Chinese were industrious and thrifty, establishing themselves in mining, restaurants, laundries, farming, fishing, clothing, furniture manufacturing, and cigar making. They were actively recruited by large agricultural interests, which recognized their talent for constructing irrigation systems and their skills in land reclamation, especially in the Delta area of the Sacramento Valley.[32] Chinese success fueled resentment. Anti-Chinese sentiment was claimed to be based on economic and moral grounds: the Chinese lowered wage rates, replaced white laborers, added to unemployment. Further, the Chinese were attacked for their exclusiveness and the close nature of their community. In 1877 a special committee of the legislature stated that Chinese immigration was "a dangerous unarmed invasion of our soil."[33]

The Workingman's Party

A severe economic depression in the mid-1870s aggravated anti-railroad and anti-Chinese sentiments. At the same time grievances over railroad freight rates, uncertain water rights, and monopolistic landholdings were rising. Together these issues created fertile conditions for political organizing. The California Workingman's Party, based in San Francisco, blamed the Chinese, as well as the big corporations—especially the railroad—for California's economic troubles and claimed that local and state officials were corrupt. As Bill Deverell points out, the Workingman's Party made its lasting contribution by introducing working-class politics and demands into California's mainstream political process. The Workingman's Party advocated the eight-hour day, abolition of the convict labor system, prohibitions against Chinese immigration, the popular election of political leaders, and unionization of workers.[34]

Protests from workers, business leaders' concerns about the power of the railroad, and the electoral strength of the Workingman's Party altered the balance of power in the state legislature, allowing dissent and pushing through a constitutional convention to rewrite the California constitution. By 1878 the Workingman's Party had elected eleven state senators and seventeen assemblymen, and controlled more seats in the legislature than did the Democrats. The new legislature focused its energy on developing a new state constitution, which was accepted in 1879. Debate over the new constitution caused a group of Democrats and Republicans to abandon their parties over the issue of regulation of the railroad. These dissidents formed a Non-Partisan Party to put a brake on reforms, foreshadowing the development of the Progressive Party.[35]

The reform agenda of the Workingman's Party, based on curbing the power of large corporate interests, encountered real opposition; its anti-monopoly sentiment was attacked as "agrarian and communistic." U.S. Supreme Court justice Stephen Field, for example, was a prominent California Democrat who regarded business regulation as a desire to "break down all associated capital by loading it with unequal and oppressive burdens." Democrats in general looked askance at business regulation, viewing it as a failure to recognize that "great corporations, with large aggregate capital, are necessary to the vast enterprises of the age and to modern civilization and progress."[36] At the same time, however, there was a strong reform undercurrent even within the Democratic Party that tried to introduce legislation to reform public and private water rights and to legislate support for public education, conservation, and consumer protection. The constitution that did pass removed broad areas of policy from the discretion of elected lawmakers (who were seen as pawns of the railroad) by creating regulatory commissions composed of appointees, including a Railroad Commission. It also set out new procedures for state action, foreshadowing the more far-reaching Progressive reforms that came some thirty or so years later. It attempted to expand the tax base by extending taxation to the newly emerging sources of profit linked to the development of corporations and new banking institutions. These included taxes on bonds, stocks, franchises, money, and credits.

In the same year of 1879 the Workingman's Party won the offices of mayor, sheriff, treasurer, auditor, district attorney, and most other municipal officials in San Francisco. The party's victory ensured that city government would be union-controlled, as the party was strongly backed by San Francisco working-class union members.

The Anti-monopolist Sentiment

The Workingman's Party collapsed in the 1880s, but the anti-monopolist sentiment lived on, internally dividing both the Republican and Democratic Parties. Among the anti-monopolists was George Hearst, who in 1880 acquired the San Francisco *Examiner* and used the power of the press to expose the monopoly of the railroad in the state. He and other prominent men occupied a dominant position within the California Democratic Party. These anti-monopolists formed the heart of the early twentieth-century Progressive reform movement. But unlike their radical counterparts, the Republican and Democratic anti-monopolists saw a role for large-scale enterprises, if those enterprises were regulated. They were impressed with corporate efficiency and productivity, and believed government should not interfere in the economy except to moderate excess. The role of government, from this perspective, was to create favorable conditions for businesses and capitalists (such as farmers who needed predictable shipping rates) and to allow business to regulate itself. Government should not attempt to fundamentally restructure the economy and eliminate large corporations.

2 · REFORMERS ASCEND TO POWER

The California Progressives

BY THE TURN of the twentieth century, political unease permeated California. Movements of opposition were forming, dissolving, and reorganizing. These movements included labor unions, farmers' unions, business organizations, and political parties. Individuals, searching for ways to express themselves politically, associated themselves with first one group or idea and then another: conventional parties, the Nonpartisan Party, the Workingman's Party, insurrectionist anarchism, the Socialist Labor Party, utopian land colonies, producer cooperatives, and groups espousing the ideas of Henry George and Edward Bellamy.

Against this backdrop of turmoil and change a modern political reform movement coalesced, part of a nationwide movement for reshaping government so it would better correspond to the technological, industrial, demographic, and economic forces that were changing the country from an agricultural nation to a capitalistic urban one. This was Progressivism, represented by Theodore Roosevelt at the national level and by Hiram Johnson in California.

Given the economic and political dominance of the railroad in California and its embodiment of the evils of industrial and economic monopoly, the California Progressive movement has often been explained as a revolt against the stifling power of the railroad. Recent historical analysis, however, has portrayed a more complex political landscape. The railroad may have provided the focus for Progressives in California, but when it came to implementing reforms, a complicated set of relations developed among the various players: machine politicians, urban reformers, the railroads themselves, and more radical elements, such as organized labor. The railroad, though vilified as strangling the state, was invited by urban reformers to the discussion table and even into their organizations. Further, the Progressives had agendas for change that went beyond curbing the power of the railroad and included urban reforms and strategies for natural resource management.[1]

Progressivism as a Movement and an Ideology

Progressivism and its reforms are important to an understanding of California's evolution because of the enduring nature both of the movement's political reforms and of its political ideology. Progressives were preoccupied with the question of land use, both urban and rural, and instituted programs, policies, and regulations for land use that remain today. The Progressive period laid down the fundamental structures that led, over time and after tinkering, to much of the physical landscape we see today. The Progressive theme of "the greatest good for the greatest number" echoed from city halls to the national forests by way of regulations for land use.

As a movement for social change, Progressivism was made up of several different tendencies. George Mowry's seminal work described its leadership as "seized by a group of supreme individualists, well-educated and bound together by a particularistic point of view, a remembrance of things past, a new code of morality, and more than the normal dash, perhaps, of a sense of indignation and a desire for power."[2] While the movement has been shown to have been broad enough to include labor (at times) and social reformers, much of the leadership of the Progressives consisted of upper-middle-class, university-trained professionals.[3] They were affluent and well organized, and had access to the press and to power. Yet they saw their programs as intended for all people, shying away from class analysis and also political parties, which they perceived as corrupt machines fostering special interests. In the area of political reform, they worked for cross-filing, the initiative, and the recall as reform measures that they claimed would increase direct democracy and decrease the influence of parties; they saw parties as antithetical to democracy. They introduced to government the professional civil service and policy-setting appointed boards and commissions.

Progressives were seduced by the success of the rising capitalist system of industrial production. They developed a new vision for government, inspired by the successful models of efficient corporations that used scientific expertise and modern management techniques. One strong thrust of their reform movement was better knowledge, combined with a more honest system of government, in the hands of civil servants but advised by volunteer boards and commissions where politics would play little or no role. They developed new governance structures so as to apply business precepts to government and developed a concurrent ideology: local governments were to be run like business organizations, where the bottom line was a balanced budget and good service.

Progressives were concerned with the physical. "The urban environment, the physical embodiment of the new social order presented to these men of taste a material form they could mold for the protection of the social whole. . . . Behind every one of their improvement plans lay the belief that environmental reform was the most important disciplinary order upon which the new civilization of cities would rise." The built environment was seen as the vehicle to stimulate economic activity by creating an infrastructural framework and a regulatory land order.[4] This applied equally to rural lands, such as forests.

Aspects of the Progressive platform appealed to the working classes: The Progressives advanced social welfare programs, old-age pensions, the eight-hour workday, and women's suffrage. These programs were supported by organized labor in the late nineteenth and early twentieth centuries, a time of great unrest manifested in thousands of strikes and serious violence. Progressives understood the need for social reforms to maintain peace, believed in them as enlightened measures, and incorporated them into their campaigns and programs. They formulated a modern agenda combining social reform with political reform. The underlying philosophy was to sanitize the political system by removing parties and therefore strife (politics was to be replaced by intelligent management) and to accomplish at least part of this through regulation of the physical environment.

John Buenker describes two distinct, and in some ways contradictory, strains in Progressivism. One aimed to remove the machinery of government as far as possible from the voters because they were seen as the problem, while the other sought to open up the political process still further by allowing popular participation in decision making at levels where it had never before taken place.[5] Both supported the institution of the recall, the referendum, and the initiative and the appointment of boards and commissions, as well as other reforms. The result was an expectation of democratic participation and influence, without the political structures to implement the democratic impulse.

The Rise of the Civil Service

Because political parties had run governments through their elected officials and appointees, the "patrician" strain of Progressives considered parties one of the major obstacles to good government. The reformers believed that political parties, and hence politics, should have very little to do with government; especially at the local level, the function of government was to create the conditions for a city to work. The built environment was to be utilized, or shaped, to stimulate economic activity and to minimize the costs of production and circulation of goods within a city.[6] That is, the role of government was to provide and administer services, such as garbage collection, street cleaning, road paving, and the like, so that the city would be efficient. Politics, to the Progressives, simply infused the process of admin-istration with bias and favors. They were reacting, in part, to machine poli-ticians in big eastern cities who rewarded supporters with city jobs and ran working-class candidates chosen by the party. Progressives had a different vision, one that emerged from the growing professionalization of disciplines involving specialized, technical knowledge. It required a different kind of politician and process: a politician independent from party pressures (a code term for special interests) and a process that relied on professional expertise, subject to the ultimate will of the voters through referenda, recalls, or initi-atives. Richard Hofstadter has pointed out that the movement for direct democracy—represented by the referendum, recall, and initiative—was also, in effect, an attempt to realize ideals of personal responsibility and good citizenship as exercised by the Yankee individual. This was a distinctly un-party-like, un-machine-like approach to politics.[7] It combined a reaction to the obvious problems of large industrial eastern cities—overcrowding, disease, poverty, crime, and social unrest—with a belief in the possibility of creating a logically ordered environment based on technical knowledge. At the core of any social problem was the physical fabric of the city, its chaos and physical disarray. Zoning codes, the relocation of nuisances, housing standards, building codes, the construction of parks: all were technical fixes put in place through the elaboration of new rules based on the belief that the order of the physical environment could remedy society's urban ills.

The idea of professionalizing city government was supported by the rise of city-planning professionals who brought their new technical knowledge to planning, elevating questions of administration out of the morass of party politics and favoritism. Progressives pushed the creation of the civil service so that a professional core of technically trained, nonpartisan man-agers would be in charge of administering the city. Progressives also further institutionalized the use of the appointed policymaking board or commis-sion, made up of volunteer professionals, often drawn from the business world. Such entities would hold hearings and then establish policy for the specific departments of the city, county, or state. For example, the appointed zoning board or the appointed planning commission would determine what land uses were appropriate and what building types should or should not be allowed in order to achieve a better physical environment. Politically, this approach reflected the Progressives' ambivalence toward government. While reforming government and putting professionals inside the apparatus of government through the civil service, Progressives also put in place a sys-tem that would check the autonomy of government bureaucrats. The idea was that the appointed board or commission, made up of disinterested ex-perts, would establish policy. The policy would then be carried out by the professional civil service. So, for example, in the area of planning, a local planning commission would be made up of local real estate agents, bankers, and real estate insurance representatives; at the state level, in the area of forestry, a board would be made up of timber industry representatives. Progressives believed that those who were financially involved in a particular sector would have greater knowledge about how that sector should be regulated and would serve in an objective way on appointed boards and commissions. Progressives thought that these business representatives would apply their special knowledge in the public interest. In their view a professional civil servant could not sufficiently understand the requirements of a particular sector and so needed the guidance of those who were directly involved.

In essence, for Progressives, government had the responsibility to stimulate economic activity and to improve the social order through new rules and institutions that would order the physical environment. The political implementation of this vision was to take place through nonpartisan local elections, the civil service, and appointed board and commissions. Citizens would keep the system in check, ensuring its accountability through the power of initiative, referendum, and recall—even though they had been distanced from actual decision making, which would become the domain of experts. For the people, then, democracy was reduced to a simple act of voting rather than participation in decision making. Progressives disconnected politics from democracy, gutting the politics, the very activity by which the broad public acts together to build democracy. In its stead Progressives put managerialism.

Tools for Direct Democracy: The Referendum, the Recall, and the Initiative

Progressives in California instituted the referendum, the recall, and the initiative statewide in 1911. These measures were intended to bring the government closer to the voters by giving voters the tools of direct democracy, thereby returning democracy to the individual citizen and directly empowering voters so that they were no longer dependent on parties to effect change. An initiative for a new law, for example, could be placed directly on the ballot by citizens, if they were able to organize and to get enough signatures for the initiative to qualify. This meant that if the legislature or the local city council was not addressing issues the voters felt were important, the voters could intervene directly by passing a reform measure that would be incorporated into law. Both the referendum and the recall were guided by the same political philosophy of giving the people direct access to government. However, there was a catch. Qualification for the ballot required signatures from a certain percentage of registered voters. Although this was not an insurmountable obstacle, especially at the local level, it did create a real hurdle for organizations that had small financial resources, for collecting signatures is a time-consuming and expensive process.

These reforms broke the power of the two major political parties in the state in just a few years and made it extremely difficult for third parties to survive. They created conditions whereby "candidates must depend upon individual political merchandising. . . . [they] think of personal machines, personal followings, individual campaigns, and not in terms of party organization."[8]

Boards and Commissions

By reforming state politics through removing the functions of the political parties and instituting boards and commissions, Progressives actually opened the door for the greater involvement of "special interests." Boards and commissions are appointed representatives of the interest they are supposed to regulate; it was thought that in this manner experts would be involved in decision making. Who better to make policy decisions than those intimately involved? But the assumption that these appointees would make their decisions on a scientific and technical basis rather than on their economic interest turned out to be mistaken. The net result was further distancing of government from the people. Members of boards and commissions could not be recalled since they were not elected, and the nature of the boards and commissions put financially interested people in charge of policing themselves. Boards and commissions also undermined the nonpartisan and professional civil service, since its function was to implement decisions made by those boards and commissions.

The perverse result of a professional, nonpartisan, apolitical government rid of political machines was an era of unprecedented corruption. "By 1920, a new lobby began to make its appearance. It included labor, agriculture, the women's clubs, teachers, a vast range of business interests, reform groups, and what not, all jockeying for power and undercutting each other."[9] With no party discipline left, a vacuum had been created in Sacramento.

California Progressives Come to Power

By the early 1900s growth in California had exceeded all expectations and was transforming the indigenous landscape in all areas of the state. Extensive, mechanized agriculture and irrigation systems reworked rural lands, and rapidly developing urban centers spread across the landscape. Los Angeles was growing fast, overtaking San Francisco in numbers and economic strength, and the East Bay cities were growing too. The problem of control of the rate of change was perceived by all, but for different reasons. For business the problem was technology, competition, price, and reliable supplies. For preservationists it was the lack of protective regulation and the specter of resource depletion. For small business the problem was restoring democracy and economic competitiveness; for small farmers it was the threat of land monopoly and decreased access to water; for labor it was fair working conditions and the perceived competition from Asian immigrants. The Progressives believed that their ideology of apolitical governance based on the principles of scientific efficiency would meet these challenges, at both the state and local levels.

Important differences between the northern and southern parts of the state were solidifying during this period. The differences would be expressed in views on social policy and, later, environmental management. In the early twentieth century northern and southern California were primarily economic rivals, though both agreed on the desirability of growth. Indeed, the prominent families in the Progressive movement, such as the Spreckels, Hearst, and Hellman families, had important interests in both parts of the state. Leaders in the north and the south found common ground in their opposition to the railroad's near monopoly and huge political influence, as well as in their support for economic growth, but their local political agendas differed.[10] One major difference was the presence of a strong labor union movement in the north and strong anti-union sentiment in the south, led by the already powerful *Los Angeles Times.* Los Angeles was characterized by a more homogeneous and wealthier population, San Francisco by a heterogeneous population of immigrants. There was also rivalry between the two cities based on San Francisco's position as the state's banking and industrial center. Such differences made for uneasy alliances and eventual struggles over power in the legislature.

Reshaping the Political Process

In 1907 journalists and civic leaders came together in Los Angeles to establish a new statewide reform organization—the Lincoln-Roosevelt League. Participants from southern California had been encouraged by the success of Progressive ideas at the ballot box in Los Angeles, under the sponsorship of the Los Angeles Non-Partisan Committee. In Los Angeles, as in most of the nation, Progressive ideas, such as nonpartisan local elections and establishment of a civil service, were being introduced at the municipal level. Thanks to the leadership of influential men such as John Randolph Haynes, Los Angeles was at the forefront of Progressive political reforms in the state. The platform of the Lincoln-Roosevelt League "called for the emancipation of the Republican party in California from Southern Pacific domination, the selection of delegates to the next Republican national convention who were sympathetic to Roosevelt's policies, the election of free and honest legislators, the direct election of United States senators and direct primaries for the nomination of candidates for all state and local offices."[11]

In 1910 the growing Progressive movement elected Hiram Johnson as Republican governor of California. His election brought the elite and middle-class reformers into power on a platform that included social reform. The reformers argued that it was important to prevent special-interest groups from controlling state power for their own purposes. Progressives felt that only a nonpartisan approach would defuse mounting class conflict as well as the political power of the railroad.

There was also political pressure organized around working-class issues, as activists called for major structural reform, including social welfare laws and land reform. The issue of land monopoly lived on. Support for the cause was fueled by growing anti-foreign sentiment arising from the apparent economic success of Asian immigrants, who were perceived as a direct competitive threat. Progressives feared this attractive grass-roots radicalism and organized to oppose it as much as to oppose the stranglehold of the railroad. Progressives believed class interests could be transcended and that there was a greater good all rational people could agree upon. As Hiram Johnson explained in his "state of the state" address:

> It is in no partisan spirit that I have addressed you . . . it is in no partisan spirit that I appeal to you to aid. Democrats and Republicans alike are citizens, and equal patriotism in each. Your aid, your comfort, your highest resolve and endeavor, I bespeak, not as Republicans or Democrats, but as representatives of all the people of all classes and political affiliation, as patriots indeed, for the advancement and progress and righteousness and uplift of California. And may God in His mercy grant us the strength and the courage to do the right.[12]

This was a typical Progressive approach: appeal to nonpartisanship and to the greater good, rather than to parties or ideology. With regard to the railroad, the aim of the Lincoln-Roosevelt League was not to put the companies out of business, but to reduce their influence in politics.[13]

Johnson's 1911 address also emphasized government efficiency, social reform measures, and the repudiation of exploitation of politics and natural resources by private interests. The Progressives introduced a social reform agenda in the 1911 legislative session; they understood the importance of basic equity issues, even though their approach to equity was very different from that of the grass-roots radicals. Regulation, not redistribution, shaped the legislation. That year women's suffrage was overwhelmingly passed, and elections of local candidates and other offices became nonpartisan.

These offices included judges and school officials, and later expanded to include county and city officials. The legislature also approved direct primaries, as well as the initiative, the referendum, and the recall. These measures were hailed as providing the electorate with the tools of direct democracy. Taken together, they were a powerful blow to the state's political parties, and thus to the ability of the railroad to influence party nominations. For example, nonpartisan local elections meant that candidates could no longer run as representatives of political parties and therefore could not always count on the party's financial and organizing support.

The 1911 legislative session resulted in the overall weakening of the political parties, which gradually withered as political emphasis shifted toward individual candidates and away from the party machine that had relied on neighborhoods and on broad involvement to maintain momentum. But as one ward leader in Philadelphia explained, reflecting on the role of the political machine in that city, "votes like babies, require both time and labor to produce. Neither are dropped down chimneys by storks."[14] The ward leader was referring to the time and effort involved in cultivating voters, getting them to come out and vote. A political party is in a much stronger position to make such efforts than an individual politician. Machine politicians knew their constituents as human beings; they cultivated them, helped them in time of need, and counted on them to participate when the time was right. Progressives, in contrast, pushed for areawide elections, further distancing the nonpartisan candidate from his electorate because he now no longer represented a district, but rather all the people. Thus differences and personal relationships were collapsed into a winner-take-all contest. This is not to say that parties no longer had any role in local elections. They certainly supported candidates, funneled money to them, and helped to get out the vote. Nevertheless, the overall effect was to dampen party politics in the state by placing restriction on party organizations that made them large, unwieldy, and powerless. Ironically, as Jackson K. Putnam pointed out, parties had often served to moderate, regulate, and forestall demands of special interests, as well as to implement them. Parties served as sources not only of funds but also of social ideas and programs that were often at odds with the demands of special interests. In effect, the party helped shield officeholders against undue influence of lobbyists.[15]

Early Opposition

By 1913 the Progressive agenda had begun to arouse opposition. Conservatives reacted to reform by organizing groups to fight what they called "Socialism." The California chambers of commerce and various commercial bodies joined together to condemn pending Progressive legislation and to try to repeal regulatory laws passed in 1911. Altogether fifty measures were singled out as injurious to business. The Progressives also faced competition from the left, with the rise of the Socialists, who received 80,000 votes in 1912, the third highest showing in the nation. A Socialist mayor had been elected in Berkeley and a Socialist assemblyman in Los Angeles. In Los Angeles one of the staunchest Progressive reformers, John Randolph Haynes, openly espoused Socialist ideals. He recognized, however, that the Progressive Party had a much better chance of succeeding with reform than did the Socialist Party,[16] and so joined in the Progressive efforts rather than supporting the Socialist Party.

Progressives embraced the prevalent anti-alien attitude, passing an anti-alien bill that made it illegal for the Japanese to own land in California. By this time, the intense anti-Chinese sentiments had been shifted to the Japanese, who had already achieved noticeable success in farming. Anti-Japanese legislation helped Governor Johnson maintain his middle-class and working-class support. The Japanese, like the corporations, were viewed as a threat to economic opportunity—but it was the Japanese, not the land monopoly of the farming corporations, who were blamed for undermining the competitive position of white small-scale farmers due to their success. Concern over racial homogeneity increased as the economic and social homogeneity of the state declined. The middle class feared it would not be able to compete with the Japanese, who were described as racially different, but also as efficient, thrifty, ambitious, and unwilling to remain "mudsillers."

The Death Blow to Party Politics: Cross-filing

The Progressives continued the dismantling of political parties. In 1913 cross-filing was introduced. This permitted any candidate for partisan public office to file for any party's primary and to win, if he obtained a plurality. As modified in 1917, cross-filing required each office seeker to win his own party's nomination before accepting the nomination of another party. This system left party politics in a state of confusion. For example, in 1918 Republican James Rolph won the Democratic gubernatorial nomination but ran behind incumbent William Stephens in his own party's primary. He was then disqualified, leaving the Democrats without a candidate. Cross-filing profoundly altered California politics, putting the candidate above party affiliation and above platform, and it strengthened the chances of reelection for moderate incumbents. The winners were most often those with the most backing from the media, the more energetic individual campaign, the most extensive assistance from interest groups, the biggest financial resources, and the highest level of name familiarity. (Cross-filing was finally abolished, only to be reinstituted by initiative in 1996.) Continuing on his path to rid politics of parties, Governor Johnson in 1915 demanded formal statewide, nonpartisan elections. This proposal was defeated in a referendum put on the California ballot by the legislature, which itself had endorsed the idea.[17]

As a result of the political changes brought about by the Progressives, a new sort of political power began to emerge in Sacramento to replace the party: the lobbyist. Special interests, no longer able to participate in an effective party system, began to send their own lobbyists directly to the state capitol. "The responsible heads of industry and former legislators have taken their [parties'] place," wrote Chester Rowell in 1913 in the *Fresno Republican*.[18] The individual officeholders, deprived of their party's shield and support, had to face the complex and often contradictory pressures of constituents, as well as following their own sense of what was right. This led to an institutionalization of pragmatism. Caught in constantly conflicting demands, the new Progressive politicians learned to shape programs by reconciling opposing interests through negotiation and compromise.[19]

Regulating Big Business

Governor Johnson's leadership in political reform did end the railroad's obvious manipulation of party politics, but its economic might remained to be dealt with. To curb railroad control over shipping rates and rail routes, Johnson strengthened the existing Railroad Commission and expanded its mandate to include all public utilities, such as electricity and gas. The resultant Public Utilities Commission was regulatory, but not anti-business. The railroads were preserved as major California corporations, as were other major corporations, including the Pacific Gas & Electric Company.[20] The idea was to foster competition between corporations in a regulated environment and thus ensure a reasonable profit and a level playing field for them, not to break them up or eliminate them. "Their reforms were aimed more at a rational reordering of the state's business and entrepreneurial playing field."[21]

Under public regulation competition between corporations could be reduced to a minimum, and the commission's implicit role was to protect the corporations in their monopoly power. Like their national counterparts, California Progressives believed that large corporations were economically more efficient than multiple small companies, so they developed a structure that would maintain the integrity of the large corporation, even protect its profits, while also regulating it to curb the potential excesses that came with its monopolistic control of a sector of the economy. Progressives introduced managed competition and rate structures that were arrived at through consultation with the corporation at hand. A constant, reliable income stream was essential for these large companies. This would ensure profitability and sufficient income to invest in upgrading and expanding services. Too much real competition might reduce profits so that services might suffer or stock-holders would not have good returns. The Public Utilities Commission was an important regulatory innovation, maintaining high levels of service while also assuring a decent rate of return for the private company. As Bill Deverell points out in his important book *Railroad Crossing,* William F. Herrin, Southern Pacific Chief Council, was said to have welcomed the Progressives and their ordering of the railroad system. "I think no railroad manager would agree to dispense with government regulation at the cost of returning to the old conditions."[22]

An element of Progressive reforms, as we have seen, was the concern to make government more accessible to the individual voter. To this end, Progressives introduced open public hearings. All boards and commissions, such as the Public Utilities Commission, held public hearings before they made policy determinations. But often the regulated corporations, with their staff lawyers, engineers, and experts in all issues involved with their regulation, were in a stronger position than the public, which was not so well or so consistently represented. Democratic process was thus often more form than substance.

> There was something which the machine busting governor and applauding people did not see very clearly or take into consideration [with the institution of the Public Utilities Commission]. The day of domination and exploitation of the State by one large public utility corporation [the Southern Pacific] was passing, and the new day of domination and exploitation by several public utility groups— water companies, electric power companies, gas companies, telephone companies uniting with the old railroad group—was at hand. And very silently, in face of the popular uprising, they were looking on, alertly, intelligently preparing to adjust themselves to the new condition for continued exploitation of a people blindly struggling for relief from the yoke of a single corporation that had for so long dominated them.[23]

The result of these Progressive measures has been debated. Arthur Lipow criticized the Progressives for stripping individuals of effective organizations and making politics a matter of personality rather than program and party organization.[24] Carey McWilliams, an astute and critical observer of California politics, argued that "the initiative has been skillfully used by the special interests it was supposed to curb." Jackson K. Putnam held that progressivism replaced laissez-faire political behavior with institutionalized activism, in which California constituents expected their officials to perform and to deliver social services through a pragmatic, balancing, moderate, but activist, process.[25] Since most of the Progressive reforms are still in place today, we will examine them in some detail, particularly as they affected land-use policy and democratic politics.

Resource Conservation and Management

Among the many pressing issues that Hiram Johnson chose to address, one of the most important for the state at the turn of the century was the management of its natural resources, an area that had previously received only intermittent and haphazard attention. In 1911 he stated:

> In the abstract all agree upon the policy of conservation. It is only when we deal with conservation in the concrete that we find opposition to the enforcement of the doctrine enunciated originally by Gifford Pinchot and Theodore Roosevelt. Conservation means development, but development and preservation; and it would seem that no argument should be required on the question of preserving, so far as we may, for all the people, those things which naturally belong to all.[26]

Governor Johnson's supporters had invited Gifford Pinchot, Roosevelt's chief forester, to speak on Johnson's behalf during the campaign, associating California Progressives with the national movement. Johnson himself was not a crusading conservationist, but he realized the political importance of the issue. The Roosevelt administration had set important precedents in the management of natural resources based on the principle of management for use. The greatest good for the greatest number for the longest time, or "conservation for use," was the slogan of the period. It reflected the growing confidence in scientific understanding of resources and the developing science of silviculture. Forests could be managed in a way to provide timber over the long term. Roosevelt's conservation programs were accompanied by the energetic creation and reorganization of departments and agencies, the U.S. Forest Service and National Park Service among them.

The Roosevelt administration had established a National Conservation Commission in 1908, one of several study commissions. Its mission was "to inquire into and advise . . . as to the condition of our natural resources, and to co-operate with other bodies created for a similar purpose by the states."[27] Roosevelt used study commissions widely to analyze situations and then propose policy based on those studies.[28] A point of pride was the voluntary nature of these commissions, which cost the government nothing yet gave it the benefit of input by some of the best minds in the nation. "Thanks to the members of the Executive and Legislative branches of the Government, already with full-time jobs, and to the experts, the work was done."[29] This, of course, meant that only people of means could participate in the formulation of policy suggestions. In addition, it established a very subtle, but significant precedent: the government itself—its own merit-based civil service—was not a source of authoritative information. Rather, outside experts were needed to supply the knowledge to inform legislative decision making. In fact, this approach is still institutionalized today in the form of appointed boards and commissions at the state and local level. The reliance on appointed boards and commissions undermines the legitimacy of the nonpartisan expert civil service, whose members are chosen by examination. Instead, decisions are made by political appointees as if they were nonpartisan experts; experts they may indeed be, but in the service of a particular economic interest. This process not only casts doubt on government as a source of reliable information and weakens its ability to carry out policy, it also opens the door to contestation: after all, any expert study can always be questioned by other appointed experts, employed by an opposing point of view.

Establishing Boards and Commissions

Following the federal model, Governor Johnson established a Conservation Commission in 1911. Composed of three persons appointed by the governor to work without compensation, the commission received $100,000 over four years to hire experts to conduct studies and prepare reports on natural resource preservation. The commission's mandate directed it to look at forestry, water, the use of water, water power, electricity, electrical and other power, mines and mining, mineral and other lands, dredging, reclamation, and irrigation.[30] It was on the basis of the reports of this commission that the Johnson administration began to develop its resource management initiatives.

By January 1913 the Conservation Commission had produced a 500-page report for the governor and the legislature. Mineral lands—including oil and gas—did not receive much attention because the commission viewed them as primarily the responsibility of the federal government. In the area of fish and game (an area that already had its own commission), the Conservation Commission emphasized the need for greater conservation. The commission concentrated its efforts on two main areas of resource management: forestry and water.

Managing Forests

The commission's philosophy regarding natural resources, especially timber, came out of the national Progressive tradition. Management for use based on scientific knowledge was the guiding principle. At the federal level, Gifford Pinchot served as the first head of the Division of Forestry. He, like Carl Schurz before him, had been trained in scientific forest management in Europe and believed that forests could, and should, be shaped and managed to enhance yield. Silviculture, as it had developed, recognized the importance of watershed management and the importance of the forests to groundwater recharge and water supply. Roosevelt Progressives, impressed with the efficiency of large-scale enterprises, believed that the resources of the nation should be made available to such enterprises and harnessed for economic growth, though in a regulated environment. It was the role of the state to ensure continued timber supply to the nation, and therefore government had to actively engage in timber protection and management so that economically efficient companies could then turn these raw materials into finished products for the nation's needs.

"The large-scale ownership of standing timber was to become so important and fundamental an innovation as technical advances in sawing and transportation, and, similarly, the corporation was to become the means by which the abundance of production could be organized." In a 1911 report the Bureau of Corporations recognized that the increasing centralization of control in the lumber industry was no longer a matter of technical advance or "any economy of large manufacturing plants," but purely a matter of business organization. This organizational structure could lessen the worst effects of fluctuating production and thereby alleviate economic stresses in the lumber industry, as in other manufacturing sectors. Thus, Progressives at the national level encouraged corporate exploitation of natural resources, believing that if such activities were conducted according to scientific and corporate principles, everyone would benefit. Pinchot developed a program of forest management that was based on rational planning to promote efficient development of the natural resources of forest regions. His was a utilitarian, highest use, multiple-use policy.[31]

The California Conservation Commission, operating within this national context, deplored the unregulated environment of private monopolies of resources because it tended to create two distinct social classes (owners and nonowners). In the commission's view, this was inconsistent with the principles of American democracy. The Conservation Commission upheld the more Socialist side of the Progressive movement (as represented by Randolph Haynes and others) by questioning monopolies and advocating government intervention and participation for the public interest. It specifically suggested that the state acquire or take custody of large areas of cut-over lands and reforest them. Reforestation was considered the most urgent task because of the fear of running out of timber. If the state had to assume responsibility for reforesting after a private company had harvested all the standing timber, then so be it. The commission also advocated the expansion of redwood parks and the development of a state capacity to fight fires.

Already in the last century preservationists had voiced concern about the dangers of fire, and in the first part of the twentieth century fire prevention became one of the overriding concerns in forest management.

In 1911 the existing Board of Forestry was given the power to force owners of forest lands to eliminate fire hazards on their land through a series of regulations. Although the board had no money to enforce these regulations, this was a first step toward regulation of private forest practice in the state. In 1912 the Conservation Commission met with representatives of the timber industry to discuss the important issues regarding forest lands in the state. By this time the industry had formed the California Forest Protective Association, a lobbying trade association. In general, they all agreed that a state capability to fight fires was a good idea—if the state paid for it from general tax funds.

The association and the commission also agreed on the need for reforestation, the association advocating that the state take responsibility for reforesting by purchasing already cut-over lands and planting them for the future, even though there was no money to do so.[32] Progressives believed that the relationship between government and business should work to assist business, and although the commission deplored monopoly, it still upheld indirect government assistance for the greater good.

By 1915 the commission had drawn up several pieces of forestry legislation for consideration, including measures to prevent forest fires, reforest cut-over lands, and consolidate existing resource-related commissions into a Department of Natural Resources. This legislative agenda was slowly implemented over the following decade. In addition, following several years of intricate and acrimonious struggles, the legislature passed the Forestry Act of 1919. This act reorganized the Forestry Board into an agency in the "image of a large corporation." There were to be four representatives, one from the timber industry, one from the livestock industry, one from agriculture, and one from the public at large. These four would constitute the State Board of Forestry, which was to develop policy for the state forester to administer.[33] The composition of the board, in true Progressive fashion, represented the industry it was to regulate. It joined the ranks of the other standing commissions, replete with the same inherent tensions between preserving the resource and promoting business interests.

Until this time the state's forests had been administered by a Board of Forestry with a weak mandate and managed by a state forester who held policy power. The state forester, whose name was Homans, believed in state intervention in private forest practice. He and his board feuded over proper state policy for nearly a decade, until the new board was put in place with additional powers that included greater enforcement authority and the power to set fire-prevention standards. This new board formalized the state's interest in forestry matters, but it also institutionalized a strong industry role in the determination of forest policy, to the detriment of the state forester's authority.

The timber industry itself was divided about the best way to maintain profits and a continuous flow of timber. Overproduction and low prices were a constant. "The annual production of lumber in the United States reached an all-time high in 1906 and 1907 . . . The tremendous capacity of the mills and the increasing availability of substitute building materials combined to glut the lumber market."[34] Some large operators wanted the federal government to create more reserves to ensure future timber supplies, and to intervene by setting regulations and standards that all in the industry would have to abide by equally. But any regulations or restrictions worked against small-scale itinerant operators, as they lacked sufficiently large supplies of timber to manage for the long term and could ill afford not to sell while waiting for prices to firm up. Not even all large operators could agree on federal or state regulation, because some regulations were more favorable to some firms and less so to others at any particular point in time. Nationally, there were the same issues regarding size of timber companies and forest policy. Under the Forest Reserve Act, for example, the government was to sell its timber to the highest bidder. This discouraged the smaller logger who either did not own land abutting the reserves or did not have transport for logs, and who therefore did not feel it was worthwhile to bid against the large lumber companies or syndicates. Large lumber companies seemed to have gained significant advantages with Forest Service policy and practices.[35]

The Special Case of the Redwoods

The California redwoods had been noted as a unique and valuable resource even by the Spanish explorers. At that time the redwoods stretched from the Santa Lucia Mountains in Monterey County northward to the Oregon border, a vestigial remnant of the pre–ice age forest. By the 1880s, except for a few groves in Santa Cruz, San Mateo, and Monterey Counties, no unlogged stands remained south or east of San Francisco.[36] Calls for their preservation were heard in the late nineteenth century, but those efforts had little tangible success.

In 1901 the Sempervirens Club was founded to save redwoods in Big Basin, 35 miles south of San Francisco. The Sierra Club and several Bay area women's groups joined this effort. Public and railroad support encouraged the legislature to appropriate $250,000 to establish the redwood forest in Big Basin as one of the first state parks. The railroad was an early booster of redwood preservation because redwoods were seen as a great tourist attraction, one that could be served profitably by the railroad. Although the commercial timber value of the trees was not yet fully appreciated, there was reluctance to use public funds for the purchase of park lands. In 1908 philanthropist and member of Congress William Kent, acting to prevent logging of the redwood forest just north of San Francisco, purchased what is now known as the John Muir Woods State Park. He had unsuccessfully lobbied for the creation of a redwood park while in Congress, even though there was strong public interest in such a project, and the northern counties themselves supported the idea of a redwood park. The parks that had been created had mostly been made up of unsold lands that were still in the public domain. From 1905 to 1911 Humboldt County's boards of trade, chambers of commerce, and local women's clubs petitioned Washington and campaigned locally for the creation of a redwood park, with little success. Kent himself had views that were quite extreme in comparison to most Progressive politicians; he believed that private land ownership was at the core of American economic problems. From this standpoint he pushed for the federal government to control all aspects of the remaining public domain and to prevent private enterprise from grabbing the rest.[37]

The Save the Redwoods League

Post–World War I timber demand in California accelerated logging in redwood country. The rot-proof qualities of the redwood had been discovered, and it had become accepted as a building material. Consequently, the redwood counties no longer saw their future in tourism. Rather, they envisioned the potential of an economy based on timber harvesting. This trend prompted a group of natural scientists from the University of California and Stanford University, joined by local women's clubs, to form the Save the Redwoods League in 1918.

The academics in the league were motivated by scientific interest: Since the redwoods were the oldest and tallest trees known, they deserved to be preserved as scientific laboratories in which questions of evolution and progress might be elucidated. Evolution and its implications—scientific, religious, and racial—were of great scientific interest. Some of the league members were interested in eugenics, at the heart of which was the theory of the superior individual or race. The survival of the redwoods over millennia was seen as a fascinating example of eugenics, from which much might be learned regarding the evolution and survival of biologically superior species. There was widespread awareness of the scientific value of the redwood as the "living link" with past ages. Redwood forests, then, should clearly be set aside as teaching centers, living laboratories.

In its early years the Save the Redwoods League, unlike other preservationist groups, adamantly opposed the idea of the federal government preserving redwood parks for recreation. National parks were seen as degrading the inspirational value of the lands preserved and destroying their primitive character. They popularized places that should be used for learning, not recreation. The league believed the redwood forests to be essentially untouched by human activity, and ardently wanted them preserved for that very quality, as examples of pristine nature. Yet for millennia before European contact California had supported the highest population densities, as well as some of the highest population concentrations, of Native Americans in North America. Several hundred thousand Native Americans had lived there, interacting with the environment, setting fires, harvesting, fishing, and in some areas engaging in agriculture. Native Americans had burned and managed the redwood forests to optimize browse for ungulates and to obtain vegetable products and basket-making materials. On the north coast they managed forests, brush, and grasslands with the use of fire.[38] So the notion of the redwoods as examples of pristine nature to be preserved and observed for its primeval qualities was, to some extent, illusory, though nonetheless powerful as an image. This flawed idea of nature as wild, untarnished, and original is still current today and serves as a strong motivation in preservation efforts. The Save the Redwoods League advocated the preservation of places where human activity would not be allowed, implicitly viewing humans as somehow separate from nature rather than as an intrinsic part of, and active participants in, the natural world.

The league combined an ideology of preservation for study, inspired by Social Darwinism, with a strong distrust of federal intervention in what it deemed state affairs. Consequently, it turned toward private philanthropy and state and county efforts to save redwoods. The organization did not believe in actions that were hostile to industry, such as condemning redwood lands as scenic byways, or for highways or park land. In the league's view, although it was the state's responsibility to maximize the public good, state action should not be substituted for civic action. If the population at large was not willing to purchase significant redwoods outright, for example, then those forests would simply not be preserved.

Members of the league were committed to the capitalist system of free enterprise and were anti-federalists. As Newton Drury, one-time president of the organization and later director of the National Park Service, explained, "There are some fundamental concepts . . . that are more important than conservation. Free enterprise, and things of that sort."[39] Consequently, the league's efforts were successful only to the extent that it could raise money to purchase exceptional groves of redwoods when industry agreed to sell them.

The Save the Redwoods League was also deeply involved in advocating and supporting Progressive reforms at the state level, based on a vision of government's role as regulatory but not interventionist. The league's interest in science and evolution and its Progressivism fit hand in hand. It could support the creation of expert boards and commissions that would provide policy guidance by outside, volunteer experts. The league "contended that salaried government administrators were not free men and should not make policy." To the extent that the public sector grew in decision-making power, those decisions would be based on "scientific politics."[40] Politically active, the league proposed institutional changes in the state regulation of forest practice, park development, and management. It advocated a comprehensive system of resource management by boards and commissions, and the creation of a statewide park commission with jurisdiction over all present and future parks (to be acquired through philanthropic means). It favored legislation for land planning in redwood country, through a program for statewide land planning, and it pushed for the creation of a Department of Natural Resources that would house the state's Division of Forestry and Division of Beaches and Parks. The organization had a far-reaching vision of natural resource management in the state and powerful allies in the state legislature. The Save the Redwoods League was the quintessential Progressive organization, advocating limited federal government intervention, voluntarism, and the use of state boards and commissions with policymaking power.

In the 1920s further Progressive governmental reorganization consolidated the functions of some fifty-eight state agencies into a few comprehensive departments. The cabinet system was established, as well as the line-item veto, which gave the governor the right to veto items in the state budget after it had been passed by the legislature. Also in the 1920s the Department of Natural Resources was founded as a combination of the various agencies administering mining, forestry, and fish and game. It subsumed the state Mining Bureau, the office of the state mineralogist, the Department of Petroleum and Gas, the office of state oil and gas supervisor, the office of state forester, the state Board of Forestry, the California Redwood Park Commission, the San Pasqual Battlefield Commission, the Mount Diablo Park Commission, and the state Fish and Game Commission.[41] With the creation of the Department of Natural Resources and the establishment of a Division of Parks in 1927, natural resource management became a permanent part of state bureaucracy.

The efforts of the Save the Redwoods League, supported by the Sierra Club and the Sempervirens Club, led to the creation of four major redwood state parks: Humboldt Redwoods State Park on Bull Creek and the South

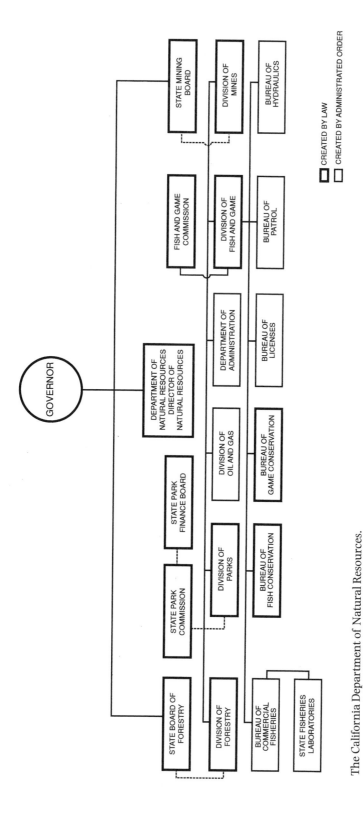

The California Department of Natural Resources.

(From Elsey Hurt, California State Government [Sacramento: Supervisor of Documents, 1936])

Fork of the Eel River; Prairie Creek Redwoods State Park; Jedediah Smith Redwoods State Park, encompassing the plains of Mill Creek and the Smith River in Del Norte County; and the small Del Norte Coast Redwoods State Park.

The State Park Commission

In 1927 the California legislature officially created the state Park Commission, part of the newly created Department of Natural Resources, to oversee state parks and especially the coastal redwoods. The legislature provided funds for a survey of lands suitable for new state parks and approved the sale of $6 million worth of state park bonds, to be privately matched, for the acquisition of new properties. In 1928 the voters approved the bond measure.

The Park Commission then hired Frederick Law Olmsted Jr. to undertake the survey. Olmsted was the son of the landscape architect who had designed many famous parks, including Central Park in New York, and who had consulted on the Golden Gate Park in San Francisco. The younger Olmsted had been involved in promoting city and regional planning within the nascent planning profession. His report guided state park acquisition for years. Olmsted organized his park plans around a scenic highway that ran from the Mexican border to the Oregon border—a response to the beginnings of automobile touring. His proposals were modest. For example, he calculated that only about 3 percent of the redwood forest could be saved, and these were primarily forests in the easily accessible flatlands that contained spectacular trees. The groves in the flats were irrigated by the rivers of the northwestern part of the state; because of the rich alluvial soil, the trees grew to extraordinary heights. These were the specimens considered worthy of protection.[42] Despite the nineteenth-century understanding of the importance of watershed protection, in the early twentieth century the issue of protecting the watersheds surrounding the preserved groves was not raised—only to cause heartbreak later.

Managing Water

The issue of water management in California continued to be controversial and unresolved. It was obvious to Progressives that the state's future economic growth was predicated on water development and that the current situation was untenable. By the time Governor Johnson came to office, there were 20,000 existing water rights, and more were being added every day. Most of them had been filed for monopolistic or speculative reasons. Early on, the Conservation Commission proposed the establishment of a water commission, an administrative board that would review water-rights claims and begin establishing new water law. The water-commission proposal was

State redwood parks

Klamath River, Humboldt County, 7 miles from mouth, 1926. (Fish and Game Commission; courtesy of California State Archives, Office of the Secretary of State, Sacramento)

rejected by the legislature, just as it had been in the previous century. Opposition also came from large southern California water companies. By 1913, however, the Conservation Commission convinced the legislature that adjudication of water-rights claims was a necessity in view of the increasingly dire situation. That year the legislature passed a law providing for the establishment of a state agency to control and distribute California water, though the new agency was not given the power to challenge or change the existing structure.

Thus a Water Commission was established, but with modest purview and powers, a concession to the opposition. It was able to accomplish little because of court challenges, inadequate funding, and insufficient power to enforce its decisions.[43] Water-law reform was an important step toward a more modern economic order in the state, one essential for continued economic growth. However, it had the potential to pit powerful economic elites and geographic regions against one another. The Wright Irrigation Act, passed in 1887, had fostered a proliferation of irrigation companies—many of which eventually failed—in the Central Valley and in southern California. Most private irrigation schemes went bankrupt. The Wright Act had many defects and gave rise to many lawsuits. In the words of Donald J. Pisani, "the Wright Act proved as much of a boon to lawyers as it did to land speculators." By 1897 a new law was passed that did away with the district concept and required a majority of all landowners, representing a majority of the property values of land susceptible of irrigation, to petition the board of supervisors before an election to form a district could be held. Further, it required a two-thirds vote, rather than a simple majority, to create a district. Bonding authority was also tightened up. Yet the district approach had made its mark and had a profound effect on the approach to improvements in cities. "It failed to transform California's vast wheat ranchos into small, intensively cultivated family farms, as the law's proponents had hoped. In fact, it promoted piecemeal, uncoordinated development of the state's water supply."[44]

But the geographically unequal distribution of water in the state meant that everyone had to look to the same sources for water. Those sources were concentrated in the northern part of the state and in the Sierra Nevada mountains. The challenge was how to maximize the use of this water and how to distribute it equitably, even to points south. Power companies, newcomers on the scene, also had great interest in the way the state regulated water. The companies had taken advantage of the state's chaotic water laws to establish control over some of the state's waterways to generate water for power. They paid nothing for the use of this water, established themselves as the owners of the water rights by appropriation, and built the value of those rights into the capitalized value of the individual companies. Rate-payers were at the mercy of power companies, which could essentially charge whatever the market would bear. In the face of these interests, the Water Commission could do little to advance the cause of water-law reform.

One of the major tests for the Progressives in California in the 1920s was whether they could overcome the opposition of powerful utility interests and already established agriculture, in order to develop a comprehensive, state-financed water and hydroelectric plan. The idea of a state-financed plan for water development was backed by many agricultural interests in the San Joaquin Valley. Suffering from low agricultural prices and drought, they had come to the conclusion that only the state could effectively provide the amount of water needed for agriculture in the valley. Central Valley farmers organized into the California Irrigation Association to lobby for water development, following a proposal by Robert Marshall, who in 1919 had outlined a water plan centered on a reservoir on the Sacramento River above Redding that would feed two parallel aqueducts running down both sides of the Sacramento and San Joaquin Valleys. Marshall's plan built on the work of William Hammond Hall in the 1880s, which was never implemented. The state would finance the project and make the water available to all who desired it.

Marshall's proposal was strongly opposed by existing irrigation districts and private power companies. Pacific Gas & Electric spent nearly half a million dollars to defeat the proposal because it gave preferential rights to publicly owned water and power companies, undermining the position of PG&E and Southern California Edison. Though Progressives pushed to have Marshall's plan accepted, the proposal was defeated first in the legislature and then three times as a ballot initiative during the 1920s.[45]

The Federal Presence in Water Development

In 1902 Congress passed the Newlands Reclamation Act in response to the need for large-scale and coordinated water development in the arid West—another land-use–oriented policy in the Progressive tradition of concern for physical development. Only a state or the federal government had sufficient resources to build such expensive and substantial systems. Further, the Jeffersonian ideal of small family farms continued to influence Congress and to serve the interests of advocates of irrigation systems. Building federally funded irrigation systems, western senators and others argued, would allow small family farms to be established in these arid lands, spreading prosperity. Irrigation would produce an ideal democracy; communities built on a foundation of irrigation (small farms) would offer all the advantages and none of the disadvantages of urban life—they might even serve as the foundation for a new ethical code and higher civilization.[46] This was powerful imagery for a nation facing labor unrest, crowded cities, and the transformative effects of modernization. It also conveniently ignored the already existing pattern of land monopolization, a result of previous federal land policies.

The Newlands Reclamation Act of 1902 was intended to meet both these objectives—the expansion of agriculture and the settlement of small family farms. (Senator Newlands, the act's sponsor, was a Nevadan who had married into a family that had made a fortune in silver mining. He owned several houses in California and often lived in the state.) The act provided for federal water development to irrigate the lands of small farms in the arid West. To qualify for federally developed water, farms could be no larger than 160 acres (per household member), harkening back to the Jeffersonian agrarian ideal and the 1862 Homestead Act. The Newlands Act required a farmer who owned more than 160 acres before irrigation to sell the excess land within a period of ten years after receiving the irrigation water, and to sell at pre-water prices. Larger farms would be entitled to receive federally subsidized irrigation water, but under the ten-year limitation. After ten years all lands in excess of 160 acres would have to be sold off at pre-water prices. Otherwise those lands would stop receiving the irrigation water or farmers would have to begin paying the full price of the water to irrigate them. But for nearly thirty years the Newlands Reclamation Act remained only a promise; nothing was built and frustration continued to mount.

California farmers continued to press for the federal government to provide subsidized water, but they wanted the acreage limitation changed. The number of farms in California had increased from about 73,000 in 1900 to more than 150,000 by 1935, and during the same period the average farm size had dropped from around 400 acres to around 200 acres. But the percentage of land in large holdings "not only remained high but rose dramatically. In 1920, for example, sixty percent of the land was in farms of a thousand acres or more, and within fifteen years, the percentage had increased to seventy [percent]."[47] Thus the pattern of land monopolization continued, further concentrating land ownership.

Small farmers were in an especially difficult position. Often their lands were not encompassed by an irrigation project or they could not afford to purchase irrigated lands. Federal reclamation activities did not begin until the mid-1930s with the construction of the Central Valley Project. Large farmers experienced anxiety and discontent out of fear that as long as the federal 160-acre limit was on the books, it might someday be enforced, thus forcing them to comply with the requirement of selling off lands in excess of the limit after the ten-year period had passed. In general, farmers resented federal intervention in natural resource policy, feeling that resource management was a state issue, yet they were also unhappy with the inherent limitations of locally initiated irrigation development. Such fears and anxieties made farmers, especially those in the Central Valley, politically active. The large farmers, claiming to represent all farmers, formed powerful farm lobby organizations, including the California Farm Bureau, to advocate for their interests in Sacramento.

Water management in the state would only become more complicated. All levels of government were implicated in water. There was not only state oversight (such as it was) and local irrigation districts, but also federal involvement in water development and distribution. The prospect of federal water development was greeted with enthusiasm because it would ensure the construction of sufficiently large systems, yet it also provoked fear and resentment of federal intervention in what was seen as fundamentally a state prerogative—the control of water. A better alternative would be for the federal government to give the state the resources with which to develop water itself. This tension, still unresolved, continues to have a profound effect on water management and politics today.

The Owens Valley

"The Owens Valley was located in what was politely referred to as 'undiscovered California'," northeast of Los Angeles.[48] It too was shaped by federal land-disposal laws and water-development policy. A high desert valley, it had been home to the Paiutes, a Native American tribe whose members practiced a form of light agriculture and irrigation. When settlers came to the valley, they thought it showed great agricultural promise, but large-scale water development and distribution would be necessary to take full advantage of its potential. Farmers settled in the northern portion of the valley, where there were more streams fed by the Sierras, and developed modest irrigation systems. The southern portion of the valley was more arid, though the Owens River flowed through it into Owens Lake, which was wide and deep enough to support paddle-boat transportation across it. Still, to irrigate from the Owens River would require cooperative regionwide irrigation.

In 1903 the valley was explored by the Federal Reclamation Service to determine the amount and quality of its unclaimed land and the possibility of storing water for irrigation. The valley seemed to have good potential for water, and accordingly an irrigation scheme was developed by the Reclamation Service in 1904, which included identification of two suitable reservoir sites the service intended to purchase. Meanwhile, Los Angeles was suffering from a drought, and the city began to look at the water of the Owens Valley as a possible source of supply. In the spring of 1905 Fred Eaton, a former mayor of Los Angeles, was directed by William Mulholland, the newly appointed superintendent of the Los Angeles Department of Water and Power, to go to the valley, secretly acquire options on key properties bordering the Owens River, and then claim its water under the doctrine of riparian rights. The rancher from whom the land was bought had himself fraudulently obtained it from the federal government by using dummy entrymen to file claims at the state land office. On most of these claims the rancher had paid only a deposit and had not kept up his payments. He had no title to the lands, but held on to them while buying out nearby farms. Despite this illegal ownership, Los Angeles was still able to buy the lands and acquire title to them. Other lands purchased by the city had originally been claimed for development by the Inyo Land Company under the provisions of the Desert Land Act, yet the acreage—12,433 acres—was far larger than could have been envisioned in the act. Thus Los Angeles ended up with large landholdings bought up secretively from owners who themselves had abused the federal land-disposal program and had engaged in fraud.

Los Angeles also outmaneuvered the Federal Reclamation Service by purchasing lands the service had designated as suitable reservoir sites, and which it intended to buy. Outfoxed, the Reclamation Service had to bow out of water development in the Owens Valley. "Had the nation's public land laws achieved greater success in establishing a denser pattern of small holdings in the valley's southern region, the larger number of irrigated farms and the more intensive use of the Owens River for agriculture might have deterred Los Angeles' advance into the Owens Valley."[49] And had federal land-disposal laws been enforced, the pattern on the land in the Owens Valley might have been quite different. Instead, fraud served to make the Owens Valley a colony of Los Angeles, providing the city with its water. This forever closed the door on the possibility of developing a farm-based regional economy or on any other future that required water. By late 1909 Los Angeles had acquired over 82,000 acres of land and appurtenant water rights, encompassing nearly the entire southern half of the valley as well as substantial acreage in the north.

The Fish and Game Commission

In 1912 the California Board of Fish Commissioners was renamed the Fish and Game Commission. It was financially independent from the state budget because of its annual fee for hunting licenses. It had a small army of game wardens and a full-time staff attorney, and starting in 1914 it even published its own journal, *California Fish and Game Quarterly*. The Fish and Game Commission's mission was to preserve the state's wildlife resources and make them available for hunting and fishing. As protector of these resources, the commission was doomed to continual conflict with the eco-

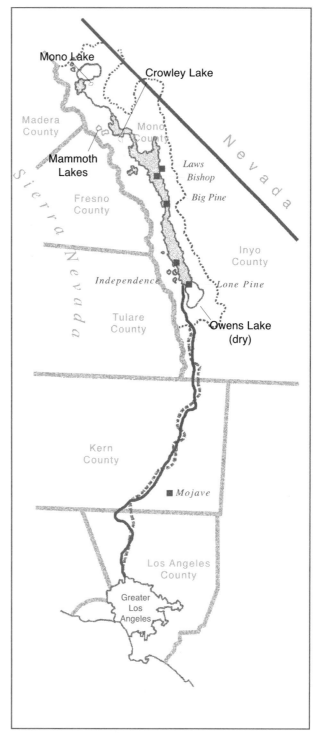

Mono Lake

Crowley Lake

Madera
County

Sierra

Mono
County

Mammoth
Lakes

Laws
Bishop

Big Pine

Fresno
County

Nevada

Nevada

Inyo
County

Independence

Lone Pine

Tulare
County

Owens Lake
(dry)

Kern
County

■ Mojave

Los Angeles
County

Greater
Los
Angeles

1st Los Angeles Aqueduct

2nd Los Angeles Aqueduct

Mono and Owens Basin

County Boundaries

Land owned by Los Angeles
Department of Water & Power

The Los Angeles Water Project, Owens Valley Aqueduct

nomic development and exploitation of forest and other resources that could adversely affect fish and wildlife.

The commission was most active in the area of fisheries management. Among its responsibilities was the regulation of the growing commercial fishery in the state. The commission found itself "in strange and treacherous waters . . . as mechanization revolutionized fishery production after 1910. Twentieth-century fishermen pushed out to sea with much enthusiasm but little information and . . . [the commission], hitherto a rather clubby association of biologists and aristocratic outdoors enthusiasts, had suddenly to police a highly capitalized and politically muscular industry." Starting at the turn of the century, as the California economy industrialized, so did its fishing industry. Fishermen used boats with fossil-fuel-burning motors, and processors used mechanical power to process the fish. "The new fisheries and the technology to develop them emerged from a complex interaction of market forces," as well as environmental change. The ocean fisheries of southern California eclipsed those of the Sacramento–San Joaquin watershed in importance, and fish packing became an important industry. By the early 1920s California led the nation in the volume and value of its fishery produce. But real growth was spurred by World War I. "Like most Americans, Californians began substituting higher-grade foods for grain in their diets as their real incomes rose after the turn of the century." Farmers needed high-protein feeds to raise livestock in the new intensive, factory-style operations, and this opened up a new market for fishmeal, a high-protein fish by-product. Pressure on the fishery resources of the state grew by leaps and bounds, but the powers and scope of the Fish and Game Commission did not keep pace.[50]

Ideas about Nature: The Tension between Preservation and Conservation

The Progressive movement at the national level, under the leadership of Theodore Roosevelt, had brought the question of natural resource management to the nation's attention. Roosevelt believed that the federal government had a responsibility to manage its resources for the greatest good for the greatest number. This conservation-for-use approach—Progressive conservation—was highly utilitarian and based on scientific management. The fundamental objective was to enhance economic growth in a managed framework, so that resources would be husbanded and not rapidly depleted.[51] Progressive conservationists were influenced by the growing field of natural science and sought to develop scientifically based systems for nat-

Salacchini canned fish products, Monterey, California, 1919. (Photograph by P. H. Ayer for Fish and Game Commission; courtesy of California State Archives, Office of the Secretary of State, Sacramento)

ural resource management so as to preserve the vital elements of natural systems while simultaneously exploiting them.

Progressive conservation faced a challenge from another approach, that of preservation. The rapid exploitation of the nation's natural resources, the growth of large industrial cities that were overcrowded and polluted, and the disappearance of species: In the East, by the early nineteenth century, these factors had already inspired a movement of reflection and concern. Writers such as Thoreau, painters such as Catlin, and naturalists such as Audubon had called for the creation of protected natural reserves and the preservation of certain fragile species. The reserves were to be places where there would be no intervention in nature, so that it could be preserved in pristine condition—without the presence of human beings. Rapid environmental destruction was palpable to the nineteenth-century explorers who combed the West. One year there were buffalo, the next they were gone. Catlin and Audubon, for example, saw their tasks as recording peoples and bird species, respectively, as rapidly as they could before extinction. The threat of extinction lent urgency to their preservation advocacy. Their appeals resonated with numerous publics, from the Romantics to the emerging middle class, melding with concerns over the enormous urban changes wrought by the industrial revolution. Many people were repulsed by the dense, unhealthy, and dangerous industrial cities that were sprawling across the landscape. Nature, in contrast, was clean and capable of nurturing fundamental spiritual values that could not be found in the cities.

These two approaches to nature and natural resource management— conservation and preservation—came into conflict in California. The classic story of the struggle over building a dam in Tuolumne Canyon in Yosemite National Park, the so-called Hetch Hetchy controversy, illustrates these opposing points of view and also the role of the federal government in resource development. In California the strong intellectual and emotional commitment to the preservation of the Sierra Nevada mountains that had found expression in the Sierra Club, among other groups, confronted another, equally powerful commitment—to Progressive conservation, the embodiment of Progressive ideology. The conflicting views were embodied by two men: John Muir and Gifford Pinchot.

The Hetch Hetchy Dam

Conservation and preservation: At the start it seemed as though they shared a common purpose, the wise management of the nation's natural resources and its most spectacular landscapes. But when business leaders claimed that San Francisco needed to expand its water supply to support future growth, and proposed damming the Tuolumne River, preservationists argued that the Hetch Hetchy Valley of the Tuolumne River, which formed a canyon of the Yosemite National Park, should not be sacrificed for such a purpose. This canyon, it was argued, had park status (as part of Yosemite) and was as beautiful as Yosemite, if less grand. Muir led the fight against the construction of the dam, while Pinchot, as head of the National Forest Service, was the articulate spokesman in favor of construction. The Hetch Hetchy saga, which has been well told elsewhere, is complex and cannot be reduced to a face-off between the two men. There were other players, both public and private, and with strong economic interests at stake. Still, Muir and Pinchot do represent the two main emerging streams of thought about natural resource management.

On paper, Yosemite National Park included the Merced River drainage and the entire headwaters of the Tuolumne River watershed.[52] Unlike the policy for national forests, the policy toward national parks was that they were not open to any form of resource development, even development regulated by federal officials. This was a way of maintaining what was believed to be their pristine condition. The mayor of San Francisco, desperate for new water sources for the city, had pressured Congress to pass a parks bill that would allow rights of way through national parks for "domestic, public, or other beneficial uses." His proposal was based on the precedent established in the park creation legislation, which allowed limited building, grazing, lumbering, and even farming.[53]

On the basis of this legislation, in 1901 the city applied for the right to turn the Hetch Hetchy Valley into a reservoir, but the request was turned down by the interior secretary, who did not want to set a precedent of violating a national park. The city tried again in 1906, after the great earthquake and resulting fires, and this time the proposal received a far more favorable reception by Progressives Roosevelt and Pinchot.

The Forest Service had been established the year before. As its head, Pinchot had a vision of natural resource management that went beyond the forests already within the scope of the Forest Service, to include all remaining forest reserves and national parks. He was an empire builder who campaigned to have existing national parks incorporated in the Forest Service and made subject to the same management-for-use philosophy. Pinchot had come to California on several occasions and was acquainted with Muir. Muir had taken Pinchot and Roosevelt camping in the Sierras, and was convinced that they were as moved by the beauty and natural riches in the mountains as he. But Pinchot could find no reason for the preservation of the Hetch Hetchy Valley of the Tuolumne River when it could clearly be put to utilitarian use for the generation of electricity. That Yosemite Valley was preserved seemed to him enough, and there were indeed pressing urban needs for water. The conservation philosophy, after all, was to use resources wisely to serve human needs. In this he was supported by U.S. senator from California, William Kent, the same individual who had donated Muir Woods. Kent saw the Hetch Hetchy dam as an efficient and democratic use of resources because the water system would be municipally owned, thus combining two of the important tenets of Progressive conservation.[54] Consequently he and Pinchot supported the dam builders despite preservationists' expectations that national parks would continue to be off-limits to development; Kent, in fact, authored the legislation. Dam construction was approved by Congress in 1913, leaving a deep sense of betrayal among preservationists. Muir died the following year. Preservation and conservation forces have continued to oppose each other throughout the twentieth century, notably over development in the Sierras, but also throughout the state and across the country.

Reshaping the Urban Landscape

The changing political and economic realities at the national level were felt even more intensely at the state and local levels. Like their counterparts elsewhere in the country, the California Progressives were concerned with cleaning up government at all levels, but the reform of municipal governments seemed particularly urgent. San Francisco and Los Angeles were the state's largest metropolitan areas. Such cities were seen as crucibles for economic activity, whose success would then infuse the rest of society. But political corruption impeded economic progress and created inefficiencies. Progressive measures for the cities were aimed at reforming municipal government—by removing it from the influence of self-serving political machines—and at modernizing the cities by providing the necessary infrastructure for commerce through planning and physical improvements. Better street lighting, efficient garbage pickup, improved electric and water systems, sanitary disposal, and intelligently planned transportation corridors were all part of the urban agenda of the Progressives.

This urban agenda was buttressed by the rise of engineering—sanitary engineering in particular—as well as the growth of planning, a product of efforts begun in the late nineteenth century. "The complexities of the metropolitan dilemma required that new explanations be made in terms of rational systemic processes that could mold development toward specified ends."[55] The components and functions of a city needed to be organized and coordinated, and the idea of land uses serving to segregate activities—for example, separating industrial from residential areas—took hold. A related idea was that of segregating people more efficiently—rich from poor, one race or ethnicity from another. Implementing these ideas became possible through the rise of planning and its tool kit, especially land-use controls, such as zoning. Zoning would achieve a more efficient city, which in turn would encourage commerce and facilitate the transaction of business.

Old-time ward bosses in eastern cities, the products of "corrupt" politics of the Gilded Age, had governed by a different principle—patronage, which meant taking care of people as potential voters. As a result, local government was perceived as inefficient and dishonest, run by party machines that were responsive to an "ignorant proletariat"—an inefficient anachronism in the face of modern forms of organization. Addressing these issues directly, the Progressive platform appealed to the glorious, and tangible, achievements of science and industry. Nationwide, this movement was captured by the descriptive phrase "city efficient," the slogan of the rising planning professionals. At the local level, Progressives also supported social reform legislation and believed that municipalities should own their own water and power utilities.

Besides desiring to bring the principles of business efficiency and good management to local government, Progressives wanted to use the professional expertise residing in the business sector. There was a general movement to bring together the two sectors, business and government. Business leaders created and/or allied themselves with "good government" leagues and thus came to exercise a powerful role in the routine administrative work of municipal government. Describing their work as nonpolitical, the business leaders funded private research bureaus that recommended improvements in municipal government operations, and established public commissions that pursued social reforms compatible with property rights. Business leaders prided themselves on their role as providers of information to local voters and congratulated themselves on their effectiveness in shaping election outcomes.[56] But electoral reforms were also a method to transfer political power into the hands of a new elite and to distance government from the people, particularly with the institution of nonpartisan local elections.

During this time business leaders and their organizations forged a political role for themselves that matched their ideology. They worked closely with mayors, governors, and members of municipal, state, and federal legislative councils as informal advisors and quasi-public consultants to bring about the reform measures they believed would improve government.[57] Progressives believed that city government should be administrative rather than legislative, a matter of executing rather than of determining policy. As a prominent business leader of the time stated, a city (Los Angeles, in this case) was "simply a huge [business] corporation. . . . [whose] citizens are the stockholders, and [whose] purpose is not to produce dividends but to promote the well-being of the community and to conserve the interests of the people as a whole."[58]

Business organizations, pushing the Progressive agenda, believed that business values would ensure progress and prosperity for the general community. In their eyes, business transcended class issues and was a value in and of itself. As Frederick J. Koster proclaimed in his inaugural address as president of the San Francisco Chamber of Commerce in 1916: "I have said that the Chamber of Commerce is not of a class for a class; and yet we are in a sense, a class—a class upon whom it is fair to lay a great burden of responsibility, responsibility for the development of fairness because where that does not exist the community cannot thrive; responsibility toward causing the community to properly protect investments made within its bounds."[59]

Los Angeles

Los Angeles had suffered under the shadow of San Francisco, a city that had grown quickly into the undisputed commercial center of the state. Bankers and investors had settled in San Francisco, growing rich off the gold country of the Sierras, from investments in the Arctic, from salmon canneries, tanneries, land reclamation and speculation, Hawaiian sugar plantations, and hydroelectric power generated in the Sierras. They transformed "vast realms into a 'treasure trove' of commodities, bought and sold on the city's markets."[60] Such investors and investments directed from urban centers wove a web of interrelations between city and countryside that transformed nature while enriching the cities. These financial webs, invisible to the eye, intimately linked the city and the country.

Settlers in Los Angeles initially were a different sort than the entrepreneurs who arrived in San Francisco. Progressivism was so vigorous in Los Angeles because the city was inhabited by native-born Americans, for the most part, and not by European immigrants dependent on the machine. "Like the reformers, these newcomers were revolted by the debasement and irresponsibility of local government in the United States and appalled by the prospect that the sordid political practices of corrupt eastern cities might prevail in Los Angeles."[61] They sought to create a city that was not a city, a place of single-family dwellings and gardens. They were aggressively anti-metropolitan; a suburban home epitomized their vision of the good community. They believed that the harmony of society depended on the uniformity of its members and sought companionship in their immediate families, distancing economic and civic interests from their social lives. In Los Angeles people were distinguished by race rather than by nationality, and nonwhites were isolated geographically. Ethnic groups existed "in intimate economic dependence, but in more or less complete cultural independence of the world about them," and a diffuse urbanization pattern was deliberately established that segregated land uses and people.[62] This segregation, both of land uses and of people, was intrinsic to the city's growth pattern and was reflected in the growing power of the idea of zoning—a way of embedding the city's social structure through land use. Los Angeles had no large concentrations of industrial activity—indeed, compared to San Francisco, it had little industrial activity at all—and commercial activity was segregated from the residential areas.[63]

Political power in Los Angeles resided in the city council, even though the mayor and the council were in theory an independent and balanced executive and legislature. The council had the right to appoint many of the mayor's subordinates and to order public improvements without his consent. It could override his veto of any ordinance. Councilmen were elected by district, and hence those elections could be controlled by powerful economic interests during the nominating process.

The Southern Pacific Railroad Company was widely known to play an influential role in Los Angeles politics. Between 1865 and 1900 the Southern Pacific machine remained in power because it managed not only to satisfy the city's major business interests, but also to adapt its own operations to the city's political parties and governmental constraints. Though the city was divided between Democrats and Republicans, at the local level the parties had little to quarrel about. They agreed on the essentials, accepting that the district-based councilmen held the power and allowing the machine to generally control the local elections.[64]

Los Angeles politics was unique in one respect: the presence of Harrison Gray Otis, the influential owner of the *Los Angeles Times*. He chafed at the power of the railroad, and he detested organized labor; consequently he used the newspaper to lambaste both. In one of the more spectacular struggles of the late nineteenth century, Otis led the Free Harbor Campaign, uniting the business community against the Southern Pacific Railroad's bid to have a harbor built in Santa Monica and to control it. This would have greatly enhanced the Southern Pacific's already substantial power in the region. Otis's Free Harbor Campaign successfully lobbied the federal government to undertake the building of an independent harbor in San Pedro—a major victory for Otis. As Bill Deverell points out, this defeat of Southern Pacific shows that it was not the all-powerful entity that it had been made out to be, and that it could be defeated.[65]

During the 1890s Otis and others like him created the institutional foundations for the effective participation of businessmen in urban policymaking. One such organization, founded by Otis in 1893, was the Los Angeles Merchants' Association, which merged with the Manufacturers' Association in 1896. The group set out to master the threat of future depressions and establish control over labor relations.[66] Los Angeles businessmen regarded labor's dominance of San Francisco politics with apprehension and supported Otis's political activities aimed at eliminating the possibility of organized labor efforts in Los Angeles. Trade unions in Los Angeles faced determined opposition from manufacturers and the "outright hostility of Los Angeles' aggressive and influential realtors and merchants." They also faced a surplus of native-born skilled labor, workers who shared the business viewpoint that organized labor was subversive.[67] Many Los Angeles business leaders were determined to establish conditions that would reduce labor strife and cripple the strength of organized labor. To ensure the success of their ideas, these powerful individuals began to reform municipal government in Los Angeles.

There was also a core of Progressive reformers, including John Randolph Haynes, a physician and president of the Direct Legislation League, known for Socialist sympathies. Haynes, though quite a bit further left than many of his colleagues, chose the middle ground out of a belief that the electoral success of California Progressivism could be a vehicle for far-reaching social reform and had a much greater chance of success than the Socialist Party. Consequently, Haynes invited many of the "wealthiest and most conservative businessmen in Southern California" to serve as vice presidents of the Direct Legislation League. Ever the pragmatist, he was always "willing to accept a quarter of a loaf if I cannot get half and half if I cannot get a whole."[68] The Direct Legislation League in Los Angeles came to be the engine behind the electoral reform proposals of the Progressives, including the initiative and the referendum processes, though it opposed the recall. The disciplined and well-financed Merchants and Manufacturers Association (organized by Otis to combat unionization in the city) gave its lukewarm support to the Los Angeles Municipal League, acquiescing in the call for the adoption of the recall and referendum as part of a joint political platform. Such direct legislation was the vehicle to rid local government of the influence of parties.

Charles D. Willard of the Municipal League invited the Southern Pacific to enter into a partnership for civic development and to contribute to the reform platform and measures pushed by the League, such as the institution of a professional civil service and nonpartisan local elections. Such reforms were seen as a way to insulate city employees and administration from political bosses. There is considerable evidence that other business interests—including the public utility corporations and gambling combines—also supported such reform measures. But in addition Progressives pushed for municipal ownership of public utilities in order to sever the connection between private enterprise and governmental authority. The Los Angeles Department of Water and Power is one result of such efforts; another is the city-owned Los Angeles Harbor. The Progressives had planned the municipalization of gas, telephone, and street railways, but did not get that far.

Despite the strong anti–Southern Pacific campaign and the denunciation of machine politics in the city, both the machine politicians (handpicked by the railroad) and the new urban reformers belonged to the Los Angeles establishment.[69] The Southern Pacific was regularly included in deliberations on reform activities and was represented in some business Progressive groups. After all, the railroad was important to the continued economic growth of the state. Finding a common basis on which to proceed toward reform was more important than dismantling the railroad, for that would have been economic suicide for the state.

No other interest group rivaled the Progressive business leaders in their ability to influence urban policymaking during this period. Labor did endorse Progressive candidates when they ran on issues favorable to labor interests, such as an eight-hour day. But lacking the resources and access to power that the Progressive businessmen enjoyed, organized labor also adopted more confrontational strategies and even (on occasion) supported the competing Socialist Party. By following a course of bargaining with internal rivals and accommodating differences, the Progressive businessmen were able to maintain a common class front, and in this way they effectively directed the decision-making process to create a political system that established regulated competition and a favorable business climate.

Progressives agreed that the function of city government was administrative rather than legislative, a matter of executing rather than determining policy. The reforms Progressives put in place severed local politics from state and federal politics by throwing out political affiliations for local elections. Candidates had to appeal to the whole electorate—districts also had been jettisoned—placing a priority on publicity over familiarity and on finances rather than favors. Reforms weakened local groups and associations, including organized labor, and increased the importance of metropolitan institutions, such as daily newspapers, civic clubs, and business and commercial organizations. They created a distance between local citizens and city government that was never recaptured. After 1913, when all the reforms had been put in place, candidates were without exception of little distinction. Campaigns avoided critical issues, such as the relationship between business and government, and focused on law enforcement, personal morality, and other noncontroversial matters. So long as the bureaucracy functioned and real estate investments were profitable, people were content.[70]

Charter Cities and Special Districts

In the late nineteenth century the business community (including the Southern Pacific Railroad) stimulated tremendous growth through boosterism and real estate speculation. Local governments were weak and relatively poorly financed. Their inability to raise money was beginning to hamper further urban growth. Infrastructure projects—harbors, water and power systems, sewage disposal systems—required public financing. Such projects, though necessary, were beyond the capacity of the business sector to provide.

The solution to this dilemma was the creation of charter cities. This invention gave local jurisdictions the financial autonomy they needed to raise money for large infrastructure projects. The first step was taken in 1879, in the form of a constitutional revision that instituted municipal home rule for cities. In 1888 cities were allowed to adopt a freeholder's charter, and Los

Angeles was the first city to do so. This status, in effect, allowed a city to draw up its own municipal constitution and to finance large-scale infrastructure projects by creating municipal bond referenda. It also permitted cities to hold annexation elections, thereby incorporating promising real estate into their boundaries. Urban special districts were created to raise the money and implement the needed infrastructure. This followed the pattern already established by the Wright Irrigation Act, whereby special irrigation districts could be formed by interested parties. In this instance, however, the special districts were urban-based and largely initiated by the local governments themselves. For example, sewage districts were created for the purpose of raising money, through bonds or taxation, to build sewers. The California constitution empowered charter cities "to make and enforce all laws and regulations in respect to municipal affairs subject only to the restrictions and limitations in their charters."

In effect, local cities that adopted municipal home rule in the form of charters became autonomous governments able to raise money and pass regulations governing all municipal affairs. As a result of Progressive reform, local cities could, and still can, undertake any infrastructure projects they desired, so long as they could find sufficient votes to pass the bond measures. Local business interests, in their role as advisors to local elected leaders, often devised the infrastructure projects to be built.

Once a special district was created, it would supervise the construction of projects and might continue to exist in order to ensure the maintenance of that particular infrastructure. Special districts operated as separate governments, often having an elected board that made policy decisions. The law did not require all districts to follow the same rules or to have the same structure. Each district could establish its own system of internal government and hire employees and managers separate from the local municipality, providing services separate from what the city might provide. They were a kind of shadow state, run by remote elected or appointed boards, making for another layer of government distanced from the electorate.

The freehold charter reform that made possible the creation of charter cities liberated cities from state oversight and gave them great financial autonomy. This autonomy furthered the pattern of fragmentation of local governments through the proliferation of special districts, contributing to haphazard and autonomous urban development and poor public accountability—a situation that continues to this day.[71]

The Los Angeles Aqueduct

One of the most ambitious projects accomplished with charter city power was the construction of the Los Angeles Aqueduct. The aqueduct furnishes an excellent example of urban control over and transformation of the rural hinterland, tying the future of the rural area to that of the city and the growth-producing activities of urban capital. Not waiting for state or federal help, southern California interests organized for water and power development by using the city's own bond-issuing authority.

Supported by the Chamber of Commerce, the Merchants and Manufacturing Association, the Realty Board, the Municipal League, politicians, and newspapers—notably the *Los Angeles Times*—voters in 1905 passed by 14 to 1 a bond issue that paid for the development of the Owens Valley Aqueduct. Construction was completed in 1913. At the time, the aqueduct delivered four times as much water as the city could use; today, more than eight decades later, it still provides a great deal of water for the city of Los Angeles.

The aqueduct, the most expensive in the world at that time, was an engineering masterpiece and brought water sufficient for 2 million people to southern California. For the Owens Valley, however, this water transfer began a profound ecological transformation, a process of desertification. The Owens Valley was a fertile and potentially prosperous agricultural area, originally inhabited by Native Americans and then taken over by immigrant settlers. The diversion of water from the Owens River into the Los Angeles Aqueduct left Owens Lake a dry, dusty depression in the land. The aqueduct captured the lower portions of numerous streams that were tributaries to the Owens River, leaving creek beds lined with dead trees. By 1933 Los Angeles had secured 95 percent of all water-bearing grounds in the valley, and 85 percent of the town property in the valley.[72] The residents, no longer able to pursue agriculture as a way of life, bombed the aqueduct many times. But the purchase of land and water rights made much of the popular protest futile, another testimonial to interplay between urban and rural development in the state and to the perverse results of the federal government's magnanimous land-disposal policy.

A city work force of up to 3,900 men worked on the project for six years until the aqueduct was completed. In seventy-three separate annexation elections held between 1906 and 1930, Los Angeles voters expanded the city's boundaries from 43 to 442 square miles. Real estate interests welcomed this water-based territorial expansion. In 1930 city voters endorsed a bond issue to develop water from the Mono Basin, once again fearing water shortages in case of drought. This additional water arrived through the Los Angeles Aqueduct in Los Angeles in 1940.

Territorial expansion was one of the founding principles of Los Angeles, a place with an agreeable climate and abundant land. From the beginning, land developers had a major role in determining the shape and expansion patterns of the city for their own interests. But the extent of urbanization

Owens Valley, Big Pine area, pre–Los Angeles Aqueduct, 1909. (Photograph by A. A. Forbes for Fish and Game Commission; courtesy of California State Archives, Office of the Secretary of State, Sacramento)

Owens Valley, south of Big Pine, pre–Los Angeles Aqueduct, 1910. (Photograph by A. A. Forbes for Fish and Game Commission; courtesy of California State Archives, Office of the Secretary of State, Sacramento)

would have been greatly circumscribed had it not been for the structure of the nation's system for disposal of public land. "Had the nation's public land laws achieved greater success in establishing a denser pattern of small holdings in the valley's southern region, the larger number of irrigated farms and the more intensive use of the Owens River for agriculture might have deterred Los Angeles's advance into the Owens Valley." The city removed most traces of abandoned rural life as quickly as possible; houses and barns were bulldozed or burned, and trees and orchards were either cut down or uprooted.[73] The relationship between the Owens Valley and Los Angeles is perhaps not unusual; large metropolitan areas depend on their hinterlands for resources for growth. Yet it is a striking example of the destructive effects that urban development can have on the far-off rural resource base, and it powerfully illustrates how urban development shapes the rural ecosystems and their economic potential.

San Francisco

San Francisco had been the center of California's business community since the time of the gold rush. Its founders "saw the Pacific Basin as *mare nostrum*, a virgin bonanza literally tributary to the city they claimed as their own." Their investments created a wealthy and united business community. Nearly all the city's businesses were owned and operated by San Franciscans on an imperial scale.[74] The dynamics of city politics were very different from politics in Los Angeles. In San Francisco there was a well-organized and powerful union presence. Although labor unions wanted to advance within the existing system, they also pushed for reforms that helped shape the Progressive reform agenda. White workers, who were particularly well organized in the Bay area, were pushing for full participation in the economic realm, advocating the eight-hour day and workman's compensation.[75]

From the 1880s to 1896 organized labor and the Democratic Party forged an alliance. Under the Democratic leadership of "Boss" Christopher Buckley (known as Blind Boss Buckley), working-class candidates achieved success in San Francisco.[76] Then a municipal reform movement, led by the city's elites, began to challenge the Democratic hold on the city, which was seen as corrupt. A key figure in this municipal reform movement was James Duval Phelan. The son of an Irish immigrant who had made a fortune in gold mines, real estate, and banking, Phelan owned vast tracts of land in the south Bay area. He wanted to make San Francisco into a model of moral and aesthetic order, and to create conditions for coherent urban growth— including growth of his own extensive property holdings. In 1892 Phelan, a Democrat, led a group of reformers, mostly professionals and businessmen,

Urban development in the San Fernando Valley after the Owens Valley Aqueduct: Van Nuys, looking toward Burbank, 1927. (Photograph by Spence; courtesy of Air Photo Archives, Department of Geography, University of California, Los Angeles)

who were concerned that Blind Boss Buckley's tactics were hampering the city's growth. Phelan defeated Buckley and was himself elected mayor.

Consistent with municipal reformers across the country, Phelan's supporters wanted to impart their sound business principles to city government and clean up the city. They also proposed a "city charter that would forever banish arbitrary rule by ward politicians whom immigrant voters kept electing to office." The new city charter proposed decreasing the number of elected officials, creating citywide instead of district-based offices, and establishing a civil service. The new charter was defeated at the ballot box, but Phelan, undaunted, solicited the assistance of organized labor and got the charter passed on a second attempt. The charter included the initiative and the referendum, a provision for the eight-hour day, and a minimum wage.[77] Despite his strong connections to the business elite, Phelan supported municipal ownership of utilities, a stance that earned him the enmity of the Market Street Railway, the Spring Valley Water Company, San Francisco Gas

& Electric, and the Southern Pacific Railroad.[78] He cooperated with the labor movement and gained reelection several times, instituting favorable regulations for labor while at the same time pursuing municipal reform measures.

Phelan envisioned San Francisco as the capital of America's new Pacific empire, a rival to Paris in its urban planning. As a young man he had spent two years in Europe and returned to San Francisco determined that his city should learn from European cities and not American ones. He promoted this idea through the civic groups he helped found, including the Young Men's Commercial Club, the Bohemian Club, the Merchant's Association, the San Francisco Art Club, and the Native Sons of the Golden West. Phelan believed that the gifted, the educated, and the wealthy should hold positions of leadership.[79] He and his fellow Progressives had a vision of San Francisco that followed Progressive lines but also included better, grander physical design and land-use planning. Herbert Croly, editor of the *Architectural Record,* in 1906 predicted that "San Francisco will dominate the other cities of the Pacific Coast in much the same way as New York dominates the other cities of the Atlantic Coast. . . . It will be the center of the prevailing financial and industrial organization and the abiding place of the men who will give form and direction to the intellectual life of that part of the country."[80] Already the Bay area had two major universities (Berkeley and Stanford), a significant natural history museum, and an influential scientific community. But the city of San Francisco had no aesthetically fitting physical plan, no vision for growth and development, and the elite were concerned that this would hamper its ascent to greatness.

The Association for the Improvement and Adornment of San Francisco, made up of Phelan's cronies, in 1904 commissioned Daniel Hudson Burnham to prepare a new physical plan.[81] Burnham was one of the nation's most renowned architects and had already designed such plans for Washington, D.C., and Cleveland. He went on to do the well-known Chicago plan. His plan for San Francisco featured tree-lined boulevards, new public buildings, stadiums, a new system of neighborhood parks, playgrounds, and more. San Francisco would be an imperial city, a neo-baroque triumph with great parkways linking open areas, squares and boulevards with fountains, roadways in harmony with the landscape, and community gardens.[82]

The 1906 earthquake derailed Burnham's plan; after the quake many businessmen argued that such large-scale plans would slow down the city's recovery and allow its rival Los Angeles to overtake it economically. The failure of the Burnham plan, however, did not deter Progressives in their vision of a larger planning unit for the San Francisco Bay area. They thought of the Bay area as a logical and efficient governmental unit, one that would, if properly developed, encompass their own landholdings that were still on the urban fringe. Accordingly, Phelan and his associates launched the Greater San Francisco movement with the hope of creating a metropolitan borough system similar to that of New York. San Francisco business interests were simultaneously seduced by the notion of governmental efficiency through regional coordination and threatened by the growth of other cities around the bay.

Oakland, a major port served by the Western Pacific, Santa Fe, and Southern Pacific Railroads, was growing rapidly. With electric trolley construction and massive real estate development, the city's population doubled in the decade between 1900 and 1910 from 75,000 to 150,000. In 1905 Oakland commissioned its own beautification plan to compete with that of San Francisco and hired Charles Mulford Robinson, another famous designer, as planner. Robinson, like Burnham, laid out a huge plan of public open space, emphasizing expansion of parkland around Lake Merritt and the establishment of new neighborhood parks and playgrounds, as well as what eventually became the East Bay Regional Park System. Robinson's plan surpassed Oakland's jurisdiction by including lands outside the city limits, but the city did carry out some of its feasible ideas, such as conservation of open space around Lake Merritt and the construction of several parks.

Berkeley's growth was even more spectacular. The university town tripled its population in the period between 1900 and 1910, from 13,000 to 40,000, and residents lobbied to have the state capital moved there from Sacramento. Here too, there was attention to design and style. Berkeley architects Bernard Maybeck and Julia Morgan left their imprint on the city, setting an architectural precedent for the entire Bay area. After the earthquake, southern Marin and northern San Mateo Counties also grew. San Francisco's growth rate lagged behind that of the Bay area as a whole, and it was dramatically outstripped by Los Angeles.[83]

Perceiving the threat of economic competition from other Bay area cities, the San Francisco elite determined to make San Francisco the dominant regional center. Failing to obtain agreement on the Burnham plan, they turned in 1912 to a state ballot initiative proposing a governmental consolidation of the Bay area cities. Consolidation was promoted as an efficiency measure: transportation would be better coordinated, and government would be less wasteful. The plan promised to bring the Bay area's governance on a par with that of New York City. San Francisco was to be to the Bay area what Manhattan was to the larger New York metropolitan area. Business interests also argued that since the Bay area functioned as one economic unit, it made sense to have one unit of governance. But the East Bay, particularly Oakland, strongly objected, and the initiative failed. The vision

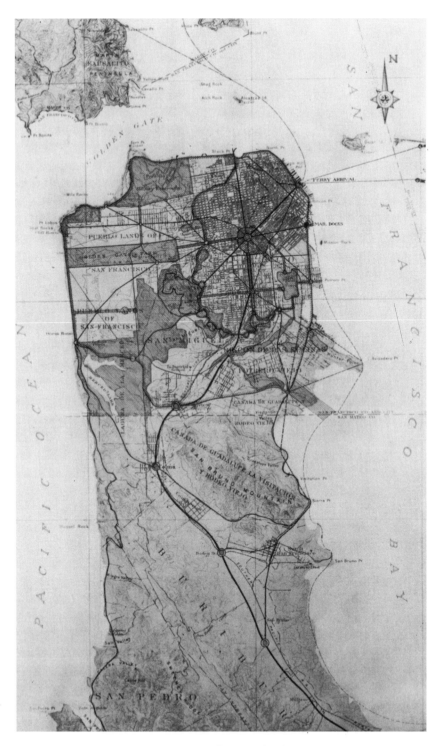

Burnham plan, map of San Francisco and peninsula, showing circuit and radial arteries, 1905. (Courtesy of the Bancroft Library, University of California, Berkeley)

of a united Bay area has lived on, however, as has the dream of coordinated land use and infrastructure planning.

In southern California planning issues never involved the same grand urban vision as in the Bay area. Rather, land development and growth were the dominant concerns, not natural beauty or urban splendor. San Francisco and Los Angeles have continued to diverge politically and in their respective local cultures.

The Progressive Legacy

Despite the presence of the Democratic and Republican Parties, as well as other social movements, no other group rivaled the Progressive businessmen in their ability to influence the shape of urban policymaking in San Francisco and Los Angeles during the early twentieth century. And despite regional rivalries, when it came to state-level political reforms, Progressives throughout the state, north and south, united to elect Hiram Johnson in 1910.

The Progressive era established the state's institutions and reformed its governance structure from top to bottom. Political reform was inspired by an idea that appropriate use of physical space—proper land-use planning—would yield proper social relations and economic efficiency. Consequently, many of their reforms dealt with land use, such as zoning, as well as natural resource management.

Driven by a Jeffersonian vision of democracy that put voters in charge of, or close to, decision making, Progressives put in place the referendum, the recall, and the initiative. These measures, they believed, gave citizens the tools to make government immediately accountable and, beyond that, even gave them the power to make law. Progressives made county and municipal elected offices nonpartisan and often pushed for at-large elections over district elections, with the belief that this would bring out the greatest good for the greatest number and reduce the influence of special interests. They eliminated the role of parties except at the state level and instituted cross-filing and the direct primary. They established the professional civil service and created specialized boards and commissions to make decisions for the civil service to carry out.

Progressive reformers believed they were standing up for democracy through these measures, which were often portrayed as necessary to rid politics of corruption. To such reformers the public welfare was much too important to be left to professional politicians, especially if they were corrupt and used their positions to enhance party power. They believed that the way to govern cities was to place their affairs in the free hands of "capable businessmen," "free men," who would "discharge their duty . . . without regard to claims of political support."[84] Appointed boards and commissions were put in charge of policy issues at all levels of government. But, as Stephen Skowronek has pointed out, "the rise of the independent commission in modern American government ultimately shattered political responsibility and judicial discipline in the exercise of regulatory power and left the state itself in internal disarray."[85] Progressives, suspicious of centralized governmental power, supported charter city legislation and the special district. These were to revolutionize local government, encouraging the proliferation of local jurisdictions and making for fragmented governance.

The weakening of political parties throughout the state and the deliberate breaking of ties between the local party machine and the state-level party by the institution of nonpartisan local offices created a vacuum. Politics shifted to the individual politician, especially at the local level, since candidates represented only themselves, not a party or a party platform. Voters were seen as individual decision makers who could band together to use the new tools of the initiative, the referendum, and the recall. These were seen as vehicles for citizens to express themselves and to gain direct access to the political system. Progressives saw democracy as an individual practice, not as a collective enterprise, harking back to the Jeffersonian independent yeoman of the mythological frontier. And their reforms made government more remote from voters, less accessible. An at-large representative was more difficult to meet than a district representative; a special district board or commission was hard to influence and even to understand.

City politics was reduced to managerialism, so that social issues no longer implied political choice but mere technical analysis that could and should be undertaken by professionals or experts. Little by little government was distanced from the people, democracy becoming an exercise in choice among individual politicians rather than a practice of engagement.

In Sacramento, to replace the access that had been available through parties and patronage, a system of special interests became organized into trade associations. The associations hired professional lobbyists stationed in the state capitol. These professionals lobbied individual politicians, supported them with campaign contributions, and winnowed out supporters among other party members or among other legislators. Progressive reforms, aimed to reduce corruption, opened the door to a more powerful and perhaps more insidious form of corruption that is still with us today.

3 · TRANSITIONAL INTERWAR YEARS

Establishing Business Associationalism

THE PROGRESSIVE PERIOD in California established the main structures of government and politics that would guide the state's development. Progressive reforms systematically incorporated business interests into government policymaking through appointed boards and commissions, and weakened political parties by eliminating them at the local level and by other reforms. Gradually, business associations were integrated into the structure of government, both by participating on boards and commissions and by serving as advisory groups for government policymaking. This was a natural evolution from Progressivism, which became known as business associationalism. It was a form of relationship between business and government that evolved at both the state and national levels, nurtured and encouraged by Congress and by President Herbert Hoover. Well adapted to Progressive political reforms, business associationalism was based on a philosophy of a free market and a government whose role was to foster a good business climate. The central principle of the American political tradition—the supremacy of society over the state—demanded that government and law should adapt to, and serve, the freely developing society, so that society commanded the state, not the state the society.[1]

The Federal Context

At the national level, during the interwar period business associationalism was incorporated into government by President Hoover. The president's "New Era" was built on a combination of modern, large-scale organization and free-market principles, according to which the role of the state was to coordinate organized social groups—farmers, consumers, workers—under the umbrella of corporate enterprise. The belief was that big business would take responsibility for the general economic welfare through the workings of the marketplace and that the free hand of the market would simultaneously establish social order. Hoover pioneered the coming together of industrial trade organizations at the federal level, for the purpose of coordinating strategies and establishing price structures. This would assure long-term viability for business, which would translate into prosperity for all.

Alan Wolfe describes these new relationships as the "Franchise State," in which the boundary between the public and private sectors becomes uncertain. There is substantial delegation of public authority from the central state to quasi-private bodies, building on the Progressive tradition of delegating policymaking to appointed boards and commissions made up of those interests most implicated in the particular sector. A vivid and long-lived example of this approach comes out of the agricultural sector: the Cooperative Extension Service. Various agricultural corporations—generally the trusts that had been attacked in the Populist days—supported cooperative, state-funded demonstration projects to disseminate agricultural information. To this end they supported the passage of the Smith-Lever Act in 1914 creating the Cooperative Extension Service, funded by public and private money. The agents who went out in the field to talk to farmers about technical advances in agriculture also became the organizers of local farm bureaus, helping farmers become better organized among themselves along trade association lines. Farm bureaus, in turn, shaped the programs of the Cooperative Extension Service. In this way, federal money was used for agricultural experiments that would improve agricultural practices and productivity, as well as create a farmers' organization that could, in turn, help shape agricultural programs and research.[2]

During the Depression, President Franklin Roosevelt used this pattern as well, choosing as the chief business planner of the National Industrial Recovery Board (quickly declared unconstitutional by the Supreme Court) Gerald Swope of General Electric, who planned to give trade associations sweeping authority to regulate production, prices, and trade. General Electric was one of the largest and most strategically important industries in the United States.

The National Industrial Recovery Act was devised to help the country emerge from the Depression by institutionalizing the work of trade associations in government policy. Trade associations met to establish the basis of cooperation among the actors in the same industrial sector. They established guidelines so that all the players would abide by the same rules and not undercut each other by unfair competition. Roosevelt hoped to use the act to control prices and production, a sort of "partnership in planning," based on the principle of industrial self-regulation with the state as enforcement agency.

The inclusion of industry in national economic decision making during this period set a precedent for the expectations of industry for broad sectors of the economy. Federal agencies were transformed into the administrative arms of private industries. The professional civil service carried out policy that had been shaped by industry.[3] In the area of agriculture, the Farm Bureau advocated that the Agricultural Adjustment Act of 1933—aimed at supporting the agricultural sector through the Depression—be administered directly by the Farm Bureau in conjunction with the Cooperative Extension Service. Like some other pieces of recovery legislation, this act was struck down as unconstitutional (in 1936), but not before it had achieved some of the aims of the Farm Bureau, such as the exclusion of farm tenants from any assistance under the act.[4]

Franklin Roosevelt's New Deal, based on encouraging industrial participation in the setting of public policy, shaped government into an administrative state centered on semi-public corporations. The federal government's assets supported the economy—replacing the role of Wall Street—but left profits in the hands of the corporations. Still, as Elias Hawley has pointed out, there remained a fundamental tension between the rise of giant business corporations, tending toward monopoly, and the ideology of laissez faire, local rights, and competition. Therefore, throughout this period there was an oscillation between policies aimed at limiting the size of businesses, at breaking up the trusts and removing the unfair advantages of big businesses, and a belief that concentration of economic power was the inevitable and desirable result of mass production and an advancing technology, that competition resulted in a waste of natural resources and human life and energy. In this latter scenario, the role of the state was to establish a government that could supervise the big corporations, in part by bringing them into the governmental planning process.[5]

California

Hoover's plan to create an "American System" by stimulating cooperation between the free market and government had its California counterpart in the activities of the California Development Association, founded in 1921. This association coordinated the state's various business organizations as part of a vision of cooperation between business and government "that envisioned the former as the senior partner." The board of directors included prominent southern California business leaders. The association became involved, for example, in "the unification and co-ordination of effort" among the various government agencies charged with water development, in the belief that poor water development was an impediment to economic growth. As R. E. Miller, vice president of Pacific Gas & Electric, stated, only "organized business leadership" could accomplish "sound development and growth of California."

To facilitate and accelerate water development, the San Francisco and Los Angeles Chambers of Commerce financed State Engineering Department planning studies aimed at comprehensive management of domestic water use, irrigation, industrial water use, and flood control. The state legislature later reimbursed the chambers of commerce and, satisfied with the initial planning work, made further appropriations.[6] Not surprisingly, these studies concluded that the state needed further water development and proposed an ambitious state water project.

Serving the Needs of Agriculture

Much of California's political, economic, social, and environmental landscape was shaped by large-scale agriculture during the early twentieth century, despite the state's predominantly urban population and the strong growth of industrial production. The scale of operations was unprecedented: there were more large-scale farms in California than anywhere else in the country. More than one-third of the biggest farms in the entire country were located in California in the 1930s, including the following:

- 30 percent of the large-scale cotton farms of the country
- 41 percent of the large-scale dairies
- 44 percent of the large-scale general farms
- 53 percent of the large-scale poultry farms
- 60 percent of the large-scale truck farms.

A. P. Giannini, founder of the Bank of Italy (later the Bank of America), was financing fully half of the state's cotton crop by 1929. He funded the producers, processors, and manufacturers, securing the prominent position of urban capital in this large-scale agricultural development. He also used the guarantees provided by the Federal Reserve Board to cushion credit crises of major farm groups, such as the California Apricot & Prune Growers Association or the California Bean Growers Association.[7] These strong urban-rural financial interconnections and interdependencies created common interests between sectors of urban capital and agriculture that wielded political clout in the state legislature.

The large landholdings were, of course, the physical legacy of the Spanish and Mexican land grants, and the results of federal land-disposal policies. By the twentieth century the Southern Pacific Railroad had holdings amounting to 2,598,295 acres (in agricultural production and in oil) in the southern part of the state, while the Kern County Land Company controlled about 1 million acres in Kern County. The Chandler-led syndicate of the *Los Angeles Times* owned extensive rural lands in the southern part of the state, including the Tejon Ranch. The syndicate included representatives of the Title Insurance & Trust Company of Los Angeles, the Firestone tire family, and others. The Chandlers also owned land throughout the Los Angeles basin, in the Imperial Valley, and in Mexico and Hawaii.[8] The landholdings of the largest farm corporations—such as J. G. Boswell, Miller & Lux, the Kern County Land Company, the Newhall Land & Farming Company, and the Irvine Company—often were nineteenth-century ranchos. In addition, "new large holdings emerged in the twentieth century through transfers and through the partial breakup of the huge Miller and Lux holding" in the Central Valley, demonstrating the success of large-scale farming in the state.[9]

With capital at its disposal, corporate agriculture could implement pioneering technologies that greatly increased productivity—that is, intensity. The growth of irrigated agriculture increased the numbers and acreage of intensive crops that demanded seasonal hand labor: citrus grapes, fruit, vegetables, melons, cotton. The rise of intensity only made large-scale farms more profitable. "Together with crop intensification and large-scale production organization has come commercialization of agriculture, higher capitalization and high expenditure for wage labor."[10] But such increasingly sophisticated farming required better state-level structures to assist its development. Agriculture needed more elaborate marketing structures for more efficient distribution and sales, and better physical infrastructure, such as reliable irrigation systems. The system of regulatory boards and commissions that had been established by the Progressives provided a good structure to build on and matched the ideology of business associationalism.

The Roots of Industry Self-regulation

Earlier administrations had institutionalized regulatory boards and commissions throughout state government, and then further professionalized this approach. "Co-ordination, specialization of functions and centralization of authority were the dogmas of the new administrative cult; efficiency, the objective; and a trained, technically competent, and specialized civil service the instrument."[11] In 1917 an appointed expert committee, the Committee on Efficiency and Economy, was charged by the governor with formulating a comprehensive plan for overhauling California's government. The committee's recommendations encompassed the advice it received from affected interest groups and in several areas, including agriculture, further incorporated business protection and promotion into state policy.

In the post–World War I period California agriculture was increasingly directed through membership-based groups, such as marketing associations. The activities of the associations were supported by assessments on crop volume or value, favoring large grower interests. Marketing associations grew to handle a large percentage of California production, further consolidating the power of large growers.[12]

In 1919 the California Fruit Growers Exchange drafted, and the legislature adopted, a specific fruit standardization law. Under this act, 50 percent or more of the producers in any branch of fruit growing could set standards for the packing, shipping, and grading of over a dozen different varieties of fruit. Although this act was struck down by the California Supreme Court, it was representative of the type of support the state was willing to lend to organized sectors in the farm economy. The state was ready to help the larger scale, better organized farmers by establishing industry standards that would then become compulsory for all farmers.

Under the aegis of the newly established state Department of Agriculture, during the 1920s farm organizations came together to formulate virtually every piece of agricultural legislation. Fruit growers, for example, took the initiative and continued to seek the expansion of the state fruit-standardization program to stabilize competition. Likewise, the California Dairymen's Association and the civil servants in the Department of Agriculture's dairy division together developed new dairy standards not only to protect public health but, as in the other sectors, to regulate competition by setting compulsory standards. The agricultural sector used the state to regulate competition, eradicate disease, maintain standards, and improve marketing. Although large producers' interests were not necessarily opposed to those of small producers, the large producers were able to achieve many advantages for themselves through farmers' organizations and legislation, due to their dominance in the organizations and their political power.[13]

By 1921 California producers had formed several important and enduring farm organizations. Gradually, these organizations set the terms of the market for producers in the state and, as in other parts of the country, developed a coordinated strategy against labor.[14] The Valley Fruit Growers of San Joaquin County, the Sun-Maid Raisin Growers Association (which included 75–90 percent of the raisin farmers), the Western Growers Protective Association, the California Growers Exchange, and others consolidated large-scale grower interests into trade lobbying groups.

Immigrants and Farm Labor

Throughout its history, California has attracted a steady flow of people looking for a better way of life. Even in aboriginal times, Indians migrated to the region. As a neighbor to three other western states, a borderland to Mexico, and a gateway to the Far East, California lured (or imported) immigrants from all over the world. In the nineteenth century came the Chinese. Originally brought to California to build the railroads, they entered the agricultural sector after the completion of the transcontinental and other major lines. As the need for cheap farm labor escalated, they were joined by Japanese, Mexican, and Filipino immigrants.

The strategy of agriculture was to use industrial organization to concentrate production and distribution, and gradually to reduce its labor costs by relying on immigrant labor on a seasonal basis only. Mechanization was used to displace many year-round farm workers, thereby increasing the use of cheap migrant labor at harvest time.[15] Preharvest operations required few workers, but demanded large capital outlays in machinery, which only the largest farms could afford. Readily available seasonal workers were required during harvest time. This approach to farming created, proportionately, the largest rural wage-earning class in any state in the nation. In California, 57 percent of all persons gainfully employed in agriculture were seasonal farm laborers. California agriculture built a rural proletariat of individuals who were largely "[of] alien race [Chinese, Japanese, Mexican], propertyless, and without ties . . . to the soil."[16] This type of agricultural system was quite different from the popular image of the Jeffersonian homesteads idealized in political debate.

As early as 1913 the state recognized the lack of suitable housing and prevalence of substandard living conditions for immigrants by creating a Commission of Immigration and Housing. The commission's chairman, Simon Lubin, had Socialist tendencies. He believed in coordinating private and local government activities, and tried to develop public-private associations to build urban housing. The commission denounced the poor housing and work conditions of agricultural workers in California's rural areas, making enemies of many large agribusiness farmers. "For more than a score of years, the state camp inspectors of the Division of Immigration and Housing (as it came to be called) have done yeoman work. Struggling against the obstacles of public apathy, inadequate staffs, resistance of employers unwilling or unable to do better, reluctance of local officials to apply penalties to their neighbors for violation of state camp sanitation laws they have sought ceaselessly to attain better conditions."[17] They achieved only marginal success. Lubin could do little to combat the strong agricultural interests at the state level, which showed no concern for improving immigrant workers' housing conditions.

The migrants, however, were not always content to remain docile workers. They organized collective bargaining units, and the International

Transient camp, interwar period. (Department of Social Welfare; courtesy of California State Archives, Office of the Secretary of State, Sacramento)

Transient camp, interwar period. (Department of Social Welfare; courtesy of California State Archives, Office of the Secretary of State, Sacramento)

Workers of the World formed the Agricultural Workers Industrial Union Local 111, though with limited success with regard to employers. In 1922 Mexican workers in Fresno formed the Grape Pickers Union of the San Joaquin Valley, and that same year Mexican cantaloupe workers organized in Brawley. As the numbers of Mexican immigrants grew, along with their ideas of mutual aid based on cultural patterns of cooperation and labor organizing, so did the hostility and opposition of the agricultural interests.

Mexican farm labor strike at Corcoran, 1933. (Courtesy of the Bancroft Library, University of California, Berkeley)

Mexican farm labor strike camp, 1933. (Courtesy of the Bancroft Library, University of California, Berkeley)

The growers' associations, better financed and more thoroughly organized, united farmers in opposition to labor organizing and eventually squelched farm worker organizing and strikes. The associations organized to set uniform wages and to recruit and distribute labor, and in 1933 they formed a special organization, the Associated Farmers, to fight labor unrest. The Associated Framers (AF) was formed by the Agricultural Labor Subcommittee of the state Chamber of Commerce. Its membership included the president of the state Chamber of Commerce, the president of the Farm Bureau Federation, and representatives from PG&E, Southern Pacific Railroad, Calpak (California Packing Association), and the Bank of America. Major contributors included large growers, packers, processors, railroads, banks, marketing cooperatives, utilities, and oil companies.[18] The AF was largely successful in its union-busting efforts, as well as in setting the prevailing agricultural wage, because of its influence on relief payments at the county level. The AF dictated relief levels to local counties (which were often in the pockets of the farm employer groups) and then would offer agricultural wages at that same "prevailing wage." If the unemployed did not take the available agricultural work, they would be forced off relief and at the same time converted into strikebreakers. In this way farmers were able to set agricultural wages. Not satisfied with curbing labor activity, large growers lobbied effectively through the American Farm Bureau Federation to exclude farm workers from any labor legislation in Congress. This meant that farm workers were not included in the New Deal worker protection legislation.

Between 1920 and 1930 2 million people came to California. From the Imperial Valley in the winter, the migrants followed the harvest up the state, moving from camp to field, field to camp. In August 1927, 11,500 Mexican laborers and their families were counted moving north by motor vehicle over the Ridge Route to the San Joaquin Valley. "Many more moved than were counted."[19] These workers continued to live in labor camps in miserable conditions.

In addition to economic depression, the Midwest experienced devastating drought in 1934 and 1936, which sent the "Dust Bowlers" streaming westward from the Great Plains, in addition to waves of migrants from the American South—whites and blacks—reeling from the lack of federal assistance to sharecroppers, tenant farmers, and small farms during this period. Planters in the Cotton Belt had begun letting go their sharecroppers and tenants, retaining the few necessary to operate tractors and paying them by the day. "A cotton planter in the Mississippi Delta . . . had 160 sharecropper families. He purchased twenty-two tractors and thirteen four-row cultivators, let go 130 out of 160 of these families, and retained only thirty for day labor."[20] A count at the California border recorded 221,000 persons entering the state by automobile alone between mid-1935 and the end of 1937.

In 1931 the unattached migrant men and boys seemed to be overrunning Los Angeles. Ten thousand a month were arriving, mostly by freight train. The fear of an invasion of vagrants led to a suggestion that they be stopped at the border. By 1935 the rate of arrival had increased drastically: in April of that year over 77,000 people entered the state. In May a bill was introduced into the state legislature to prevent indigents, or those likely to become public charges, from entering California. The Los Angeles Chamber of Commerce urged the use of hard labor prison camps for vagrants as a means of discouraging indigents from moving to California and Los Angeles in particular. Finally, in February 1936 Los Angeles police officers were sent to various border stations to turn back migrants entering either by automobile or by freight train. Not only was this approach ineffective, it was declared illegal by the state attorney general. Immigrants kept pouring in, with over 27,000 people coming to search for work in the two-month period of September and October 1936.[21] Worst of all, the immigrants found almost no work available, despite the seasonal requirements for labor in the agricultural sector.

In 1927 the Department of Industrial Relations, Division of Housing and Sanitation, assumed the duties of the Commission on Immigration and Housing. This shift disengaged the state from its commitments to provide work for California's immigrants and unemployed, obligations that were then taken up by uncoordinated agencies and public-private enterprises. For example, east of Salinas, a "shanty-town" for 200 people was started. Immigrants were able to buy a small plot of land (50 x 120 feet) for $200, paying $50 down and having four years to pay the balance. The state also established Social Adjustments, Inc., to set up nonrelief families on an acre of land at a low rent. This agency supplied seeds and a hoe, and a contract that required the renter to complete, within the first year, a handmade shelter (usually adobe) on the land. These small farms were established where part-time work was available, where there was fertile soil and water. The Shore Acres plan, established in 1933 near Los Angeles by the Security First National Bank of Los Angeles, boasted of 600 successfully established families. At Mineral King in Visalia, another alternative farm was established in 1937 consisting of ten families cooperatively farming 530 acres. They received a loan of $5,000 from the Federal Farm Security Administration (a short-lived New Deal program) to finance operations the first year. Other such experiments were set up with no long-lasting success, since there was no long-term institutional commitment. That they should have been undertaken at all demonstrates the tenacity of the ideal of the small farm, but a prevailing social Darwinist ideology, the improving economy, and large-scale ownership of agricultural lands doomed such programs to failure.

More the norm were the so-called Hoovervilles, shack towns throughout the San Joaquin Valley made of tin oilcans, burlap, cardboard, and rags, inhabited by people hoping for agricultural work. Many camps were provided by growers, and though work was seasonal or part-time, they became places of permanent, if miserable, occupancy.[22] Yet there were other agricultural systems in place at the same time. For example, in 1920 Japanese immigrants owned 45,056 acres of agricultural lands and controlled 80–90 percent of the vegetable and berry production and 80 percent of the tomato crop in the state.[23] Clusters of Japanese farms appeared in fertile areas, such as the Santa Clara Valley and the Agnews area. All members of the Japanese family contributed their labor, working intensely to create highly productive farms. Although there were anti-alien land laws prohibiting the Japanese from owning land, children born on American soil, the Nisei, could hold title. Because of their success in farming their own lands, Japanese farm workers were less willing to work for low wages, and hence were gradually replaced by cheaper labor, mainly Filipinos and Mexicans. Japanese farmers also formed marketing cooperatives and developed farm technologies to suit their special brand of garden farming. They invented scrapers and levelers as well as row sprayers, implements appropriate for smaller fields. They pioneered the greenhouse production of vegetables, especially celery and seedling starts.[24] White American farmers felt threatened by Japanese success and worried that the Japanese would outcompete them through their intensive farming methods and low labor costs due to the use of family labor. Resentment against the Japanese culminated in the World War II internment of the Japanese immigrants and their families, and the wholesale expropriation of their lands.

Agricultural Water: The Central Valley Project

As large-scale agriculture acted to ensure its dominance in the state with the development of self-interested legislation promoted by trade associations, it also turned its attention toward further water development. In 1920 Colonel Robert Bradford Marshall had written a report, published by the California State Irrigation Association, that proposed a series of dams on the tributaries of the Sacramento and San Joaquin Rivers, including a major dam on the Sacramento River. Grand canals were to lead down the east and west sides of the Sacramento and San Joaquin Valleys to transfer water from the Sacramento River to the San Joaquin Valley. The main canal down the west side of the valleys was to cross the Carquinez Strait by means of an

Japanese deportation, 1942. (Social Welfare: War Services; courtesy of Caliifornia State Archives, Office of the Secretary of State, Sacramento)

Japanese deportation, 1942. (Social Welfare: War Services; courtesy of California State Archives, Office of the Secretary of State, Sacramento)

inverted siphon across the Benicia harbor. Export of water from the Kern River to the Los Angeles area was also proposed.[25]

An important element in water planning in the state was power distribution. Under the 1920 Federal Water Power Act and the successor act of 1934, the Federal Power Commission was authorized to grant fifty-year licenses for hydroelectric development—licenses that with few exceptions were granted to private monopolies, establishing a precedent and pattern of expectations for power companies.[26] The privately held Pacific Gas & Electric Company strongly opposed the public distribution of electric power that might be generated by federal- or state-funded dam construction. This posed an obstacle to water planning and the implementation of any projects. Three times already in the 1920s, PG&E had successfully mounted well-financed campaigns to defeat initiative measures aimed at implementing Colonel Marshall's plan. Though regulated by the Public Utilities Commission, formerly the Railroad Commission, PG&E waged a campaign against the project because of the public power provision, which would permit a public entity to distribute electrical power, rather than a privately held, publicly regulated utility like PG&E. The company spent more than half a million dollars, exclusive of regular advertising, to defeat the plan.[27] Despite PG&E's campaigns, the desire to increase water deliveries persisted. It was argued that additional water would bring potential agricultural lands into production, expanding the state's agricultural base. This would be especially favorable to the establishment of family farms and would bring the additional benefit of alleviating land subsidence caused by increased groundwater pumping to compensate for a lack of reliable irrigation water. By 1930 the state engineer, A. D. Edmonston, had completed his report (another in the long series of state-generated reports on water development), concluding that the federal government should develop California water.

Committed to states' rights, the state legislature in 1933 managed to pass the Central Valley Project Act allowing a bond for a state-built system to be placed on the ballot. This was the culmination of years of state water planning and over ten years of intensive engineering, investigation, and research. The act included the possibility of public distribution of electric power. Once again Pacific Gas & Electric mobilized to oppose the project, hiring consultants Fred G. Athearn and Clem Whitaker to mount a campaign against the bond. Besides influencing the legislature through paid lobbyists, PG&E also contributed to farm organizations, the building trades, taxpayers' associations, industrial groups, chambers of commerce, and political candidates, thus maintaining its access and influence. Trade alliances wielded tremendous political power as well, and in 1936, a Depression year, PG&E contributed $59,938 to national and state power company alliances.[28] Other power companies across the country, as well as investors in PG&E and the Southern California Gas Company—including the Sun Life Insurance Company of Montreal, the General Electric Employees Securities Corporation of Jersey City, and Sigler & Company of New York—exerted what political pressure they could to defeat the act. Stakes were high for all of them. Public wheeling (distribution) of power would set a precedent for other state-funded projects and could put them out of business.

Southern California voiced the greatest opposition to the act, although the San Francisco Chamber of Commerce also opposed it. The California State Grange and the California Farm Bureau Federation endorsed the project, as did the state irrigation districts. With 33.4 percent of the electorate voting, the act narrowly won, by a vote of 459,712 to 426,109.

In the end, the bonds were never put up for sale. The state could find no buyers in the Depression era, so the federal government stepped in to build the largest integrated public water and power project in California, subject to the regulations administered by the U.S. Bureau of Reclamation—especially the Newlands Reclamation Act of 1902 that restricted the receipt of irrigation water to farms of 160 acres per household member.

The federally funded Central Valley Project (CVP) broke ground in October 1937 with the digging of the Contra Costa Canal. In 1938 construction began on Shasta Dam, completed in 1944. The master plan called for the construction, in several phases, of forty dams and storage reservoirs, twenty-five or more canals stretching nearly two thousand miles, and twenty-eight hydroelectric plants—a massive infrastructure project that was to radically alter the state's ecosystems and future land uses.

Meanwhile, farmers were pumping millions of acre-feet of water from the ground. Groundwater levels continued to plummet, and the costs of well drilling rose dramatically. Earlier in the century, wells 55 feet deep had been sufficient, but no longer. Small farmers could not afford to sink deep wells, some going to 2,500 feet. And if a farmer could pay the costs of drilling, then the cost of electricity for pumping the water proved prohibitive. In addition, the quality of the water being pumped, especially in Kern County, was deteriorating, as a result of invasion by salts and boron. Pumps became so heavily encrusted with minerals that they had to be pulled from the wells and scraped several times a year. Other unforeseen problems were developing as well. After years of irrigation, high concentrations of minerals and salts had accumulated in the upper few feet of soil, impairing plant growth. The common solution was to flush excessive salts into natural drainage channels leading to the sea or some other place; in the all but landlocked southern Central Valley, this meant flushing into the San Joaquin River. But because the San Joaquin was a source of irrigation water, downstream irrigators were upset about the contaminated water that drained into the river from upstream ranches. Industrial wastes and fertilizers joined the salts and other minerals, damaging the downstream cropland. Expanding agricultural water needs were transforming the environment, permanently harming the lands in the Central Valley and changing its water regimen.[29]

In addition to the question of who should distribute the power created from the Central Valley Project were the equally important questions of who was to control the project, under what conditions, and, of course, to whose benefit. The 1902 Reclamation Act was the main body of law guiding the distribution of water for the CVP. It had the declared purpose of settling the arid West with small irrigated farms, fulfilling the Jeffersonian ideal of a nation inhabited by independent yeoman farmers. During the Depression, there was great unemployment and oversupply of seasonal agricultural labor. The CVP was seen as a means to give these people farms, to build rural land ownership and prosperity. More than 750,000 migrants to California were from farm families, so it was argued that the CVP would help them become farmers in their own right. The Federal Resettlement Administration (1939) of the Department of the Interior, in cooperation with the Department of Agriculture, was created to resettle people on agricultural lands. Reclamation projects were an important part of this policy in the arid West.

The resettlement policy was conceived to accomplish several purposes. It would provide people with land, make them independent, help create a prosperous small farming class, and alleviate pressure on the cities caused by the migration of unemployed farmers. There were no jobs in the cities, and members of Congress were concerned about the movement of more people to already overcrowded industrial centers. Fears of class violence preoccupied politicians, who wanted to prevent organized political movements that might push for a radical restructuring of the capitalist economic system. The CVP in California promised to bring thousands of acres of land into agricultural production and thus to provide a livelihood for numbers of displaced farmers. "Looking forward to the availability of irrigation water for approximately 2,000,000 acres of fertile undeveloped lands on the western side of the San Joaquin Valley, the Bureau of Reclamation in 1942, enlarged the Delta-Mendota Canal plans to provide additional capacity for irrigation of several thousand acres."[30]

However, in the southwestern San Joaquin Valley, large farming corporations saw the potential of new irrigation water with a different eye. They preferred to maintain a plentiful supply of cheap seasonal labor and did not want to encourage the rise of small, independent farmers. Additionally, large land speculators opposed the proposal because the acreage limitations would force them to sell their lands and would undercut their opportunity to sell at a profit. PG&E also opposed the plan unless it was given the distribution rights to the generated power.

By the mid-1940s farmers' opposition to federal control of the Central Valley Project and additional projects was vehement. A campaign was launched to oppose the enforcement of the 160-acre rule, and the rhetoric was heated. Ralph Taylor, executive secretary of the Agricultural Council of America, had this to say: "The very farmers who put up the original funds to campaign for the Central Valley Project, so that a new water supply could be developed for their lands, now face a fight to escape being dispossessed of their lands by Secretary of the Interior Harold L. Ickes under the Ickes plan to turn the Central Valley area into a Federal colonization project."[31]

Like other politicians, Bradford S. Crittenden—a state senator, chairman of the Interim Legislative Committee, and a sponsor of the CVP in 1931— had changed his position by 1944, when the nation's economic condition had improved. Crittenden stated, "[Interior Secretary Ickes] not only wants to set up a communistic socialistic agricultural program in areas to be irrigated by the Central Valley's project, but in the whole Central Valley Basin."[32] Crittenden was joined in this opinion by the state Chamber of Commerce, the Farm Bureau, and nearly all large economic interests in the state. As the politics heated up, the Bureau of Reclamation abandoned its project to extend the CVP up the southwest side of the San Joaquin Valley. These "westlands," potential farmland for thousands, were owned by Standard Oil (218,000 acres), other oil companies (264,000 acres), the Kern County Land Company (348,000 acres), Southern Pacific Railroad (200,000 acres), Tejon Ranch Company (348,000 acres), Boston Ranch Company (37,000 acres), and other private owners of more than 1,000 acres each.[33] No water development would come to that part of the state for some time, either for large landowners or for the thousands of farmer migrants who might have settled there with federally subsidized water for small farms.

Central Valley farmers continued to lobby for access to water with no acreage limitations. Though they had initially supported federal construction of the project during the Depression, they adamantly rejected the 160-acre limitation. As they saw it, the acreage limitation would have meant the end of large-scale irrigated farming in the state because unsubsidized water would have proven too expensive, making their crops uncompetitive. The implications of enforcement of the act were revolutionary indeed, given the concentration of agricultural land ownership in the receiving area. Enforcement of the act might have meant settlement of thousands more farmers in the Central Valley, creating a very different political, economic, and farming landscape—including the position of agricultural labor.

The vision embodied in the 160-acre limitation, of a state filled with small farmers and small towns, once again slipped away. Large growers turned their attention to state purchase of the CVP, rather than comply with the law and break up their large landholdings. State Engineer Edmonston emerged as the standard bearer for the buy-back movement, but the federal government refused to sell.

Industrially farmed land, W. H. Mettler Ranch, 1944. (Courtesy of the Bancroft Library, University of California, Berkeley)

Ecological Ramifications of the Project

The building of the CVP brought about an environmental transformation in the state. Water, abundant in the north, was conveyed to the south—a change that had effects on natural systems in the state that went far beyond what had been anticipated, and far beyond the ability of engineers to control. Water was moved in tremendous quantities from one part of the state to another by removing millions of acre-feet of water from the Sacramento River via pumping from the Delta. This dramatically reduced the amount of water available to that immense wetland. At the same time, in some parts of the San Joaquin Valley, newly irrigated lands became salinized and sterilized by their conversion to agricultural use. The topography of the valley was changed by the use of heavy equipment, leveling, the compaction of soils, and the removal of all existing vegetation and animal habitats.

The CVP also involved building dams on the rivers that flowed into the Central Valley. Water that formerly flowed unimpeded into the valley, especially during wet years, was now stored, unavailable to nourish existing ecosystems. For example, Tulare Lake, in the southern half of the San Joaquin

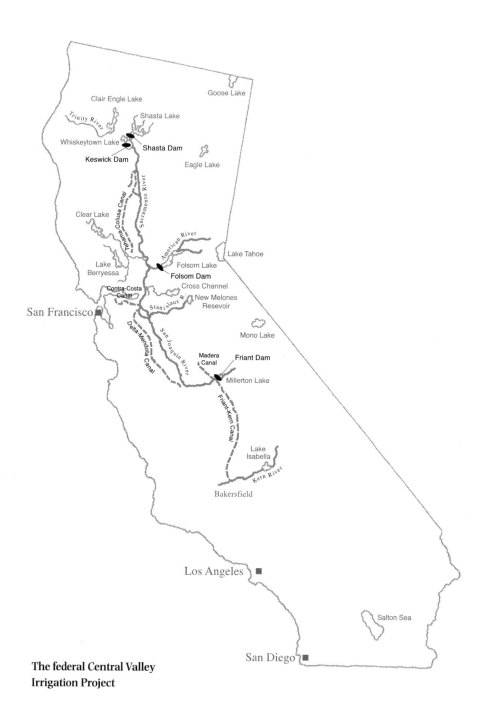

Clair Engle Lake

Goose Lake

Trinity River

Shasta Lake

Whiskeytown Lake   **Shasta Dam**

Keswick Dam

Eagle Lake

Sacramento River

Tehama-Colusa Canal

Clear Lake

American River

Lake Tahoe

Lake Berryessa

Folsom Lake

Folsom Dam

Cross Channel

Contra-Costa Canal

New Melones Resevoir

Stanislaus R.

San Francisco

Mono Lake

Delta-Mendota Canal

San Joaquin River

Madera Canal   **Friant Dam**

Millerton Lake

Friant-Kern Canal

Lake Isabella

Kern River

Bakersfield

Los Angeles

Salton Sea

San Diego

**The federal Central Valley
Irrigation Project**

Valley, disappeared permanently. Formerly a closed watershed with swamps and marshes, covering an expanse up to 50 miles long and 30 miles wide, in wet years it had supported a significant inland fishery and had provided feeding ground for birds and other animals, and habitat for valley flora. The Yokut Indians had established several villages around the lake, which had richly provided for the subsistence needs for nearly 19,000 people.[34] Buena Vista Lake, another inland body of water, once found southwest of Bakersfield where the Kern River comes into the San Joaquin Valley, also disappeared.

The Central Valley was once a vast expanse of alkali flats, grassland prairie, and marshlands composed of tule beds, oxbow lakes, and freshwater bogs. In the Sacramento area forests of willow, oak, cottonwood, and sycamore covered about 775,000 acres. The rivers supported golden beaver, mink, and river otter. Grizzlies and black bears made seasonal migrations to hunt the salmon and freshwater fish, such as the thick-tail chub. There were other indigenous fish, too, such as the Sacramento perch, as well as sturgeon. Great flights of ducks, geese, swans, cranes, and shorebirds wintered on hundreds of thousands of acres of marsh, overflow lands, and waterways in the valleys and the Delta, and around San Francisco Bay.[35] But the damming of nearly all the rivers that irrigated this complex and rich ecosystem brought about a profound ecosystemic change. With no more water available for the indigenous ecological systems, many withered or collapsed. The wetlands shriveled, along with the fauna they sustained, the grasslands were transformed into agricultural lands, and the native vegetation was removed or converted. Hills were leveled, valleys filled. The land was transmogrified, for irrigation development was yet another form of land-use planning.

Rise of Corporate Agriculture

The patterns of water subsidy, combined with the emerging structures of agricultural marketing, made it difficult for smaller scale agriculture to compete. Corporate agriculture made use of modern, rational business techniques that urban financial investors could bank on and that produced reliably good yields. Banking institutions were oriented toward the industrial farm and its requirements, rather than toward other types of farming units that either did not provide the same amount of return on investment or did not fit into emerging accounting and production methods. Although small farmers did exist and survive, the dominant form of "factories in the field," as Carey McWilliams called them, was reinforced by the Central Valley Project and sustained by cheap agricultural labor. The imperatives of corporate agriculture created a class of poor, itinerant farm workers.

Still, corporate agriculture faced the prospect of government enforcement of the 160-acre limitation. The economy was doing better, and corporate agriculture lobbied for the state to take on its own water development project, which would have no restrictions. Agricultural interests convinced the legislature to pass the State Water Resources Act, which affirmed the state's intent to manage and develop its own water resources, and to create a new agency to carry out this purpose: the state Water Resources Board. This was the first step toward freedom from federal oversight. Creating its own Water Resources Board would enable California to build its own state water project, with no federal strings attached, in a situation in which "oil, railroads, power companies, publishers, interlocked with ranchers, realtors and bankers to manipulate much of California's irrigated land."[36] In 1947 the Water Resources Board was charged with making a comprehensive inventory of the water resources of the state, including every possible source and use of water. The board did so and developed projections of California's future water needs based on a scenario of tremendous growth. The following decades would be dedicated to fulfilling these growth predictions and building the necessary state infrastructure. Growth would be energy-, land-, and water-intensive, as though there were no limits to expansion.

States' Rights

States have a built-in antagonism to the federal government, and this antagonism is structured in the governmental system of the United States. The federal Constitution devolves great power and authority to the states, which they defend with great energy. "As the various levels of U.S. government were partially bureaucratically and professionally reorganized, the fragmentation of political sovereignty built into U.S. federalism, and into the divisions of decision making authority among executives, legislatures, and courts, was reproduced in new ways during the twentieth century."[37]

This historic tension between federal and state governments was both used and fueled by agricultural interests rejecting the limits imposed by federal law. California farmers considered the situation an unjust and inappropriate meddling in the rights of private property and state autonomy by the far-off federal government. Confounding private property rights with states' rights was a clever and effective approach to lobbying for state control of water development. Agricultural interests developed this approach despite the fact that they had originally been the very forces pushing for federal water development. But when federal development came with strings attached, they were no longer so pleased. Opposition to federal involvement was broad and well connected to the political elites in Washington in part due to interlocking dependencies between the agricultural sector and the

Lower Klamath Lake

Goose Lake

Rhett (Tule) Lake

Honey Lake

Clear Lake

Lake Tahoe

Mono Lake

Tulare Lake

Owens Lake

Kern Lake

Buena Vista
Lake

Lake Elsinore

■ Coastal Salt Marsh
■ Riparian Forest
■ Freshwater Marsh
■ Saline & Alkaline Lands
▥ Coastal Brackish Marsh
☐ Lakes

California's original waterscape, before large-scale human transformation

state's financial syndicates and investors. These were powerful entities that saw their future in the ability to grow and expand, and access to water was crucial. Federal involvement in water development was never the state's first choice; rather, it occurred by necessity and, though welcomed at the time, never settled well. It came with restrictions that kindled the ever present resentment that states have toward federal rules. Agricultural interests ably ignited this situation, when it suited them and when it was financially advantageous to do so.

The combination of political power at the state level (and alliance against the federal government), the concentration of wealth and land through interlocking directorates that spanned urban and rural landscapes, along with a cheap and readily available labor force, set the stage for California's path of infrastructure development for continued economic growth. Corporate power was assisted by state boards and commissions, by cheap water, and by cheap labor. All of these translated into changes in land use.

Rural Power Reaffirmed: Reapportionment

Even though the agricultural sector of the state was powerful and provided much of the state's economic prosperity and growth, the sharp rate of growth of southern California in the 1920s and 1930s alarmed agricultural interests and cities in the northern and central portions of the state. The implications of continued population growth in Los Angeles County meant it would merely be a matter of time until the urban south dominated the state legislature under the prevailing system of apportionment. Urban interests would overwhelm rural legislators, affecting the existing balance of power and setting up a conflict between the urban and rural regions of the state.

California, from an early date, was highly urbanized. Even in 1900 more than half of the population lived in urban areas. The rural counties had already tried in 1911 to figure out a way to maintain their ability to control state policy, and had proposed to change the weight of representation to favor rural counties. To do so they exploited the deeply rooted anti-urban sentiment of American society. Rural legislators pointed to San Francisco politics as the epitome of evil city politics—corrupt and union-controlled. The unvoiced subtext, of course, was the threat to corporate agriculture—with its reliance on cheap, unorganized labor—posed by the rise of strong labor unions in control of a major California city's politics. This rural anti-union sentiment was shared by Otis Chandler, owner of the *Los Angeles Times,* who provided the rural interests with a strong urban ally. At that point, attempts to change the apportionment in the legislature failed, but not for long.

Los Angeles continued to grow, especially in the 1920s. San Francisco and Oakland, threatened by the economic success and population growth of Los Angeles, came to share the disquiet of the rural counties about the political power certain to be conferred on southern California by increased representation in the legislature. Together, northern California cities and a wide array of rural interests began to develop various reapportionment schemes for legislative consideration. In 1926 a coalition of business trade associations, working hand in hand with the conservative agricultural and financial interests of the state, engineered a reapportionment plan to ensure continued control of the legislature by rural interests. The state Farm Bureau Federation was a strong supporter of this change, as was the Chamber of Commerce.[38] This plan was passed by the legislature.

Two years later, in 1928, this reapportionment plan, called the "federal plan," was confirmed by 61 percent of the voters. Under the plan, no county could have more than one state senator and not more than three counties might be combined to form a single senatorial district. This meant that less than 6 percent of the voters of the state elected a majority of the state's forty senators. Los Angeles County, with 39 percent of the population, had one senator for 3.5 million people. El Dorado–Alpine–Amador Counties, with 24,920 residents, also had one senator. The city and county of San Francisco, with a population of 750,000, had one senator, as did Mono-Inyo, with a population of 12,270.[39]

The "federal plan" shifted control of the Senate from urban to rural areas of the state. Initially, some urban interests, such as the Los Angeles Chamber of Commerce, had opposed this legislation, but they came to understand that they would have greater leverage in the legislature if the more conservative rural interests dominated the Senate. If Senate representation had been based on population, then growing cities, such as Los Angeles, would have more representatives. Urban dwellers had inherently different concerns than rural inhabitants, so increasing their representation could upset the status quo, diverting state resources to meet social demands rather than directing them to business-guided expenditures. Thus, the dominant economic groups of the state, many with land-based assets, regardless of sectional divisions or geographic location, supported the "federal plan" because it offered them the assurance that business as usual would be maintained. The Senate would continue to be controlled by rural interests and their urban business allies.

Unanticipated Consequences: The Influence of the Lobbyist

Progressive reforms had effectively eliminated the role of parties at the local level and had dramatically reduced their power statewide. The withering of political parties created a political and policy vacuum into which stepped

special-interest lobbyists, known today as "the third house."[40] They comple-
mented business associations by serving as their day-to-day contact with
the legislature and their spokespersons in the offices of legislators. The most
prominent lobbyist was Artie Samish, a "guy who gets things done." His
brilliance consisted in recognizing that, in the absence of a political machine, he could convert interest groups and trade associations into machines that functioned independently of a political party. Whether teachers,
reform groups, labor, or agriculture, the competing interests all wanted
something from the state government, but they no longer had a party discipline to adhere to or any coordinating mechanism to allow them to reach
consensus or establish priorities. Samish filled that gap; he understood how
to put the police power of the state at the service of business. Samish assisted business in its drive for "control measures aimed at fixing prices and
eliminating 'unfair' competition and 'unfair' trade practices after the
manner of the NIRA codes." Under his guidance, California perfected the
regulation of general business by statute, and business associationalism
flourished.

For example, in 1931 the legislature adopted the Fair Trade Act, which
provided that no agreements and combinations among business were illegal
if the purpose was to ensure a reasonable profit. This permitted manufacturers to set a price for their commodities and to require retailers to observe
the figure. In 1933 this act was strengthened by allowing firms that suffered
from price-cutting activities on a fixed-price item to sue the offenders. The
state used its power, paid for by taxpayers, to eliminate "cutthroat" competition among businesses, resulting in an enormous saving for the particular
industry and creating a climate of business in which only certain well-con-
nected firms could survive and thrive.

Samish "invented a new type of machine carefully designed to meet the
peculiar requirements of California politics." Converting the interest group
into a machine that functioned independently of political party gave organized economic interests a distinctive advantage: a party machine could be
challenged at the polls, but interest groups could not. Samish understood
the weaknesses inherent in California's Progressive reforms. Not only did he
enhance the power of trade associations in government policymaking, but
also, in the absence of parties and given the possibility of a cross-filing
system, Samish found himself in a position to nominate and elect candidates in many districts by the expenditure of nominal sums. To assist these
efforts, he and his former colleague, Clem Whitaker, created the first con-
sulting company in California to specialize in political campaign organizing.
Together the two men mastered the manipulation of public opinion
through publicity and promotion. Samish worked the legislature, Whitaker

public opinion. Whitaker ran initiative and recall campaigns, managed campaigns for political office, and defined the shape of political campaigning in the state for years to come. Whitaker specialized in initiative campaigns, and his company was in the business of organizing campaigns both for and against initiative and referendum measures. When faced with the possibility of public wheeling of electricity, PG&E turned to Whitaker for help. Whitaker also ran the California Feature Service, which provided material, editorial and otherwise, to rural newspapers, helping to shape public opinion on behalf of his clients.

Obstacles to Political Change

Before 1920 California Progressives, reform Republicans, had made California a weak one-party state, given the power of lobbyists and special interests. The Progressive Party had melted into the Republican Party, and Republicans had a better than three-to-one lead in registration. Democrats could be elected to the legislature, but largely because the direct primary law of the state permitted candidates to appear on all ballots without indicating their party affiliations. The Depression and anti-Hoover sentiment did help elect Roosevelt supporter William Gibbs McAdoo as the state's Democratic senator in 1932, and he was succeeded by Sheridan Downey, also a Democrat, in 1938.

Still, formal Republican dominance did not entirely reflect the political currents of thought in the state. There was a proliferation of attempts to build alternative forms of economic cooperation to survive the Depression. But these alternative ideas and movements faced difficult obstacles in a political climate that was suspicious of cities and apathetic regarding the power of the voting public. Existing political parties were weak, and it was nearly impossible to organize new ones because they played so little role in governance any longer.

Yet because the Depression was a period of tremendous dislocation and social and economic stress, nontraditional candidates emerged to attempt to address the crisis. Upton Sinclair, the author and frequent Socialist candidate for office, pushed the limits of the political system put in place by the Progressives: he switched his registration to Democratic and ran for governor in 1934. Sinclair put forward a plan to "End Poverty in California" (EPIC). The EPIC platform was based on people being able to produce for themselves, establishing "production for use" cooperatives throughout the state to get people off welfare. Sinclair's following was especially strong in southern California. EPIC managers stressed the importance of registering as Democrats, and Sinclair's popularity pushed Democratic registrations above Republican for the first time. He offered people in the state a different vision of how an economy could be organized. The 1935 legislature considered a production-for-use bill due to the strength of the EPIC/liberal vote. A numerous minority in the Assembly and a handful in the Senate favored the bill. This pro-EPIC group in the legislature was led by Culbert Olson, who was elected governor in 1938. The production-for-use bill, which came within two votes of passage, would have provided state aid for cooperatives and for state reopening of closed factories.[41]

Despite this legislative failure, over one hundred self-help cooperatives were started in southern California alone during this period, based on the principle of mutual aid. A response to the Depression, these cooperatives provided people with work—making things, fishing, or growing crops—producing goods that the cooperative could then trade for other food goods or other necessary items. This was a nonmonetarized, trade-based economy that provided people with what they needed to survive. These subsistence-based alternatives to the capitalist, money-based economic system created a small parallel economy based on barter. The cooperatives adhered to democratic principles; each cooperator had a vote. They demanded from each according to ability and gave to each according to need. The units governed themselves by the principle and practice of peaceful action. Nondiscrimination was the rule in most units. People willing to work and to contribute to the common good were admitted regardless of race or nationality, economic or social status, religion, or political affiliation.

Los Angeles County, the center of EPIC activities, also constituted the main self-help center in the entire nation, with nearly 45 percent of all cooperatives in the United States. The city and county governments, perceiving that these cooperatives could help reduce expenditures on unemployment relief, began as early as 1932 to furnish them with food, staples, oil, gas, and other items. In 1933 the federal government, through the Federal Emergency Relief Administration, began to make grants to approved cooperatives for production purchases. In return for labor, cooperators received food, clothing, furniture, household necessities, and various services. Examples of cooperative ventures included the Unemployed Citizens' League of Santa Monica, unit no. 299, which operated an auto repair shop, a fish-processing plant, a mechanical workshop, a shoe repair shop, a furniture and stove repair shop, a clothing renovation shop, and a barbershop. The cooperative also owned two motor boats, used for fishing. A portion of the fish was distributed for immediate consumption, some was used for exchange for vegetables or other goods, some was sold. That which was not used immediately was smoked, pickled, or dried and stored for future use. As part of the barter system, members of one cooperative would work in exchange for goods from another cooperative.[42] But despite their uncontested success at getting people off government relief, cooperatives were soon seen as subversive despite their modest numbers, threatening business interests and capitalism as a form of economic organization.

The 1934 gubernatorial campaign was bitter. Newspapers were solidly against Sinclair, and cooperatives were targeted by the opposition. Conservatives described them as forerunners of communism, and began to harass them, hampering their development through pressure on state and local governments.[43] Sinclair's writings were used to portray him as a dangerous

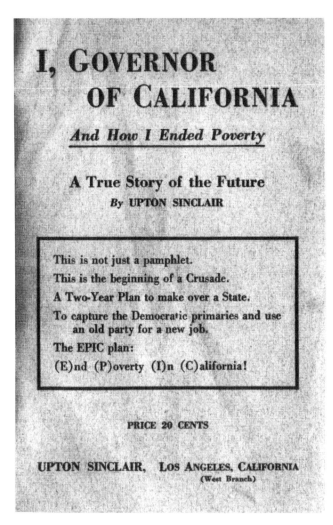

EPIC brochure, 1933, cover

THE EPIC PLAN

1. A legislative enactment for the establishment of State land colonies whereby the unemployed may become self-sustaining and cease to be a burden upon the taxpayers. A public body, the California Authority for Land (the CAL) will take the idle land, and land sold for taxes and at foreclosure sales, and erect dormitories, kitchens, cafeterias, and rooms for social purposes, and cultivate the land using modern machinery under the guidance of experts.

2. A public body entitled the California Authority for Production (the CAP) will be authorized to acquire factories and production plants whereby the unemployed may produce the basic necessities required for themselves and for the land colonies, and to operate these factories and house and feed and care for the workers. CAL and CAP will maintain a distribution system for the exchange of each other's products. The industries will include laundries, bakeries, canneries, clothing and shoe factories, cement-plants, brick-yards, lumber-yards, thus constituting a complete industrial system, a new and self-sustaining world for those whom our present system can no longer employ.

3. A public body entitled the California Authority for Money (the CAM) will handle the financing of CAL and CAP. This body will issue scrip to be paid to the workers and used in the exchanging of products within the system. It will also issue bonds to cover the purchase of land and factories, the erection of buildings and the purchase of machinery.

4. An act of the legislature repealing the present sales tax.

5. An act of the legislature providing for a State income tax, beginning with incomes of $5000 and steeply graduated until incomes of $50,000 would pay 30% tax.

6. An increase in the State inheritance tax, steeply graduated and applying to all property in the State regardless of where the owner may reside. This law would take for the State all money above $50,000 bequeathed to any individual and all money above $250,000 bequeathed by any individual.

7. A law increasing the taxes on public utility corporations according to the value of the franchise.

8. A constitutional amendment revising the tax code of the State, providing that cities and counties shall exempt from taxation all homes occupied by the owners and ranches cultivated by the owners, wherever the assessed value of such homes and ranches is less than $3000. Upon properties assessed at more than $5000 there will be a tax increase of one-half of one percent for each $5000 of additional assessed valuation.

9. A constitutional amendment providing for a State land tax of 10% upon unimproved building land and agricultural land which is not under cultivation.

10. A law providing for the payment of a pension of $50 per month to every needy person over sixty years of age who has lived in the State of California three years prior to the date of the coming into effect of the law.

11. A law providing for the payment of $50 per month to all persons who are blind, or who by medical examination are proved to be physically unable to earn a living; these persons also having been residents of the State for three years.

12. A pension of $50 per month to all widowed women who have dependent children; if the children are more than two in number, the pension to be increased by $25 per month for each additional child. These also to have been residents three years in the State.

Facing page and above: EPIC brochure, 1933, plan

Socialist. He lost the election. Cooperatives, as an alternative model to the dominant economic paradigm, began to fade.

Republicans won the governorship again, and the state remained Republican, even though Franklin D. Roosevelt, a Democrat, had been elected president during the Depression. Still, there was potential for change: the increase in California's population due to immigration inflated Democratic voter registration. From 1930 to 1940 Democratic Party registration went up by more than 431 percent. One possible reason for such a dramatic increase was that voter registration certificates were often used as a means of proving residence for the purpose of securing relief or civil service jobs.[44] Whatever the reason—voter registration, economic distress, or a Democratic president—Culbert L. Olson, a Democrat and strong EPIC proponent, was elected governor in 1938. He had made a reputation in the California Senate by opposing the oil industry's practice of pumping tidelands, which created pollution and subsidence, and he singled out the Standard Oil Company for criticism. He ran on a platform favoring the public ownership of utilities, creation of more production-for-use cooperatives, and protection of labor rights through collective bargaining. In the campaign against incumbent governor Frank Merriam, a Republican, he denounced the forces and influences controlling the governor's actions: Standard Oil and its affiliated corporate interests, privately owned public utilities (such as Pacific Gas & Electric), stockholding building and loan associations, the cement trust, large processing and packing firms, and the mastermind behind all of these special interests, Harry Chandler of the *Los Angeles Times*.[45]

Cooperative commissary, collection of food, Unemployed Citizen's League, Santa Monica, 1933–34. (Photograph by B. Sloan; courtesy of the Bancroft Library, University of California, Berkeley)

Cooperative barbershop, c. 1933–34. (Photograph by B. Sloan; courtesy of the Bancroft Library, University of California, Berkeley)

Issuing food at the cooperative, c. 1933–34. (Photograph by B. Sloan; courtesy of the Bancroft Library, University of California, Berkeley)

Cooperative sewing room, c. 1933–34. (Photograph by B. Sloan; courtesy of the Bancroft Library, University of California, Berkeley)

Once in office, Olson found himself stymied at every turn by the very interests he had campaigned against. The Republicans, fearing his election to office, had converted to civil service nearly all the previously appointed positions in state government, depriving Olson of the opportunity to effect change through appointees. The legislature was less than compliant. So in 1939, for example, despite the governor's strong support, an attempt to restrict the activities of lobbyists was roundly defeated in the legislature. Sponsored by Assemblyman Hugh P. Donnelly, a Democrat, the measure would have required all lobbyists to register and provide full information regarding the interests they represented and the terms of their employment. Olson's other efforts to reduce the power of lobbies were also defeated, as were his attempts to abolish cross-filing and promote prolabor measures. Olson's support of public ownership of utilities put him squarely in opposition to some of the most powerful interests in the state; this and his lack of support in the legislature doomed him to be a one-term governor, elected on his reform platform but stalemated at every turn, leaving the state in the same hands as before.

In the 1942 gubernatorial race, Culbert Olson was defeated by Earl Warren, California's attorney general. Warren's political philosophy emphasized "local government and the decentralization of power." "Leadership, not politics" was the keynote of Warren's campaign, which was managed by Clem Whitaker and received the support of nearly all the state's metropolitan newspapers. The newspapers referred to Warren as a "nonpartisan candidate for governor." Warren even received a large vote in the Democratic primary, made possible by the state's cross-filing provision (404,778 votes to 514,144 for Olson). Olson's campaign had been criticized for its overemphasis on partisanship and on the differences between the parties. Clearly, the state's voters had grown to believe that politics and parties had no part to play in elections. Warren used this to his advantage, declaring at the Republican state convention in 1942 "that the campaign was: 'not a contest between the Republican and Democratic parties.'" The Republican platform closed with a pledge of "nonpolitical government" and a request for support: "We call on all loyal citizens of the great State of California to forget partisan politics."[46] The rhetoric of politicians, it seemed, had not much changed since Hiram Johnson's 1911 appeal to the state legislature to put aside partisan politics, but in reality special interests, organized through business associations, had taken the place of political parties. Once again, alternative visions—embodied in the EPIC campaign, the dreams for small-scale irrigated agriculture, and political reform—had been pushed aside.

Timber

The crisis in the timber industry across the country due to overproduction, low prices, and poor private forest management was felt in California as well. The state Board of Forestry had not been able to develop effective regulations for private forest management because the industry itself was divided about what approach to take. At the federal level there was great concern as well over management of the nation's private forests. Forest Service leadership believed there needed to be federal rules to guide the management of private forests, otherwise the nation's timber-producing capacity would be put at risk. New Dealers sought to establish policies that would provide for economic growth through intelligent planning and management of the nation's resources.

The help that the timbermen received from the Forest Service during the Hoover and Roosevelt administrations set a precedent of expectations on the part of industry. During the Depression industry sought relief from President Hoover, who in 1930 appointed the Timber Conservation Board, charged with equalizing production and consumption. T. Mason, a lumberman on the board, proposed that it coordinate public and private timber supplies so that the volume logged would not exceed the volume grown, and any deficiencies would be made up by sale from the national forests. This approach set a precedent for the role of the public forests—to supplement and/or assist private forest production—even though by this time 80 percent of the nation's forests were privately held and contained over 90 percent of the growth capacity of timber in the country.[47]

The New Deal had put people to work for the Forest Service constructing roads and trails, building fire lookouts, clearing fire lines and breaks, and working on other projects with the Civilian Conservation Corps (CCC). In California the CCC made lasting contributions to both federal and state forests in the construction of ranger residences, lookout towers, crew houses, garages, warehouses, bridges, firebreaks, roads, and telephone lines. These improvements also helped private forests, especially the fire-fighting infrastructure that was put in place. The war then shifted the government's attention from maintaining forests to emphasizing their strategic value as a source of timber. National forest policy was altered to meet wartime needs. This included assistance for the timber industry through scientific research, pricing policy, and, during the war, provision of labor for the private timber mills.

In keeping with the ideology of the New Deal (investing to create economic growth), foresters and forest planners were concerned to find ways to halt the degradation of the timber resource in the United States. Forest Service administrators felt that the federal government needed to establish a framework of regulations that would guide private forest practice—requiring, for example, that trees be systematically replanted after harvest. Hearings on the condition of forests in private ownership were held over several years at the federal level to establish the need for federal oversight. Earle Clapp, acting head of the Forest Service, advocated a system of state regulation in the mid-1930s, guided by minimum federal requirements. This was consistent with the historic pattern of federal-state relations. Given a decentralized governmental system, the federal government's role was to establish overall regulations that the states would then be responsible for enforcing. If states dragged their feet and failed to set up an acceptable program, only then would the federal government step in and do so in their stead. For a time, Clapp's strong positions were influential. In 1941 the Joint Congressional Committee on Forestry published its report, confirming the need for better forest management and stating that "private owners, the general public and the federal government [were to blame] for perpetuating the uninhibited exploitation of forests and other natural resources."[48]

The attempt by the federal government to regulate private forest practice spurred industry into action. Already organized into trade associations, the industry actively lobbied against the federal rule setting that had been advocated by Clapp. Strong industry pressure led to President Roosevelt's appointment of J. Philip Boyd of Weyerhaeuser to head the Lumber and Timber Products Division of the War Production Board. Boyd developed policies to put the Forest Service at the service of the timber industry.

Even so, fear of possible federal intervention spurred the Council of State Governments, encouraged by the timber industry, to put forward a model Forest Practice Act in 1940. Both the council and industry wanted to keep the federal government from regulating forest practice nationwide. The council was motivated by states' rights concerns, and industry felt it would have more influence at the state level than at the federal level to influence the development of laws in its interest.

Business associations had increasingly used the Council of State Governments as their vehicle to respond to the threats of federal rule making by pressuring the states to develop their own regulations, shaped by direct industry input. This approach to preempting federal rule making—having the Council of State Governments develop a model act for states—was followed over the next several decades in many sectors, enforcing state autonomy and precluding federal intervention, in a further evolution of business associationalism.

Although California was never considered a big timber state, unlike its counterparts to the north or midwestern states such as Minnesota, its forest resources were considerable, consisting of redwood, pine, and fir. An important part of the timber resource lay in the northwestern part of the state in redwood forests. As commentators on California forestry have noted, most of the conflict between preservationists, conservationists, and the timber industry focused on the redwoods. These noble trees continued to inspire reverence as well as scientific curiosity. So throughout the Progressive and New Deal periods, while the trees were being logged, constant pressure was applied in Sacramento regarding forest practice in the redwood region. However, the 1926 "federal plan" of apportionment had put so much power in the hands of rural senators that no amount of public pressure seemed to make much difference in the regulation of private forest practice at the state level.

Acknowledging the continuing tension over timber and the need for coordinated state action, Earl Warren called on W. S. Rosecrans, a businessman concerned with conservation, to discuss California's forestry problems. They agreed that the state needed to strengthen and reorganize the Forestry Board, an institution with a checkered history. Following conventional Progressive procedure, Rosecrans turned to private industry to draw up a list of possible appointees. These included three representatives from the timber industry and one each from agriculture, livestock production, and water development. The nominees were appointed, with Rosecrans, the public representative, as chair. By 1944 the Board of Forestry was a reestablished entity that fully embodied the ideology of the Progressive reformers of the earlier period. True to form, it was composed of those economic interests most vitally affected by regulation of private forest lands: those who knew the most about the economics of the industry, those who had the most to win or lose as a result of how the regulations were structured. Rosecrans later described the board's area of responsibility as working out a balanced program that considered public opposition to "bureaucratic control." "Our program had to fit the State's political philosophy. . . . A democratic, grass-roots program, it has been developed in keeping with the American tradition of free enterprise. So far as the regulatory phases of it are concerned, these are in close contact with the people concerned, are initiated by the timber owners and operators and are put into practice more by education than by enforcement."[49] Nominally concerned with conservation, the Forestry Board under Rosecrans epitomized the approach of business associationalism. The formal inclusion of business interests in the functions of state government to elaborate the rules to govern themselves was the fruition of Progressive reform and the application of Progressive ideology.

The actual forest practice rules were developed during 1944 and 1945 by Senator George M. Biggar of Covelo (a rural town in northern California)

and Professor Emanuel Fritz of the forestry school at the University of California, Berkeley. They first submitted the rules to the Forest Protective Association (an industry group) for modification, then presented them to the legislature, which passed them in 1945. The Forest Practice Act established
four forest districts in the state and set up forest practice committees, made
up of local timber owners in each district, to formulate rules, which would
then be submitted to the state board for approval. Any rules proposed by the
committees first had to be approved by a two-thirds majority of the local
timber landowners in each district. Changes in the rules had the same requirement. The rules promulgated under the 1945 act were weak and went
virtually unenforced. Rules included minimum cutting diameters, care of
residual trees from logging damage, snag and slag disposal, fire prevention
safeguards, and fire protection measures. There was no regulation of the
conversion of timber land to other uses, such as grazing; as a result, this was
easily done and was widely resorted to as a means to escape compliance
with the rules.[50] It was clear that the bounds of the state's regulation of forest practice were set by industry with the primary intent of ensuring favorable economic conditions for industry.

Chairman Rosecrans had the following to say about the new structure:
"The Forest Practice Act is working out very well. It is administered on a live
and let live policy. . . . A democratic and grass roots approach has been used
. . . this is forestry by the people. It is getting results."[51]

This was a clear example of associationalism—industry self-regulation
sanctioned by the rural timber and agricultural interests that dominated
legislature. DeWitt Nelson, head of the California State Division of Forestry
under Warren, explained this approach: "There was still the threat of federal regulation, and I have always believed that the timber industry chose
the lesser of two evils, shall we say; that they would much rather have state
regulation than federal regulation, which I think is still the way that it
should be."[52]

Local timber interests took the opportunity provided by the threat of federal regulation to establish a minimum-diameter law in 1943, prohibiting
the commercial cutting of coniferous trees measuring less than 18 inches in
diameter, unless a permit was obtained from the state. This legislation was
endorsed and pushed by the California Protective Association, a timber
business association, to placate growing public criticism about poor timber
practices, and especially to stave off possible federal legislation.[53] The industry used the state's police powers to enforce those standards against operators who tried to compete by selling more cheaply and cutting smaller
stands. Small operators had lower overhead costs and could afford to sell
timber cheaper than the larger operators. The larger operators were anxious

to establish the minimum cutting thresholds so that they could maintain their profit margins. Forest regulations served the same purpose as the marketing regulations developed in the agricultural sector—using state regulatory authority to further the interests of the most powerful segment of the industry.

In fact, overall timber-harvesting techniques were not substantially changed by the new regulations. The laws merely codified normal industry practice, making it harder for marginal operators to survive. Degradation of the resource continued. One of the most debatable aspects of forest practice was its effect on watersheds. Previous conclusions about the relationship between deforestation and flooding, derived from Marsh's scientific analysis of the role of forests, had led to the preservation of the mountains in southern California and other measures. However, the current Forestry Board's regulations made no provisions with respect to protection of watersheds or water quality. This seemed a deliberate oversight and was criticized severely from the beginning by the public as well as by the Department of Fish and Game.

The Department of Fish and Game, already well established and with a long institutional history devoted to the promotion and protection of fisheries, over time developed an antagonistic relationship with the Department of Forestry, which enforced the rules adopted by the Forestry Board. Many times experts from Fish and Game testified to the Board of Forestry regarding the devastating effect that poorly regulated timber harvest practices were having on the state's fisheries, especially salmon. The agencies' fundamental antagonisms were summarized by DeWitt Nelson, head of the Division of Forestry during this period, who commented, "The Department of Fish and Game has the ultra-preservationist concept. All streams must be preserved in their pristine purity, and the fish are more important than a timber industry."[54] Watershed protection and more stringent forest practice laws for private landowners were blocked at the state level because the Board of Forestry was appointed by the governor and confirmed by the Senate, which was in turn dominated by rural interests and powerful economic interests.

Fisheries and Wildlife

Exploitation of California fisheries grew with the increase in population. In addition, the tremendous growth in the number and size of factories and cities greatly aggravated stream pollution. Agriculture also contributed to the problem: irrigation reduced stream flows and also contaminated streams with fertilizers in the return irrigation water. Hydroelectric power development interfered with the natural flow of streams and their fish life. Fisheries were under siege, and salmon runs were being severely affected.

The fishery industry, like other industries, organized trade associations: the California Salmon Fisher's and Canner's Association, the California Abalone Association, the California Bay Fishermen's Association, the California Shrimp Association, the California Tuna Association, and the Association of California Sportsmen's Clubs. Such groups felt the effects of stream degradation caused by poor timber practices, and they organized against the destruction of virgin timber resources. Among their members and supporters were some of the wealthiest individuals in the West, such as Isaac Zellerbach, president of the giant Crown-Zellerbach Paper Corporation, who was interested in wildlife and fish conservation and served for many years on California's Fish and Game Commission.[55] Of course, Zellerbach's personal interest in conservation did not change the fact that the wood products industry is one of the greatest culprits in the destruction of fish habitat and pollution of waterways.

The Fish and Game Department had an independent source of income through licenses and a commercial fishing tax it collected. This fund was used to conduct research, propagate fish, and conduct department operations. The commission also imposed restrictions on stream pollution and obstruction through administrative orders. It applied for court injunctions to stop dumping and tried to persuade private enterprises to dispose of their wastes responsibly. It worked to persuade hydroelectric plants to install fish ladders and other devices to allow the passage of fish. Even so, in 1924 the commission estimated that 3,000 fish ladders should have been installed, but only 600 were in place, less than half of which were in proper functioning order.[56]

Fish and Game relied on different sections of the state penal code to do its job. To keep the Sacramento Basin waterways free for running salmon, it used individual statutes to inspect irrigation and power dams, and to order operators to build fishways or entire hatcheries at state expense, if their obstructions were impassable. This approach meant that the costs of complying with state law were passed on to the public sector rather than being paid by the industry responsible for violating the law. Despite paying to install fish screens, Fish and Game still was not able to get farmers to comply with the law and screen their irrigation ditches to keep fish out. The commission protested to no avail that farmers and others who used the state's water for free ought to pay something to protect the fish. Farmers refused, and the legislature did not budge either. During the New Deal the Civilian Conservation Corps established a free program of screening canals, but such an effort was not financially possible for Fish and Game.[57]

John Enos dam, no fish ladder, with at least 60 fish an hour trying unsuccessfully to get over dam, unknown date. (Photograph by Fisher for Fish and Game Commission; courtesy of California State Archives, Office of the Secretary of State, Sacramento)

Defective fish ladder at the Carmel River bridge, below the dam, 1929. (Photograph by E. S. Cheney for Fish and Game Commission; courtesy of California State Archives, Office of the Secretary of State, Sacramento)

Example of Fish and Game Commission's proposed fish screen for irrigation ditches, unknown date. (Fish and Game Commission; courtesy of California State Archives, Office of the Secretary of State, Sacramento)

Despite its independent budget, Fish and Game suffered insurmountable obstacles in its attempt to protect the state's natural resources. The structure of law that guided the commission obliged it to work on a case-by-case basis, which required a great deal of staff time and effort. Gentlemen's agreements and an occasional lawsuit were the meager tools of the commission, which addressed each violation individually. This approach was insufficient to deal with the wholesale destruction of fishery habitat by irrigation districts and power companies after 1915, and continued watershed degradation. Fish and Game appealed fruitlessly time and again to the Water Rights Division of the state Public Works Department to guarantee minimal flows of water through Central Valley dams to maintain fisheries. The interests supporting fish were no match to those behind timber, agriculture, and water.

In an exceptional instance, in the early 1920s the commission took its case to the public when attempts to work through regular channels failed to stop the Electro-Metals Company from damming the Klamath River. "The company mounted a very powerful cost-benefit argument in its behalf. The dam, it said, would generate more income for the local economy than would

the salmon fishery, which a local editor called a 'small enterprise of only local importance' and which in any event produced only one-sixth of the Pacific Coast commercial salmon pack. A local newspaper denounced the Fish
and Game Commission as the tool of the 'idle rich' and 'dangerously near to
becoming a menace to the industrial expansion of the state.'" The Klamath
was the largest remaining free-flowing river on the Pacific Coast. The commission took its case directly to the people through a ballot initiative measure opposing the dam, and the initiative succeeded after Fish and Game employees in all parts of the state campaigned vigorously for passage. Such
techniques, however, were never repeated.[58]

The Fish and Game Commission attempted to keep fish harvests at sustainable levels for several different fisheries. It made various attempts to regulate the sardine harvest, but its rule-making powers were actually quite
weak. It also tried to protect salmon fisheries. The run on the Sacramento
River in 1930, for example, was only 20 percent of what it had been twenty
years before. The commission tried in vain to convince the legislature to prohibit all salmon fishing on the Sacramento, but the objections of the fishermen's association prevailed. Likewise, the future of the tuna harvest was
of great concern, but the commission could do nothing to restrict fishing.
Despite the agency's seniority and prestige, it could only recommend actions

"Save the Fish on the Klamath River," unknown date. (Fish and Game Commission;
courtesy of California State Archives, Office of the Secretary of State, Sacramento)

to the legislature. The state lacked a unified fish and game code until 1933, and only in 1940 did the commission become a constitutionally endowed body, to which the legislature granted plenary powers. This was only because of a statewide initiative that was passed in 1940, establishing a model Fish and Game Commission law. The legislature itself showed no leadership in this area.[59]

The growth of the fishing industry made problems of oversupply worse. During the period 1919–33, the fishing industry in California increased production fivefold, and the state became the nation's second-largest fishery. The problem was that fishers supplied more fish than could be marketed, causing a decline in the value of the commodity, reminiscent of the timber industry. Not only did the commission face the problem of conservation of the resource over the long haul, but it also had to confront the problem of control of production and distribution, competition, and the constantly fluctuating business cycles.

As in other commercial sectors, the state stepped in to regulate the industry. The commission created a State Fish Exchange to regulate the relations between supply and demand by imposing restraints on production and prices, and creating special markets. All fish dealers were licensed by the state. In 1919 the legislature established a Bureau of Commercial Fisheries at the behest of the tuna fishermen, who appealed to state government to aid their depressed industry as European markets disappeared. In these ways state police powers were used to attempt to stabilize a volatile industry and market. Zellerbach, head of the appointed Fish and Game Commission, explained the commission's philosophy: it was to "function as a business concern with a similar form of management, centering all responsibility [in] the three Commissioners."[60]

Despite these efforts California's fisheries continued to decline as fishermen scrambled to take as many fish as they could. The Fish and Game Commission was unable to do much about it because of its intrinsically split allegiances—protecting the resource and promoting economic development—even though its job was to place itself between the fisheries and the market failures. Overexploitation led to the dramatic crash of the sardine populations off the coast of California at the end of World War II, which has been called "one of the most egregious disasters in the history of U.S. wildlife management. As Lance Scofield [U.S. Bureau of Fisheries] had predicted it would, *laissez-faire* permitted the sardine to 'adjust itself at an economic level . . . [just as] the buffalo did.'"[61]

The California Fish and Game Commission historically was somewhat more responsive to the need of preserving the resource than were most of the other natural resource boards and commissions, but it eventually succumbed to the pressures of the commercial fishing interests. Unlike many of its counterparts, however, Fish and Game also found itself fighting other enterprises to keep fisheries viable. This put it in opposition to some of the most powerful rural interests of the state: oil, timber, and agriculture.

Federal Housing Policy

It is perhaps surprising to think of the 1920s and 1930s as the period when much of the nation's urban planning methods and a national housing policy were put in place, yet many urban policies were indeed developed and implemented during the period of Hoover's business associationalism and then the New Deal. The process by which this occurred was typical: the federal government proffered financial assistance programs and set standards—guided by the real estate developers. The federal government then provided oversight and money to encourage states to implement federal rules and programs.[62]

Just as in other industrial sectors, the story of American real estate development is one of increasing growth—in the size of the enterprise, the average scale of development, and the size of land parcel. Scale in land development brought efficiencies. Building residential subdivisions on vacant land at the suburban fringe could reduce per-housing-unit costs, increase profits, and at the same time provide less expensive housing than the previous house-by-house approach. California's speculative developers and builders devised critical advances in construction practices and community planning. They consolidated land subdivision, construction, and sales into a single organization.[63] Because of the scale at which subdividers operated (especially beginning in the 1940s), they performed, de facto, the function of American city planning. They operated by the motto that "private innovation precedes public action" and worked to have the federal government incorporate much of that private innovation in its regulatory framework.[64]

Federal involvement began in earnest when the urban real estate boom collapsed with the rest of the economy because of the Depression. Under Herbert Hoover's guidance, the federal government stepped in to protect and prop up this sector, just as it had done for agriculture and timber, among others. As commerce secretary (1921–28), Hoover had formulated, endorsed, and enacted policy and programs designed to encourage residential construction, extend home ownership, and set neighborhood standards.[65] With the assistance of the National Association of Real Estate Boards (the major industry trade association), the government developed the Federal Home Loan Bank Act to create a series of discount banks for home mortgages. These would stimulate residential construction and increase

Table 2. *Yearly Landings in Pounds: Salmon*

Year	Coastal Ports	Sacramento Area Ports	Coastal Rivers	Total Pounds
1916	5,592,216	3,450,786	1,896,592	10,939,594
1917	6,085,997	3,975,487	999,097	11,060,581
1918	5,933,346	5,938,029	1,221,813	13,093,188
1919	7,208,382	4,529,222	1,408,123	13,145,727
1920	6,066,190	3,860,312	1,207,317	11,133,819
1921	4,483,105	2,511,127	996,700	7,990,932
1922	4,338,317	1,765,066	1,131,741	7,235,124
1923	3,736,924	2,243,945	1,109,391	7,090,260
1924	6,374,573	2,640,110	1,000,586	10,015,269
1925	5,481,536	2,778,846	1,265,371	9,525,753
1926	3,863,677	1,261,776	958,926	6,084,079
1927	4,921,600	920,786	669,543	6,511,929
1928	3,444,306	553,777	480,483	4,478,566
1929	4,033,660	581,497	429,714	5,044,871
1930	4,085,650	1,213,698	703,546	6,002,894
1931	3,666,841	941,605	686,065	5,294,511
1932	2,649,204	1,264,987	703,990	4,618,181
1933	3,657,661	454,253	446,520	4,558,434
1934	3,921,530	397,572	—	4,319,102
1935	4,773,112	888,868	—	5,661,980
1936	4,093,475	949,179	—	5,042,654
1937	5,934,996	974,871	—	6,909,867
1938	2,170,921	1,668,376	—	3,839,297
1939	2,238,755	496,933	—	2,735,688
1940	5,160,393	1,515,588	—	6,675,981
1941	2,946,030	844,963	—	3,790,993
1942	4,063,306	2,552,944	—	6,616,250

Table 2 *(continued)*

Year	Coastal Ports	Sacramento Area Ports	Coastal Rivers	Total Pounds
1943	5,285,527	1,295,424	—	6,580,951
1944	7,021,848	3,265,143	—	10,286,991
1945	7,912,754	5,467,960	—	13,380,714
1946	7,196,527	6,463,245	—	13,659,772
1947	8,104,297	3,380,484	—	11,484,781
1948	5,860,915	1,939,801	—	7,800,716
1949	5,531,021	899,090	—	6,430,111
1950	5,867,346	1,202,890	—	7,070,236
1951	5,849,530	1,343,171	—	7,192,701
1952	6,536,890	738,081	—	7,274,971
1953	7,136,223	869,696	—	8,005,919
1954	8,599,579	900,961	—	9,500,540
1955	9,656,996	2,320,746	—	11,977,742
1956	10,274,902	1,139,585	—	11,414,487
1957	5,176,909	321,824	—	5,498,733
1958	3,656,841	—	—	3,656,841
1959	6,768,699	463	—	6,769,162
1960	6,221,445	—	—	6,221,445
1961	8,637,907	—	—	8,637,907
1962	6,672,861	—	—	6,672,861
1963	7,859,186	—	—	7,859,186
1964	9,481,215	—	—	9,481,215
1965	9,737,775	—	—	9,737,775
1966	9,446,995	—	—	9,446,995
1967	7,401,729	—	—	7,401,729
1968	6,951,931	—	—	6,951,931

Source: California Department of Fish and Game, "The California Marine Fish Catch for 1968 and Historical Review 1916–68," *Fish Bulletin* 149 (Sacramento, 1970), 58.

Table 3. *Seasonal Landings in Tons: Sardines*

Season	Reduction Ships	San Francisco Area	Monterey Area	Los Angeles Area	San Diego Area	Total Tons
1916–17	—	—	7,710	17,380	2,440	27,530
1917–18	—	70	23,810	41,340	7,360	72,580
1918–19	—	450	35,750	32,530	6,810	75,540
1919–20	—	1,000	43,040	16,580	6,410	67,030
1920–21	—	230	24,960	11,740	1,520	38,450
1921–22	—	80	16,290	19,220	910	36,500
1922–23	—	110	29,210	33,170	2,620	65,110
1923–24	—	190	45,920	35,040	2,780	83,930
1924–25	—	560	67,310	96,330	8,820	173,020
1925–26	—	560	69,010	61,990	5,710	137,270
1926–27	—	3,520	81,860	64,720	2,110	152,210
1927–28	—	16,690	98,020	67,900	4,650	187,260
1928–29	—	13,520	120,290	119,250	1,420	254,480
1929–30	—	21,960	160,050	140,540	2,620	325,170
1930–31	10,960	25,970	109,620	38,490	80	185,120
1931–32	31,040	21,607	69,078	42,656	264	164,645
1932–33	58,790	18,634	89,599	83,605	62	250,690
1933–34	67,820	36,336	152,480	125,047	1,746	383,429
1934–35	112,040	68,477	230,854	178,818	4,865	726,124
1935–36	150,830	76,147	184,470	138,400	10,651	560,498
1936–37	235,610	141,099	206,706	138,115	4,594	726,124
1937–38	67,580	133,718	104,936	109,947	383	416,564
1938–39	43,890	201,200	180,994	146,403	2,800	575,287
1939–40	—	212,453	227,874	96,827	112	537,266
1940–41	—	118,470	165,698	175,592	1,202	460,584
1941–42	—	186,589	250,287	148,912	1,585	587,373
1942–43	—	115,884	184,399	201,510	2,868	504,661

Table 3 *(continued)*

Season	Reduction Ships	San Francisco Area	Monterey Area	Los Angeles Area	San Diego Area	Total Tons
1943–44	—	126,512	213,616	135,311	2,690	478,129
1944–45	—	136,598	237,246	178,294	2,767	554,905
1945–46	—	84,103	145,519	173,110	951	403,683
1946–47	—	2,869	31,391	194,774	4,768	233,802
1947–48	—	94	17,630	101,154	2,463	121,341
1948–49	—	112	47,862	131,830	3,922	183,726
1949–50	—	17,422	131,769	186,433	3,281	338,925
1950–51	—	12,727	33,699	303,752	2,910	353,088
1951–52	—	82	15,897	111,774	1,351	129,104
1952–53	—	—	49	5,635	27	5,711
1953–54	—	—	58	4,111	323	4,492
1954–55	—	—	856	67,099	510	68,465
1955–56	—	—	518	73,943	—	74,461
1956–57	—	—	63	33,564	16	33,643
1957–58	—	—	17	22,255	—	22,272
1958–59	—	—	24,701	79,264	6	103,971
1959–60	—	—	16,109	21,146	1	37,256
1960–61	—	—	2,340	26,436	102	28,878
1961–62	—	—	2,231	23,295	2	25,528
1962–63	—	—	1,211	2,961	—	4,172
1963–64	—	—	1,015	1,895	32	2,942
1964–65	—	—	308	5,717	78	6,103
1965–66	—	—	151	535	33	719
1966–67	—	—	23	311	10	34
1967–68	—	—	10	61	—	71

Note: Season = June–May.
Source: California Department of Fish and Game, "The California Marine Fish Catch for 1968 and Historical Review 1916–68," *Fish Bulletin* 149 (Sacramento, 1970), 57.

A brail load of sardines being unloaded from a purse seiner, 1929. (Fish and Game Department; courtesy of California State Archives, Office of the Secretary of State, Sacramento)

home ownership by providing the facilities for long-term loans payable in installments, mortgage deductions, and other federal policies. The Reconstruction Finance Corporation, created in 1933, provided loans to banking institutions, life insurance companies, building and loan societies, the railroads, and farm mortgage associations to boost the real estate sector. Such programs helped underwrite the risk of development for the developer.[66]

The New Deal period made permanent these major financial institutions, many of which still serve to back the housing market today. The federal rules elaborated to guide their lending policies became national standards, including routine redlining in black and Jewish neighborhoods (a practice that continued into the 1970s). Financing from the Federal Housing Administration (FHA) made it cheaper to buy a new suburban home than to rent a comparable structure in the city, encouraging suburbanization and the gradual departure of the middle class from inner-city neighborhoods. FHA financing discouraged the construction of multifamily projects through unfavorable terms compared to those available for single-family dwellings at the urban fringe. Finally, the "FHA established minimum standards for home construction that became almost standard in the industry."[67] These institutions, including the FHA and the Reconstruction Finance Corporation, permitted the stronger home builders to weather the Depression. With financing mechanisms in place and standardized codes for all builders es-

tablished by the federal government, large-scale subdivisions could prolif-
erate under the protective umbrella of government programs. Of course,
only well-capitalized builders could participate and meet the minimum
standards that had been established by the big players. Federal government
housing programs, through their patterns of incentives, were a major con-
tributor to the suburbanization of the United States and the departure of
the middle class from the nation's cities. Later the federal highway building
programs reinforced this pattern. The beginnings of disinvestment in many
of the nation's cities can be traced to the policies of the New Deal period.

Los Angeles: The "Crabgrass Frontier"

Southern California was perhaps the leader in large-scale land development
in the United States. Many of the forms of land use and the institutions and
arrangements necessary to develop large tracts of land were pioneered
there. The problem of land-use planning was acute in Los Angeles because

"This Tract is Exclusive," Los Angeles, 1940s. (Courtesy of the Southern California
Library for Social Studies and Research, Los Angeles)

of the rate of population growth. The settlement of the outlying territories in Los Angeles was the work of promoters who encouraged the thousands of upper- and middle-class families that wanted to live in a city but retain a rural setting, thereby perpetuating the vision of the early developers. With the increased availability and use of automobiles, dispersed development accelerated. The federal policies developed to assist the housing sector nationwide simply facilitated an already well-established industry in southern California and exacerbated the problems of sprawl. Yet as Greg Hise points out in *Magnetic Los Angeles*, it is important to realize that this multicentered spatial dispersion had an intrinsic logic and coherence. It grew out of the garden-city ideal, incorporating community planning, that included homes, transportation, churches, parks and recreation areas, and shopping facilities. The project of home building included the layout of subdivisions and establishment of the relationship between home neighborhoods and the location of business and industrial centers. The purposeful linking of industrial and residential development was axiomatic.

At the same time builders were developing new housing at the urban fringe—in places like the San Fernando Valley, which had recently received Owens Valley water—the Los Angeles city council realized that uncoordinated growth would be inefficient and also could create insurmountable infrastructure problems. In April 1920 the city council appointed a city planning commission, one of the first in the country. Then, in 1922, a county planning commission was created to coordinate development in the unincorporated parts of the basin. In its first nine months it was inundated with proposals for more than eight hundred new tracts in unincorporated areas. A private group, consisting of the editors of the three leading Los Angeles newspapers and individuals from the Southern California Development Association (formed at the suggestion of a special committee created by the Automobile Club of Southern California), sponsored the design of a metropolitan highway plan by the Olmsted brothers, Harland Bartholomew, and Charles Cheney.[68] Despite these initial efforts to anticipate and plan for this growth, cities and counties spent most of their time and efforts simply keeping up with the pace of speculative development: providing sewers, storm drains, schools, and roads. Soon the attempt to establish a general plan to guide development was overwhelmed, and the political will to force such an effort was lacking. The opportunities to establish parkways, preserve open space, and work cooperatively on a regionwide basis were defeated by the tenacity of impatient private developers and the proliferation of new municipalities in the basin, each with its own planning authority, which it exercised independently of others. Local control over local land use meant that small incorporated cities within Los Angeles County, or even within the city of Los Angeles, had no obligation to take the plans of neigh-boring entities into account while making their own. In addition, there was a proliferation of special districts set up to finance, build, and administer various infrastructure construction and maintenance needs, and the bal-kanization of the region continued to accelerate with the growth of popula-tion. The essence of local government was to facilitate growth, its function administrative rather than political. And expansion was the region's pri-mary business. A growing population opened opportunities in construc-tion, manufacturing, and commerce, and if immigration had diminished, the result would have been disastrous.[69]

Federal programs designed to assist the faltering housing industry, begin-ning in the 1920s, contributed to the problems of unmanaged growth since they were mostly concerned with supporting the viability of the private home-building industry and left planning issues entirely to the locals. Local control over local land use was already a jealously guarded prerogative, and it was easily confounded with the protection of private property rights. Here again, federal support and guidelines were welcome, but not oversight over the planning process or guidance in how private property should be used.

There was another side to Los Angeles, too: its increasing ethnic diversifi-cation and the development of poor neighborhoods. During the first quarter of the twentieth century, the already existing ethnic diversity of Los Angeles escaped the attention of most white Angelenos. In parallel to the thunder-ing pace of subdivision development for the middle class, there was another reality, closer to the center of town—ethnic neighborhoods. Building on a long established population of Californios, from 1900 to 1930 thousands of Mexicans immigrated to Los Angeles, especially during the years of the Mexican Revolution.[70] Mexican immigrants built the interurban railroad system of Los Angeles, and were some of the first workers in its growing in-dustrial sector, which included tire manufacturing, steel, and meat packing, located primarily on the city's east side. The Mexican community grew in this eastern part of Los Angeles, providing low-wage labor for industry. Slums (called barrios) developed to house these workers.

The Anglo population left downtown and East Los Angeles to the foreign-born, Mexicans, and blacks. Since Mexicans were the largest immigrant group, they made up significant proportions of many of these communities. With the Depression, however, the pool of jobs dried up. Employers no longer needed cheap foreign laborers, and Los Angeles began deporting unemployed Mexicans back to their homeland. Mexicans were seen as com-peting for scarce jobs and were considered a threat.[71] In 1931 the California state legislature enacted a law making it illegal for any company doing busi-ness with the government to employ "aliens" on public jobs, and accordingly many private companies refused to hire workers of Mexican origin.[72] Repatriation occurred without any concern for citizenship status, length of residency, health conditions, or age factors. Entire trains, as well as ships, were filled with Mexicans being sent back to Mexico. Many nationals left without official intervention and paid their own way under pressure from the government and anti-Mexican sentiment.[73] It is estimated that approximately one-third of the Mexican community in Los Angeles returned to Mexico during the 1930s.

The slums that had been built near parts of downtown also became targets for redevelopment by the city after the Depression. Private developers considered some of the neighborhoods Mexicans lived in as prime real estate because they were so close to downtown. Through their business associations, builders began to formulate plans to redevelop these areas, using federal redevelopment laws and subsidies. Since builders were incorporated into the city's policymaking boards and commissions by appointment, they were able to shape the city's plans and influence redevelopment strategy. Federal housing policy, which had been prompted by concerns about the lack of low-income and affordable housing, was ultimately shaped, through the able manipulation of building trade associations, to help builders provide housing largely for the white middle and working classes. (Later, after World War II, it also helped provide housing for the growing African American working class in segregated neighborhoods.) Federal housing policy never really addressed the housing needs of poor people, and slums continued to be the housing norm for that sector of the population. Federal housing policy encouraged those who could afford it to leave the inner city for new housing at the edge of town.

Although future years saw struggles over urban form, the distribution of growth, equity, and power, the idea of metropolitanism in Los Angeles—integrated regional planning balancing jobs with housing and maintaining a strong urban core, parks, and open space—was buried by the frenetic pace of development, stalemated by local control over local land use, and subverted by federal housing policy. In addition, the structure of local government itself worked against metropolitanism, since it was largely made up of boards and commissions (planning commissions, zoning commissions, and others) whose members, drawn from the local development community, had direct economic stakes in the further expansion of urban development.

San Francisco: Quasi Metropolitanism

The San Francisco Bay area continued to try to push forward its metropolitan planning dream of the Progressive period. The Regional Planning Association of San Francisco Bay Counties, formed in 1925, recaptured many of

Meat packing in Los Angeles, 1928: Packing and butchering, Cudahy Packing Company. (Courtesy of the Los Angeles Public Library, Security Pacific Collection)

the earlier ideas put forward by Mayor Phelan, who had first promulgated the idea of regional planning for the Bay area. But the regional rivalry between San Francisco and Oakland, fueled by the suspicion that San Francisco wished to dominate other communities, continued, and a rival East Bay Regional Planning Association, put together by an ambitious East Bay realtor, weakened the San Francisco regional plan. Even at the level of basic infrastructure development, the two sides of the Bay were reluctant to cooperate. For example, San Francisco had assumed that it was building a regional water system when it developed a plan to dam the Hetch Hetchy Valley for the Tuolumne River water, but Oakland residents suspected that this was another San Francisco scheme to deprive them of home rule. (Other cities in the East Bay did ultimately use Hetch Hetchy water.) Instead, Oakland constructed its own independent public system, the Pardee Reservoir on the Mokelumne River of the Sierra Nevada mountains, administered by the East Bay Municipal Utility District.[74]

Mexican garment workers, 1943: Rosie Albrann (age nineteen) and Ramona Fonseco (age seventeen), outside of Barenveld Shirt Factory, San Fernando. (Courtesy of the Los Angeles Public Library, Shades of L.A. Archives)

After World War I many roads were built in the Bay area to accommodate the increasing use of the automobile. Nearly all new building construction included garages, and there was pressure to build yet more roads to handle the greater amount of traffic. The Golden Gate Bridge was built in 1937, as was the Bay Bridge, funded by the federal government as part of a federal public works project during the New Deal. But the Bay area, in contrast with Los Angeles, seemed to maintain more of a sense of metropolitanism, despite the intraregional rivalries. This was, after all, the home of the scientific elite of the state and of the nascent preservation organizations, such as the Sierra Club. Growth was more concentrated, partly due to the Bay area's natural topography, which presented some natural obstacles to the pattern of sprawl prevalent in the south. Only in the 1950s did the suburban pattern really take hold in the region.

Still, business associationalism structured the patterns and ambitions of the Bay area. Prominent developers, bankers, and insurance company representatives were at the forefront in defining the direction of growth in the region. The struggles over metropolitanism for the Bay area, led by San Francisco, were restricted to this elite. Metropolitanism was not a grassroots political movement; planning issues were the domain of those with a financial interest, and it was for financial reasons that metropolitan planning was either supported or opposed. Contrary to the situation in southern California, where development interests simply wanted a free hand, there were factions in the Bay area that wanted to exert greater control. Though the cultures of business associationalism in the north and south differed, in both regions it was clear that business associations determined the patterns of land use and development.

Slum, Fickett Hollow, Los Angeles, 1940s. (Photograph by Leonard Nadel; courtesy of the Los Angeles Public Library, Security Pacific Collection)

View of downtown Los Angeles, north of the Los Angeles River, 1936. (Photograph by Spence; courtesy of Air Photo Archives, Department of Geography, University of California, Los Angeles)

The Success of Business Associationalism

Urban and rural infrastructure development—a form of land-use development—underwritten by the federal government largely as a result of the New Deal, was a powerful force in further transforming the natural landscape of California and in establishing a pattern of segregated urban land uses and urban sprawl. The Central Valley Project was the most significant of these large-scale projects, but urban land development also was facilitated by federal largesse, which provided access to financing for builders and buyers, and subsidized the bridges and roads necessary for further growth. California had received an enormous influx of immigrants during the Depression years, a ready work force for the war industries that quickly geared up in the subsequent period and made California an industrial leader. Combined with a powerful agricultural economy, California's natural resource base seemed like a bottomless well from which to draw the resources necessary for economic growth. Rural and business interests, anxious to retain their hold on Sacramento, engineered reapportionment of the state Senate in their favor, aiding business associations to infiltrate the structures of government.

Progressive reforms, aimed at ridding the state of corrupt party politics, left a vacuum of leadership that was filled by business interests with a clear notion of what they wanted and needed from state government. There was consensus about the desirability and importance of economic growth throughout the state, an attitude buttressed by the Depression. But the Depression focused much more attention than before on the equity of distribution. Socialist movements of opposition to the status quo became almost legitimate, though the fundamental structures of the state that had been put in place during the Progressive era ensured the long-term success of large property and business interests. Those interests had used the new approach to government to institutionalize a strong interdependence and alliance between the forces of economic growth and the state's governing institutions; the withering away of political parties at the local level was but one of those new changes. Another business-initiated reform passed during the Depression, whose impact was not regretted until much later, was the Riley-Stewart Act of 1933. Faced with serious budget constraints, the legislature passed a provision—advocated by the Commonwealth Club—that any increase in noneducation state spending that exceeded 5 percent must be approved by a two-thirds vote of both houses of the legislature. In the 1960s the 5 percent threshold was removed.[75]

The regulatory boards and commissions put in place by Progressives "were less creatures of the state's progressive movement than culmination of lengthy drives by interested business groups."[76] They served to consolidate the franchise state through business associationalism, a system whereby business groups were formally empowered by the state to regulate themselves, establishing norms and codes that then became the standards for an entire sector. Often these norms and codes were designed to cartelize sectors, reducing competition and requiring all to abide by the same procedures.

At the close of World War II Earl Warren, a Republican, was elected governor, remaining in office until 1953. He was so popular that he captured both the Republican and Democratic nominations in 1946. Warren espoused nonpartisan politics, reiterating the Progressives' anti-party approach. Despite the momentary rise of opposition parties reacting to the hardships of the Depression, the state was dominated by Progressive-style Republicans who believed in the incorporation of business associations in the rule-setting processes of state government and applied their precepts to the regulation of land uses and natural resources.

4 · THE PROBLEMS AND POLITICS OF GROWTH

> The attempt to isolate segments of public policy for decision by those most directly affected is common in American politics and is a general problem.   Grant McConnell, *The Decline of Agrarian Democracy* (1953)

CALIFORNIA'S ECONOMY boomed with the World War II military buildup. "Aircraft factories rose out of the pea fields and orange groves of Southern California, while quiet northern fishing villages along San Francisco Bay suddenly became the shipbuilding centers for the war."[1] The economic growth induced by the war industries and their federal subventions brought about yet another set of profound transformations in the state's natural landscape to meet expanding needs for housing, schools, water, and roads. The postwar decades were marked by political transformation—the state Senate was reapportioned to reflect the preponderance of urban dwellers, shifting the balance of power to the cities—and the emergence of the modern environmental movement. Reapportionment represented a significant break with the past, opening the door to political change. With new blood in the Senate, visions of possible alternative paths for the state and its future met entrenched interests head-on. Rapid growth was visibly transforming a landscape that people had become accustomed to and which they associated with the good life in California. Poorly directed, uncoordinated, and unrestrained growth began to meet with organized opposition. The patterns on the land and the growing regional inequalities in California were, in part, an unintended consequence of federal largesse. Federal investment in the war industries created demand for more housing, which was built using federal subsidies (the FHA and Veterans Administration home loans, for example) based on Depression-era housing policy. This inexorably led to greater urban sprawl and an unequal distribution of benefits.

World War II, "the fabulous boom," as it has been called, brought tremendous industrial growth, while the agricultural and land-development sectors continued to thrive. California's increased industrial capacity now, for the first time, posed a real challenge to eastern industrial supremacy.[2] This growth was helped by generous federal spending. Los Angeles alone handled more than $10 billion in war production contracts, creating new industries and new plants for the production of durable goods. Growth in California continued after the war, especially in Los Angeles. The city's highly dispersed geographic pattern was perfect for the modern industrial plant—a one-story structure on the edge of built-up areas. Transportation facilities in Los Angeles were good. The climate was right for aerospace manufacturing, particularly with the Mojave Desert nearby, providing a major testing area.

Paralleling the developing aircraft industry was the growing automobile industry, soon second in size and scope only to Detroit. Regional headquarters of large corporations, such as the Prudential Insurance Company, began to move to Los Angeles. Prudential began to buy agricultural lands in the Central Valley and urban real estate, continuing the pattern by which large companies in California had become involved beyond the urban context, having interests in both urban and rural land. The construction of the West Coast's first integrated blast furnace and steel mill at Fontana, east of Los Angeles, was another significant step in California's industrial development. People immigrated to California to fill the jobs created by these new industries. To take just one example, the wartime influx of African Americans into Los Angeles County created the third largest concentration of blacks outside the South.[3] In 1950 the resident population of California increased by 53 percent, second (in the twentieth century) only to the growth experienced in 1930 when it increased by 66 percent.[4]

Although California's spectacular growth was clearly linked to federal spending in the state, federal and state officials claimed that "the wartime partnership between government and business had proved capitalism capable of an almost unlimited expansion that would obviate the need for redistributive policies."[5] Awarding government contracts to private companies was not considered part of government's redistributive policies. Rather, the philosophy of business associationalism, or the franchise state—state police powers and financial underwriting—guided and used by business, now formed part of standard American business practices.

The Problems of Planning: The Federal Context

With the surge of land development brought about by postwar prosperity, questions about how best to plan land use were of national concern. Nationally, the pattern of development—building suburbs—was visibly leaving the city behind, with poor housing and poor people. In response, the Department of Housing and Urban Development (HUD) in the late 1950s and early 1960s began pushing metropolitan planning as a condition for federal funds at the local level. Federal money de facto pushed the creation of regional planning organizations, whether states and localities were ready for them or not.

As we have seen, how to plan had been a concern throughout the twentieth century and had found especially fertile terrain during the New Deal. The case for metropolitan (regional) planning had been most fully developed in the 1930s by Lewis Mumford and the Regional Planning Association of America (RPAA). The RPAA, under Mumford's intellectual leadership, had put forward a vision of "organic" regions where cultures and habits would be maintained through the methods and patterns of building, and cities would be integrated economically with the surrounding regions, fostering interdependence—as with farms or regional industries. New Dealers, concerned with how to foster economic growth in poor areas, and how to solve the problems of uncoordinated planning and economic development, applied these ideas to rural areas, not urban regions. For example, they suggested that the Central Valley Project be organized along regional principles to foster small farms and small towns in an integrated development scheme, including irrigation development. Small farms, it was thought, would absorb many of the unemployed Depression immigrants displaced by mechanization and the Dust Bowl. But large-scale growers were strongly opposed to these ideas, which threatened to break up their landholdings, and regional planning for California's Central Valley was never realized.

Regionalism by New Dealers had a different emphasis from that of Mumford, featuring economic development and territorial planning, "integrating regions with disparate cultures and resource bases into the larger American industrial economy, eroding cultural distinctiveness in the process."[6] But even this type of planning was seen by Californians as too interventionist, because it meant that land-use decisions would be made, or at least shaped, by regional and state regulations, potentially taking decision-making power out of the hands of the locals. Only in Tennessee, with the Tennessee Valley Authority, was the New Deal conception of regional development ever implemented.

Still, the idea of regional planning lived on, and the suburban explosion of the 1950s that deepened regional economic disparities, transportation problems, and inner-city decline inspired federal programs aimed at improving coordination among the multitude of local governments in the same region. So, for example, to encourage coordinated transportation planning, a substantial amount of federal highway planning money was made available to the states for major urban-area transportation studies. By 1960 approximately two-thirds of the nation's existing 212 metropolitan areas were engaged in some type of areawide planning, assisted by federal money. Federal aid programs for highways, mass transit, and open space began requiring

The San Fernando Valley, 1950. (Photograph by Spence; courtesy of Air Photo Archives, Department of Geography, University of California, Los Angeles)

metropolitan planning as a condition for funding. In 1965, the year of its creation, HUD made funds available with the provision that areawide organizations of locally elected officials, known as Councils of Government (COGs), were formed to coordinate regional growth and development and to disburse federal funds. Other regional planning requirements and assistance programs were enacted in the 1960s, concentrating on metropolitan areas and their regions. These federal initiatives required states to create regional planning organizations in order to receive federal funds. California was one of the states that did so.

Housing

The lack of sufficient, decent, and affordable housing in many of the nation's urban centers continued to haunt policymakers in Washington. In the early 1940s the problems surrounding urban blight and the lack of affordable housing were addressed in a government publication, *Handbook on Urban Redevelopment for Cities in the United States,* issued by the FHA. The publication proposed a federal role in the building of affordable housing and outlined a metropolitan approach to the problem of urban deterioration so that housing development would meet the needs of an entire region. The National Housing Act, passed in 1949, was intended to reward returning veterans with adequate housing and also included a provision to build 135,000 units of public housing annually, to help the urban poor. Six years later, when the legislation expired, only about 200,000 units had been built. After 1954 federal funds for urban renewal could be used for other purposes, such as developing commercial, industrial, and public infrastructures. At the same time, under the rubric of urban renewal, existing housing was destroyed to make room for the other federally supported uses (such as commercial). That housing was never replaced, leaving even larger numbers of poor people with inadequate housing.

As the country emerged from the war in strong economic condition, however, there was increased resistance to any government intervention in the marketplace. The building industry and local government associations mounted a campaign against any programs that might remotely involve direct federal participation in the construction sector, or threaten state and local autonomy in matters of land use and development. The building industry was vitally interested in federal support, but not federal intervention, and forcefully made the case that private enterprise was the appropriate vehicle for providing housing in the United States.

Federal policymakers, responding to the desires of the home-building sector and of local governments, developed incentive systems to encourage developers. These incentives included a finance infrastructure that encouraged home ownership through home mortgage insurance. "In the decade after the war Congress regularly approved billions of dollars worth of . . . mortgage insurance for the Federal Housing Administration." Congress also created the Veterans Administration mortgage program, similar to the FHA, and "it accepted the builders' contention that they needed an end to government controls but not to government insurance on their investments in residential construction."[7] In this way, by the late 1940s and early 1950s, concerns over the existence of slums and the lack of affordable housing were transformed into a program of federal support for the home-building industry.

The large-scale, private home-building industry that emerged full-fledged after the war, underwritten by federal programs, permitted the pervasive suburban-sprawl pattern of land use that is so prevalent across the United States today. The availability of new housing at affordable prices accelerated white flight out of the city centers, leaving behind poor housing and poor people, often minorities—exacerbating the problems these federal programs were created to help solve.[8]

Earl Warren: A Nonpartisan Republican versus Special Interests

Earl Warren, an avowed nonpartisan, was elected governor by a wide bipartisan margin in 1938. His approach to governance seemed to be another testament to the success of the Progressive reforms. He won the primary with the support of both Republican and Democratic voters who appreciated his promise of a nonpolitical approach to governing. During his campaign, he took no stand on major issues beyond promising "economy in government." It seemed for a time that the Progressive vision of clean government would be realized, but gradually the gridlock caused by their reforms became apparent. As governor, Warren attempted to use his office to initiate programs he felt would enable the state's economy to grow in a healthy and equitable way. He was stalemated at nearly every turn, despite his overwhelming popularity with the voting public.

During his first two years in office, Governor Warren was able to obtain victories for some of his social programs, including additional state aid for education in poorer school districts and expanded unemployment insurance. He also established child-care centers for children of working mothers. Warren then took up the issue of state health care. By approaching the California Medical Association (CMA) for its support, he thought he would pave the way for successful legislation. However, the CMA members violently opposed any such program and hired Whitaker & Baxter, the public relations firm that had run Warren's victorious campaign, to put together a public-opinion campaign to oppose Warren's compulsory health insurance program. The successful campaign was financed by mandatory assessments on every member of the CMA and featured newspaper editorials, advertising, billboards, and direct lobbying of legislators. Such mandatory trade group assessments were, and are, a significant source of lobbying funds for special interests.

As it turned out, health insurance was only one of Warren's social legislation proposals. He also called for the revamping and liberalizing of unemployment relief, the continuance of old-age pensions, the creation of a Department of Mental Hygiene, a commission on political and economic equality to study minority problems (a first step to a fair employment practices commission), a school of industrial relations to prevent "regressive" labor legislation, state inspection and licensing of hospitals, and "serious consideration of urban development."[9] This agenda was certainly unexpected from a Republican governor and raised concern on the part of the business community. The 1945 legislative session frightened old-line Republicans, and the Democrats did not trust Warren's sincerity.

By 1946, with the war ended, Warren continued to pursue his social programs. Once again he asked for health insurance, and he also proposed creation of a fair employment practices commission. He addressed the problems of housing, employment, urban redevelopment, public health and safety, education, and conservation. The war boom had created new industries and a population explosion, and Warren wanted the legislature to act to meet the emerging needs for infrastructure construction. The legislature did appropriate funds for sewers, sanitation, and hydraulic improvement. These funds were distributed to cities and counties to be spent in accordance with the wishes of local jurisdictions. Warren had wanted the state to keep control of this money, but in characteristic fashion, local jurisdictions successfully lobbied the legislature to appropriate funds with no strings attached.

Reelected to another term by both parties in 1946, Warren again pressed for health insurance and action on fair employment to break down racial prejudice. He believed the state was responsible for the poor, the hungry, the sick, and the unemployed, and saw that higher taxes were called for to meet these and other needs. Consequently, Warren outlined a tough fiscal policy with no tax cuts and proposed a new tax, on gasoline, to finance a statewide highway and freeway program—thus taking on the oil industry lobby in addition to the California Medical Association.

Predictably, the oil industry, in alliance with the trucking industry, worked with lobbyist Artie Samish to defeat the gasoline tax proposal, even though it was generally recognized that California's economy was now dependent on easy travel by automobiles and trucks, and thus needed new highways, streets, and roads. Warren reasoned that those who used the roads should pay for them. Eventually, by denouncing the undue influence of special interests, Warren was able to shame the legislature into passing his gasoline tax, but he obtained little else.

The legislature largely followed the line of the state Chamber of Commerce, voting against much of Warren's social legislation, which it claimed would only create another unnecessary state bureaucracy. Yet the legislature did act in other domains, passing special-interest bills that were backed by Artie Samish and the lobbies he represented and coordinated. "The power that emanated from Samish's suite in the Senator Hotel was greater than that which came from the Governor's office."[10] Given the structure of state government, where the Senate was dominated by rural interests and there was no political accountability to parties, Republicans did not consider it important to support their own Republican governor. For his part, Warren did not demand party loyalty, as he chose to pose policy issues in nonpartisan terms. The people had voted for Warren the individual, and he had run nonpartisan campaigns. Still, without the support of his party, he could accomplish little.

In the area of natural resource management, however, Warren's positions gave Republicans nothing to worry about. He was strongly in favor of state ownership of the tidelands and the oil they contained, and was opposed to the 160-acre limitation on ownership of federally irrigated farm land in the Central Valley. Further, he opposed the expansion of federally operated power plants and was in favor of private utilities owning and developing power in California. In these areas he defended states' rights and corporate prerogative. It was in social policy that Warren believed there was an important role for the state.

Warren's reputation grew nationally, and he was considered presidential material—enhancing his prestige but not his clout in California. In 1950 he asked again for a health insurance program and a state fair employment practices commission, to no avail. He wanted a further extension of the state highway program to be financed by the gas tax, and a continuation of the gross receipts tax on the trucking industry. He pushed for legislation to improve the state hospital system and to provide better mental-health programs and more and better schools, all without success. He also placed the blame for the increasing pollution of California's water and streams on the oil industry, calling on it to pay the costs to remedy this pollution, but in vain.[11]

Despite Warren's popularity with the public (he was elected governor three times and served from 1939 to 1953), and his faithfully Progressive, nonpartisan approach, many of his social programs were defeated. Samish, the organizer and director of what has been called an "invisible government," was the real power in Sacramento. When Warren submitted a budget, the legislature duly went to work on it, but so did Samish. Together with assemblymen and senators, Samish and his clients (including, for example, the utilities, the retailers, and oil interests) rewrote the budget and laid out the strategy for reshaping it along lines that were more favorable to them. They then went over to the Capitol and ensured that their version was enacted. In the end, because Warren did not address himself to the fundamental problem of lobby capture of the legislature and the disproportionate power of rural interests in the Senate, his proposals were consistently defeated. Progressive reforms had eviscerated any political accountability that might have brought about change. Special interests were involved at every level of government, from choosing candidates and financing their campaigns to shaping legislation and rewriting the state's budget. Local governments remained antagonistic to efforts at the state level to coordinate infrastructure development and planning, preferring to go their own way with state-provided money.

Earl Warren, unsuccessful in his several bids to become the Republican candidate for president, was appointed by President Eisenhower to the Supreme Court, where he proved an able and forward-thinking chief justice. Goodwin Knight, California's governor for the next five years, was far more conservative than Warren. In addition, the rise of McCarthyism cast a shadow on the state's politics and the Republican Party.

Then, in 1959, cross-filing was abolished by a coalition of Democrats and frustrated conservative Republicans (it was reinstated by referendum in 1996). Combined with Republican in-fighting over McCarthyism, this left the state open for fresh political blood. In 1958 pragmatic liberal Democrat Pat Brown was elected governor of what had become the third most populous state of the nation. With the support of the first Democrat-controlled legislature in decades, and in a prosperous economy, he successfully initiated programs that had eluded Warren. Brown was able to fund mass transit programs and an expanded university system. He built roads, fought housing segregation, and built the State Water Project. The State Water Project, long coveted by large growers in the Central Valley, provided taxpayer-subsidized infrastructure for the state's continued growth. It involved building another huge conveyance system, largely parallel to the existing Central Valley Project that had been built by the federal government, but irrigating the west side of the valley.

Throughout this phase of expansion, the effect of the pace and scale of growth on the quality of life in the state sparked concern about urban and environmental degradation. Much of what Brown proposed had dramatic effects on land use. The most obvious effects were changes in natural ecosystems due to increased water diversions and dam building, the expansion and intensification of agriculture through irrigation, and the furthering of suburbanization by freeway building. Infrastructure projects by their very nature involve land development, though even now their transformative effects are often not fully considered by means of environmental impact reports.

Addressing the Problems of Growth

To begin to address some of the problems engendered by the state's phenomenal growth, and spurred by federal planning money, the California legislature created a state Planning Office in 1959. Located in the governor's office, it developed a state planning guide. At the same time, Governor Brown appointed a Coordinating Council on Urban Policy to study the growth problems affecting the units of local government in the state's metropolitan areas. This council was an elite group of twenty business, labor, and professional leaders, all of whom had expertise in urban problems. Two years later, its report urged the creation of one multipurpose regional district in each of the state's metropolitan areas, to be responsible for regional planning and at least one additional function taken from the following list:

- Air pollution control
- Metropolitan water supply
- Metropolitan sewage disposal and drainage
- Metropolitan transportation, terminals, and related facilities
- Metropolitan parks and parkways
- Metropolitan law enforcement
- Metropolitan fire protection
- Urban renewal
- Civil defense
- Any other areawide functions requested by the respective metropolitan areas.

To implement this proposal, the council recommended that the state legislature authorize the proposed multipurpose districts, to be elected by majority vote within each of the state's metropolitan areas.[12] The proposal met with hostility from officials of many cities and counties unwilling to give up any of their local land-use powers.[13] Representatives of the League of California Cities and the County Supervisors Association of California who had served on the council offered dissenting opinions in the final report. They opposed metropolitan-area multipurpose districts, as well as proposals to improve the laws concerning incorporation, annexation, and special districts, and they rejected the idea of a state metropolitan area commission to oversee the process of regional metropolitan planning in the state.

Despite resistance from local governments and counties, and internal dissent, the council in 1963 pursued the idea for a state metropolitan area commission, though with a modified scope. The commission, which would consist of five members appointed by the governor, would review all proposals for annexation, incorporation, and special-district formation.[14] (The proposal followed the Progressive political form of an appointed board removed from democratic accountability.) The council had thus narrowed its view of the problems of growth to a matter of establishing coherent jurisdictional boundaries—once again a land-use, physical planning approach. A state commission would presumably make rational jurisdictional decisions based on its regional perspective. Jurisdictional boundaries, of course, were very significant since they could affect the racial, economic, and social composition of cities, but the proposed approach skirted the issue of regional planning and reduced it to better boundary making, map drawing. Nevertheless the powerful County Supervisors Association of California was strongly opposed even to this proposal, which to them still represented centralized decision making in the capital. Instead, the association and its chamber of commerce allies backed alternative legislation that created Local Agency Formation Commissions (1963). These were county-level commissions throughout the state, charged with determining local jurisdictional boundaries within the counties themselves.

Local Agency Formation Commissions

Local Agency Formation Commissions (LAFCOs) were established in each county. They consisted of five commissioners: two county supervisors, two commissioners representing local cities, and the fifth member chosen from the public by the other four members.[15] LAFCO boards were empowered to approve or disapprove any petition for incorporation, special-district formation or dissolution, and annexation. Any incorporation or annexation approved by the LAFCO went on to the relevant county board of supervisors, which then decided whether or not to grant a petition for an election in the proposed city or annexed territory. This legislation clearly reflected the political power of the County Supervisors Association of California by placing final power with the supervisors; also apparent was the influence of the local chambers of commerce, which wanted to maintain as much local control as possible over land-use decisions. By creating mechanisms that sustained their own decision-making powers, local and county officials ignored and subverted the initial impetus for the legislation—uncoordinated, inefficient, and wasteful patterns of growth. This approach also maintained a distance between decision-makers and local residents and voters, placing critical policymaking acts in an arena that was nearly invisible to the ordinary person.

As Gary Miller has shown in *Cities by Contract*, this LAFCO structure resulted in a highly politicized process, despite its apolitical form. The LAFCO structure treats decisions about annexation and incorporation as administrative problems needing rational analysis in the Progressive style, reducible to a map. Yet such decisions determine a city's socioeconomic composition by gerrymandering jurisdictions along race or class lines. LAFCO decisions determine a municipality's tax base by endowing or removing income-generating land uses (such as commercial strips). The LAFCO structure assumes that a separate board of appointed representatives of local government will approach issues in a comprehensive manner and that the regulatory process itself will lead to just and intelligent decisions. But, in fact, LAFCO boards and their decisions are an important part of the maintenance of local conditions for economic growth and are, of necessity, tied into the local "growth machine."[16] By creating jurisdictional boundaries favorable for economic growth, LAFCOs ensure the local municipality sufficient tax revenues to sustain itself. Areas with minimal economic activity and growth—such as poor neighborhoods—may be, and often are, gerrymandered out of other areas where there is greater potential for revenues and development.

LAFCOs form yet another layer of governmental decision making, in addition to all the special districts that exist at the local level (water districts, sewer districts, streetlight improvement districts, and so forth), and their decision-making process, although not secret, does take place outside the public's realm of everyday knowledge and scrutiny. LAFCO activities are rarely monitored. The officeholders are officials elected to other posts but appointed to LAFCO boards, presumably removing them from the pressure of special interests. But this ensures that LAFCO boards are also insulated from the public and sheltered from any direct, democratic accountability. A LAFCO board cannot be recalled, for it is not elected. Further, decisions about annexation and incorporation often seem arcane and seem to lack immediate relevance, even though they have significant long-term impact on the quality of people's lives and the structure of the metropolitan area. Therefore, LAFCO matters do not attract much attention, which further insulates the public officials from public scrutiny. Political institutions like LAFCOs make it nearly impossible for people to participate in government, to exercise their democratic responsibilities.

The state legislature created LAFCOs to solve California's escalating growth and planning problems. It chose to throw the problem back to a local political elite—an appointed board—a reflection of the political power of local chambers of commerce and local governments, consistent with Progressive ideology of managerial government and the long-standing American fear of centralized government. The larger problem of coordination and planning remained unresolved. Local governments, each operating according to its own needs, cannot produce coordinated planning, for their interests are structurally antagonistic: what one municipality gains, another loses. It is a zero-sum game, since there is no mechanism in place for tax sharing, for example. And by removing the processes of political decision-making from public accountability, LAFCOs helped keep local governments concerned principally with the needs and desires of the business sector because business provides a local municipality's income. Instead of solving problems of growth, LAFCOs perpetuated them.

Councils of Government

In the early 1960s, with increased federal money available for regional planning, Councils of Government were formed in southern California, in the San Francisco Bay area, and eventually in San Diego and the Sacramento area. These COGs, made up of locally elected city and county officials, are voluntary associations that serve in an advisory capacity and rely for the majority of their funding on member contributions and federal funds. COGs disburse federal funds, conduct research and hearings, and make policy recommendations, but members are free to act as they will and are free to withdraw at any time.

Appointed from a restricted arena of elected representatives, the COG follows the Progressive notion of using an appointed board to establish policy directives rather than a directly elected group of representatives vested with regulatory power. COGs are not constituted to be accountable to the public at large or organized to act as democratically representative bodies. Although their mission is to coordinate planning among multiple jurisdictions in a region, because there was so much opposition to their existence in the first place, COGs have no power to implement programs or enforce policy suggestions, except through the incentive of providing funds. They exist as forums for information gathering and as disbursers of federal and state planning money. When COGs must address regional policy questions, home-rule ideology usually prevails, with each jurisdiction jealously protecting its turf. This makes regional consensus about metropolitan planning policy and coordination elusive at best.

Duplication, waste, and lack of accountability are only some of the results of a decentralized and fragmented system that is derived from the belief that local land-use decisions are the purview solely of local government.

Local Mobilizations

Although business interests and the associations of local government defeated attempts to better manage growth, individuals and grass-roots groups continued to try to curb the effects of growth in the places where they lived. The 1950s and 1960s were decades of tremendous transformations in the state's land use. Redwood harvests peaked at unprecedented levels to satisfy the surge in construction in the state. Agricultural lands on the urban fringe were subdivided with ease and rapidity.[17] Large-scale land development had come into its own in the West; this was the era of the "merchant builders"[18]—the Eichlers, Lewises, Lyons, Kaufmanns, and Broads. These landowners and developers created California's current suburban form by taking advantage of federal programs by playing on Americans' anti-urban biases and racism to engage in the "vast production of new residences . . . shift[ing] the center of gravity . . . from the urban core to the periphery."[19] They often bought lands on the urban fringe, years in advance, if they did not already own them as a result of a Spanish land grant having been passed on in one way or another. They counted on growth, as they still do today, planning whole new cities and neighborhoods, including commercial and industrial areas and schools.

The Bay area offers a dramatic example of this suburbanization process. Between 1940 and 1970 the population of the nine-county area nearly tripled, but after 1945 the population of San Francisco and Oakland actually declined. Virtually the entire postwar population growth of the region occurred in the suburban periphery. By 1970 only about one-quarter of all Bay area residents lived in the old core cities.[20]

The suburbanization of the Santa Clara Valley south of San Francisco is a classic example of the process that occurred in many places in California. The valley was ideal for prune growing and by 1915 was producing more than one-third of the world's prunes, as well as apricots and walnuts. Santa Clara County adopted a master plan in 1934 aimed at orderly and coherent development. By 1940 about 50,000 people lived in the city of San Jose, whose chief industry was canning, packing, and processing the products of the surrounding farms. Farther north, Stanford University was the hub of the smaller city of Palo Alto. In 1950 Lockheed and Westinghouse (federal defense contractors) built major plants in Sunnyvale. Santa Clara communities were vigorously competing to attract housing, shopping centers, and factories. The county master plan, overwhelmed by the pace of urban development, was jettisoned. By 1954 land development had occurred in a haphazard fashion, creating a patchwork of farms and subdivisions.

The growing suburban population demanded that local government provide the same services available in fully urbanized areas. At the same time, farmers tried to hold onto their land and got the state legislature to enact a Green Belt Exclusion Law in 1955 and an Agricultural Assessment Law in 1957. These laws created large zones specified as farmland, excluding any other development. But unbroken tracts of land were ideal for developers. They began to bid up land prices. Farmers, tempted by the potential for large profits, one by one began to approach nearby cities to annex their lands. LAFCOs, predisposed to create favorable conditions for growth, allowed the annexations to go forward. Using zoning to protect agricultural lands proved inadequate in the face of rising land prices and pressure from urban residents for urban services, and the valley filled rapidly with new development.

Such growth was the norm around the Bay area and in Los Angeles. Sonoma County's population tripled during the 1940–70 period. The southern portion of Alameda County also felt the effects of this suburban boom, and by the 1950s commercial agriculture there, too, was virtually nonexistent.

Expansion triggered local movements of opposition. For example, the continued in-filling of San Francisco Bay to create more land for development, along with proposals to export more water from the Sacramento River (the Bay's primary source of fresh water) for agricultural expansion and urbanization for southern California, met with increasing public resistance. The Bay's valuable wetlands and estuaries were being destroyed, imperiling the future of this important ecosystem and public amenity. The Berkeley general plan of 1960, enthusiastically embracing growth, provided for the filling of more than 2,000 acres of San Francisco Bay. An area extending 2 miles west into the Bay beyond the city's present shoreline was slated for housing, industry, a community college campus, and an airport.

Panoramic view of the Livermore Valley, Alameda County, 1865. (Courtesy of the Bancroft Library, University of California, Berkeley)

In 1962 a group of Berkeley residents, led by wives of University of California faculty, formed a group called Save San Francisco Bay.[21] The founders believed that regional planning was needed to control shoreline development: there were thirty-two cities and nine counties on the water, each pursuing its own growth agenda. Of the 276 miles of Bay shore, only about 5 miles was owned and used for recreation by the public. The group appealed first to the only regional government organization established to address the problems of regional growth coordination and planning: the Association of Bay Area Governments (ABAG). The association, a Council of Government, had just been created as a forum for discussion of regional planning issues. It was formed to address the planning coordination problems that the multitude of Bay area local jurisdictions and counties could not resolve, such as transportation and housing, and to meet the growing public concern over the physical degradation of San Francisco Bay. It was also a conduit of federal and state planning money. Save San Francisco Bay members naturally asked ABAG to address the issues of planning coordination around the Bay, since it was made up of all of the Bay area jurisdictions and seemed the perfect forum for planning land use. But the combination of lack of real regulatory power and the strongly held belief in local control over local land use meant that ABAG was structurally and politically unable to address the issues of land-use planning controls around the Bay.[22]

The members of Save San Francisco Bay were not deterred in their pursuit of Bay shore protection. They turned to the state legislature for action. As a result, in 1965 the Bay Area Conservation and Development Commission (BCDC), a single-purpose regional planning agency, was created by the state legislature to supervise development around the Bay. BCDC consisted of twenty-seven appointed members broadly representing the interests touching the Bay.[23] The legislature gave it a narrow mandate over any "substantial" change or development within a 100-foot-wide strip of shoreline. Filling could be authorized if public benefits clearly exceeded public detriment. Although the creation of BCDC was seen as an important step forward in regional planning for the Bay area and preservation of the Bay, the structure of the agency reflected the political legacy of the Progressive era. Its appointed members were not subject to recall, its decisions not subject to public approval, its purview narrow, and its creation an addition to the numerous existing special-purpose administrations.

Suburban expansion, often on prime agricultural land, triggered concern about the loss of these lands and the need to define the edges of cities. Between 1945 and 1968 California is estimated to have lost to development more than 1 million acres of prime agricultural land. The property tax system contributed to this loss. Taxes on California farmland escalated greatly because of the increased value of nonagricultural uses of such land; between 1950 and 1965 agricultural property taxes increased from 6.7 percent to more than 15 percent of net farm income. The opportunity to earn large profits from conversion to urban land uses was irresistible to some, economically necessary for others. These pressures, in addition to the failure of agricultural zoning in the Santa Clara Valley in the previous decade, spurred the state legislature to pass the Williamson Act in 1965.[24] The Williamson Act, still on the books, created a landowner–local government contract, preventing development for a minimum of ten years. Land in the agricultural preserve is taxed on the basis of farm use. However, the act's weak provisions are not effective at keeping the land in agriculture once its value has significantly increased, as the penalties for exiting the preserve category are relatively minor compared with the potential profit from land sales, and each county can determine its own enforcement policy. Further, since the 1978 passage of Proposition 13, the initiative to reduce property taxes, the main attraction of the Williamson Act has been undermined.

Opposition to growth developed in other areas, too. Napa County in 1968 used zoning to prevent the transformation of valuable vineyard property into suburban tracts. Napa County was destined to become a bedroom community to San Francisco until citizens mobilized to put pressure on the board of supervisors to create an agricultural preserve that included the county's entire valley. Agriculture was made the primary use allowed on the land with a minimum parcel size of 20 acres (increased to 40 acres in 1978).[25]

Road-building plans also sparked a great deal of local activism. The state Highway Commission was an important part of the growth machine of the state. It was supported by, and its members recruited from, the trucking industry, the auto clubs, the petroleum industry, the heavy-equipment manufacturers, auto makers and dealers, concrete producers, general contractors, the lumber industry, rock and aggregate producers, and the state chambers of commerce. The Highway Commission froze California's transportation system into a single-focus, auto-dependent approach, buttressed by the gasoline tax, which could be used only to build more roads.[26]

Road construction was a national obsession during this period, and California aggressively took up the challenge of upgrading its highway system. Governor Pat Brown was an enthusiastic supporter of road construction and encouraged an active Highway Division. Because the division was governed by a commission composed of seven members appointed by the governor, it was insulated from public pressure and accountability—in true Progressive style. The governor was an advocate of growth and construction, and he appointed commissioners who represented this point of view and economic interest.

At least fifty areas in the state were fighting Highway Division plans in the 1960s. San Francisco residents, appalled at what massive highway construction was doing to their city, effectively stopped further construction in the central waterfront area; both Marin and Napa Counties turned down freeway proposals that would have encouraged suburban development in regions devoted to open space and agriculture.[27] In Monterey and Carmel, the battle against the state Highway Commission was waged and lost; for three decades Santa Barbara managed to halt the building of the freeway that would divide the downtown in two.[28] It was built only in the early 1990s, separating the historic downtown from its coastal zone with several lanes of freeway.

A favorite and economical method that the Highway Commission used for highway improvements was to maximize the use of state land to minimize cost. Highway 101 in the northern portion of the state was targeted for improvement; the least expensive route involved cutting through portions of the Prairie Creek Redwoods and Jedediah Smith Redwoods State Parks. The plan called for removing broad swaths of trees, including some of the oldest in the redwood region. After bitter fighting, local mobilizations defeated the plans for improving Highway 101—a sign of the increasing scope of concern of organizations like the Sierra Club and their growing political power.

Another epic battle of the 1960s involved a proposal by Walt Disney and his entertainment company for a major ski resort in Sequoia National Forest, with the cooperation of the Forest Service. As early as 1949 Sequoia National Forest, carrying out the federal recreation mandate for the national forests that had been enacted by Congress, called for bids for ski development in the Mineral King area. None came. In the 1960s the idea surfaced again, with a project proposed by Walt Disney Productions. In January 1965 it purchased two tracts of private land in the Mineral King Valley, advancing the status of the proposal. The Sierra Club, which in 1949 had supported ski development in Mineral King, announced its opposition to the proposed massive recreational development in May 1965. In 1966 the Forest Service signed a three-year development contract with Walt Disney Productions to begin planning the ski resort, and in the following year the state of California adopted a final route for a new state highway to Mineral King to serve the resort. In 1969 the Sierra Club filed suit against the development, and the court issued a temporary injunction. Although the road to preservation was long and complicated, by the early 1970s "the battle for Mineral King was no longer a one-sided affair in which a few environmentalists attempted to stave off development. . . . Taking advantage of the increasing urban sensitivity to wilderness preservation that was sweeping across California, the

Sierra Club had become a formidable adversary." Finally, in 1978, the Carter administration reversed the federal government's support for the development and announced it would instead support the addition of the area to Sequoia National Park, removing it from Forest Service jurisdiction.[29] This, among several other anti-development fights, catapulted the Sierra Club, California's oldest conservation organization, into full-fledged environmentalism.

One of the most long-lasting and difficult of the efforts to control development in California took place in the Lake Tahoe area. Among the deepest lakes in the world, Lake Tahoe is one of California's most beautiful scenic attributes. Its environmental problems, due to urbanization and deforestation, are substantial: severe soil erosion, irreversible water degradation, and deteriorating water quality. For nearly a century there had been proposals for its protection, which by the 1970s had resulted in nearly 70 percent of the land being set aside in state parks and national forests. Nonetheless, rapid postwar urbanization on private land near the lake had begun to seriously degrade its purity. In the late 1950s environmentalists, scientists, and others began to call for control of growth around the lake. Political authority is divided among five counties bordering the lake, two state governments (California and Nevada), and the federal government (controlling Forest Service lands). This was a classic case of the challenge of controlling growth across jurisdictions. Each local jurisdiction felt it could individually profit from growth, and those that were more inclined to impose stricter land-use controls knew that if they denied growth it would simply move across the jurisdictional line, contributing tax revenues to the rival jurisdiction.

In 1957 a nonprofit organization was formed for Lake Tahoe's protection and "orderly development." The Nevada-California Lake Tahoe Association undertook to elaborate a coordinated approach to the worsening problems in the basin. But as soon as the association began to study the basin and propose regional controls, local interests expressed concern. After consultation with the representatives of the three Tahoe chambers of commerce, in an attempt to promote cooperation and unity, a council organization similar in concept to ABAG was created, called the Lake Tahoe Area Council. It was incorporated in Nevada, represented all basin interests, and operated as a nonprofit clearinghouse for ideas and problems. Yet the allure of development quickly undermined this effort. Just as this organization was establishing itself and beginning to develop a comprehensive planning survey and plan, the executive director of the council suddenly resigned to become planning director of a major new construction project in Nevada's Washoe County. Regardless of pleas for further study, the new development was approved by the Washoe County commissioners, effectively undermining the efforts of the Lake Tahoe Area Council. Still, planning directors and representatives from each of the five county planning commissions persisted. They met with the Lake Tahoe Area Council planning committee to form the Tahoe Regional Planning Commission—yet another attempt at voluntary cooperation, since the commission's powers would be only advisory.

Disappointingly, the Tahoe Regional Planning Commission's 1964 master plan was little more than an extrapolation and extension of existing trends into the future, offering little in the way of change. Although the poor sewage disposal that had been degrading lake water quality led to expanded and improved sewer systems in the basin, the problem of water-quality protection persisted. This more than anything, according to Douglas Strong, provided the impetus for California state assemblyman Edwin L. Z'Berg (D) to attempt to create a regional authority for the entire basin. Environmentalists continued to pin their hopes on the regional intervention of the federal government, but the question of the control of growth was a state and local government issue, consequently outside federal authority. Z'Berg, the powerful chair of the Natural Resources Committee, cobbled together an agreement for regional planning with Nevada state representatives.

In 1978, over the strenuous objections of the city of South Lake Tahoe and the Greater North Lake Tahoe Chamber of Commerce, and in spite of Governor Reagan's tacit opposition, Z'Berg created a Tahoe Regional Agency that possessed regionwide and bistate jurisdiction. Reflecting Nevada's generally anti-regulatory stance, the agency that was established in the final version of the bill was much weaker than Z'Berg had originally proposed, and as a result, growth continued, especially casino building on the Nevada side. People again turned to the federal government for a solution, but its tools were restricted to water-quality protection. The other extreme, declaring the lake a national park or monument, and coming up with the money to purchase all the private property interests surrounding the lake, was out of the question. Citizen groups continued to try to influence the situation. The Sierra Club and the League to Save Lake Tahoe filed lawsuits to make proposed developments comply with the law, while yet more casinos were being built on the Nevada side of the lake.

The dynamics of this situation resembled closely those of the Bay area when residents organized to oppose continued in-filling of the Bay. The major difference, however, was that Lake Tahoe was shared by two states, which could not come to agreement about its long-term management. Local economic interests, buttressed by the nation's laws protecting private property interests, proved more powerful than environmental arguments and a sympathetic California state legislature. The structure of governance simply gave localities the final say in land-use decisions. Federal involvement was limited to federally owned lands and to infrastructure improvement through the application of the Clean Water Act and money to build better sewage-disposal plants. Its role was confined to encouraging cooperation among the local jurisdictions; it had no legal basis to compel cooperation. Consequently Lake Tahoe's water quality has continued to slowly deteriorate, and although some of the most egregiously destructive land-development techniques have been curbed, development around Lake Tahoe continues, producing air pollution, erosion, and general degradation.

In the debates over growth and its management, local governments were often seen as the source of the problem of uncoordinated and destructive growth. Through the League of California Cities and the County Supervisors Association, local governments had successfully organized to stymie efforts at regional coordination of land use and planning. They did pass local growth-control ordinances (or else citizens voted them in by initiative), reflecting citizen wishes and concerns. But because these ordinances were confined to individual municipalities, they could do little to change the effects of overall growth. They could not alleviate such problems as increasing traffic, the conversion of agricultural lands to urban uses in adjacent jurisdictions, or increased pollution. There was no forum in which the larger questions could be effectively addressed and discussed, and no way that local concerns could be placed in a larger context to arrive at a common direction. Public frustration over the effects of growth continued.

Natural environments and rural landscapes were disappearing. The urban quality of life was deteriorating. The modern environmental movement began to coalesce in opposition to these changes, which were eroding the California people had come to believe was theirs. In a little over one hundred years, a semi-mythic image of California had emerged, part Sierra Club, part land of opportunity, in which nearly everyone could benefit from modern economic development. Californians had developed a very strong sense of place and identity that was being challenged by the rapidity of change.

California Tomorrow (and Other Idealistic Proposals)

Under Governor Pat Brown, the state Planning Office produced no statewide planning document, and the Governor's Commission on Metropolitan Problems restricted its scope of study to urban California. There was no comprehensive structure that could develop policy to address the urban and rural transformations that were taking place. Out of frustration with the state's inaction in the face of frenetic and seemingly unlimited subdivision construction, California Tomorrow, a nonprofit educational institution, in 1962 published a plan called *California Going, Going . . .*, whose opening statement said that "although the dough looks good, the cake is not rising, and the reason is simple: nobody wrote out a recipe. . . . In other words, there is in California a serious, progressively disastrous lack of coordinated land planning and development."[30]

The document advocated a sweeping reorganization of government to enhance more efficient central planning, based on a broad vision informed by scientific knowledge. Planning was to be carried out by planning experts. The organization believed that regional problems could never be met by independent local governments and that there was a need for regional planning commissions throughout the state with the power to implement an overall state plan. In effect, California Tomorrow advocated implementing the very proposals Brown's Council on Metropolitan Problems had initially put forth, but took them a step further to include the state's rural areas in recognition of the relationship between urban growth and rural transformation. The council had proposed the creation of a multipurpose regional planning district in each of the state's major metropolitan areas. These districts would also have been responsible for other specific area functions, such as air pollution control or transportation. The districts would have been elected by majority vote. The California Tomorrow organization focused on the limitations of local sovereignty that left certain cities, like Oakland, to cope with the heavy burden of decaying downtown centers, as well as housing and job inequities, while higher paying jobs, a better tax base, and decent housing moved to the suburbs. (This was a trend that LAFCOs tended to encourage.)

California Tomorrow believed that regional government could and should act as a redistributive entity and actively redress revenue and housing inequities. Opposition to such government lay in race and class bias. As it was expressed in the organization's quarterly magazine *Cry California* (1967): "Regional governments have not been created, in part because the white majority doesn't want to face the full range of economic and social problems of the regional cities where, in fact, they live. The whites have gone to the suburbs along with industry, thus avoiding having to pay their just share for the education and housing of the black minority in the central city." For California Tomorrow, establishing functional regions organized along utilitarian lines—like water-service delivery areas or transportation basins—and to be implemented by a regional government was the way to redress inequalities between the inner city and the suburbs and to pool resources to make cities livable for all. The group advocated creation of a statewide growth management plan that would guide the efforts of the newly created regional governments, as well as determine open space, preserve beauty and facilitate efficiency, preserve agricultural lands, and protect California's natural areas. California Tomorrow's approach seemed to reflect a growing consensus among policymakers and the land-use intelligentsia that there was a need for regional mechanisms to control land use and urbanization.

Private organizations at the national level echoed California Tomorrow's critique of the problems of uncoordinated management and put forth their own proposals. These organizations included the Urban Land Institute (the research and policy-generating arm of the large-scale development industry), the American Law Institute, and the Ford Foundation.[31] These analyses tended to indict local land-use controls and urge the creation of statewide authorities to oversee local governments as the way to overcome local parochialism, racism, and inner-city decay.[32] Rational land use, they argued, was based on integrated development guided by regional mechanisms and would result in economic development and civil rights for all.[33] This vision of land-use reform was based on the belief that a more rational use of land would contribute to economic efficiency by raising corporate profits, lowering government budgets, and creating jobs. Local governments were seen as too beholden to local special interests and as the cause of fragmented land-use planning. The answer was to remove power from the locality. Other issues, such as how to ensure democratic accountability of the proposed regional planning institutions to local populations and better distribution of growth and jobs, were not raised by these organizations. California Tomorrow addressed the questions of power and equity more directly than most other regional planning advocates, perhaps anticipating the events of 1965. It differed from previous Progressive-era regional planning approaches in its awareness of issues of power, race, and class—incorporating sociological and political elements—and in its commitment to democratic participation. Nonetheless, it echoed some of the Progressive beliefs in rational, scientific management.

The Watts Rebellion

The 1965 Watts rebellion in Los Angeles was the reaction to a prevailing pattern of poverty and exclusion. Unequal regional development, exacerbated by the long-standing federal abandonment of cities to the benefit of suburban expansion, left older black neighborhoods behind. Then and there the problems and politics of growth came to a head. The Watts rebellion was about the politics of growth, a politics that favored the white working and middle classes, supported and sustained by state and federal programs and incentives, such as redlining. Watts residents did not experience the fruits of tremendous economic growth in the state. There were no programs to bring housing or jobs to their neighborhood. Such alienation predictably resulted in violence.

Watts rebellion, 1965. (Courtesy of the Southern California Library for Social Studies and Research, Los Angeles)

The rebellion was a grass-roots cry of protest by the black community about the unequal distribution of growth in the city and its disproportionate burden of joblessness, poor housing conditions, and a generally degraded environment. The Kerner Commission, the Kaiser Committee, and the Douglas report (all federal commissions appointed to study the rebellion and come up with policy recommendations), three years after the fact, pointed to exclusionary zoning as the cause of inner-city ghettos. Each commission advocated a policy of regional intervention to increase housing development, assuming that its cost would be within the reach of poor people and that more housing production in itself would eliminate segregation.[34] (This, of course, ignored the fact that a great deal of housing was being built, but at the suburban edge, unavailable and unaffordable to poor people or with restrictive covenants.) Those groups that had been advocating regional growth management—California Tomorrow, the Urban Land Institute, and others—were not to be found in the aftermath of the outbreak of rage and frustration expressed by the Watts rebellion.

The rebellion could have been the symbol of the need for regional government, for fundamental reform of the pattern of federal subsidies and the policy of redlining, and for a general reevaluation of urban policy, but instead it was exploited by conservative forces in the state. Rather than searching for approaches to begin to address the problems of poverty, racism, and exclusion that could be alleviated through social programs and better planning, policymakers, led by the successful Republican gubernatorial candidate Ronald Reagan, developed an agenda of law and order that blamed the victim. Instead of viewing the Watts rebellion as a consequence of unmanaged, opportunistic growth and racism, Reagan and his followers saw it as a result of unchecked criminal elements.

Ronald Reagan's Rise to Power

Ronald Reagan became governor in 1966, rallying the forces of law and order to reestablish "normalcy" in the state in a period of tumultuous social activism. Reagan successfully used the Watts rebellion, as well as student demonstrations in Berkeley (the Free Speech Movement), to push his agenda of repression. Under government led by Democrats the problems of the black community had been subsumed under the need for better planning (with a few exceptions like open housing legislation) and the management of growth—and then virtually ignored. With a conservative governor they became problems of law and order. Planning—statewide, regional, or otherwise—was anathema to Republican thinking.

Legislative mandates and federal rules for assistance required the governor's Office of Planning to write and publish a California Development Plan, which it did reluctantly in 1973, after Reagan had been in office seven years.[35] It was an outline for continued economic exploitation of the state's natural resources by the private sector; no substantive changes in state resource management were proposed. There was little or no discussion about comprehensive planning, and certainly no plan. Reviewers from the federal funding agency (HUD) were critical of the report and pointed out that "the major obstacle to environmental planning appears to be the concern on the part of some state officials that planning means excessive State control over land use."[36] Efforts to ameliorate and coordinate land-use decision making at the state level would prove frustrating with an anti-government governor in office, well-organized and powerful local governments, public hostility toward state land-use planning, and the opposition of the building industry. The governor, ideologically ill-disposed to such state-led activities, provided no leadership. Local residents were given the responsibility of monitoring complex and overlapping local governments—multiple special districts, appointed boards and commissions—and their land-use decisions, with no greater tools for understanding, accessing, or influencing the process.

Citizen Activism

Governor Reagan, despite winning handily on a conservative platform, was burdened by a Democratic legislature and a public that expressed rising discontent over the state's management of natural resources, over industrial pollution, and over the continuing problems of urban growth. The 1969 Santa Barbara oil spill, one of the first on U.S. shores, placed environmental issues in the lap of the governor, on the world's television screens, and in people's consciousness. Residents were incensed, outraged, unbelieving. "Santa Barbarans became increasingly ideological, increasingly sociological and . . . increasingly 'radical.' Increasing recognition came to be given to the 'all powerful Oil lobby'; to legislators 'in the pockets of Oil'; to academicians 'bought' by Oil and to regulatory agencies that lobby for those they are supposed to regulate."[37] This new awareness of the interrelations among industry, research institutions, and environmental degradation spurred citizens to put pressure on the state legislature, the federal government, and local officials to account for their environmental records. The Santa Barbara area became an anti–oil drilling bastion. The spill brought environmentalism into its own, and over the next twenty years there was a significant change in the public's perception of the environment. The spill inadvertently ushered in a decade of environmental protection legislation that for the first time established standards of accountability.

One aspect of this new environmental awareness was the successful passage of local ordinances for growth control. The city of Petaluma (in Sonoma County), on Highway 101 north of San Francisco, had seen requests for building permits jump from 59 in 1971 to 891 in 1972.[38] Developers, ready to house San Francisco commuters looking for cheaper single-family dwellings, proposed to build housing developments in the eastern part of the city, leapfrogging outward, passing over the multifamily-dwelling pattern of the older parts of town and leaving it to slowly decay. The city, responding to citizen pressure, developed the first growth-limitation policy in the nation. It was a point-based housing allocation plan for single-family dwellings, rewarding developers who complied with the city's housing policy, which allocated 8–12 percent of the annual quota to low- and moderate-income housing.[39]

For the city of Livermore, air pollution, overcrowded schools, an impending shortage of treated water, and an overloaded main sewage treatment plant resulted in a 1972 growth-control measure that concentrated on requiring infrastructure provisions for proposed new subdivisions.

Fed up with the lack of state leadership in the area of growth and tired of the detrimental effects on daily life, local citizens took to the ballot box to try to develop local solutions for the management of growth. These were local

Workers cleaning up oil spill, Santa Barbara beach, 1969. (Courtesy of the Robert Easton Collection, University of California, Santa Barbara)

Public reaction to the oil spill, Santa Barbara, 1969. (Courtesy of
the Robert Easton Collection, University of California, Santa Barbara)

defenses of place. By the end of the 1960s several growth-management systems were in place up and down the state, including Santa Cruz and Santa
Barbara Counties, Redlands, Davis, and Riverside, among others. Each of
these efforts was shaped to meet the perceived problem at hand, and each
treated the phenomenon of growth differently. Thus, despite the Republican
governor's unwillingness to provide leadership in this area, and the reluctance of local and county governments to cooperate at the regional level,
widespread discontent with the status quo inspired grass-roots attempts at
local solutions. This approach also suited the decentralist, anti-state attitude
of most citizens, cities, and counties, notwithstanding the inherent limitations of this approach.

Oil spill, Santa Barbara, 1969: the image that flashed across the nation. (Courtesy of the Robert Easton Collection, University of California, Santa Barbara)

Public demonstration against oil drilling, Santa Barbara, 1970. (Courtesy of the Robert Easton Collection, University of California, Santa Barbara)

The only significant exception to this pattern of addressing growth problems on the local level was the passage of the 1972 statewide Coastal Protection Initiative. Over the years, developments along the coast had been slowly
but surely privatizing California's beach access, restricting the coast to those
affluent enough to purchase beachfront property. The building trades, local
jurisdictions, and other interests had prevented legislative agreement on
this topic. But it united California's voters sufficiently for them to pass an
initiative for coastal protection (discussed in greater detail in chapter 5).

By 1970 regional growth-management efforts had failed, but at the
grass-roots level there were many local efforts to control the local effects of
the state's growth. Because they were scattered, individual, and unsystem-
atic, these efforts did little to shape or curb the momentum of growth in the
state, the continuing proliferation of special districts and fragmented authority, or the effect on the landscape.

California Tomorrow, Revisited

Still not to be defeated, California Tomorrow again developed a plan for the
state. The 1971 *California Tomorrow Plan* was not about land use only, or
about housing, or about water or smog or jobs. This time it was a comprehensive plan. It proposed a state planning council, composed of the governor and ten of his appointees to be confirmed by the legislature. This
council would prepare, and update yearly, a state plan that would address infrastructure (transportation, power plants, transmission lines, waterworks, and other basic facilities) and include a bill of rights for a livable
environment. The *California Tomorrow Plan* called for the creation of ten
or so regional governments with regional legislatures, directly elected, that
would absorb many of the single-purpose regional agencies already in
place. Each of these regional agencies was responsible for developing a regional plan.[40]

California Tomorrow's proposals were widely circulated and discussed
among policymakers and growth activists. However, the plan had little effect on the legislature beyond providing an important background for the
environmental protection bills that passed in the early 1970s, such as the
California Environmental Quality Act. California Tomorrow's proposals
were too threatening to the established power structure and too elitist for
the general public. California Tomorrow saw the connection between urbanization and environmental degradation much more clearly than most at
that time. Local jurisdictions and chambers of commerce were threatened
by the prospect of a new institution that would be directly democratically
accountable and would assume the responsibilities of myriad obscure special districts and special-purpose agencies. As for the general public, re-

gional government decision making about land-use planning would have been far more transparent and accessible than proposals for regional legislatures.

Instead, public discontent with the status quo turned on local government as both the problem and the solution. Better local regulations, it was thought, would solve the problem. Deeply entrenched suspicion about higher levels of government and centralized decision making, fueled by local development interests, made regional mechanisms unthinkable. Further, legislative initiative in this area was unlikely because of the dependency of legislators on those very economic interests for their reelection. Local government seemed the only point of access. The local focus corresponded with the predominant belief in local control, and it was a scale that could be mobilized by outrage when land development seemed to destroy that which had become habitual. And it also folded into the protection of individual private property values, a compelling motivation for action.

Natural Resources and Growth

The state's methods of natural resource management—particularly of timber and water—were even more disturbing to the budding statewide environmental movement than urban growth, and this issue brought the environmental movement together. Environmentalists tended to see nature as other, as wilderness, as not urban, just as the preservationists had seen it. Their attention was focused on finding ways to preserve natural wonders from economic exploitation and human intervention. They paid little or no attention to urban-rural interactions and linkages or to "nature" or environmental degradation in the city outside of the general issue of air pollution.

California, home of such groups as the Sierra Club, was seen as a leader in addressing the emerging environmental issues and in fostering environmental protection movements. One of the most controversial and well-known of these movements was, and still is, the struggle to preserve the redwoods.

The Timber Industry

Although logging had begun in the mid-1800s, it was not until the 1950s that the timber resource was seriously exploited in the West. Once there was no longer any "free" (uncommitted to mills) timber left in Washington and Oregon, loggers and the large timber firms turned their attention to California. The great suburban expansion of the 1950s created a huge demand for wood. "Gyppo" loggers (small operators) who could no longer make a living in the Pacific Northwest moved into California, with the large timber companies on their heels. The increased demand for timber, however, combined with its relative scarcity in the Northwest, gradually changed the whole social structure of the redwood industry as families sold their property to timber companies and people migrated to the northern counties for work in the expanding industry.[41]

Timber interests were well organized and had great power in the legislature due to the state's unbalanced Senate apportionment that gave rural counties more votes than the more populated urban counties. The timber industry still developed the forest practice rules through its representatives on the Forestry Board. As with most boards and commissions in the state, the Forestry Board made rules primarily to protect the industry from unfair competition from within its own ranks. For example, it specified the minimum size of tree that could be harvested in order to regulate the activities of the smaller "gyppo" operators who did not have access to the larger stands but who could undermine the price of timber by selling smaller logs at lower prices. The state Department of Forestry retained its fire-fighting role, assuming little responsibility for forest management. The department had originally been given weak powers of enforcement, and subsequent legislatures had done nothing to enhance its mandate. The Forestry Board called the shots.

In the early 1900s, when the timber industry was still small, there was wide support in the redwood counties for preservation as the base for the development of tourism. When logging gradually overtook tourism as the basis of the economy, attitudes changed dramatically. In the 1950s and 1960s timber-related employment drove the local economies. There was little positive sentiment for the regulation of private timber practices, and little awareness of or concern for the finite nature of the resource. However, in the late 1960s a lumber market recession caused smaller companies to suffer decreases in production and to close mills. The rise of larger corporate operations signaled a structural change in the industry.

Corporations diversified and began to integrate all aspects of the industry—from logging to processing to marketing the product. Previously these tasks had been undertaken by distinct sectors of the timber industry. "Logging jobs in the state decreased from 7,161 in 1956 to 4,202 in 1974 . . . the average number of jobs in the lumber and wood-products sector . . . stabilized at 50,000."[42] However, local workers continued to identify their livelihood with the timber industry, even as the industry was increasingly mechanizing to reduce its labor needs. No one in the industry acknowledged that the resource was diminishing because the prevailing practice was to cut as much as possible for short-term profit rather than to manage the resource for long-term, sustained yield. Other short-term management practices included clear-cutting and inadequate replanting. Higher profits could be made in this manner, and the land could then be resold for other purposes. The long-term impact on the economic health of the local communities was not part of the companies' considerations.

California's Cathedrals: The Imperiled Redwoods

Throughout the 1950s small changes were made in the Forest Practice Act in response to public protest over the accelerating degradation of the redwood resource. The 1950s were the period of greatest logging. Each year the redwoods fell at a rate three times that of any year prior to 1950, reaching in 1958 an annual cut, unmatched before or since, of 1.2 billion board feet.[43] By the end of the 1950s only about 10 percent of the original 2 million acres of redwood belt remained uncut.

Tractor logging had been introduced and approved by the Board of Forestry, allowing logging on previously inaccessible slopes and causing great damage. By the mid-1950s the Bull Creek watershed surrounding Humboldt Redwoods State Park had been denuded. The winters of 1954 and 1955 brought unusually heavy rains, and stacks of harvested logs, awaiting removal, were carried away by the raging waters of Bull Creek and transformed into battering rams. When the waters abated, 525 giant redwoods had been knocked over in Rockefeller Grove, 50 acres of the flat had washed away, and the creek had been damaged.[44] This caused an uproar among preservationists and conservationists, and catalyzed the Sierra Club, which until this time had been content to follow the leadership and philosophy of the Save the Redwoods League, into aggressively advocating federal purchase of a redwood national park. The league, throughout, still opposed state or federal purchase of redwood lands and continued to raise private money instead, consistent with its historic position. Further, the league believed that the best redwood acreages had already been set aside in the four redwood state parks. However, with the loss of Rockefeller Grove, the Sierra Club parted ways with the league.

Bills were introduced in the legislature to reform the Forest Practice Act with regard to its lack of protection of streams and migratory fish resources, but all were defeated despite the lobbying efforts of the Sierra Club and the Izaak Walton League. The rural dominance of the legislature made reform impossible. The Board of Forestry, put on the defensive because of the devastation caused by the floods, ordered a study of the state's Forest Practice Regulations with respect to streams and watersheds. The study, accompanied by hearings in the northern counties, exonerated the timber industry and the Forest Practice Regulations from responsibility for the damage.[45]

When Pat Brown came into office in 1959, he ushered in a period of greater openness, encouraging questioning and debate in government, including debate over natural resource management. Consequently, the Department of Fish and Game began to more publicly challenge the effectiveness of the existing Forestry regulations with regard to stream protection. Again on the defensive, the Board of Forestry held public hearings in 1962 to gather public input about California's forest practice, particularly concerning logging damage to streams. David Pesonen of the Sierra Club, future director of the Department of Forestry under Governor Jerry Brown, testified to the damaging effects of timber practices. The Associated Sportsmen of California and the California Wildlife Federation expressed concern over logging damage to streams and advocated legislative remedies.

All the protest came to nothing. Instead, beginning in 1960 the Board of Forestry began to approve large clear-cuts in the region. Brown's appointments, not surprisingly, were industry people. In 1961 the board approved the Arcata Redwood Company's proposal to clear-cut 823 acres in an area adjacent to and in view of the Redwood Highway, north of Orrick. Until this time there had been a tacit agreement that the redwoods along the Redwood Highway (the northern portion of the scenic highway proposed by Olmsted) would be left to stand as a parklike strip. As a visual buffer, it seemed to lessen public awareness of the extent of logging in the region and pleased the Save the Redwoods League. But clear-cutting was a more profitable logging method, and in 1962 the Simpson Timber Company and Weyerhaeuser also obtained permission to clear-cut. The next year nearly all other timber companies followed suit.[46]

The state legislature remained deaf to pleas for conserving the redwoods and developing better forest practice until 1966, when the rural interests lost their legislative dominance in Sacramento. Before then, agricultural and timber interests had enjoyed a historic alliance based on their common concern over fire protection and protection of private property rights. Supporting each other in the legislature, they formed an undefeatable bloc.[47]

Immediately following reapportionment, the Assembly Committee on Natural Resources, Planning and Public Works, chaired by Democrat Edwin Z'Berg, for the first time established a Subcommittee on Forest Practice and Watershed Management. Charles Warren, Democratic assemblyman from Los Angeles, held the most comprehensive hearings about forest practice in the history of the state and issued a report about the redwood region that was intended to stimulate the creation of a redwood national park. The balance of power in the state was beginning to change in favor of the urbanized areas that held most of the state's population.

Warren's hearings precipitated the introduction of eleven bills to amend the Forest Practice Act. The bills included proposals to do the following:

- Expand public membership on the Board of Forestry and the Forest Practice Committee
- Expand the purposes of the act to include protection of other values than timber productivity
- Require that timber harvest plans (THPs) be subject to approval by the state forester (rather than the board)
- Allow the board to adopt rules independently of the regional committees
- Control soil erosion and protect streams.

All the bills were uncompromisingly opposed by the Board of Forestry, by the timber industry, and by the state Chamber of Commerce. None was passed that year (1966) or the next. The only bill that eventually passed allowed the Bay area counties of Marin, Santa Clara, San Mateo, and later Napa to adopt their own forest practice rules.[48]

After more than half a century of proposals for a national park, a compromise Redwood National Park Bill was finally passed in 1968, without Governor Pat Brown's support. The governor instead suggested implementing the old Olmsted scenic highway plan. Ultimately, however, neither reapportionment nor the park's creation had much effect on state regulation of forest practice or on the forest practice of the timber companies in the redwood region. Brown's Forestry Board appointees continued to be hostile to the regulation of private logging, and the Division of Forestry continued to uphold the industry's position as well. The national park boundaries were largely restricted, like the state parks, to preserving the most magnificent specimens growing in the flats. The park did not encompass any watersheds. The state Board of Forestry consistently approved THPs as long as they conformed to the industry-formulated Forest Practice Act and Rules, resulting in the clear-cutting of several watersheds surrounding the park and up to the park boundaries. Such practices continued despite the lessons of the 1954–55 Rockefeller Grove floods, which demonstrated how clear-cutting of surrounding watersheds could destroy an entire grove.

Conservation and preservation organizations lobbied extensively to expand the boundaries of the national park and to reform the state's forest practice. But the timber companies ignored public sentiment and continued to cut old-growth redwood even in areas that had been long proposed for park inclusion. There were no compromises. Animosity between the two groups mounted.

In 1969 a favorable log-export market for young-growth timber led to logging in Marin and San Mateo Counties, areas that were heavily urbanized in comparison to their northern counterparts and were not dependent on the timber industry for their economic survival. Bayside Timber Company obtained a permit to log from the state board and received other necessary permits from the San Mateo County Planning Commission. Local citizens—including Claire Dedrick, who later served as secretary of resources under Governor Jerry Brown—were outraged and appealed to the county board of supervisors, which denied the local permits on the basis of problems of road access. Bayside Timber appealed the denial and won, based on a 1956 opinion of the California state attorney general that the 1945 Forest Practice Act preempted the county's logging permit system. However, the county, encouraged by Dedrick, did not accept this decision and appealed.

The 1970 decision by the First District Court of Appeals *(Bayside Timber v. Board of Supervisors of San Mateo County)* was a bombshell. The court ruled that the 1945 Forest Practice Act was unconstitutional because it unconstitutionally delegated regulatory authority to an industry that was pecuniarily interested. This was a formidable blow to the ideological underpinnings of Progressive-era boards and commissions, challenging the principle that it is those very interests who are most capable of rule-making because of their insider understanding of the conditions facing the "regulated" industry. The *Bayside* decision left California with no enforceable forest practice rules.[49]

Over six months went by before emergency regulations were signed into law empowering the existing Board of Forestry to adopt rules effective for 180 days. "The Board responded by readopting most of the former rules."[50] The appeal decision had no effect—the status quo remained.

The Legislature Steps In

Assemblyman Z'Berg, chairman of the Assembly Natural Resources Committee, held hearings that same year to begin formulating new legislation regulating forest practice. His Republican rival in the Senate, John Nejedly, chairman of the Senate Natural Resources Committee, did the same. Z'Berg's bill was perceived as more environmental, Nejedly's as more oriented to industry. When Nejedly's bill arrived at the Assembly Natural Resources Committee, Z'Berg refused to let it be heard. This action caused much resentment between the two houses and delayed for a year any action on new forest practice. Finally, a compromise was worked out with the help of the attorney general's office. The Z'Berg-Nejedly Forest Practice Act of 1973 retained most of the provisions of the Nejedly bill.[51]

The new act established a new Board of Forestry composed of nine members, five from the general public, three from the forest products industry, and one from the range livestock industry. The appointments were to be made by the governor, subject to confirmation by the state Senate, and were to be selected on the basis of expertise. The act mandated that the "Board shall represent the public interest." Both of these requirements come straight out of the Progressive era. The act also required "giving consideration to values relating to recreation, watershed wildlife, range and forage, fisheries and aesthetic enjoyment," but did not establish any priorities among these.[52] The language of the act remained at the level of generalities. Developing the specific rules for implementation lay, once again, with the regional forestry commissions. The board established three forestry districts in California and appointed a nine-member Technical Advisory Commission for each district to advise the board on the development of the technical rules.

That the legislature assumed responsibility only for the general framework of regulation, leaving the development and implementation of the specific rules to the regulatory boards, was a direct legacy of the Progressive era. Once again, if the politically appointed members of the board or commission were fundamentally opposed to the intent of the law, they could effectively stymie the legislature's purpose, since the board was responsible for developing those rules necessary to implement the intent of the law. This was the case with the Forestry Board and regional commissions appointed by Governor Reagan. The redwoods continued to be harvested as before.

Decades of activism on behalf of the forest, especially the redwoods, had achieved little due to the regulatory structure put in place by Progressive reforms and its enduring political ideology. The assumptions of the Progressives—that putting politically appointed volunteers most pecuniarily interested in the outcomes of government regulations in charge of developing the regulations would result in thoughtful and informed decisions—proved fallacious. Such a structure does not take into account the long-term public interest or what might be considered ecosystem management for sustainability. Rather, it is driven by the short-term competitive needs of the economy, even when members from the general public are involved in addition to those with vested interests. There is no impartiality in this system, and perhaps more significantly, the structure is not democratic.

Water Development: Never Enough

Water Politics Heat Up

In the 1950s, while Los Angeles and the Bay area suburbs continued to expand and their industrial capacities grew, large agricultural interests in the Central Valley were still chafing at the restrictions of the federal reclamation law that came with the federally subsidized water from the Central Valley

Project, even though those restrictions were never enforced. President Truman's reclamation commissioner, Robert Straus, actually explained to farmers how to get around the acreage limitation through "technical compliance" by giving each stockholder 160 acres if the farm was a corporate entity or deeding land to relatives and children, and other such devices.[53] But besides the unlikely possibility that the federal government might enforce the laws, the federal water project simply did not deliver sufficient water for the large growers to be able to expand irrigated agriculture to all of their lands. San Joaquin Valley landowners along the southwestern side and at the southern end of the valley needed additional water so they could bring those lands under much more profitable irrigated production. Growers also adamantly refused federal water under the conditions of the reclamation law and organized to obtain water from the state, with no strings attached.

However, the state legislature's historic aversion to developing coordinated water planning and creating coherent water law was a substantial obstacle to further water development. There were also significant conflicts among water uses and users: electricity versus irrigation, fish versus electricity and irrigation, upstream versus downstream users, Central Valley versus the San Francisco Bay area, northern California versus the central and the southern parts of the state. In addition, California's water agencies had multiplied and become a patchwork of sovereignties operating in isolation and secrecy. "By 1956 one official tabulation showed that thirty general and forty special enabling acts had accumulated on the statute books. These acts had been used to create 165 irrigation districts, 69 county water districts, 55 reclamation districts, 39 water districts, 35 county waterworks districts and 19 municipal water districts." This did not even include the 1,460 mutual water corporations, 456 commercial water companies, and 207 municipal water operations.[54] In 1962 California had more than 4,000 public and private water-related entities, of which more than 3,000 were concerned with some phase of water distribution. The rest were dedicated to flood control, drainage, and reclamation. Fifty-two agencies were handling various phases of water development, water rights were split among eight agencies, and pollution control was handled by fourteen agencies. Flood control was divided among three agencies. Here again, the emphasis on local control of the resources was a result of Progressive-era legislation, making democratic access difficult for the ordinary citizen.

By 1956 a single state Department of Water Resources (DWR) was created by a special session of the legislature, called by Governor Knight. All other state-level agencies that had dealt with water were abolished. A state Water Board, made up of appointees, was created to oversee the new agency. In 1957 the new department issued its *California Water Plan,* a grand design for water projects that were to meet the ultimate needs of the entire state for the foreseeable future. The plan called for the construction of 370 reservoirs, with networks of canals, tunnels, siphons, and pumps. The key to this plan was the damming of the Feather River, a tributary of the Sacramento and the state's heaviest flowing, wild (undammed) river. The plan was to control floods and collect runoff water for delivery along a 750-mile route, first to the San Francisco Delta, then to the San Joaquin Valley through an aqueduct along the west side, and finally to southern California.[55] The Feather River water would form the backbone of a state-built water project, promising freedom from federal regulation and oversight for large-scale Central Valley farmers.

While this plan was being developed and studies were being conducted on alternative routes of development, the Feather River Project Association—a business association created by big San Joaquin Valley landowners, the heads of corporate farms, land management firms, and railroad executives—began a relentless campaign in favor of the state-built water project. They hired Whitaker & Baxter, the public relations firm that had been started in the 1930s with Artie Samish. The Feather River Project Association lined up those large-scale farmers who for several decades had been lobbying the state to build them a new irrigation water-delivery system that they would have a hand in designing.

> Bloodless, efficient organizations, they [the farming corporations] were geared to compounding dollars for their owners and stockholders. Their future lay in irrigated Farming. The men who controlled them, along with much else in California, were unanimously dedicated to the proposition that the only way to beat the Bureau of Reclamation's 160-acre limitation on water for farmers was to have the state, rather than the federal government, operate a water distribution system. In this way their lands would escape fragmentation by the acreage auctioneer.[56]

The California Water Plan included northern California's other major rivers: the Klamath, the Trinity, the Mad, the Eel, the Van Duzen, and the Russian. They were to be harnessed in the future to bring nearly all of the state's rivers into the service of irrigated agriculture and urban land development—the ultimate transformation of the state's original water regimen. Planners of the 1950s saw nature as completely malleable and gave little thought to possible future consequences. This attitude on the part of the state water planners and the economic interests that would benefit has not changed much over time, although with the rise of modern environmental thinking, the ambitious state water plan was challenged.

But at the time, the Feather River was the most easily dammed because of the configuration of its canyon and so was the first river to be harnessed for the State Water Project. The dam would be considerable, since the river's watershed encompassed 3,900 square miles of Sierra watershed. It was estimated that the dam could store 3.5 million acre-feet of water. The water was not to be diverted directly from the dam site (the Oroville Reservoir); instead, the dam was to regulate the flow of Feather River water into the Sacramento River, which would then flow into the Delta. The additional water available from the damming of Feather River would be pumped out of the Delta into a major storage basin, the San Luis Reservoir near Los Baños. An aqueduct, going south down the west side of the San Joaquin Valley, would make water available for irrigation there, and the rest would eventually be pumped over the Tehachapi Mountains and into the infrastructure of the Metropolitan Water District of Southern California.

The Central Valley Project did not irrigate the west side of the San Joaquin Valley, where some of the largest landholdings in the state were located. The State Water Project, however, would allow hundreds of thousands of acres there to be irrigated for the first time, benefiting large-scale farmers—those with landholdings exceeding the 160-acre limit that applied to federally subsidized water—who were among the strongest backers of the state-built water project. These landowners, and their holdings, included the following:

- Kern County Land Company (owned by Tenneco, Inc.), 223,534 acres
- Tejon Ranch Company (20 percent owned by the Times Mirror Company, publisher of the *Los Angeles Times*), 38,689 acres
- Southern Pacific Land Company, 15,060 acres
- Southern Pacific Company, 11,605 acres
- Buena Vista Associates, 25,254 acres
- Belridge Oil, 24,627 acres
- Occidental Land and Development Company (an oil company), 14,462 acres
- General Petroleum, 16,619 acres
- Shell Oil, 15,353 acres
- Standard Oil, 89,810 acres
- Blackwell Oil Company (controlled by the Lazard Frères banking company), 21,910 acres.[57]

The Feather River Project Association, corporate backer of the State Water Plan, had found urban allies in the northern part of the state. The Santa Clara Valley, growing rapidly, strongly supported the project, as did other communities in the south bay. The big agribusiness corporations needed support from southern California to make the State Water Project happen. They hoped that their water development scheme would dovetail with the long-range thinking of the Metropolitan Water District of Southern California (MWD), the powerful agency that dominated water distribution in the south. Although MWD received its water from the Colorado River, this supply was threatened by Arizona's claims, which that state had presented to the Supreme Court. MWD was concerned that if water for southern California appeared to be available from a large alternative source, such as a state water project, its claim on the Colorado would be jeopardized. Further, there was always the possibility that northern Californians would lay claim to the northern water, leaving MWD with nothing.

> In smoke-filled rooms the joint-venture proposal was broached to southern California's water chieftains. Met's people, however, were lukewarm. They had no intention of pulling the valley rancher's chestnut out of the fire. True, they foresaw the day when they would import northern water, but they wanted it on their own terms. And on their own timetable. They could afford to bide their time and, by so doing, drive a harder bargain with the ranchers of the San Joaquin who were measuring alarming declines in each year's water table or who were up against water of deteriorating quality as well as quantity.[58]

The MWD wanted a state constitutional amendment guaranteeing its water deliveries from the project. Northern Californians were uneasy with this and demanded the protection of water rights in the areas of origin of the water. There was great concern about the effects of further water withdrawal on the Sacramento Delta and San Francisco Bay. The north feared that since southern California contained most of the state's population and most of the votes, water allocations could shift away from the north by a simple vote. The politics of water development were as contentious as ever, but Governor Brown, an adept politician, stepped in to offer a sophisticated, if slippery, compromise: the State Water Resources Development Bond Act (known as the Burns-Porter Act), to be put before the voters. The act specifically guaranteed protection of water rights in the areas of origin of the water, and provided that $130 million from the sale of the bonds be designated for loans and grants to public agencies for construction of local water projects. To gain support of southern California voters, the act required the state to guarantee the contracts for the sale and delivery of water during the lifetime of the bonds—guaranteeing that the water promised would be delivered. The Feather River Project Association put its weight behind a campaign to convince voters of the need for further water development. The bond act barely passed, with southern California delivering a narrow victory and the forces of big agriculture exerting a tremendous amount of pressure.

Eighty percent of the burden of paying for the project fell on urban water users. Kern County corporate farmers received their water at bargain rates. They accomplished this in four ways.

1. In 1961 they persuaded the county's residents to create the Kern County Water Agency, through which every taxpayer would end up funding the imported water. This meant that the urban residents of Bakersfield absorbed most of the costs.
2. The growers obtained a special water rate, reduced by the amount of revenue generated by power sales at Oroville Dam.
3. Kern County landowners benefited from another subsidy. Water is usually assessed on the size of the water conveyance system, but in this case, they managed to be charged on the volume of water used. This favored the farmers since farmers did not have to pay for the larger system they needed to deliver peak summer flows, and only paid for the water itself.
4. The final subsidy was a special rate for surplus water negotiated with the state and with the MWD. The State Water Project delivered more water to the urbanized part of southern California than it needed (despite a campaign in favor of the State Water Project that claimed southern California would face imminent water shortages if the project was not built), so Kern County farmers agreed to purchase the excess water at about the cost of its transportation instead of at its true cost. This amounted to paying about $13 per acre-foot instead of the $43 per acre-foot that urban dwellers were paying.

The State Water Project consisted of a dam on the Feather River, and joint construction, ownership, and use of the San Luis Reservoir with the federal government. By 1967 both the Oroville Dam on the Feather River and the San Luis Reservoir were completed. The Feather River water flows into the Sacramento and down into the Delta, from which water is pumped to fill the San Luis Reservoir, as well as to supply the old Central Valley Project.

One of the major selling points of the State Water Project was that it would provide farmers with enough water so they could stop the overdrafting of groundwater supplies by pumping. Instead, groundwater pumping continued unabated, while the new water was used to bring previously unirrigated lands into irrigated agriculture, essentially developing new farmlands.[59]

The State Water Project was the culmination of decades of agitation and pressure by big agriculture for state-controlled water development and de-

livery. At first, agricultural interests had been all too happy to accept federally subsidized water. It was better than no irrigation water, and it made
possible the large-scale development of irrigated agriculture in the state.
California became one of the most productive agricultural areas in the
world. But federal water came with restrictions, and these threatened to
break up the large agricultural holdings that had been consolidated in the
late nineteenth century, fruits of federal land-disposal policy and the Spanish land-grant system. Large-scale agricultural landholders in the mid-
1950s were large, diversified, often urban-based corporations. Owned by oil
companies, publishing firms, land-development companies, and insurance
companies—the economic motors of the state—they were unwilling to
abide by federal laws if that meant giving up their agricultural empires.
State-developed irrigation water was the alternative, and the agricultural
corporations were well positioned to pressure the state into building them
an additional water-delivery system, allowing them to bring even more land
into production, at the taxpayers' expense. The social, economic, and land-
use ramifications of this system of agriculture were significant, as were the
costs to the urban dwellers of the state. These concerns, however, were not
aired as part of the public debate over water development, even though going forward with construction of the State Water Project did require a popular vote. The long-term environmental consequences of the project, beyond
increased damage to the Delta—more marginal agricultural lands brought
under production, the increased use of pesticides and herbicides, salinization, and the potential for increased suburban growth—were scarcely
raised, nor were the collateral land-use effects.

The Social Costs of Big Agriculture

Immediately after World War II, there was a labor shortage in the Southwest
and in California. Many Mexicans came over the border illegally by wading
across the Rio Grande or riding in on the buses of the growers' labor contractors. Because of pressure by large-scale agriculture to maintain a supply
of inexpensive labor, in 1947 the U.S. government legalized some 55,800 immigrants. An additional 19,000 Mexicans had already been brought into
the country as "braceros," or emergency labor, after U.S. government agreements with Mexico in 1942 and 1944. In 1949 four-fifths of the 107,000
braceros for that year were legalized undocumented immigrants. In 1951
Congress codified the Mexican agreements into Public Law 78, authorizing
the government to import braceros for growers that needed them. No other
industry in the United States had had this kind of privileged labor supply,
paid at a federally sanctioned lower wage than American labor would com-
mand. The Farm Bureau Federation was an active force behind this policy,

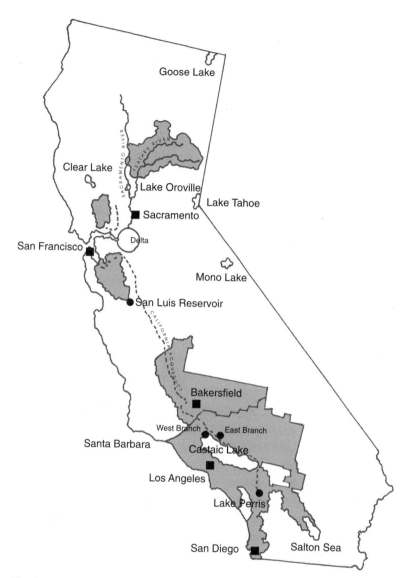

Goose Lake

FEATHER RIVER

SACRAMENTO RIVER

Clear Lake

Lake Oroville

Lake Tahoe

Sacramento

Delta

San Francisco

Mono Lake

San Luis Reservoir

CALIFORNIA AQUEDUCT

Bakersfield

West Branch   East Branch

Santa Barbara

Castaic Lake

Los Angeles

Lake Perris

San Diego   Salton Sea

The State Water Project

continually lobbying Congress and the Department of Agriculture. It was only in 1964 that this policy was allowed to expire.

Still, agricultural interests did not give up easily. From the ashes of the PL 78 program rose the 1968 green card program. To obtain an immigrant visa, Mexicans needed only to untangle some red tape and furnish proof of a job in the United States. If a person established residence during the four-month grace period, he or she could then obtain a "green card," which allowed visits to Mexico and return to the United States.

This Mexican-based farm labor system worked best for large growers. According to the 1964 farm census, 60 percent of California's 81,000 farms used no hired labor, while 7 percent of the state's large farms employed 75 percent of total farm labor. Clearly, it was corporate agriculture that benefited from the labor policy. The termination of the PL 78 program opened the door to farm labor organizing, and in 1965 the first California grape strike and boycott was organized by the young United Farm Workers of César Chávez—a significant development in challenging long-standing labor policy.

In a now classic study published in 1947, anthropologist Walter R. Goldschmidt compared two rural towns of similar size in the San Joaquin Valley, one surrounded by modest family farms, the other by large corporate farms.[60] The investigation revealed shocking differences in the quality of life in each. Dinuba, surrounded by small farms, had three times the number of schools and parks than did Arvin, surrounded by large farms. The small-farm community supported sixty-two business establishments, compared to thirty-five in the large-farm community, a ratio of nearly two to one. People in Dinuba had a better average standard of living than those in Arvin. Dinuba also had better city infrastructure than Arvin: paved sidewalks, paved streets, sewage, and garbage pick-up. The small-farm community had more than twice the number of organizations for civic improvement and social recreation, two newspapers, and more public participation in government decision making. Finally, there were no great differences in wealth in Dinuba, while in Arvin there was more poverty.[61]

The rural poverty that characterized Arvin was a reflection of the incomes and position of the workers on the corporate farms. Farm workers have fewer rights than any other segment of American labor. Not until 1955 did they become eligible for Social Security, and not until 1966 did Congress amend the fair labor standards acts to give farm workers a minimum wage of $1.65 per hour. Farm workers were not eligible for state or federal unemployment insurance, though nearly half of California's farm labor force was unemployed for twenty-seven weeks or more a year. Working conditions for many farm workers were abysmal, as is still often the case. Inadequate numbers of toilets (or none at all) in the fields, inadequate drinking water, and use of back-breaking, short-handled hoes for weeding were some of the most obvious problems in addition to poor housing and low wages. The impact of these conditions, combined with extreme land concentration and factory-like farming, created substantial regional inequalities. Over the years, farm workers became largely Mexican (replacing the successive waves of Chinese, Japanese, and Filipino workers who preceded them), maintaining the historical racial dimension of California agriculture's income inequality.

The building of the State Water Project, providing water to the large farms on the west side of the San Joaquin Valley, subsidized the expansion of this system of agriculture. Increased water, subsidized by taxpayer dollars, did not, and would not, increase the prosperity of local communities. Industrial agriculture—not only in California but throughout the Southwest—is characterized by substantial degradation of human communities and living conditions. Before industrial agriculture, rural communities' fates were tied directly to the agricultural economy. Where there were family-owned and -operated farms, profits tended to be spent in rural towns, supporting stores and services, fostering a large and viable rural middle class. Smaller, family-based farmers rely on rural towns for their civic and social identity.

Corporate agriculture operates differently. Farm inputs, such as fertilizer, seed, tractors, and irrigation equipment, are purchased more cheaply far away. Large-scale farmers tend to bypass local public and commercial services and establishments, preferring to shop in distant cities and to purchase education, police protection, and recreation from the private sector for their own exclusive use rather than from the local municipality. The public involvement of the largest industrial farmers is focused not on supporting the local community, but on lobbying and selling at the state, federal, and international level. There is no middle class, and instead the economy has a bimodal income distribution, polarized between rich and poor.

The social consequences for these two different community types are substantially different. Recent studies of the Westlands Water District of the San Joaquin Valley show that 215 farming operations averaged over 2,000 acres with mean annual sales of $1.5 million per farm, suggesting an extremely rich agricultural region. Fifty percent of the total population, and 70 percent of Latinos, were employed as farm labor. Twenty-five percent of all families, and over 50 percent of the Latino families, lived below the poverty line. Up to 20 percent of the households in the Westlands census tract lacked plumbing, compared to less than 1 percent for the state as a whole. These correlations between farm size and community impoverishment have been found consistently throughout the Central Valley as well as in the Southwest overall.[62]

Thus the trends identified by Goldschmidt's 1947 study demonstrating the negative social and economic effects of large-scale farming on local communities have held over time and have been shown to be intrinsic to the system of corporate farming. Nevertheless, federal and state irrigation projects continued to be justified as bringing the possibility of rural prosperity through the expansion of the farming community. Far from creating the Jeffersonian dream of a nation of small yeoman farmers on the public domain, public water subsidy has vastly enriched some few immensely large farmers while leading to the exploitation of labor and impoverished rural communities. Democratic institutions have suffered at the local level, and the entire process of decision making about subsidized water development has been carried out in a less than candid manner by the interests with most to gain from further water availability.

Not only do towns surrounded by big farms have a less well-developed civic culture and less active democratic institutions, but they are also characterized by high numbers of poor immigrant workers who tend not to be citizens and thus have no right to participate in local democratic institutions.

Agricultural water subsidy in the Central Valley has contributed to topsoil depletion caused by the use of huge agricultural machinery, salinization from poor drainage on marginal soils, and chemical pollution, as well as the transformation of the landscape itself through leveling and earth moving. The State Water Project was another giant step in the radical transformation of nature in the Central Valley.

The Urban Link to Rural Water Development

The State Water Project served two purposes, one obvious (allowing further agricultural expansion) and the other less immediately apparent. The second purpose involved the urban dimension: availability of water made it possible for new towns to spring up on inland sites in southern California—towns that otherwise might have been impossible to build. It was for this eventuality that the MWD finally backed the State Water Project. Southern California had enough water to support the current residents, and even to sustain some modest growth, without the building of the project. But landowners who held onto the vast ranchos of the Spanish era (at the urban fringe of the Los Angeles basin and in the Central Valley) were eager to develop these lands. The owners of these huge holdings—the Irvine Ranch, Newhall Ranch, Newhall Land & Farming Company, Tejon Ranch, and others—greatly benefited from the State Water Project, since it enabled them to build more subdivisions and new towns in the Los Angeles basin as well as to expand their agricultural production, most especially in Kern County.[63] Water development thus served the large landholders for both urban and rural land transformation. Once again the boundary between urban and rural development interests in the state was impossible to draw.

Further Danger to the Delta

The State Water Project meant a further alteration of California's original water regimen. The Sacramento Delta took on ever increasing significance in water projects as the giant well from which the state filled its aqueducts. The Delta is the hub of the entire 50,000-square-mile Central Valley river network, a vast, complex, and poorly understood ecosystem. In one way or another, all the rivers, streams, and rivulets of the entire Central Valley watershed flow into the Delta. Pumping from the two water projects together has put a tremendous strain on the Delta ecosystem. It has allowed the intrusion of saltwater. Native fisheries have been destroyed for lack of enough water to sustain the fish. Spawning fish are often killed in the pumps. If this is not enough, fish are also confused because of the reverse water flows caused by pumping, inhibiting natural migration patterns. All in all, many of the fisheries are jeopardized. A trade-off on paper was developed, whereby in exchange for more water from the Delta, farmers would agree to pump less groundwater (its depletion was causing ground subsidence and higher energy costs for deeper pumping). But more Delta water diversion meant further damage to the system. Entire species were threatened with extinction. And in the end, both occurred—continued groundwater pumping and more water diversion from the Delta.

The State Water Project was a major piece in completing the puzzle of continued land development and agricultural growth in the state. It refueled the engines of economic growth by providing another transfer of natural resource wealth, paid for by the taxpayers, to those large property owners that stood to gain the most.

More Water Politics

Beyond the State Water Project remained the State Water Plan, which had outlined an ambitious further capture of nearly all of the state's rivers. The Eel River was the next river to be harnessed for the state's growth. In 1968 the Army Corps of Engineers proposed a dam on the Eel at Dos Rios, a small town in Round Valley. The valley was the reservation home of the Yuki, a tribe that had lived there for at least 9,000 years. The dam would have flooded the valley, drowning it under 300 feet of water, inundating reservation lands and prime agricultural land. The Yuki were to have received 2 acres of hill land for each acre of flooded flat land, though Yuki had always been flatland dwellers and farmers and would have had difficulty sustaining themselves on hillside acreages. The town of Covalo would have been relocated entirely. The Army Corps intended the water to be tunneled through the mountains to the Sacramento River. Timber interests favored the dam because it would reduce the flooding of the Eel, which often caused a great deal of damage.

The threats to the Eel River caused environmental groups to lobby for the protection of the remaining wild rivers in the north of the state. The activists hoped to permanently alter the State Water Plan by putting these rivers off-limits. This would have far-reaching consequences for further water development planning in the state, as the State Water Project was only the first step in developing more water. In 1972, with the leadership of Senator Behr of Marin County and the backing of Reagan's trusted associate Norman Livermore, secretary of the Resources Agency (who obtained the governor's support), wild river status was conferred on the remaining rivers in the northern part of the state. The defeat of the Eel River / Dos Rios Dam project and the passage of wild river protections signaled the end of major water development projects for a time. It implemented the concept of wild rivers protection in the state, a major environmental victory.

Political Change: Reapportionment

For decades, rural interests had dominated the state legislature by controlling the Senate. The "federal plan" had created a situation such that by 1960 the ratio between the population of the largest and smallest senatorial districts was over 400 to 1. Northern California's 40 percent of the population was represented by 70 percent of the senators. Measures requiring a two-thirds vote in the state Senate could be blocked by fourteen senators representing 5 percent of the population. Southern California was inequitably represented in Senate committees, further reducing its political power.[64] Although changing this system would be difficult, southern California legislators were increasingly dissatisfied and pressed for reform.

During the 1950s several proposals for constitutional amendments to modify the "federal plan" had been introduced in the Assembly, to no avail. A ballot initiative was put forth (the third in a series of attempts) to modify the apportionment plan enacted in 1926. This initiative, the Bonelli Plan, Proposition 15, had the bad luck to be politically associated with another important measure on the ballot, Proposition 1, the $1.7 billion Water Resources Development Act—Governor Pat Brown's State Water Project bond act. Proposition 15 would have dramatically reduced rural and northern California county representation, which could have jeopardized Governor Brown's delicate balancing act in getting northern and southern interests to agree on Proposition 1. For this reason, Governor Brown opposed the reapportionment proposition, though he recognized that there was a serious problem of inequitable representation. Reapportionment lost, and the Water Resources Development Act narrowly passed. Equitable political representation was a lesser priority than growth-inducing water development.

Brown subsequently appointed a Study Commission on Senate Apportionment. Hearings conducted throughout the state showed only lukewarm discontent with the "federal plan" and only a moderate desire for change. The commission put forth some recommendations, and the governor placed them on call for the 1962 special session of the legislature, asking for a constitutional amendment that would then be put on the ballot for the November general election. The Assembly passed a bill that increased representation for Los Angeles and other populous counties; not surprisingly, the bill died in Senate committee. The rural-dominated Senate had little incentive to change its own composition. Another initiative was then put on the ballot to expand Senate representation, Proposition 23. This, too, was defeated, but narrowly.

In March 1962, while the Assembly and Senate were debating the recommendations of the Governor's Commission, and before Proposition 23 was qualified for the ballot, the U.S. Supreme Court took its first look at the "federal plan" as it was developed in the state of Tennessee. In *Baker v. Carr* (369 U.S. 186), Justice William Brennan wrote that claims of denial of equal protection under the Fourteenth Amendment did constitute a reason for looking at apportionment. There was a flood of suits across the country asking the courts to require the principle of "one man, one vote" in both houses of a state legislature.

In December 1964 a special three-judge Federal District Court panel, in a two-to-one decision, ruled the plan of representation of the California Senate unconstitutional. The court mandated the legislature to reapportion the Senate as its first order of business, and the court retained jurisdiction to act in the event that senatorial districts were not "fairly, adequately, and validly" redistricted by July 1, 1965.

One of the first reactions by rural senators was to call for splitting California into two states. The proposal was considered seriously, with 25 of 40 state senators cosponsoring the proposal. Although it passed the Senate, the proposal died in the Assembly.

The state legislature had no choice but to address the issue of reapportionment. But the two houses could not agree on a plan. The matter went back to the courts, with the Federal District Court deferring to the California Supreme Court. The California Supreme Court then ordered the legislature to reapportion both Senate and Assembly according to population and to do it by December 9, 1965. No district could depart from the ideal size by more than 15 percent, with a majority of members of each house to be elected by voters of districts containing at least 48 percent of the total population of the state. The legislature went back to work and, to avoid a court-determined reapportionment scheme, produced its own plan.[65]

Reapportionment was a major change in California politics, as it gave urban populations more representation. One of the effects of this change was that the legislature began to take environmental questions into consideration. By 1970 the legislature had passed the California Environmental Quality Act and instituted an environmental impact assessment process that applied to both state and private development projects. The legislature, with better urban representation, expanded the scope of natural resource protection issues it was willing to address. As we have seen, it tackled reform of forest practice legislation, the establishment of wild rivers protection, and the creation of water quality reform.

Assemblyman Jesse Unruh, Assembly Speaker from Los Angeles, introduced yet another significant change in the California legislature. Unruh felt that unless legislators were paid a living wage and worked full time, they would continue to be susceptible to the influence of lobbyists and would not see themselves as professionals, paid to represent their constituents back home. He succeeded in pushing through a package of reforms, creating paid staff for representatives and implementing a year-round legislature, making California's state government one of the most professional in the nation.

Environmentalism and the Legislature

The reforms in the state legislature were part of a fundamental political change in the state. With urban interests more accurately represented, concerns of the contemporary world could now be introduced and discussed in the legislature. The society at large was undergoing profound turmoil and change. The civil rights movement had made a big impact on politics, and new attitudes about representation and equality were beginning to develop. The anti–Vietnam War movement had picked up the political momentum from the civil rights movement. Government was opened to greater scrutiny. Decision-making processes were starting to become more transparent and accountable. These trends and currents certainly affected politics in California.

Perhaps the most significant event influencing legislative representation and policymaking in the state was the Santa Barbara oil spill. This event catalyzed the emerging modern environmental movement in the state and catapulted it to the forefront of public visibility. Protecting the environment became the issue of the day. It seemed like a nonpartisan issue, safer politically than civil rights or the Vietnam War (though Democrats and Republicans often lined up differently on the votes). George Milias, Democrat on the Assembly Natural Resources Committee and the Select Committee on Environmental Quality, explained the nonpartisan nature of environmental questions in an interview in 1970:

> If you study the make-up of the big conservation organizations, at the top leadership level you find strong representation by people in both parties. So I have always said that it is not a partisan issue, it stands on its own. It is certainly to the disadvantage of the issue to try to make it a partisan thing. . . . The environment issue was like an iceberg. It had been there for years but most of it was not visible. There was a tremendous body of public opinion that had been growing and growing, until all of a sudden it was just enormous. Then a few things happened. There was the Santa Barbara oil spill. Some more literate individuals began to come out with publications like the *Population Bomb*. You had quite a bit of talk about pesticide problems and DDT in fish and other wildlife. All of a sudden people got very, very uptight about the environment, and that's why it became a big issue in 1970.[66]

In 1970, after the Santa Barbara oil spill, Governor Reagan devoted one-third of his state of the state address to ecology. He said, "There is no subject more on our minds than the preservation of our environment, and the absolute necessity of waging an all-out war against the debauching of our environment."[67] Everybody wanted to protect the environment—Republicans, Democrats, industry, and the public. But when it came time to actually regulate polluters, sentiments became more complicated. Business leaders claimed that pollution prevention programs were bad for business. Decisions for legislators became politically charged and party divisions more acute.

Among the many environmental bills that were introduced, a Conservation Bill of Rights was authored by Assemblyman Edwin Z'Berg. His bill would have placed environmental protection at the same level as human rights. He also proposed the creation of an environmental quality study council to take over responsibility for environmental protection in all fields, including solid waste management. The idea encountered a wall of opposition from members of the Reagan administration, who claimed the council would exert "virtual dictatorial control over every aspect of life in California."[68] Also joining the chorus of opposition were Democrats, considered liberals, who feared that this type of strong environmental legislation would shift the distribution of power among bureaucracies, creating new ones that might diminish their own influence.

Still, this early period witnessed an explosion of environmental legislation and new ideas. There was legislation to halt oil drilling in the Santa Barbara Channel and to protect the San Luis Obispo coastline from drilling. Senator

Petris of Oakland introduced a bill to ban the use of smog-producing car engines by 1975 (SB 66). Another bill would have banned cars from the core area of nineteen major California cities. A bill to require that beverage containers be refundable or biodegradable was presented and defeated in 1970. Attempts were made to increase state or regional participation in local planning decisions, also defeated. Unruh proposed to set up a powerful state environmental quality control board (AB 2180), killed in committee in the Assembly.[69] Some of the bills seem prescient or radical today, yet with the rise of the environmental movement in the early 1970s there was a sense that much could be accomplished legislatively, that problems were urgent, and that solutions needed to be substantial and unmitigated. Almost none of the environmental bills passed, but at least there was a political atmosphere that permitted the airing of big problems and substantive discussion.

The most significant accomplishment of the decade was the passage of the California Environmental Quality Act, modeled on the federal Environmental Quality Act. The California legislation went beyond the federal because it required public hearings and government response to all questions raised by the public. The act also covered major private developments, which the federal law did not. The other major piece of environmental legislation was the state's air pollution regulations, requiring the phasing out of leaded gasoline and the development of the state's own air quality standards, tougher than those of the federal government. These laws and others put California at the nation's forefront in environmental protection.

Growth and Environmentalism Come to California

Political change in the state in the late 1960s and early 1970s made California one of the most innovative states in the nation. It was seen as a leader in environmental protection and political professionalism. Political reapportionment redressed the long-standing rural hold on the Senate and established population-based representation, favoring the cities. All of this, however, was built on a slippery foundation. The structure of government put in place by the Progressives remained, with its business-oriented boards and commissions, proliferating special districts, and depoliticized and fragmented local, regional, and special-district governments. The economy prospered, and ever more houses were built at the urban fringe, drawing resources and jobs with them, restructuring the landscape and distribution of wealth. Democratic participation in the decisions about the direction of growth and its environmental impacts was limited, constrained by the structures of governance and decision making, and the way the issue was conceptualized.

Governor Pat Brown was one of the key architects of continued growth. He masterfully negotiated a compromise between the state's big agricultural interests and the powerful Metropolitan Water District of Southern California to enable the building of the State Water Project, creating another huge water conveyance system, but without federal acreage limitations. Big agriculture had finally won the no-strings-attached water conveyance system it had coveted for so long.

Despite urban areas increasing their political clout in the legislature through reapportionment, growth as usual continued on an ever increasing scale. Much of the decision making that was driving growth still took place behind the scenes, at the level of boards and commissions, special districts, and special elections—reinforcing the very development patterns that were of concern to the urban-based environmental community. Local political fragmentation and lack of responsiveness to public desires were still the norm for urban growth, and regional inequalities deepened.

The state legislature, within significant structural limits, began to develop legislation to address environmental degradation, but some of the most significant initiatives were citizen-led, like the Coastal Protection Initiative. The growth infrastructure, ably developed by Governor Pat Brown, had brought with it environmental and social costs that would be the sources of contention in coming decades.

5 · UNFULFILLED VISIONS

The Jerry Brown Years

THE POLITICAL REFORMS of the 1960s brought California into a new era. The state now had a professional legislature, a representative Senate and Assembly, and a prosperous economy. Much of the drama of the activism of the late 1960s and early 1970s had already been played out by 1975, when the voters elected a governor who appeared to be a representative for the age: Jerry Brown, an articulate and well-educated young politician who ran as an independent candidate. Jerry Brown was the son of former governor Pat Brown, a liberal Democrat (see chapter 4). By the time the younger Brown was elected, environmental issues had become issues of state. Alternatives for change to enable the consumer society to survive in the long term were debated as part of the public discourse. A spirit of optimism reigned. Under Brown there appeared the hope that the historic changes that seemed to be taking place in the culture—new attitudes toward authority, the environment, war, race, and work—would be reflected in and integrated into state politics and institutions.

Why did the promise of the period turn sour? The mid-1970s was a critical time in the evolution of the state, as well as the nation, for during those years efforts to create a more open democratic process, as well as a more sustainable economic future, seemed to gain momentum. Yet in the end politics as usual, and the accompanying cynicism, prevailed, dashing the hopes of voters, contributing to apathy, and plunging the state into a nihilistic process of dismantling government and discrediting its programs. The collusion between business interests and politicians increased, and the political realm became increasingly irrelevant to people's daily lives. Many of the reasons for the contemporary degradation of civic society and politics can be found in the disillusionment of the 1970s, both in California and nationally.

Setting the Stage: The Rise of Environmentalism

The late 1960s and early 1970s were years of political struggle. In the United States, the Vietnam War divided families and generations, and also split the Democratic Party. The student uprisings of May 1968 in Paris caused political turmoil that reverberated throughout Europe and was echoed by the events at Kent State University and other anti–Vietnam War protests in the United States. These years marked the beginnings of the postmodern age of relativism and immigration, of world music and global markets.

The tumultuous and violent 1968 Democratic convention in Chicago was convened only months after Robert Kennedy's assassination in Los Angeles and the same year as the murder of Martin Luther King. Richard Nixon was elected president, and the United States undertook secret bombing missions in Cambodia. There followed the Watergate political scandal that led to President Nixon's resignation, under the shadow of impeachment. This was the broad canvas against which environmental issues came to be defined and distinguished from issues of conservation or natural resource management. The organized protests of the civil rights movement and the anti-war movement had subtle and important influences on the emerging environmental movement, as did the philosophy of the anti-consumerist counterculture. Several important groups and organizations emerged in the 1960s to push for social change—from civil rights to corporate responsibility, land reform, and greater government accountability. In Europe these events had their counterparts in the form of anti–Vietnam War protests, anti-nuclear campaigns, and rising environmental awareness. Government was often the focus of protest, since it was seen as the major obstacle to social change and also the most powerful potential agent of change.

The International Context

Internationally, the environment was increasingly a matter of concern—concern that was focused upon issues of population growth and control, and diminishing resources. In 1968 the Club of Rome, a group of thirty individuals from ten countries—including scientists, educators, economists, industrialists, and others—were brought together by Dr. Aurelio Peccei, an Italian industrialist, to discuss the future of man on earth. In 1972 the group published *The Limits to Growth: Our Common Future*, a controversial but highly influential analysis of the effect of continuing the "physical, economic and social relationships" that governed the development of the world system. The book concluded: "If the present growth trends in world population, industrialization, pollution, food production, and resource depletion continue unchanged, the limits to growth on this planet will be reached sometime within the next one hundred years. The most probable result will be rather sudden and uncontrollable decline in both population and industrial capacity."[1] This pessimistic assumption was then tempered by affirmation of the possibility of altering the trends in favor of ecological and economic stability, sustainable far into the future. The report advocated both zero population growth and zero economic growth.

Consistent with mid-1960s corporate analyses of existing energy supplies, population growth, and future technological developments, the report advocated striving toward an equilibrium state (now reinvented under the rubric "sustainable development") and stressed that exponential growth of the type the West had been experiencing was not sustainable. Economists such as Herman Daly began writing about a new economic theory, steady-state economics.

In June 1972 the first United Nations world conference on the human environment was held in Stockholm. In all, 114 nations were represented. The conference produced a "Declaration on the Human Environment" and a set of environmental recommendations to guide national governments and international institutions. (This conference was repeated in Rio in 1992.) The report highlighted the development/environment issue and the importance of establishing natural resource reserves, and outlined specific techniques, such as integrated pest management. The issue of banning nuclear testing was a focus of intense debate at the conference. The conference members established the U.N. Environmental Program, which more than a decade later produced a report echoing the Club of Rome's *Limits to Growth*, while projecting even more urgency about the need for change and the state of the global environment.[2]

Small Is Beautiful, by E. F. Schumacher, was published the following year. In this influential book Schumacher, the founder and chairman of the Intermediate Technology Development Group in Britain and a student of Gandhi, set forth a compelling argument for a decentralized, small-scale, communitarian society. He drew from Gandhi's philosophy and economic principles as well as from anarchist thought. In this synthesis, economics was re-embedded in the civil society and humankind's fundamental dependence on the earth's finite and fragile resources was emphasized. Schumacher was very critical of conventional, neoclassical economics for ignoring the unique and nonsubstitutable contribution that nature makes to production. For Schumacher, "the market is the institutionalization of individualism and non-responsibility."[3] He argued for an economic system that would serve "*production by the masses* instead of *mass production*" (emphasis in orig-

Anti–Vietnam War march on Wilshire Blvd., Los Angeles, c. 1968. (Photograph by Mark Keats; courtesy of the Southern California Library for Social Studies and Research, Los Angeles)

Love-in, South Park, Los Angeles, 1967. (Photograph by Mark Keats; courtesy of the Southern California Library for Social Studies and Research, Los Angeles)

inal), and for technological development leading back to the real needs of humans and to their actual size—appropriate technology.[4]

The ideas of the Club of Rome, the U.N. conference on the human environment, and E. F. Schumacher were widely discussed—especially after the 1973 oil-supply crisis—and became a factor in government and corporate decision making. The environment, the protection of nature, and pollution control were of concern at different levels of society, from expert think tanks funded by large corporations to the mainstream environmental organizations and a growing grass-roots movement. The environment was an apparently apolitical issue, on whose importance everyone could agree. It encompassed both broad and narrow concerns at the same time, from global overpopulation to the protection of a single landscape.

The United States

In the United States, too, the public was becoming more concerned about the state of the environment. It seemed clear that the environment, increasingly threatened by human activity, required protection through state and national laws. During the Republican administration of Richard Nixon, major environmental legislation was passed that has since influenced the course of pollution control and national environmental standards. This legislation included the following measures:

- Reenactment of the Clean Air Act in 1970, substantially strengthening its standards
- Passage of the National Environmental Policy Act in 1970
- Reenactment of the Clean Water Act in 1972, also in substantially stronger form
- Reenactment of the Endangered Species Act in 1972, much stronger than it had been previously
- Passage of the Coastal Zone Management Act in 1972.

A proposed National Land Use Policy Act failed, in spite of the support of large-scale developers and other influential groups, including the National Mortgage Bankers Association and the Washington representatives of the National Association of Home Builders. These groups all supported the idea of a regulated and coordinated land market, organized and managed from above by expert, public-spirited administrators in cooperation with corporate technicians and environmental scientists. This followed their well-established tradition of working with the federal government to establish programs that placed government's police powers and financial muscle at their service. But local chambers of commerce, the local branches of the National

Association of Home Builders, ranchers, and local timber interests all mobilized to put pressure on the House of Representatives to defeat the proposal for federal land-use planning. National land-use planning would have required localities to coordinate their planning efforts, and the localities feared they would lose regulatory power over crucial growth questions. Both local businesses and members of the environmental movement, reluctant to give up local control of land-use decisions, fought centralization and coordination. Other environmental protection measures passed because implementation was delegated to state and local governments and because the laws did not seem to threaten established ways of doing business or the power of local authority, and a few were passed after pitched political struggle.

The first Earth Day was held in 1970, funded by foundations. Handbooks for improving individuals' behavior became popular, educating people on how to reduce their impact on the planet. The environmental problem was boiled down to individual choices. The social and economic context, the issues of power, politics, the role of the market—all were usually judiciously sidestepped.

Large corporations and mainstream think tanks turned their attention to the environment. Organizations such as RAND in California, Resources for the Future (created by the Ford Foundation), and the Brookings Institution in Washington, D.C., were conducting forums on the quality of the environment and identifying research needs for corporations and industrial trade associations. Industrial interests began to mobilize in the environmental area, as executives realized that pollution could adversely affect profits and that regulation needed to be developed, but along traditional trade association patterns. The regulations had to create a level playing field for industry so that all would be carrying the same costs of compliance, precluding the possibility of competitive advantage, and had to ensure that costs associated with such regulations would be passed on to the consumer.

How environmental issues were shaped and packaged, from the beginning, reflected in large measure the needs of big business. As we have seen, this had been the conventional pattern for the evolution of regulation in the United States. Large corporations were especially wary of state and local environmental regulations, as these could modify existing standards and rules, making it more expensive to operate a business. Thus there was a great push for federal rule making in the environmental arena. Federal environmental regulations followed the standard legislative pattern. Policy and standards were set at the federal level, and then their enactment and enforcement was delegated to states and to local governments. Thus, in the area of air pollution, regional air quality management boards had the final responsibility for developing the steps by which a region would attain clean air. With federal standards set, industry would have a level playing field; with local enforcement, there would be room for negotiation and compromise on such things as the time line for implementation and definition of permissible technologies.

This approach was consistent with federal government policy in general, which is characterized by a highly decentralized mode of intervention. The federal government, in environmental regulations as well as in urban policy, has functioned as a kind of "banker government," funding local agencies to conduct national programs. In this way the federal government cedes a tremendous amount of discretion and control over its programs to local political actors. These local actors then wield powerful tools to achieve political as well as economic change at the local level.[5]

In the early 1970s there was definite conservative dominance at both the federal and state levels, while at the same time there was radical political critique of the American system at the grass-roots level. Nonetheless, somewhere in the middle, there was also a flourishing culture of alternative ideas and movements, in which people were actively engaged in working to change the system. Environmental issues gained stature and legislation passed, though it was usually couched in apolitical terms and often focused on the individual as the source of the problem. In this jumbled context, full of contradictory tensions, Governor Jerry Brown took office in California.

Federal Anti-urbanism

President Nixon signed much of the nation's most significant environmental legislation, responding to the groundswell of activism across the country. At the same time, he and his administration "opposed reliance on the kinds of quasi-governmental anti-poverty agencies that had been established in the Great Society" of President Lyndon Johnson. They went to work dismantling the social programs the Great Society had just finished putting in place. The Nixon administration especially targeted those programs that had been established in the large cities to help alleviate the problems of poverty and disempowerment—measures such as the Model Cities Program, federal housing subsidy programs, and a host of public service employment and social service programs. These programs were aimed at local empowerment of inner-city residents (many of them black), a community that was not taken into consideration by most environmentalists, but one that had suffered some of the most injurious effects of environmental degradation and poor urban planning. Under the Democrats these programs had been aimed in part to keep the support of a constituency. For example, almost a quarter of the black politicians elected to local office in the 1970s had received their initial political training in the Great Society Community Action Program. Nixon also wished to remove environmental impact reviews, citizen participation mechanisms, and other such programs that "brought unwanted constituencies into the higher reaches of the federal government itself." Anti-urbanism went hand in hand with squelching opportunities for public mobilization and participation. Environmental impact reviews, now required by the National Environmental Policy Act, opened federal activities—such as redevelopment and highway building—to public notification and comment. Together with the citizen-participation programs that were part of the Great Society, they could have encouraged greater public participation in federal decision making. This was just what the Nixon administration wanted to avoid, since those who would be participating were by and large Democrats.[6]

In hindsight, one can wonder if the potential for building an urban environmental movement, motivated by the problems of urban environmental degradation and questions of human health effects, was delayed by the policies of the Nixon administration. The possibility for building an alternative path of urban development through the grass-roots involvement of inner-city residents was effectively snuffed. The Nixon administration had its own constituencies to reward with federal programs and funds—including politically supportive regions of the country, especially the suburbs and southern and southwestern metropolitan regions. Its agenda was couched in rhetoric that promoted shifting control back to the local level and increasing federal funding (through HUD) for suburbs and rapidly growing cities, mainly in the South and Southwest. Most northeastern cities made few gains or suffered growing fiscal distress. Conservative policy initiatives increased the competitive advantage of the suburbs and new metropolitan areas over the large, older metropolitan areas, which remained segregated and poorer. Environmental programs passed during the Nixon administration did little to address the problems in these cities. Nixon's urban policy weakened citizen-participation mechanisms initiated by Great Society programs that had begun to create an opening for questions of equity and environmental justice.

Federal anti-urbanism was matched in California by Ronald Reagan's political philosophy. His natural constituents were suburban dwellers, and his campaign for law and order was an implicit slam of the older, minority-dominated central cities of Oakland and Los Angeles, as well as San Francisco. Radical organizations like the Black Panthers—which had started to develop more synthetic analyses of the correlations between urban poverty and environmental degradation, and of the need for better education and better community infrastructure—were targeted as subversive and dangerous.

California on the Leading Edge

As described in chapter 4, when the 1970 legislative session opened, the environment was the top item on the agenda. Governor Reagan had made it a key issue in his state of the state address, and much legislation was proposed, though most of it did not pass. One example of moderate success in the area of planning and land use was the revamping of the Office of Planning and Research, giving it a broader mandate. Local lawmakers were required to consider the environmental impact of state and local programs, and to include conservation and open-space elements in their general plans. The California Environmental Quality Act was passed, strengthening public environmental review. Several boards and commissions were expanded to include environmental members, though the traditional form and dominance by vested economic interests continued. Environmental interests, in this view, were only another special interest that engaged in the same kinds of negotiation and compromise as all the others.

Setting an example for the rest of the country, California lawmakers crafted an unprecedented amount of environmental legislation during Reagan's administration. But the failure of most of these bills illustrates the real balance of power in the state. The proposed state environmental quality control board, for example, was defeated because it infringed on existing state bureaucracies and boards and commissions. Business interests were concerned that such a board would not be sufficiently responsive to their needs. Bills to protect the coastline were defeated in the legislature. This last issue, however, eventually became one of the most successful statewide environmental battles in California's history.

The Coastal Initiative

No discussion of California environmental politics is complete without mention of Proposition 20, the 1972 Coastal Initiative. Citizen struggles over local development proposals to put high-rises, hotels, or houses on beachfront property raged up and down the state. *Cry California,* the magazine of California Tomorrow, featured the coast in several articles. The Sierra Club engaged in a bitter internal dispute over its public stand on the proposed Nipomo nuclear power plant, and this also highlighted the issue of land use along California's coast. The creation of the Bay Area Conservation and Development Commission, the result of strong concern about in-filling of San Francisco Bay, was a precursor to the larger movement slowly developing throughout the state. During the late 1960s, coastline preservation bills were introduced, and the legislature debated the state's role in preserving coastal resources. The issue heated up after two important rulings by the

California Supreme Court: *Gion v. the City of Santa Cruz* and *Dietz v. King.* These decisions established that the old common-law doctrine of implied dedication could be extended from roadways to shoreline and beach use; the public could obtain a permanent right to use private land if it was shown that there had been previous access over a certain period of time (five years). Implied dedication created a public right to the use of private property. Before the rulings, recurrent use of private land by the public to gain access to the coast was presumed to be by license only—a license issued by the local government—and thus not a public right.

These court cases led to a flurry of bills in the legislature aimed at protecting private property rights along the beach and restricting further public access. This legislation directly opposed growing public opinion, but reflected the balance of power in the legislature. Propertied interests favored restricted access and made their opinions known. Oil interests, land developers, and utilities formed a powerful opposition that still had a virtual stranglehold on the state Senate. Governor Reagan, too, opposed coastal protection.

Labor unions, the state Chamber of Commerce, and the California Real Estate Association were all opposed to the coastal initiative. These opponents charged that the initiative would create a severe economic depression in the fifteen coastal counties, as a result of job loss, falling land values, and a drop in local tax revenues. They claimed the initiative was a "power grab" by "elitists" who wanted to take over the coastline for their own purposes.[7] They contended that environmental preservation threatened jobs.

Lack of success in the legislature led environmental groups to create a coalition, the California Coastal Alliance, to save the coast by initiative. The Coastal Alliance had little trouble gathering the necessary signatures to qualify an initiative for the ballot, and even though its funds were only a fraction of the campaign money of the opposition, Proposition 20, the Coastal Initiative, passed with 55 percent of the vote. The 1972 initiative established a Coastal Zone Conservancy Commission as a four-year interim planning agency. Its task was to develop a coastal plan and to regulate all development within 1,000 yards of the shoreline. The plan was prepared "after the most massive citizen-involvement planning program California has ever seen—hundreds of thousands of citizens received newsletters, attended hearings, filled out mail-back questionnaires or heard presentations of alternative plan proposals."[8]

Despite initial citizen involvement, environmentalists had structured a top-down planning process favoring regional or state planning as a more rational level for large-scale land-use planning. This approach only deepened the long-standing enmity between state and local government entities. Local governments resented their obligation to develop local coastal development plans and submit them for approval by the state commission. The commission staff made little effort to develop collaborative relationships with the professional planning community and local planning directors.[9] Local jurisdictions had successfully prevented the state legislature from developing programs to force regional growth management and had effectively blocked programs that would have centralized planning authority at the state level over time. Nonetheless, they were not successful at beating back a popular statewide initiative.

The jobs-versus-the-environment rhetoric that coastal protection inspired proved to be an enduring slogan in the political fights over regulation. Labor interests have traditionally allied themselves with the pro-growth development community, and environmentalists have consistently been labeled elitists. The elitist label is paradoxical in this case, however, since environmentalists were the ones defending beach access for the general public. In the end, the passage of Proposition 20 had none of the adverse impacts the development community predicted. Instead it ensured, for a time at least, that working people could have access to the coast for recreation, and it even made it possible for some to live near the coast, since provision of low-cost housing was required in the legislation.

The Energy Resources Conservation and Development Commission

Another significant piece of environmentally motivated legislation passed while Reagan was still governor. The 1973 oil crisis caught the state off-guard, as it did most of the Western world, and caused people to recognize that petroleum was a resource that required better management. Power companies and other providers were projecting high power-generation needs in the future, based on their estimations of future energy demand. The Reagan-appointed Public Utilities Commission lent a friendly ear to such arguments, as well as to those for higher energy rates. Until the early 1970s the need for steadily increasing power generation for economic growth and continued modernization had been the accepted view. But in 1973 such projections came under close scrutiny, and the voices of nontraditional energy analysts began to be heard. They pointed to energy conservation as a viable alternative to the construction of new power plants, and to the potential of nonpolluting, renewable, alternative forms of energy, such as the wind and sun.

California Assemblyman Warren, along with Senator Alquist and pro-environment legislators, cosponsored the State Energy Resources Conservation and Development Act, which put the state in the business of assessing its own energy needs and developing its own plan for the future. In 1973

Governor Reagan vetoed the bill, bowing to industry pressure. The Public Utilities Commission, the investor-owned utilities, the California Manufacturers Association, and General Electric (a major purveyor of nuclear power plants) all united to oppose the act. The act created a five-member commission in charge of determining the state's long-term energy needs and selecting future power plant sites. The utilities argued that the siting mechanism in the act would be inefficient and time-consuming and that they themselves were far better equipped to determine where power plants should be located and when. But in 1974 state legislators, having experienced gasoline shortages and seen their effect on California, passed the Warren-Alquist State Energy Resources Conservation and Development Act, and this time Governor Reagan did not exercise his veto.[10]

The act outlined the scope of the commission: forecasting, energy resources conservation, power facility and site certification, and research and development. The five commissioners were to be named by the next governor, and each had to fit one of the following criteria:

- background in the field of engineering or physical science and knowledge of energy supply or conversion systems
- member of the State Bar, with administrative law experience
- background and experience in the field of environmental protection or the study of ecosystems
- economist experienced in natural resource management
- member of the public at large.[11]

The act reflected the growing awareness of alternative energy sources, such as solar, geothermal, and wind, and the need for energy conservation. It mandated that the commission come up with prescriptions for minimum standards of operating efficiency for major appliances, as well as energy-conserving standards for lighting, insulation, climate-control systems, and other building requirements. It incorporated a funded research and development program to produce energy forecasts. No longer would the industry alone determine future energy demands or control the design of energy conservation programs.

By the time Governor Jerry Brown was elected, environmental issues were prominent in state politics. The legislature had passed several important bills—the California Environmental Quality Act, the improved Forest Practice Act, the Energy Resources and Development Commission Act, the Wild and Scenic Rivers Protection Act (see chapter 4)—and was acutely aware of public sentiment about environmental protection. Environmentalists had demonstrated their potential political power through the passage of the Coastal Protection Initiative. Although the basic structures of state government remained largely unchanged, the political climate of the early 1970s offered potential for political change and set off another round of attempts to implement alternative visions of living with the land.

Jerry Brown and the Era of Limits

Brown was thirty-six years old when he assumed office, the youngest governor on record; it is fair to say that his experience in politics and as an elected official was limited. He had been secretary of state, and an activist one, supporting the 1972 Political Reform Act and enforcing its provisions—actions that did not endear him to the legislature.

Brown's personal upbringing, preparing for Jesuit priesthood, committed him to the principles of austerity, public service, hard work, and discipline. A latecomer to environmental issues, his personal path made him receptive to many of the new, alternative ideas of the period. *Small Is Beautiful* had a profound effect on his world view, and influenced Brown in developing his "era of limits" concept, by which he meant physical, governmental, and fiscal limits, not limits to human ingenuity and spirit. He recognized the finite capacities of the earth and saw that resources needed to be conserved. Similarly, he argued, there was a limit to the capacity of government to respond to social needs. He was a fiscal conservative and did not believe the solution to problems was to start another program or pass more legislation. He saw society as an entity, with government as just one part of it. His approach emphasized self-reliance and creativity in social relations; he also cast doubt on the state's ability to effectively solve social problems. This was a refreshing approach to politics—full of possibilities and hope. Yet it also had an ominous undercurrent of a profound distrust of government, which would become dominant with the Reagan revolution.

In his campaign Brown promised a "new spirit," with politics based on principles appropriate for the age. His approach was based on three fundamental principles: (1) the inclusion of women and minorities in government, bringing California's diversity into government; (2) the protection of the environment; and (3) the intelligent use of new technologies.

Because of the large number of appointed boards and commissions in the state, as well as judgeships, the governor wields great power through the ability to confer appointments. This power can give the governor leverage with the legislature because appointments can be used as political favors and as a strategy to advance the party or special interests. We have seen how these appointments traditionally served to reinforce the power of special interests, but they could just as well be used to disempower these interests or to circumvent an uncooperative legislature. If the legislature seemed unwilling to cooperate in any specific area, carefully chosen appointees could mitigate the problem.

The power of appointment was a central vehicle for Brown's vision of inclusive state government; he appointed more women and minorities to positions of authority than any governor before or since. This was clearly a strategy on his part to open state government to the citizens, so as to have the government reflect the state's population. It was not so clear, however, that the appointees themselves had a unified political vision and strategy aimed at effecting a certain type of change, or that Governor Brown provided such a vision. It was not enough simply to appoint more women or people of color to boards and commissions; the appointees needed to have a coherent agenda with a vision for change. Further, in key natural resource areas, such as the Board of Forestry, boards and commissions of the Department of Food and Agriculture, or the Fish and Game Commission, Brown's appointees upheld traditional interests, though this time around the interests included environmentalists. In the end, the weight of the past proved overwhelming, and only minimal change took place in the internal dynamics of policymaking in these areas.

A Progressive's Progressive

Brown had campaigned for a new spirit, but he himself remained profoundly ambivalent about government. He believed in its importance for social change, as a means to ameliorate people's lives. Like the Progressives of the turn of the century, he believed that government should actively promote the public good and the general welfare in a nonpartisan manner. He saw a role for government in the balancing of the market and labor. But Brown had little patience with or respect for process and bureaucracies. He did not believe government was a substitute for social structure. Like the Progressives, Brown was an anti-politics politician because he did not see a role for partisanship or party. He campaigned without the support of the Democratic Party, without the support of organized labor. He appealed to all Californians, beyond any party affiliation, much as Governor Warren had in an earlier period. Brown also suffered from a lack of real party support in the legislature, and this was exacerbated by his perception of legislators as obstacles rather than the conduits through which a governor worked to accomplish an agenda.

Brown believed in the power of technical information. His administration relied on the development of scientific evidence as the basis for policy direction and change. Government decision making was approached as a rational process, unbiased and unaffected by power and special interests.

Although Brown was no fool, and he recognized the existence of special interests and especially their strong influence in the legislature, still he approached his own public mandate with the belief that these interests would yield in time to superior information, that he would be able to sway the legislature and business associations by reason and logic based on fact.

This belief in technical information as a guiding force for legislative decision making is strongly embedded in American political ideology. It has sustained the appointment of expert boards and commissions since the turn of the twentieth century and has justified the inclusion of special interests in the shaping of legislation. The belief in the power of technical information is part of the modern era's infatuation with science and rationality, and can be seen as part of the legacy of the Enlightenment.

The ambiguity built into Progressive political reform between special interest and expert knowledge, however, had a warping effect. Knowledge based on vested economic interest cannot be considered objective. There has been a fundamental confusion in this area in the American mind. Intellectuals and experts, detached from practice, are viewed with suspicion in most circles because of a long-standing, anti-intellectual bias in American culture, whose roots are firmly anchored in a "can do" approach. Thus, academic or civil-service experts are discounted because they lack real-world experience balancing budgets or meeting payrolls. The notion of employing technical knowledge as the basis for decision making in public policy is attractive, yet such knowledge is either purchased from or in the employ of particular interests. This creates a profound contradiction and tension about the identity of the expert and the basis of his or her knowledge. Too often expert opinion becomes an argument among hired guns—one side's scientist against the other's. Yet the idea of scientific objectivity based on expertise still provides comfort and insulation from direct political accountability and also obscures the intrinsically political nature of decision making.

In the 1970s the question of scientific expertise as the basis for decision making started to become a significant issue, particularly in the area of environmental protection, because of the different interpretations of what was happening in the environment and why. For example, in the early 1970s scientists at the University of California, Irvine, discovered a hole in the ozone layer at the South Pole and identified the use of chlorinated fluorocarbons as the problem. Industry scientists disputed this finding, and the question of ozone depletion and its effects has been debated ever since.

Brown accepted unquestioningly the Progressive notion of nonpartisan government represented by balanced boards with the proper number of experts who would come up with the most equitable and objective solution to a problem. This attitude was a novelty in state government, since the conventional wisdom, not voiced aloud, was that boards and commissions were a kind of parallel government through which a governor could achieve his policy objectives without legislative or public scrutiny. Brown did not appoint people because they shared his political or philosophical outlook; instead, he chose people who best represented the interest the seat was intended to represent. So, for example, since Board of Forestry appointments required timber interests to be chosen, Brown consulted with the industry, and the same applied to the environmental slots when they were so stipulated. This approach effectively preserved the status quo, often with stalemate and frustration, even though Brown was inspired by other motives in his selection. Brown believed in the process of negotiation among interests and in the creativity brought about by tension, and he held that a balanced outcome would result. Brown's approach to government was certainly more honest than that of his predecessors, but because it lacked direction, consensus, and vision, it failed to accomplish substantive change.

Environmental Politics in the Brown Years

Governor Brown's concern for the environment was placed on an equal footing with other areas of commitment, such as affirmative action. The environment, at least in his rhetoric, was part and parcel of any state governance issue, like economic development and transportation. This was a departure from the past and an acknowledgment that environmentalism had come into its own. More than any other administration, Brown's was concerned with the environmental effects of its actions. He appointed recognized leaders of the California environmental movement to positions of power where they could push the environmental agenda. But each of his other appointees to state offices had the same type of power. And although environmental issues now had the opportunity to compete equally in the policy debate, the result was often a stalemate. Because Governor Brown's relations with the legislature were so poor and because he did not have a defined agenda to pursue, significant environmental legislation was difficult to obtain. Environmental questions were mostly debated at the level of boards and commissions, or else individual legislators took the lead without coordination with the governor, or it was the governor who took the lead without coordination with the legislature.

In January 1975, the same month Brown was inaugurated as governor, Judge Broddus ruled that timber harvest plans (THPs, documents prepared by the timber industry for harvesting trees and then approved by the Forestry Board) were subject to the California Environmental Quality Act and had to include environmental impact reports (EIRs). This was an unintended consequence of the California Environmental Quality Act, and it had business and timber interests up in arms. The Brown administration had been in office all of twenty-one days when the ruling came down, and was entirely unprepared for the resulting outrage.

Claire Dedrick, Brown's secretary of resources, was an outspoken environmentalist who had cut her teeth on open-space preservation in the Bay area and timber protection in the landmark Bayside Timber case. She had also been active in protecting the San Francisco Bay and was a member of the board of the Sierra Club. Dedrick had been recommended to Brown by Tom Graff of the Environmental Defense Fund (Graff was a member of Brown's transition team and an influential environmentalist in state politics). A woman in charge of an agency whose professions had been traditionally filled by men—forestry, fish and game, mines and geology—Dedrick had not yet had time to establish her credentials and leadership ability in this position when Judge Broddus announced his decision.

The California Department of Forestry, as we have seen, historically identified its interests and mission with the timber industry. It was the state's premier fire-fighting agency, in charge of protecting private forest lands, the domain of tough, gruff men. Fish and Game had a different set of allegiances, to fishers and hunters. The Department of Mines and Geology had been founded during the Progressive era to map the state's geological resources in order to aid commercial interests in developing them. The appointment of an environmentalist, a *female* environmentalist, to head the agency must have been a shock to the bureaucrats. The agency's mission had been oriented toward development, not preservation, and even less toward environmental management.

Appointed in January, Dedrick had to act fast since the logging season began in April. She had to find a way to have THPs comply with the environmental impact report requirements, knowing that she ran the risk of alienating all sides. Little was accomplished in the first month, and the governor had to step in. Over a weekend in mid-February, Governor Brown assembled all of the concerned parties: representatives of the timber industry, small operators, owners of small parcels, loggers' union representatives, the Sierra Club, and relevant state government representatives. A compromise was reached, based on the concept of functional equivalent. The functional equivalent would be a more elaborate timber harvest plan, which would then serve as a modified EIR. (The THP was essentially a detailed explanation of private harvest plans for that year for a specific forest, and under the "functional equivalent" agreement, it would have to explain environmental impacts and their mitigation, such as the effects of road building on soil erosion.)

There remained the thorny problem of public review, required by the California Environmental Quality Act. The timber industry and the Department of Forestry were adamantly opposed to any public review of proposed timber harvest plans, fearful that environmentalists would make too many objections and would slow or block projects. The Department of Forestry and the Board of Forestry had never enforced previous public-review requirements, but here they could not skirt the issue. There was very reluctant compliance with the public-review requirement, and public notice of impending THPs remained a contentious issue. Still today the public feels it does not have adequate notice of or access to THPs in most instances, and industry does not like to divulge them.

When the legislature came back into session, it found that the Brown administration had developed the "functional equivalent" alternative by fiat. Members of the Assembly and Senate who had worked on timber issues, such as the Forest Practice Act of 1972, were insulted and angry with the governor and the process. These legislators had also been working on how to apply Judge Broddus's decision and they felt slighted by Brown, who had bypassed them without acknowledging their historic leadership in this area.

In March there was an emotional demonstration as loggers circled the Capitol in their trucks, claiming the compromise would put them out of work and blaming Dedrick for the situation. The Board of Forestry (still dominated by Reagan appointees) and the Department of Forestry also opposed any change, so the administration continued to wage the "functional equivalent" battle on two fronts.

For the industry and its workers, the problem was simply jobs versus trees. The Brown administration, and Dedrick in particular, was seen to care more about preserving trees than about maintaining people's livelihoods and their communities. This was the perception, despite a historic downturn in the industry. In the 1950s approximately half the labor force in Humboldt and Mendocino Counties had been directly involved with logging or associated with wood products. By the mid-1970s this had declined to 25 percent. In Humboldt County jobs in the timber industry had declined from 6,000 to 3,000; in Del Norte, from 3,000 to 1,000.[12] Despite the focus on the northern counties, most of the forest-related industrial employment has been in southern California, along the central coast, and in parts of the Sacramento region, in secondary wood processing and not dependent upon California-grown lumber.[13]

As the state's growing stock decreased, the number of trees cut annually declined. The greatest volume of redwoods had been cut in the 1950s to build the state's rapidly growing suburbs. Private growers had not been replanting systematically. The volume of cut redwood declined 41 percent between 1953 and 1975.[14] The nature of trees had changed as well: they were now smaller. The mills, built to handle the ancient behemoths, could not handle the change in tree size. This meant that the timber industry had to either retool the old mills or export the logs for processing elsewhere. The industry chose the latter alternative, thereby contributing to employment decline as mill after mill was closed. Then as now, timber workers were the ones who bore the brunt of the change, and they blamed government policy and environmentalists for their unemployment.

The environmental community was not happy either. It felt the administration had bungled the handling of the "functional equivalent" issue. At the same time the question of expanding the Redwood National Park re-emerged because of the negative effect of private forest practice on the watersheds surrounding the park, posing potentially serious threats to the trees over time in case of torrential rains. Nothing less than a moratorium on logging around the Redwood National Park area would do, especially in the fragile Redwood Creek Basin.

So once again the preservation of the redwoods was the driving force behind a growing movement to reform private forest practice. The Department of the Interior became involved in negotiations, as it was developing a plan to expand the national park. The department asked the timber companies to voluntarily refrain from cutting in certain key areas of Redwood Creek Basin for eighteen months. The companies refused.[15] At the state level, the Brown administration's approach satisfied no one, and Dedrick's deputy director resigned in protest. Finally, the administration, in conjunction with California Rep. Philip Burton, developed a jobs package for loggers who had been put out of work. This proved the key to federal acquisition of the sensitive watershed around the Redwood National Park, as it was an effort to remediate the problem of unemployment in the region. It did not, however, ameliorate the issue of the "functional equivalent."

Brown had finally made a majority number of appointments to the Forestry Board, including individuals promoted by the timber industry. His environmental appointees represented the mainstream environmental groups. Much to the chagrin of the preservationist groups, Brown's Forestry Board felt legally and morally compelled to approve THPs if they complied with the law. The board approved clear-cutting in the Redwood Creek watershed, despite the delicate negotiations the National Park Service was conducting with the industry to expand Redwood National Park. Environmentalists felt betrayed.

In the end, the watershed was preserved, as the board yielded to environmentalist pressure and instituted a moratorium on THPs for the Redwood Creek region from October to January, when President Carter signed the Redwood National Park expansion bill. But by then the industry had relaxed its opposition to the park expansion, realizing that it would be generously compensated for the lands and that its national image had been seriously tarnished by the publicity generated by the Sierra Club.

The park was expanded, but the question of regulating private forest practice was not settled. Brown's board, though more democratically representative (thanks to Brown's evenhandedness in filling the slots), was inherently disposed toward industry interests because of its structure and its institutional history. Even in its most environmentally friendly period, the board never fundamentally challenged the timber industry's policies and practices. The net result has been the continuing decline of the job base in the timber-dependent counties of the state, including the Douglas fir–producing counties of the Sierra Nevada mountains.

Brown's appointment to the board of a more genuine array of interests mitigated only the most extreme THPs. Further, Brown did not publicly support his secretary of resources and replaced Dedrick shortly after the Redwood National Park expansion was announced. The position was filled by another environmentalist, Huey Johnson, who had been director of the Trust for Public Land, an organization that uses private money to preserve land for permanent open space, which it then either manages or sells at a lower price to a public land agency. This philosophy of public-private partnership appealed to Brown's sense that government had limited resources and capacities, and that the private sector should be brought in as a partner in some undefined capacity. Huey Johnson brought this inclination with him.

The Brown administration ended up as the villain in the state's timber counties. It had essentially acted on its own with no public input, no legislative outreach to take advantage of the knowledge already accumulated in the Senate and Assembly, and most of all, no apparent respect for the dilemmas facing residents. When asked whether the administration could have done more to work with the local population by demonstrating the direct relationship between the cutting practices of the industry and the local economy's decline, Dedrick replied:

> No, and there is no point in trying to get that into their heads, you're talking about Joe six-pack. He's got a wife and five kids and a tractor rig he's got to pay for, and he doesn't know about that kind of thing. You talk to a logger and he'll tell you, and mean it, that he's a conservationist, and that he takes care of wildlife, that he cares about fish, and it's true. But they are not academics. Its silly to expect people to understand things that are way outside their experience.[16]

This attitude was pervasive in the Brown administration and among many of the state's most influential environmental organizations. These elites would identify problems, develop solutions, and attempt to impose them from the top down rather than from the bottom up, by identifying problems and then working with the locally affected communities to develop solutions sensitive to local needs and understandings. In the area of forestry, for example, neither environmentalists nor the Brown administration made concerted efforts to work with the affected timber-dependent communities. The timber resource was disappearing, industry was restructuring, jobs were disappearing. Clearly, here was a problem the state and environmentalists needed to address. They could have developed solutions with local input so there would be local buy-in. But Brown's political strategy was elitist: appoint the best people you can find, provide good ideas, communicate with the press, and things will change, regardless of local conditions or opinions.

The application of the California Environmental Quality Act to THPs and the expansion of Redwood National Park were not the final act in the long drama of preservation of the redwoods. With the park expansion, 4 percent of the original acreage was preserved in the public domain, and 10 percent of the ancient forest remained overall. The struggle to save ancient forests continues today.

Water and Agriculture: The Never-ending Story

The Peripheral Canal

The State Water Project, by the mid-1970s, had not fulfilled its contracts for water deliveries to the Metropolitan Water District (MWD) and to agribusiness interests in the Central Valley. Never mind that the MWD was still selling "excess" water to the Kern County Water Agency because there was more than enough water to meet southern California's urban needs. More water delivery *potential* was desired. As part of the original State Water Plan developed in the 1950s, a peripheral canal was to be built for additional delivery to the State Water Project. The canal would be an unlined ditch 400 feet wide and 30 feet deep, stretching around the Delta for 43 miles, with a carrying capacity of 16.3 million acre-feet of water per year—over 70 percent of the average flow of the Sacramento River.

The major supporters of the Peripheral Canal were the usual cast of characters—large growers in the Central Valley, land developers in southern California, the Metropolitan Water District, and the state's own water bureaucracy. The MWD continued to be concerned about the possibility of future water shortages with continued urban growth in the south, and farmers did not want to have their water use hampered—even though more than 80 percent of the water used in California is applied on crops, including very water-intensive crops, such as alfalfa and cotton.

The state's water bureaucracy had historically promoted water development. Many of the state's top water bureaucrats either had worked in the water development industry or were later recruited by the industry from the state. There was a revolving-door policy and a tight fraternity. When Governor Jerry Brown came into office, he immediately violated this tradition by appointing outsiders to this professional brotherhood. This made the water establishment suspicious about his plans for further water development.

With the Peripheral Canal issue, Brown and his appointees confronted a complex situation. Governor Reagan had avoided building the Peripheral Canal during his term because he was a fiscal conservative and thought it was too expensive, though his own Department of Water Resources continued to plan for its construction. This planning included an environmental impact report on the canal, produced in the last year of the Reagan administration, and the beginning of excavation for the canal a month before the end of Reagan's term. The EIR concluded that the major impact of the canal would be beneficial, though there would be some problems. The Suisun Marsh (part of the Delta), the nation's largest continuous marsh and a major wintering ground on the Pacific flyway, could suffer increased salinity.[17] The canal, the EIR stated, would be the best alternative for obtaining the desired environmental conditions in the San Francisco Bay Delta—the giant wetland area inland from the San Francisco Bay irrigated by the Sacramento River—conditions that were declining rapidly.[18]

The ditch, the first step in excavating for the canal, was lamely defended by state water officials, who argued that the fill material for the I-5 freeway, still under construction, had to come from somewhere. Even if the canal was not built, they claimed, the excavation could be used for fish raising, picnic areas, nature study, or garbage pits. It was clear that the state's water bureaucracy, after years of planning, was not going to give up the Peripheral Canal easily. As one department official said, "We have been working on this for ten years and we foresee no different decision."[19]

But there was also significant opposition to the Peripheral Canal. Among the opponents were Delta residents, especially those in Contra Costa County, whose farms and residences were bearing the brunt of saltwater intrusion. Environmentalists were also adamantly opposed to the project, fearing that it would further degrade the health of the Delta. The canal proposal included no safeguards for the Delta, no assurances that enough fresh water would be delivered to maintain its biological health. The definition of a healthy Delta had not even been established by the state. Further, there was fear that the volume of water to be sent south would be so great that it would require removing the north coast rivers from their wild and scenic status to provide the additional water necessary for the Delta's health.

Environmentalists were also concerned by the refusal of the San Joaquin Valley and southern California interests (in addition to the Reclamation Bureau, the federal agency that had been responsible for building and managing the Central Valley Project) to acknowledge any responsibility for maintaining water quality in the Delta, even though the Central Valley Project diverted water from the Delta.

Governor Brown appointed Ronald Robie to head the Department of Water Resources. Robie was well known to the water agencies and industry as the *éminence grise* of the Porter-Cologne Act of 1969, which had reformed the Water Resources Control Board. Although he and his reforms did not fundamentally threaten the status quo, Robie was viewed with suspicion by the old guard. Stewart Pyle, engineer-manager of the Kern County Water Agency, stated, "With former directors [of] DWR . . . there was direct evidence that they were working in support of the position of the customers-contractors . . . we felt we had our man in Sacramento. Well, we feel that the man in Sacramento is representing others [*sic*] than the contractor's interests."[20] Worse yet, in their eyes, Brown appointed Gerald Meral, staff scientist for the Environmental Defense Fund (whose director Tom Graff had been part of Brown's transition team), as Robie's deputy director. Meral had been very active in water issues, testifying for the need to protect the north coast rivers from development and also against the canal.[21]

Once in office, Robie immediately halted construction of the Peripheral Canal. He ordered the staff to conduct another study of the canal and to redo the controversial Reagan-era EIR. With a governor in office explaining that there were serious problems with continued growth and that the world was entering an era of limits, many expected the Department of Water Resources to come out against pursuing the construction of the canal.

Nine months later, in October 1975, the department issued its new EIR. The report endorsed the canal on the grounds that increased water-delivery capacity was essential if the state was to head off the water shortages predicted for 1984. The new canal proposal claimed that further degradation of the Delta would be averted by a complex series of water-release gates at specific points along the canal. These additional releases would help solve the problems of reverse water flow in the Delta (caused by the State Water Project and Central Valley Project pumping), easing water-quality problems and allowing the Delta fishery to recover. The project would include some extra storage facilities, but no dams on the Eel or other wild rivers of the north coast.

Governor Jerry Brown's Peripheral Canal proposal included something for everyone, much as Pat Brown's State Water Project had. Water quality for the Delta was assured, wild and scenic river protection would satisfy the north coast counties and environmentalists. Environmentalists were also promised the restoration of Delta fisheries and wildlife. More water delivery assuaged large agriculture in the San Joaquin Valley, as well as the Metropolitan Water District in southern California.

So, despite the industry's fears about Brown's atypical appointees and his philosophy of limits, once inside the DWR his men assumed the pro-development mantle of the organization, attempting to fulfill the water-delivery contracts the state had entered into with thirty-one water districts. They did not question the assumptions of growth on which the State Water Project had been predicated and the water contracts developed. There was no discussion regarding the efficiency of water use by agriculture or the choice of crops. But, as opponents pointed out, "in fact, all such contracts have clauses that limit delivery and construction obligations to cases where they are 'physically and financially feasible.' Further, SWP contracts are made in accordance with the 'Governor's Contracting Principles,' which are guidelines only, not statutory requirements. In any event, the contracts have never been tested in court and the state has made no effort to challenge them."[22]

Robie and Meral were not about to challenge over a half-century of water-development policy and practice, or interests such as large-scale agriculture and the MWD. Yet they wanted to protect the Delta and believed the compromise canal would achieve both goals—providing more water and ensuring environmental protection. "Playing no small role in influencing their judgment was the drought that hit California shortly after Brown took office and led to rationing, especially in parts of the hard-hit north, before it ended two years later, with the final year (1977) being the driest on record."[23]

In 1977 Brown publicly announced his support of the compromise canal, with the safeguards as developed by Robie and Meral. He also demanded Washington's equal participation in paying for facilities to maintain Delta water quality, since the Central Valley Project's water diversion had contributed to Delta decline. For the next two years he unsuccessfully lobbied the legislature to include the safeguards in canal bills. When the measure finally passed, it did not meet the needs of the south because the safeguards were considered too strong. The north considered them too weak. Moreover, the Department of the Interior refused to cooperate. The ensuing legislative battle was complex, with shifting alliances and positions. At first, the major environmental organizations—the Sierra Club, Friends of the Earth, and Audubon—came out in favor of the proposal because of its environmental safeguards. But the grass-roots membership of the Sierra Club, who had not been consulted about this endorsement, revolted and called for a membership-wide election on the issue. Club endorsement of the canal proposal was defeated. Little by little, the rest of the environmental community turned against the canal, deciding that the Delta water-quality safeguards were little more than a "paper cage: for water-hungry Southern California which would not stand up to contain the beast when it gets genuinely thirsty."[24]

At first glance it is curious that environmental organizations took so long to oppose the canal. But it illustrates the deep-seated acceptance of the status quo among these organizations. Any improvement is considered better than nothing. Earlier in the century Hetch Hetchy Dam had been supported by conservationists, except for the Sierra Club under Muir's leadership, because it was represented as necessary for the economic development of San Francisco. Only slowly did the major environmental organizations mobilize to oppose major dam-building proposals throughout the West.

Further, Brown's appointees had been recruited from among the environmentalists' ranks, so the organizations assumed that their best interests were being represented. Meral had initially argued against the Peripheral Canal; perhaps his change of mind meant the canal might not be so bad after all. Brown's appointments were, in some instances, the cream of the environmental leadership. But once within the framework of the bureaucracies, these individuals could not maintain their independent stance. The influence of the water-development industry was strong, and its internal justifications made sense once you were on the inside. The environmental movement lost momentum through cooptation, if only for a moment on this issue, perhaps assuming that Brown's appointees would be immune to the prevailing institutional ideology or that Brown himself would be able to withstand pressure from the powerful interests lined up behind further water development.

The Peripheral Canal was the final major piece of the grand water-development plan that so generously subsidizes agriculture in California's Central Valley. Commenting on the original State Water Project, former Governor Pat Brown observed that

> under the federal Reclamation Act, they sell that water for $3.50 an acre-foot, and it costs about $18 to deliver. So there's a $15 an acre-foot subsidy to those big farmers—Southern Pacific, Standard Oil, Kern County Land—and those people just reaped a terrific wealth there from the federal government. Now, under the state project, as it later developed, we charged them for—not the actual cost of the water because the domestic user paid for most of it—but we charged them a much higher price for the water. . . . This [state] project was a God-send to the big landowners of the state of California. It really increased the value of their property tremendously.[25]

The Peripheral Canal was the keystone of this system. It permitted agribusiness to bring more lands under production and to allow further land development for other purposes, like subdivisions. It was the culmination of business as usual, since the construction of the canal had no strings attached regarding water use, such as triggering conservation strategies or requiring the water to be substituted for groundwater. Groundwater pumping continued unabated during this period, using up the water in aquifers more quickly than it was being replenished. It was well known that there were already available technologies for irrigation that were far more water-efficient than the use of open ditches, but since subsidized California water was so inexpensive, farmers had no reason to convert to less water-intensive and more capital-intensive methods. The Peripheral Canal promised more of the same.

After nearly five years of legislative maneuvering, the legislature passed the Peripheral Canal bill in 1980. But this bill did not contain strong environmental safeguards for the Delta. Instead, the legislature chose to allow the voters to decide upon environmental safeguards, through a special ballot initiative, Proposition 8. This was a chancy strategy at best for environmental protection. At the same time, Brown appealed to Cecil Andrus, President Carter's secretary of the interior, to put the north coast rivers under the protection of the federal Wild and Scenic Rivers Act, effectively precluding any development. Andrus did so, setting aside 1,235 miles of rivers.

No sooner had the Peripheral Canal legislation become law than opponents began a referendum drive to repeal it. Eventually the repeal initiative qualified, with more than 800,000 signatures, more than any other voter petition in history. Then, in November, voters approved the legislature's Proposition 8—the Delta safeguards—to the consternation of the California Farm Bureau and the state Chamber of Commerce, which claimed this would be harmful to agriculture. There remained the Peripheral Canal legislation to defeat.

The battle lines over the canal repeal initiative formed quickly. In support of the canal the Metropolitan Water District allied itself with corporate and oil interests in the southern San Joaquin Valley, including Shell Oil, Getty Oil, and the Tejon Ranch Company (of which the *Los Angeles Times* was a large stockholder).[26] But for once, agricultural interests were not united around the issue of water development. The Farm Bureau Federation, along with two of the largest agricultural corporations of the state, J. G. Boswell and the Salyer Land Company, campaigned against the Peripheral Canal. These interests resented the environmental controls that were put in place by Proposition 8 and wanted either a Peripheral Canal with no strings attached or the "Through Canal Alternative." This proposal would have increased the flow of water through the Delta itself (not through another system like the canal), water that would have then been diverted directly by pumping from the Delta. This proposal involved no environmental safeguards.

A bitter and expensive campaign ensued over the canal repeal initiative, in which each side spent nearly a million dollars. Environmental opponents of the canal joined in an unholy alliance with both J. G. Boswell and Salyer Land Company. The canal repeal initiative won overwhelmingly, 62 percent to 38 percent. Support for the project from southern California was soft, voters feeling anxious about its cost. In the northern part of the state the project was overwhelmingly rejected. Of eight counties in the Central Valley, only one (Kern) favored the project, but not by a large majority.

Jerry Brown kept a low profile during the campaign. He had proclaimed his support for a revised Peripheral Canal and had negotiated a canal bill that the legislature had passed. But in the face of tremendous opposition, both from significant players in agribusiness and from the environmental community, he did not actively work for the canal during the repeal initiative campaign. At this time Brown was running for the U.S. Senate. Earlier, in his first term as governor, he had been perceived as friendly to farm workers, having marched with César Chávez and the United Farm Workers and having made appointments to the Agricultural Labor Relations Board who, for the first time, were not entirely anti-labor. But as a candidate for the Senate, he could not afford to further alienate large-scale agriculture. Perhaps this influenced his soft-pedaling stance, even though he had already permanently estranged agricultural interests.

The era-of-limits governor lost sight of the larger questions regarding the course of future development of the state. Rather than a vision of frugal and ingenious use of resources, through conservation and judicious management, business as usual dominated state politics. The opportunity for creative change through forward-looking leadership was lost. Agricultural water conservation would come up again, but not for pro-active reasons.

The Movement for Land Reform: Addressing the 160-Acre Limitation

Concerns about land concentration in California had generated a great deal of political activity at the end of the nineteenth century. The writings of Henry George, which pointed to the anti-democratic dangers inherent in land concentration, and the agrarian populist movement in California were both reactions to the increasing number of large-scale landholdings. The Newlands Reclamation Act had been passed in 1902 with the intent of providing the opportunity for small farmers to establish themselves in the West where water was scarce and its development expensive. In exchange for limiting landholdings to 160 acres (320 for a married couple), and living on the land (a residency requirement that ensured the peopling of the land by small farmers), a farmer could qualify to receive federally subsidized water. Much of this water, however, went to farms larger than the 160(320)-acre size legislated by Congress. Because of the pattern of land settlement in the state, immense corporate farms owned by petroleum companies, real estate syndicates, the Southern Pacific Railroad, and others were the largest beneficiaries of federally subsidized water, and they were benefiting illegally. The Reclamation Act allowed farms larger than 160 acres to receive subsidized water, but required that after ten years the farmers sell their excess land at pre-water prices. For a large owner like Southern Pacific, which owned more than 109,000 acres, this meant quite a large divestiture.

The State Water Project was a way to avoid the federal acreage limitation because the state of California had financed the project. Nevertheless, the state needed to share some of the federal water-conveyance infrastructure, because it was cheaper and more efficient for the state and federal governments to share than for each to build its own infrastructure. The San Luis Dam was one of these facilities. Its construction was included in the federal government's 1949 Central Valley Project plan, and was part of Edmonston's original plan for the Feather River Project in 1951, the backbone of the State Water Project. The state of California paid 55 percent of the construction cost of the facility, and the Bureau of Reclamation paid the rest. Shared facilities raised thorny issues, especially concerning acreage limitations. This issue added an extra layer to the problem of compliance with the law.

As we have seen, over the years the Bureau of Reclamation basically did not enforce either the acreage limitation or the residency requirements for irrigation projects. Large farmers, though, continued their campaign to have the restrictions dropped, fearing the possibility of enforcement at some time. In 1947 the U.S. Senate considered, and defeated, a bill to repeal certain parts of the federal irrigation law, including the residency requirement. Beginning in the mid-1950s a group of small farmers and their supporters in the San Joaquin Valley began organizing and confronting the big landowners, the Bureau of Reclamation, and legislators who supported the evasions of the acreage limitation in the act.

Three areas of California became the focus of the small farmers:

- The west and south sides of the San Joaquin Valley, where a state/federal irrigation project was under legislative consideration (the San Luis Westlands, future site of the San Luis Reservoir)
- The Kings River–Pine Flat district in the San Joaquin Valley, where big landowners were trying to escape the provisions of the Reclamation Act imposed on a project completed in 1954
- The Imperial Valley on the Mexican border, where the Department of the Interior had granted an administrative exemption from the Reclamation Act in 1933.

This movement began to build throughout the West, and similar movements developed in central Arizona around the Central Arizona Project, as well as in Washington around the Columbia Basin Project.

Small farmers were driven by a dream: bringing water to the Westlands of the San Joaquin Valley could provide water to 6,100 farms, bringing the population to 87,500 people: 27,000 farm residents, 30,700 rural nonfarm residents, and 29,800 city dwellers. In the words of Rep. Berni Sisk, who in 1959 was the chief San Luis sponsor, "Why will this land support four times as many people if this project is built? Because it is inevitable and historic that under the impact of reclamation laws, as well as the economics of farm management and operation, these lands will break down into family-size units, each cultivated by individual owners and their families."[27]

In 1959 the small farmers went to Washington, D.C., to oppose the authorization by Congress of the San Luis integrated state-federal project, which Governor Pat Brown had engineered and was pushing through the California state legislature. This joint approach would make it possible for the state to undertake construction of the State Water Project because the Bureau of Reclamation would help financially. The State Water Project consisted of damming the Feather River and pumping water from the Delta that was calculated to result from the dam impoundment. But that pumped water needed storage before it could be distributed to points south. Reservoir storage would permit controlled, year-round flow of the new water. The largest among the projected storage reservoirs, located south of the Delta, was the San Luis Reservoir, and the state needed federal help in building it. Governor Pat Brown and his agribusiness allies were pushing hard for this assistance, specifying that it would be free of the requirements of the 1902 Reclamation Act.

By the time the San Joaquin small farmers and their allies got to Washington, a San Luis authorization bill sponsored by California senators Tom Kuchel and Clair Engle had passed unanimously out of the Senate Interior Committee. The bill contained a clause that would have exempted from the Reclamation Act all waters delivered to a "state service area" (the area served by state-developed water)—that is, the San Luis Westlands reservoir service area. This was just what Pat Brown had wanted. The small farm activists from California reacted by creating an opposition coalition with the National Farmers Union, the National Catholic Rural Life Conference, and the AFL-CIO. Together they obtained appointments with Senators Paul Douglas and Wayne Morse, who agreed to take up the fight. They managed to have the exemption language removed from the bill, after showing who would most benefit from the exemption, given the pattern of existing land-ownership in the Westlands. In 1960 the San Luis Westlands legislation contained no exemptions.

That same year the authorization for the state part of the project was passed by the legislature and narrowly approved by the electorate in California. No exemption language was included in the bill or the ballot measure, and small farmers claimed victory, believing that the reclamation law would apply. The water delivered to the "state service area" would pass through several works, including a reservoir and a long canal, each with a 50 percent federal investment. Additionally, these joint-use facilities were to be built upon earlier federal facilities that had been constructed over a period of twenty-five years.

Facing a tough election campaign against Richard Nixon, Pat Brown needed the support of large-scale agriculture in the state. He appealed to President Kennedy for a state water contract with the federal government that would grant an exemption from the Reclamation Act for the "state service area." Kennedy agreed to the exemption, but only for the Westlands, not for the Imperial Valley or Kings River–Pine Flat areas. This meant that for State Water Project water, even though it was conveyed through state-federal infrastructure, there would be no acreage limits imposed on farmers in the Westlands. This was a partial victory for the forces of large-scale agriculture. But it did not mean the end of the legal obligation of the federal government to enforce acreage limits.

Large landowners, anticipating water deliveries, were buying more land in the Westlands project area. Westlands water deliveries from the Central Valley Project and the State Water project began in 1963, with heavy deliveries starting in 1967. Large landowners requested the water and began signing contracts—contracts in which they agreed that in exchange for subsidized water, in the *federal* part of the project, they would sell their excess land (over 160 acres) within ten years into parcels of 160 acres or less to eligible buyers and at pre-water prices. Both the buyers and the land prices had to be approved by the Bureau of Reclamation.

In the early 1970s, recordable contract sales began to take place. But they were convoluted evasions of the reclamation law. As the small farmers researched the sales from the public records in county and Bureau of Reclamation offices, they realized that the large landowners were not complying with the spirit of the law. In 1974 they organized National Land for People (NLP). In 1975 Senator Nelson, head of the U.S. Senate Small Business Committee, held investigative hearings in Washington. Nelson, while a member of the Senate Interior Committee, had already held hearings in 1964 and 1966 on the San Luis Westlands situation.

In June 1975, just a month before Nelson set his July hearings in Washington, D.C., a federal grand jury returned the first indictment ever under the reclamation law. The probe began after NLP had publicly exposed an illegal sale. After extensive hearings in July, Nelson pledged to hold hearings in Fresno. Support for these hearings came from Governor Jerry Brown, who publicly expressed his concern about the lack of enforcement of the reclamation law, and from Senator Alan Cranston of California.

Both officials called for holding up any new water contracts between the federal government and the Westlands Water District pending the hearings. This was the first time in history that a governor had taken any kind of stand for small farmers in the state and had questioned Bureau of Reclamation policy. Brown's public support for small farmers and his previous support for the United Farm Workers led many people to believe that a new era was on the horizon. For the first time in years, there were grounds to believe that some of the large holdings benefiting illegally from federally subsidized water might be broken up or that the owners would be forced to pay the true costs of the water. Either way, this would mean a fundamental change in California agriculture.

In December 1975 NLP formally asked the Bureau of Reclamation to change the rules by which it approved land sales. The bureau refused. Members of NLP then offered to buy 640 acres of Southern Pacific's excess land in the Westlands. Southern Pacific declined the offer, thereby giving NLP standing in court.

Senator Nelson did come to Fresno in February 1976. He held two days of hearings before an overflow crowd in a college auditorium, and called on the General Accounting Office (GAO) to study the Westlands. In May 1976 NLP sued the Bureau of Reclamation in the Washington, D.C., district court, asking for an order directing the bureau to change its rules and prohibit any further excess land sales until the rules were finally changed. The large Westlands growers intervened as defendants, feeling anxious about the possible outcome of NLP's petition for rule making. NLP used Senator Nelson's GAO report as part of its supporting documentation, along with many other documents showing lack of compliance with the reclamation law. In August the NLP won its suit for rule making. The judge in the case ordered the bureau to report to him monthly on its rule-making progress. Four months later, in January 1977, Jimmy Carter assumed the presidency, and a whole new cast of officials entered the Department of the Interior and the Bureau of Reclamation.

To continue putting pressure on the bureau, in May 1977 NLP again sued the bureau, this time seeking $500,000 in personal damages on behalf of three members of NLP who had tried to buy small parcels of excess land

owned by the Anderson-Clayton Corporation, land that the bureau had allowed to be sold in one block of 4,600 acres.

By August 1977 Secretary of the Interior Cecil Andrus had proposed new
reclamation rules in response to the NLP court order. These rules generally
supported a lottery distribution of excess lands "or any other objective
means," a 50-mile residency requirement (the farmer could live within 50
miles of the land, rather than having to actually live on the land), and farm-
size limitations restricted only by the number of family members. Although
this was a far cry from the reclamation law on the books and was not especially favorable to the small farmer, it would have made it more difficult for
large landholdings in federally subsidized irrigation projects to continue in
operation. There were ninety days of comment and hearings on the proposed rule. Landowners throughout the West were up in arms at the proposed changes. Full-page ads began to appear in big daily newspapers across
the country, placed by the Farm Bureau and others.

By the end of the comment period in November 1977, big money had
inspired strong opposition to any enforcement of the reclamation law, or to
its revision. Large landowners had threatened to push through Congress
bills to repeal or weaken the law. A coalition was organized to retain and
strengthen the law, and at a December 1977 conference 2,500 delegates
unanimously supported water-law proposals put forward by National Land
for People.[28]

The mid-1970s debate regarding enforcement of the 160-acre limitation
was only part of a larger questioning of the course of agriculture nationally
and internationally, and the corporate domination of production—another
aspect of the limits-to-growth movement. It was the beginning of a serious
attempt to develop alternatives to large, corporate, chemical-intensive agriculture, which had been the result of farm policy. This search for alternatives involved questioning the role of federally funded land-grant colleges
that conducted much of the agricultural research leading to more mechanization, and the use of increasingly intensive mixtures of pesticides, herbicides, and chemical fertilizers.

Questioning of university mechanization research entered into political
debates in the California legislature. The Assembly version of the University
of California budget in 1977 required "social impact reports" to be prepared
to assess the effects of labor-displacing research.[29] The United Farm Workers' protests over wages and workplace safety had raised awareness of the
relationship between university research and the structure of agriculture.
Large-scale agriculture, reliant on hired farm labor, had been effective in
lobbying the federal government for special treatment, allowing it to use
lower paid Mexican workers. The United Farm Workers organized to oppose

this policy and to raise farm workers' wages. Such activism spurred corporate interest in the development of machines that would replace farm
laborers.

Hearings were held on the university's role in shaping the structure of
agriculture through its mechanization and crop-related research. The hearings revealed that, for example, university vice chancellor Chester McCorkle
and Edward W. Carter, a member of the board of regents (both officials appointed by the governor), served on the board of directors of Del Monte Corporation, a major beneficiary of mechanization research. William K. Co-
blentz, chairman of the board of regents, was also the managing partner of
ASA Farms, a corporate tomato farm in the Sacramento Valley. Although
large farming interests had retreated from directly donating funds for university research, they had turned to "marketing orders" to generate research funding. Under the California Marketing Act (Progressive-era legislation), growers or processors could join together to form a marketing order
and impose a state tax on a specific agricultural commodity. This revenue
could then be allocated by the Marketing Order Board to cover advertising
(for example, ads promoting the drinking of milk or the eating of eggs or
pork), market surveys, or university research. The University of California
mechanization research budget of 1975–76 obtained 17.6 percent of its
revenues from marketing orders. This kind of close relationship between
corporate agriculture and the university was now being questioned. When
legislative attention was brought to bear on the potential impacts of such
relationships, all sorts of interesting connections came to light. For example, one of the biggest beneficiaries of the university-funded development of
the tomato-harvesting machine was John B. "Jack" Anderson, who farmed
62,000 acres of cannery tomatoes.

The opposition movement, represented by NLP, questioned the economic
efficiency and ecological sustainability of larger and larger farms, pointing
out that even large corporate farms of many thousands of acres often broke
down the management units for many crops into parcels of 160 acres or
less. It questioned the pattern of federal crop subsidies that encouraged
farmers to engage in ecologically harmful practices. It pointed out how the
rules imposed by private and public financing institutions did not allow the
use of more environmentally sound techniques on the basis that these were
unproven and might not yield the crop returns promised by already established techniques. In the 1970s there was a conjunction of activities challenging conventional forms of agriculture and food production, which were
of increasingly larger scale and which relied on chemical inputs, huge
amounts of water, and cheap immigrant labor.

Enforcement of the 160-acre limitations could have brought about profound change by allowing thousands of new farmers to settle the land in a way that would have transformed the settlement patterns of the Central Valley and caused a revolution in agricultural scales and practices.

In January 1978 large landowners filed and won a federal court suit directing Interior Secretary Andrus to make an environmental impact study (EIS) of any new policies before they were finally promulgated. This was seen as a stalling tactic because it was unlikely that the social and environmental impacts of changing the law would be negative. By April 1978 Andrus indicated he was willing to weaken his earlier, revised reclamation proposals before a hearing of the Senate Energy Committee. He proposed that farm size be limited to 960 acres but that landowners be allowed to sell excess land in unlimited amounts to relatives, neighbors, and longtime employees. This would have made it very difficult for small farmers to buy land unless they had inside connections.

One additional element in the struggle over land and water also perverted the intent of federally subsidized water delivery: the way in which some significant water districts were managed. For example, the Westlands Water District had voting by acreage rather than by person—that is, it was property-weighted. Thus the Southern Pacific Railroad, which owned 106,000 acres in the Westlands (part of its land grant for building the railroad, land that it had retained despite the 1902 acreage-limitation requirement), controlled 20 percent of the vote, since its holdings represented nearly 20 percent of the district.[30] Not all water districts in California operated on this principle, but to the extent that they did, they signified a dramatic departure from "one person, one vote" democratic processes. Large property owners were in a position to virtually dictate water district policy, because they controlled most of the votes. Small property owners had little say.

In recent times there has been a tendency for new districts throughout the state to be property-weighted, especially those in urban counties where population concentration is highest. Property-weighted irrigation districts mean that large property owners set the irrigation policy for the district, even though they may be in the numerical minority. Most water districts have the power to assess property taxes or fees, to exercise eminent domain, to enter into contracts, to construct project works, to issue bonds, and to charge for services. Local Agency Formation Commissions (LAFCOs; see chapter 4) are the agencies in charge of reviewing and approving or disapproving water districts and their organization, of which there are seventeen classes established by state legislation. In property-weighted districts, elections are infrequent and voter turnout is low. Further, owners of small holdings are likely to find it difficult or even impossible to appeal the decisions of a governing board. For tenants and renters, there is no recourse whatsoever. At times, the control of public government—in this case the water district—by private organizations may be complete, recreating the conditions of the franchise state in yet another arena.[31]

By 1982 Ronald Reagan had become president, and James Watt was secretary of the interior. No major legislation had reformed reclamation law under President Carter, and Secretary Andrus had weakened his positions. The EIS he had ordered was released just days before he left office, confirming that there would be greater economic development and more widely spread benefits if conditions encouraged small farms rather than big agriculture. But also by 1982 large agriculture had caught up on NLP's initial lead and was successfully exerting its influence in Congress. The mood of the country had turned more conservative, and corporate agriculture once again found favorable legislative terrain. Two bills were passed in 1982 that legitimated the Bureau of Reclamation's past violations of the 1902 law. SB 1867 and HR 5539 essentially did the following:

- Abolished residency
- Contained no mandated lottery that would have given outsiders access to land purchase, and set no acreage limitation
- Did not impose real, full costs for the use of irrigated water (Westlands irrigators have paid $7.50 an acre-foot when the actual cost was closer to $200 an acre-foot)
- Exempted about 2 million additional acres that received Army Corps of Engineers project water in the San Joaquin Valley, owned by such large landholders as J. G. Boswell (185,000 acres), Tenneco (125,000 acres), Superior Oil (35,000 acres), Getty Oil (30,000 acres), and Standard Oil (30,000 acres)
- Exempted church land from any regulation, benefiting the Mormon Church with 15,000–40,000 acres of federally irrigated land
- Exempted trusts, a device used by large landholders.[32]

Since the mid-1970s Westlands has delivered an average of 1.23 million acre-feet of State Water Project water a year to 580 farmers. By 1987 growers used 566,844 acres of land to produce crops valued at $652.7 million, subsidized by $27 million in irrigation, $11 million of which benefited the Southern Pacific Land Company.[33]

Included in the exemptions were two other areas: the Kings River–Pine Flat project, and the vast Imperial Valley. The Kings River–Pine Flat area (1 million acres) was dominated by small farms, in many cases averaging less than 100 acres. But 300,000 acres was held in ownerships larger than 160 acres; this included 90,000 acres owned by Boswell, 60,000 owned by Salyer, 13,000 by Standard Oil, 27,000 by Bangor Punta, and 4,000 by Getty Oil. In addition, each of these owners except Salyer also owned huge tracts in other federally subsidized projects.

In the Imperial Valley the tale of large farmers dominating the landscape and the politics of water continued. Irrigation waters for the Imperial Valley, in the southeast corner of California (desert lands), came from the Bureau of Reclamation dam on the Colorado River, the Boulder Dam. With the federal construction of the All-American Canal, water deliveries to the Imperial Valley began in 1942. By the mid-1970s, 61.4 percent of Imperial Valley acreage was farmed in operations larger than 1,280 acres. The valley's largest farmer was the Elmore family, which held more than 15,795 acres in 1977. Other large Imperial Valley operations included Castle & Cooke with 3,396 acres and United Brands with 6,000 acres. Southern Pacific owned about 4,000 acres in the Imperial Valley, and the Irvine Ranch Company (big Orange County landowners) about 5,000 acres. Southern Pacific Railroad, the Irvine Ranch Company, and the Holly Sugar Company (processors of Imperial Valley sugar beets) were the largest contributors to Imperial Resources Associated, the group that pressured Congress to exempt the Imperial Valley from acreage limitations. The promise of federal water deliveries attracted great sums of investment capital from Los Angeles, San Francisco, and elsewhere. Many of these investors also held vast acreages in the Central Valley.

With all this investment at stake, large-scale agriculture had a lot to lose from the enforcement of the acreage limitations. The strongly intertwined rural-urban investment structure in the state reinforced large-scale agriculture's ability to influence policy because of its economic presence in several forums: land development, transportation (oil interests and rail), publishing (Chandler family interests), banking and securities, and others. Southern Pacific, for example, was a major urban real estate holder and developer of industrial parks. It owned the world's largest coal slurry (Black Mesa), piping coal from Navajo land. In 1979 Southern Pacific's president sat on the board of directors of Tenneco, and until early 1978 a member of Southern Pacific's executive committee sat on the executive committee of Safeway.[34]

The sociological profile of the Imperial Valley mirrors that of the Central Valley in terms of large average farm size and corporate domination of landholdings—as well as one of the highest poverty rates in the nation. As Walter Goldschmidt's 1947 analysis and more recent studies conducted in the 1970s have pointed out, increasing farm size and industrialization are antithetical to organized rural community life. As farm size increases, median income decreases, even though employment rises. Unemployment is negatively associated with both farm size and mechanization—that is, large industrial farms need less labor and are employers of unskilled workers at low wages. Increased mechanization of farm work only exacerbates the situation as work becomes more piecemeal and simplified, just as it does on an assembly line. Further, this means that job training cannot be the answer to the wage and employment problems in these areas, because the industrial agricultural system requires low-wage, low-skill labor in order to remain competitive. The most mechanized agricultural counties have the most persistent poverty. Beyond widespread poverty, there are also low education levels. The per-capita income in the Westlands is among the lowest in California. The incidence of poverty ranges between 21.5 percent and 28.9 percent, and among Mexican Americans, the ratio in the Westlands ranges from 24.6 percent to 28.9 percent. The 1990 census revealed that in California the five towns with the lowest per-capita annual income were located in Fresno County.[35] The industrial agriculture system produces a bipolar society of rich and poor.

In the early 1980s, with Ronald Reagan in the White House and Jerry Brown ending his second term as governor, a chapter in California history had closed. The struggle against large-scale land ownership and control in the rural portions of the state was over. Perhaps, as the National Land for People advocates stated, the battle was lost because it was "against the warp of our time. We did not have a sufficiently large living constituency for the small farm policies."[36] But also the general political climate had changed. Jerry Brown had been elected on a platform of the "era of limits" and a new vision of possibilities to bring the state into a more open, more environmentally sensitive way of doing business, ripe with the promise of greater empowerment, a more human scale, and democratic participation. President Reagan was elected on a platform of reforming government by dramatically reducing its capacities, to the point of making it incapable of intervention. Thus Reagan's revolution was also an era of limits, but one bereft of possibilities, especially for those who were not rich. Reagan put his faith in the ability of large-scale business to lead the country, rather than relying on democratically elected representatives or even Jerry Brown's self-reliant communities.

The Revolt of the Middle Class

Ronald Reagan's campaign for the presidency rode the crest of the taxpayers' revolt against local and state governments. To many taxpayers, local and state governments seemed unwilling or unable to act in the face of a real crisis—rising property taxes that squeezed low- and middle-income homeowners. The increase was due to the tremendous inflation of land prices in the state; state law required houses to be assessed at 25 percent of the current market price.

> Throughout the suburbs of California, homeowners associations and other com-
> munity groups created a property tax revolt—a consumerist movement to reduce
> housing costs. In middle-income communities, protesters sought to lower the
> taxes on their own homes, not the taxes on office buildings, stores or industries.
> Some activists favored measures that would particularly benefit low-income
> homeowners who could not afford to pay their tax bills. Others turned their
> populist fervor against big business as well as big government, arguing that oil
> companies should be taxed to provide property tax relief for homeowners.[37]

The problem of increasing property tax rates was connected to the continued frenetic pace of growth and land development and transformation,
yielding ever greater profits as land prices and values continued to climb.
Mini-malls and high-rise office buildings went up in the affluent, desirable
parts of the city, while expansion continued on the urban fringe, bringing
increased traffic congestion to both.

Property Taxes and Proposition 13

The result of taxpayer anger was Proposition 13, a ballot initiative aimed at
reducing property taxes. But in the period between grass-roots mobilization
and the actual formulation of ballot language, the movement was hijacked
by pro-business think tanks that formulated the initiative in such a way that
two-thirds of the benefits went to business owners and only one-third to
homeowners. According to Clarence Lo, who studied the property tax revolt
movement, this development had some support from homeowners, as well
as from anti-business activists. The pro-business program was enthusiastically embraced by those who "heretofore trusted Ralph Nader to fight for
their interests as consumers and rights as citizens." Lo explains that "California homeowners built a movement with a pro-business program as they
waged a decades-long fight against unresponsive big government. . . . For
some, experiences in city hall were yet another kick that they had come to
expect from institutions that supervised them and ruled them. Others were
awakened from their complacent expectations that government had been
created to serve the public."[38] In other words, people did not trust government to do the job. Jerry Brown, for example, had talked about the need for
property tax relief, but had done nothing, just like his fellow politicians in
the legislature. For all of Brown's talk about making government more responsive, he ran his administration in a top-down manner, never attempting to disguise his well-known disdain of process and bureaucracy. Reagan's
great breakthrough, as president, was to give voice to this tremendous sen-

timent of dissatisfaction with government—a government that Brown and his administration had not been able to change in California.

The mastermind of Proposition 13 was Howard Jarvis, who seemed to be a radical anti-establishment leader. He attacked tax-exempt foundations and trusts, and proposed taxes on oil corporations and insurance company headquarters. He championed the cause of the small property owner caught in the squeeze of rising taxes. But Jarvis had spent his life as a business owner and conservative Republican, not a populist. In 1972 he became the executive director of the Apartment House Association of Los Angeles County, and in that capacity he engaged in political activity, including lobbying the state legislature against rent control. He believed that cutting property taxes would produce a building boom and spur business growth throughout California. He claimed the state was losing dozens of companies and thousands of jobs every year because business taxes were too high.[39] The property tax was one of the main problems, he felt. Because he worked with the Apartment House Association and had been active in the Republican Party, Jarvis was in a unique position to bring the small business community and homeowners together.

California had a very efficient system of property tax collection, especially for residential property. In part, this was an artifact of the system of property tax evaluation. The residential sector was assessed by computerized mass appraisal. In the case of retail stores and industrial plants and equipment, assessed value could not be determined in such a mechanical manner, because property sold less often than did homes. Business property was assessed by an appraiser's estimate and calculated manually, taking into account the cost of construction minus depreciation, benchmark land values, and the net income produced by the property. These assessment figures relied heavily on human judgment. The net result was that residential properties bore the greatest burden of assessment increases. Throughout California, net assessed value between fiscal 1975 and 1978 increased 111 percent for owner-occupied homes; the increase was only 26 percent for commercial, industrial, and agricultural businesses. The year before Proposition 13 passed, valuations on homes increased by 20 percent, while valuations of other types of property increased by 10.5 percent.

Throughout the United States, the property tax situation mirrored what was happening in California. Homeowners paid the largest increases in property tax bills, while the business share of the property tax burden nationally fell from 45.1 percent in 1957 to 34.0 percent in 1977. Not surprisingly, more and more of the public began to express their distress at paying increasingly high property taxes.

Opposition to property taxes was not new to California. In 1962 Philip

Watson, who wanted to become assessor of Los Angeles County, had run on a platform of lowering property taxes. He was backed by a group of shopping center owners and was greeted enthusiastically at local chambers of commerce throughout the county, as well as by homeowners. Watson tried to persuade the state legislature to place a referendum for a 2 percent property tax rate on the ballot that same year, but without success. In 1968 Jarvis put an initiative on the ballot to abolish the property tax. In 1972 Watson was back with another initiative for property tax reduction. He was supported by real estate boards, the California Farm Bureau Federation, and others. His campaign director was James Udall, who had served as president of the National Association of Real Estate Boards and also as the head of the Apartment Association of Los Angeles County.[40] Although all these efforts failed, they were a sign of a growing and persistent movement among small business interests to reduce property taxes. This momentum, combined with Jarvis's appeal to homeowners and the huge increases in property taxes in the mid-1970s, made Proposition 13 successful when the other efforts had failed.

The Unresponsiveness of Local Government

According to Lo's analysis, a second important factor in the property tax revolt movement was the general unresponsiveness of local city and county government to the problems of ordinary citizens.

> This was the tragic flaw of the progressive reformers in California and elsewhere who sought to do good, better than the political machine. At least the machine precinct captain was always arranging special benefits, trying to respond to the grievances of ordinary citizens. In fact, partisan machines arose not in Europe but in the United States, one of the few nations where many persons (most white men) had political rights early in the nineteenth century. Under the machine system, an alderman could fix a tax bill if a citizen could not afford to pay.[41]

But under the Progressive reforms tax collection, as well as many other governmental services, became models of impartial administration, and the fragmentation of local governments into many different entities was justified as decentralized democratic control, enhancing efficiency. In effect, the city "is in no way ruled by the people. . . . Political leaders, regardless of whether they were cohesive or divided, had great powers over citizens, including the power to shape preferences and define the alternatives on the public agenda."[42] In middle-income communities, protest movements were ignored by county government, by big city government, and even by the town governments. The five supervisors in Los Angeles County, for example, each represent over 1 million people, far more than a congressional district.

The fact that these representatives are often at odds with each other does not mean that they are responsive to regular citizens. These institutions, which the Progressives had sanitized of politics—parties and machines— were now completely unresponsive to the general public. Poor people were already familiar with this attitude, which had led to their almost complete political apathy and withdrawal. Successful small businesses in a community, however, had a very different experience. Those involved with property development—the motor of local government finance—historically had a very close relationship with local government, since they were intimately involved in zoning and development issues in the community, and generally provided important campaign contributions.[43] But even they were not able to influence a property tax reduction. Their power was limited by the higher levels of government, the county and the state, which possessed the authority to assess property tax rates.

The powerlessness of local citizens was, ironically, a direct result of traditional American values of liberty, individualism, suspicion of big government, and hostility toward power. The American system of checks and balances, the desire to eviscerate political parties because they were seen as corrupt, the professionalization of the administration, and the application of business principles of efficiency and expertise all had an unanticipated consequence as well: lack of responsiveness and accountability. From the moment the task of the political realm became achieving efficiency and having local and state government work to create favorable economic conditions, the concerns of the public sphere were reduced. The government no longer served to improve the quality of life of its citizens, so it became unresponsive and inaccessible. The multiplication of special districts, the process of checks and balances, and the corporatist model of government all contributed to the powerlessness of ordinary people.

The Unresponsiveness of State Government

Californians paid high taxes and received good services. Homeowners expected them. "Even as they railed against big government and called for slashing the property tax," homeowners kept up their appetite for improved services.[44] They wanted increases in spending for mental health, police, fire protection, prisons, schools, and transportation. Under Pat Brown's governorship, the state had entered a golden age—good freeways, good schools (and virtually free university education), and elaborate water-transport systems. Brown had built a top-notch infrastructure, but it cost money to build and maintain. Property owners bore the brunt of this expense, and because of the system of taxation, taxes went up with inflation.

There was pressure on the state legislature to change tax laws. In 1976 the Sherman Oaks Homeowners Association gathered a quarter-million letters calling for a special session of the legislature to enact tax reform. Fifteen tons of letters were delivered to Governor Jerry Brown. He met with the protesters for thirty-five minutes and established a task force to study tax reform, but did not call a special session. A year went by, the legislature continued to be deadlocked over tax relief bills, then it recessed. This stalemate continued in 1977, and Governor Jerry Brown, though publicly acknowledging the problems that high property taxes were causing for property owners, did not do much to advance a solution. Thus, for many who saw no other solution on the horizon, Howard Jarvis appeared to have the answer.

Proposition 13 reduced property taxes for all types of property, not only for owner-occupied residences, but also for apartments and businesses, whose taxes had increased less sharply. Between 1978 and 1983 taxes were reduced by about $41 billion. Homeowners received only about 36 percent of the reduction. Landowners, farmers, and the owners of commercial and industrial property received most of the savings. Southern California Edison, for example, saved $54 million in 1979; Chevron, also an owner of substantial amounts of farmland in the Central Valley, saved $47 million. Four years after the passage of Proposition 13, homeowners were paying an even greater share of the property tax burden than before. In short, business property owners received the most benefits from Proposition 13. But what alternative was there for homeowners? They were faced with unresponsive local and state governments and taxes that went up along with the ever increasing prices of housing. The economic boom of the 1970s drove up property values but created great hardship for those with fixed or low incomes.

The effect of Proposition 13 was to drastically reduce local revenues, forcing local governments into greater reliance on the state. For a few years after the passage of Proposition 13, the economy was doing well, and the state supplemented local budgets out of its own funds. But the overall result was belt tightening at the local level, a gradual erosion of services, and a greater centralization of control at the state level as the state began to fill the shoes of local government. The federal government's withdrawal from many projects was also having an impact. President Nixon had permanently reduced funding for projects in big cities, such as Los Angeles and San Francisco, and the trend continued under Carter and accelerated under Reagan. But the real effects were felt later, during the governorships of Deukmejian and ·especially Wilson, as the general state of the economy began to falter and the state government began to divert local taxes to itself.

Metropolitan Politics

The major urban areas of the state were caught between the expensive and detrimental effects of growth, and the revolt of the homeowners. Suburban flight continued, fueled by the rise in housing prices in established urban areas. New houses at the far-flung suburban fringe continued to be cheaper because of lower land costs and other long-standing subsidies. The state's metropolises continued to expand. In Los Angeles, this meant further movement toward the east. San Francisco experienced substantial downtown redevelopment, led by business. The greater Bay area experienced continued suburbanization of the area just outside the ring of mountains surrounding the established communities—Walnut Creek, Livermore, Vallejo, Petaluma. In these places, the forces of growth control had tried to exert a moderating influence, but the surrounding unincorporated county areas were only too happy to accommodate the growth the old small towns were trying to contain.

San Francisco

The year 1975 was a turning point in San Francisco politics. A coalition of groups challenged the previous regime's advocacy of redevelopment and growth, questioning the removal of low-cost housing and light industry to make room for office buildings and high-end housing. The San Francisco Planning and Urban Renewal Association, made up of the city's most powerful business leaders, labor unions, municipal authorities, and newspaper owners, had acquired as much downtown land as it could. It cleared away whole sections of the city to make room for major projects, such as the Golden Gateway and Yerba Buena Center. It created the conditions for San Francisco's boom in high-rise office construction. From 1965 to 1985, San Francisco's supply of downtown office space grew from 26 million square feet to more than 60 million, an annual growth rate of more than 1.4 million square feet per year.[45] This growth was not unopposed, but opposition grew slowly. It was not until 1975 that effects of such laissez-faire development turned neighborhoods, community organizations, and the middle class against the pro-growth politicians. George Moscone was elected mayor, and voters reformed the city charter so that supervisors would be elected by district (in San Francisco the city and county are the same).

Moscone was a passionate liberal (elected the same year as Jerry Brown) supported by minority groups, community organizations, public employees, the increasingly influential gay community, and liberal activists. During his campaign he accepted no donations over $100. Once elected, he appointed a transition commission to recruit people from the gay and minority communities and from the neighborhoods for slots on the city's boards and agencies. He appointed slow-growth leaders to the Planning Commission and the Redevelopment Agency. Although he was largely thwarted by the more conservative board of supervisors, he did manage to open up city government to a greater extent than any of his predecessors had.

During the same period, the newly instituted district elections placed Harvey Milk, a gay candidate, on the board of supervisors. Moscone and Milk represented a distinct political change in San Francisco, and this was not welcomed by all. In November 1978 Moscone and Milk were assassinated by Dan White, who was white, conservative, working class, and a former police officer. The trial divided the city. White was esteemed to be a hero by some, including the police and firefighters, who raised over $100,000 for his defense fund. The jury found White guilty of voluntary manslaughter, and he was sentenced to seven years and eight months in jail. He was paroled in 1984 and later committed suicide.

The Milk-Moscone murders shattered the reform movement. Board of supervisors president Dianne Feinstein was Moscone's successor, and she was markedly more conservative. Feinstein led the way to the restoration of the at-large supervisoral election system, reinstated a conservative majority, and expedited the construction of high-rises by developers. The promise of change toward a more community-oriented politics representing neighborhoods and people was destroyed. Once again, local government was allied with pro-development and business growth interests. Nevertheless, the ideas put forward by the slow-growth coalition—about community, human scale, democratic accountability, and inclusiveness—had made some inroads.

The Bay area was host to another level of organizing around issues of scale, density, and development. Starting in the Progressive era, plans to better integrate and coordinate the land uses around the Bay had been suggested by the elite, but had met with little success because individual towns and cities were unwilling to relinquish local control. Still, the idea of a coherent urban whole, surrounded by parks, held appeal. Starting in 1958, a group called People for Open Space (POS) was active in the Bay area, putting forward a plan to preserve a ring of parklands all around the Bay as a green belt, a form of growth control using preserved open space to define urban limits. The idea began when the East Bay Municipal Utility District (EBMUD) placed 6,500 acres of San Pablo Reservoir watershed lands on the market. A coalition of groups persuaded EBMUD to refrain from selling the lands, the first step in the envisioned ring around the Bay. POS was active in developing open-space preservation plans throughout the Bay area. In 1969 POS published "The Case for Open Space," financed by a grant from the Ford Foundation.

In the late 1970s and early 1980s, groups like POS, following in the footsteps of California Tomorrow, developed visionary proposals to balance housing and open space, adapting to the necessity of providing affordable housing, while attempting to contain sprawl and reform wasteful building practices. The ideas of appropriate technology, energy conservation, and the era of limits were expressed in POS proposals for compact, city-centered development that would meet the region's housing needs within existing and committed urban land uses by reusing abandoned industrial lands, increasing densities, and encouraging mixed use. Developments emphasizing public transportation were part of these proposals, and groups like POS worked to show how affordable such a new development approach would be compared to conventional land-use development. These proposals attracted a great deal of attention and excited people's imagination. In some ways, the work that POS undertook was exactly what the regional planning agencies, the COGs, had been established to do, but were unable to achieve because of their weak structure, lack of power, and inability to overcome interjurisdictional rivalries. The ideas of regional planning and coordination, the preservation of open space, and the densification of existing urban areas to increase transportation efficiency and encourage better communities aroused enthusiasm, but died on the political vine. Once again, local and state governments proved unwilling to respond. They were structurally entrenched in a growth formula in which local development interests underwrote city government, and city and county governments were engaged in a competitive bidding war to maintain that growth by offering the best deals possible. This was the case despite the public's apparent disenchantment with the status quo and the continuing success of slow-growth initiatives at the ballot box.

Los Angeles

The Los Angeles area in the 1970s was characterized by continued sprawl and decentralized growth. The four counties of Orange, San Bernardino, Riverside, and Ventura collectively averaged a 40 percent increase in population during the 1970s and experienced an even higher rate of employment growth.[46] Los Angeles itself was dominated by a multiracial booster coalition headed by Thomas Bradley, a black ex-police officer and councilman who became mayor in 1973. The Bradley regime drew support over the years from some of the area's largest corporate interests, such as Bank of America, the Irvine Ranch, and ARCO, which participated in enlarging the Community Redevelopment Association (CRA) mandate to encompass all of downtown.

Alternative vision for a city of the future, 1976. (Courtesy of Tom Bender, former editor, *Rain* magazine, Portland, Ore.)

New arenas for commercial developers opened as downtown lands were declared available for redevelopment. As Mike Davis explains, through the mechanism of "tax increment financing" the CRA was able to take the tax increase resulting from new development and use it to subsidize further development. Downtown redevelopers obtained special low-interest loans, free infrastructure modernization, tax abatements, and discounted prime land. "The CRA . . . quietly municipalized land speculation." Almost $2.5 billion of new investment flowed into downtown in the decade after Bradley's election.[47]

Efforts to resist redevelopment surfaced. In the area known as Pico Union, the oldest and densest Central American neighborhood in the city, located west of the downtown convention center, CRA plans were largely defeated—one of the few victories against the CRA. However, the success came at a cost, since neglect by the city created a run-down and poorly serviced neighborhood. The net result of the CRA growth coalition that elected Bradley

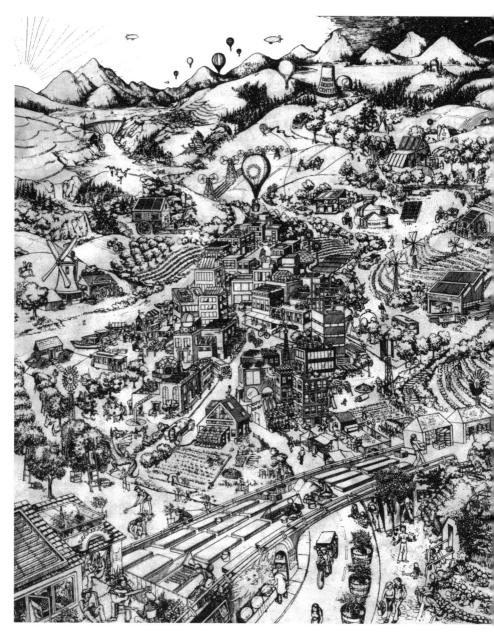

Alternative vision for city and country of the future, 1976. (Courtesy of Tom Bender, former editor, *Rain* magazine, Portland, Ore.)

mayor three times is a high-rise downtown surrounded by poor and decaying neighborhoods, continued white flight to the suburbs, a tremendous undersupply of low-cost housing, and a poorly maintained infrastructure.

During the 1970s Los Angeles and its region experienced a profound demographic change. The population continued to grow and expand farther into the hinterlands surrounding the city and county, due to lower land costs. At the same time the population's ethnic profile changed dramatically from predominantly white to predominantly Latino. This was a result of a high rate of birth among Latinos and an upsurge in migration from Mexico and Central America. Between 1969 and 1985 the number of poor Latinos in Los Angeles increased by more than half a million. The availability of this Latino work force, combined with the reorganization of industrial manufacturing away from large factories employing skilled, unionized blue-collar workers, created a very different economic base for the Los Angeles region. The consequences of these changes were dramatic when combined with the decline in government revenues due to the passage of Proposition 13.

Los Angeles entered the arena of environmental preservation in the early 1960s, when its west side residents engaged in a historic struggle to save the Santa Monica Mountains from development. As early as 1962 an 11,000-acre development at the western edge of Los Angeles in Mandeville Canyon was proposed and defeated. In 1964 a proposal for a 16,000-acre Santa Monica Mountains State Park was put forward. Topanga State Park was purchased by the state in the 1960s, but pressure for development continued. The group Friends of the Santa Monica Mountains was founded by such confirmed foothill dwellers as Mr. and Mrs. Burt Lancaster, James Garner, and Steve McQueen. They set as their goal a 20,000-acre mountain park and recruited 11,000 dues-paying members. Their initial idea was a state park with the 50-mile-long Mulholland Parkway linking a chain of parks and a network of riding and hiking trails.[48] A proposed freeway through Malibu Canyon was defeated in 1970, and finally in 1972, under Governor Reagan, a commission was put together to study the Santa Monica Mountain zone. The commission recommended careful consideration of the natural resources and the development of mechanisms to conserve them. Hearings on preserving the mountains were held in Los Angeles in the 1970s by senators Henry Jackson and Bennett Johnson.

The activists who wanted the mountains protected were well-to-do and well connected. The Santa Monica Mountain Comprehensive Planning Commission, formed in 1977, was empowered to prepare a "comprehensive and specific plan which is capable of implementation for the conservation and development of the mountains, consistent with the preservation of the resource." Finally, in 1978, after sixteen years of struggle, the Santa Monica

Mountains were designated a national recreation area, but the designation was only partially funded and lacked the power of eminent domain. The recreation area could grow only as land was purchased and was thus dependent on yearly budget allocations by the federal government. Meanwhile, the land within the designated boundaries continued to be controlled by local jurisdictions, including the city of Los Angeles, the county of Los Angeles, and Ventura County. Each of these entities continued to be susceptible to developers' plans for the lands designated as future parts of the recreation area, and development continued. Activists fought every proposal, development by development, canyon by canyon. They were motivated partly by property value concerns, partly by environmental and scenic values. Such has been the history of growth control and land-use management in southern California, faced with the tremendous influence of the development community, which has, by and large, been in partnership with local elected officials.

The Los Angeles region benefited very early on from the federal set-aside of the major mountains that surround the basin. But after the 1920s preservation efforts encountered more and more difficulties. Attempts by the Los Angeles County Planning Commission in the 1920s to establish a metropolitan vision of planning were overrun by the rapid pace and large scale of development, and pro-growth politics came to dominate decision making. Still, environmental activists managed to slow development of the Santa Monica Mountains in the 1970s and 1980s, and air and water quality became important issues for environmental groups in the basin that organized to intervene, at times successfully.

An Urban Strategy for California

Like his father, Jerry Brown was not insensitive to concerns over the pace and direction of urban growth. In early 1978, the same year Proposition 13 was passed by the voters, the Governor's Office of Planning and Research published "An Urban Strategy for California." The document stated that "the Urban Strategy is based on one overriding principle: government alone cannot solve our urban problems. The future pace of the state's economy and its physical environment depend on cooperation between public agencies and private enterprise."[49] It outlined the following priorities: (1) to renew and maintain existing urban areas; (2) to develop vacant and underutilized land within existing urban and suburban areas already serviced by basic infrastructure; (3) when urban development was necessary, to first develop land adjacent to already developed land.

Within the Urban Strategy, there was an urban action program to improve existing housing and social and economic conditions, and resolve in-

Pacific Palisades from Sunset Blvd. to Santa Monica Canyon, Los Angeles, 1970. (Photograph by Spence; courtesy of Air Photo Archives, Dept. of Geography, University of California, Los Angeles)

terjurisdictional conflicts. For example, the strategy proposed a speculative gains tax, which was aimed at dampening the inflationary effect of speculation in housing. This proposal was attacked as communistic, but it could have done a lot to slow the rate of inflation in housing costs that characterized the late 1970s and the 1980s. There were other important suggestions regarding the construction of low- and moderate-income housing, encouragement of industrial and commercial rehabilitation, and encouragement of energy efficiency through land-use planning, building code modifications, and subdivision ordinances. Property and sales tax sharing was proposed, as well as tax reform, but it seemed as though the proposals came too late in the administration, for they were by and large ignored. Soon thereafter Proposition 13 passed—a seemingly much simpler, more direct approach to the issues of high property taxation and the unresponsiveness of government.

The Enduring Legacy of Progressive Reforms

The 1970s started with a tremendous explosion of ideas and possibilities. The oil crisis of 1973 increased awareness of the planet's finite natural resources and the long-term dangers of environmental degradation. An atmosphere developed in which there could be a reconsideration of industrial and consumerist society. There were proposals for a new direction based on an era of limits, the possibilities of the imagination, and creative new approaches for humans to live on the planet. There was widespread interest in change, in meeting the challenges. Grass-roots movements to protect environmental resources had an influence, contributing to the expansion of Redwood National Park, the protection of the California coast, the slowing of urban growth, and the preservation of agricultural lands in some counties of the state. But these movements, though successful at the margins, faced structural obstacles in their attempts to implement an alternative vision. Progressive-era reformers, intending to clean up government and make it more efficient and less corrupt, had put in place a government that was less responsive to its citizenry. The special districts for urban services, managed by boards and commissions, became shadow governments, out of view and out of reach of citizens. Their land-use decisions were seen as technical and managerial and not as social and political. Further, there was a deliberate depoliticization of politics—taking out platform and ideology, and reducing its practice to electing a candidate with no ultimate accountability except to his or her contributors. This led to a lack of real analysis and of programs that could produce the fundamental changes people seemed to ready to embrace.

In his first gubernatorial bid Jerry Brown campaigned on a platform offering a "new spirit." Though he was elected by a narrow margin, he quickly captured the imagination, interest, and support of Californians. His ideas and style attracted international attention. For those seeking to develop alternatives to existing policy on environmental, social, and economic problems, Jerry Brown offered hope. He was intelligent, articulate, provocative, intellectual, and thoughtful. But Brown's ideology remained general and fundamentally apolitical. He put forth new ideas, but they were not based on a coherent political-economic analysis. He deeply believed in pluralism and the eventual fairness of the outcome through the give and take of reasonable argument, even though he could articulate and see the existence of injustices and inequalities that were the result of the existing system. He acted as though the proper set of ideas and good appointments could do away with the previous inequities. The system, in his mind, was inherently sound, though limited. Deeply anchored in American liberal political ideology, Brown mistrusted politics and government and believed it needed to be supplemented by self-reliant voluntarism. However, instead of working with organized groups, he tried to transcend them and appeal to the people as individuals at large. He lacked an understanding of the importance of movements as sources of change and of interpersonal support. As governor, he reinforced the fragmentation of groups and interests, and perpetuated special-interest politics by pitting one group against another. This approach contributed to political stalemate. Further, Brown clearly felt that the politician as individual could be a leader in social change. For this reason he was disinclined to form coalitions or to seek to identify common interests even with his own Democratic Party. This approach, too, was a legacy of the Progressive era, when politics was reduced to the individual and a party became a public relations machine organized around image making for the candidate.

Brown's two terms as governor ended with citizens more alienated from government than ever before. Local governments were beginning to experience serious fiscal shortfalls resulting from the passage of Proposition 13 and the beginning of national economic restructuring and decline. This was happening alongside continuing and accelerating inflation in the cost of land and housing. Immigration was on the rise, and economic restructuring was changing the composition and compensation of the workplace. Income polarization—the disappearing middle—was beginning to be noticeable. Affordable housing was becoming scarce. People were concerned about the profoundly disruptive impacts of unmanaged growth upon their neighborhoods. Others were deprived of any of the effects of growth. Poor communities were often the target of negative land uses, such as hazardous waste incinerators, located there under the guise of economic development. The mid-1970s rhetoric about high property taxes driving businesses out was replaced by cries that environmental regulations were bad for business and causing it to leave the state.

In retrospect, the 1970s represented a consolidation of power and wealth for the already wealthiest segment of landholders in the state. Proposition

13 had significantly reduced property taxes for business and commercial property owners, and the federal government had abandoned the enforcement of acreage limitations on property owners who received federally subsidized water in the Central Valley. These legislative decisions meant the further concentration of wealth in the hands of the large-scale corporate elites of the state. The federal government, under President Nixon, considerably reduced its contributions to the states, especially for the cities and their rehabilitation. Instead, suburbs were favored, reinforcing the pattern of white middle-class flight. Tax inequalities escalated. This disengagement policy was continued by President Carter, then accelerated by President Reagan. Cities and counties, deprived of their rich budgets fed by property taxes and federal contributions, began to cut services. And citizens, disillusioned by too many promises and too little action, were increasingly alienated. The stage was set for the disintegration of the government of the state of California.

The Real Era of Limits

THE 1980s brought about profound transformations in the ideology and role of the government in the United States. In 1980 Ronald Reagan was elected president on a pro-business, anti-taxation, and anti-government platform. During his inauguration address in January 1981 President Reagan railed against the deficits that the federal government had been accumulating, putting forth a vision of government that would be run like a business, an enduring theme. "For decades," he said, "we have piled deficit upon deficit, mortgaging our future and our children's future. . . . To continue this long trend is to guarantee tremendous social, cultural, political and economic upheavals." The deficit that year, left by President Carter, was $74 billion. By the following year it had jumped to $120 billion. The next year it ran to $208 billion and continued to grow each year of Reagan's presidency.[1]

Governmental regulation was seen to be the major impediment to economic expansion and job creation. Consequently, government policy was aimed at the reduction of regulation. This trend was already under way during Carter's presidency, when the airline and trucking industries were deregulated, but President Reagan took giant strides in pushing deregulation, the reduction of government spending in certain sectors, and tax reduction.

This conservative, anti-government ideology ignited public suspicion and cynicism with regard to politicians and politics. The Reagan revolution made use of this suspicion to promote the superiority of individualism and business values and methods in achieving social well-being. Attitudes toward government, regulation, taxation, and the role and function of politics were profoundly influenced by the Reagan revolution. An entire generation of Americans was brought up in an era when the public and political sphere shrank in importance in favor of expansion of the market. The popularity of the ideology of the efficiency and success of the market (as opposed to the state or other structures) in organizing daily life was reinforced by the fall of the Berlin wall, once again confounding democracy, a political system, with capitalism. Market-driven restructuring of government and labor laws (the application of capitalist economic principles to government) was also espoused in Britain by Margaret Thatcher who, like President Reagan, was an articulate and convincing spokesperson for the privatization or reduction of many government activities and for tax cuts in favor of increasing individual incomes.

This approach, presenting government as inefficient, unresponsive, and wasteful, has had substantial impact on what people believe is possible and ought to occur, encouraging individual maximization as the path for greater societal happiness. The Reagan revolution has influenced what people believe is right or wrong, and thus has affected how government conducts its business. Government has come to be viewed as just another service-providing sector, rather than as the privileged sphere of democratic governance and accountability. The Reagan revolution virtually obliterated any distinction between the public sphere of politics and the economic sphere of capitalism.

The conservative ideology so well articulated by the Reagan administration had its counterpart in California, first enunciated by Governor Deukmejian and then by Governor Wilson, both Republicans. It had major effects on the management of growth and natural resources in the state.

Republicans Back in the Governor's Office

Governor George Deukmejian came into office in 1982 with a conservative agenda. Echoing the Republicans at the national level, he outlined a campaign of returning control to local government, reducing government regulation, and protecting the "rights of private property" against the state. In the name of fiscal responsibility, his budgets reduced funding across the board. Local governments, feeling the effects of Proposition 13, had been bailed out by the state under Governor Brown. Governor Deukmejian cut back those budget lines to local governments, "freeing" them from state assistance.

Deukmejian's style was characterized by an emphasis on management procedures rather than goal setting. He stressed the need for "cutting government waste" and an adherence to the principles of Proposition 13—that is, legislate no new taxes, and attempt to lower existing taxes. Any innovative programs were curtailed or eliminated, including Brown's programs to promote energy-conserving office buildings and appropriate technology.

Although overall the state's economy was strong, local governments continued their descent into fiscal instability, resulting in the shutting down of county libraries and the cutting of sheriff department budgets in the more remote rural areas of the state. Poor counties, having less of a local tax base, suffered the most. Subdivision conversion on the urban fringe continued, as did development and redevelopment activities in cities, which were scrambling to find new sources of revenue.

Urban Redevelopment and Attempts to Control Growth

Redevelopment was an especially important tool used by cities to boost sales tax revenues, which were badly needed to fill the coffers left empty by the decline in property taxes since the passage of Proposition 13. This led to continued concern about growth on the part of citizens. The increase in retail development—such as mini-malls, auto malls, and shopping centers, approved for their sales tax revenues—meant that in some areas car traffic was greatly increasing, as was building density along major arteries. Local residents' quality of life was eroded by increased noise and congestion. Unwilling to trade their quality of life for increased sales tax revenues (or unclear about the relationship between the two), citizens had placed close to 100 growth-control measures on the ballots by 1986, and almost 150 by 1989. These growth-control and growth-management proposals came in all shapes and forms, each crafted to meet local needs. Yet all these local efforts actually did little to manage California's growth in the 1980s. Growth was a phenomenon that went beyond the land-use management powers of a single jurisdiction; it required larger-scale intervention. In addition, often it was the municipalities themselves that put growth-control initiatives on the ballot, preempting citizen initiatives. This was done in order to put into place regulations that would shape the growth so as to promote the fiscal solvency of the jurisdiction. This "fiscalization of land use" meant that the most successful growth-management systems were not designed to respond to citizen concerns about property values, to protect natural resources, or to create more livable communities. Rather, they were intended to ensure a community's solvency by attracting sources of tax revenues and/or paying for infrastructure.[2] This was essentially a perversion of citizen intent and ultimately contributed to citizen alienation from government, because the growth control proposed by local jurisdictions did not and could not achieve what was promised. Because the growth-management schemes were local in nature, they served only to move growth around, not to restrict it—often with disastrous consequences for the environment and the sustainability of the metropolitan area.

Financing Schools and Local Services

Proposition 13 had greatly reduced the amount of property tax revenues available to build new school facilities. The main source of funding for permanent school facilities was the state School Building Lease Purchase Program, funded primarily by periodic issuance of state bonds. But this pool of money was too small, and the eligibility standards restrictive; creative financing schemes had to be developed to handle new school enrollments. To supplement the inadequate amount of state money available, local jurisdictions developed an array of funding sources whose equity and fairness have been questioned. Developer fees became the most common method of raising funds for classrooms. These are fees charged to developers building new subdivisions. Most districts used the fees to pay for portable classrooms, while applying for state funds for permanent facilities. These fees were very unpopular with home builders, and they loaded the cost onto one class of people: the new home buyer.

Another method of school funding used the Mello-Roos Community Facilities Act. In effect since 1982, Mello-Roos permits local government to levy special taxes to finance public facilities, if two-thirds of the voters approve. If there are fewer than twelve registered voters in the district to be taxed, the landowners are the qualified voters. "That provision means that Mello-Roos works best in undeveloped areas, where the only qualified voters are developers."[3] Developers, of course, have little incentive to vote against the tax, as they will be selling the land after it has been developed. New home owners will be responsible for paying the additional tax.

The Benefit Assessment District, authorized in a 1911 Progressive-era law (part of the Progressives' special-district legislation), was also activated to build schools. It permitted the collection of special fees for improvements that directly affected property values in the district—fees to improve streets, sewers, and drainage systems in developing areas. Because implementation of the law required no vote, a city could decide to assess a new fee, and if the majority of the property owners didn't complain, the city could proceed. But this admittedly sneaky method to enhance local revenue encountered the tax-cutting wrath of the Howard Jarvis group; the passage of Proposition 218 in 1996 restrained it by requiring a two-thirds, property-weighted vote of all of the affected property owners. Local governments are currently scrambling to figure out what to do, as the law applies not only to schools but also to all other assessment districts. Its property-weighted vote requirements raise serious questions of constitutionality and representativeness. Property owners could decide, for example, to vote against paying for a lighting district in an area where they own rental property, leaving the local inhabitants to deal with the consequences.

Each of these methods of raising money for schools (one of many local public services) depended for success on continued growth and continued construction. If building halted, no new money came into the local government coffers, even though the need might have increased. This put the quality of life of local jurisdictions in direct conflict with their fiscal needs, driving much of the citizen-initiated growth-control initiatives. These methods for financing schools illustrate the increased dependence of local governments on the development industry and the difficulty of controlling growth, or even selecting desirable types of growth, because of that dependency. They also show how government at the local level has become increasingly opaque. How to provide for the growing numbers of school-age children in a period of declining government revenues and public resistance to taxation and growth was a difficult problem, since a simple tax increase was out of the question. The 1996 legislature tried to develop alternatives to this development-dependent approach to school finance, but in the end enacted no new legislation.

Budgeting by Initiative

Despite the electoral success of conservative Republicans who campaigned on a platform of fiscal austerity, voters were still adding to the state's fiscal obligations by extending its public lands. Proposition 70, the California Wildlife, Coastal and Parkland Conservation Bond Act, was passed in 1988 with a two-thirds margin. It designated pieces of land throughout the state for purchase and protection by the state Parks and Recreation Department and Fish and Game Department, and allocated $776 million for that purpose. It was one of the biggest environmental petition efforts in California history, in which more than 25,000 people collected more than 735,000 signatures in less than 4 months to qualify the initiative for the ballot.[4] Voters also passed Proposition 98, sponsored by the California Teachers Association and the rest of the state's educational establishment. Proposition 98 guaranteed the public schools and community colleges 40 percent of the state's general fund. Proposition 62, passed in 1986, instituted a two-step process for local government and special districts to raise new general taxes: a two-thirds majority vote by the local agency's governing body and a majority of voters, but all special taxes to be approved by two-thirds of the voters—surely a questionable initiative to be led by citizen voters. Proposition 62 is a good illustration of the initiative process being hijacked by a small and clever group who appealed to taxpayers' frustration and put in place yet another roadblock to effective governance.

The budget-tightening mood of the legislature, a response to the perceived public opinion, was being thwarted and modified by the initiative process. Through the initiative voters could express their sentiments on a case-by-case basis, when and if an experienced group or organization pulled an initiative together. Yet this approach created laws and expenditures that made it increasingly difficult for the legislature to balance the budget or create new programs. Large fractions of the state's revenues were preallocated by initiative requirements, which made disposable money scarce and made any programs not protected by an initiative requirement vulnerable. The legislature had less and less room to shape coherent programs and budgets because initiatives predetermined much of the state's budget expenditures. Citizens, frustrated by a perceived lack of leadership on the part of their representatives, acted on those areas they felt were of critical importance on a piecemeal basis (the only avenue available), or on those areas in which a special interest had organized a ballot alternative. This exacerbated the budget crisis of the state and reduced government's flexibility.

Toxics and Gubernatorial Politics

The battle over the governorship in 1986 was waged in a peculiar manner. Los Angeles Mayor Tom Bradley, a three-term mayor elected by a crumbling but historic coalition of Jews from the west side of Los Angeles and the city's black population (and by some of the city's most powerful development interests), presented himself as the liberal alternative to incumbent governor Deukmejian. The campaign developed around Proposition 65, the Safe Drinking Water and Toxic Enforcement Act of 1986. The initiative had three main points: it would protect drinking water, require warnings of exposure to toxics, and provide incentives and tougher penalties for enforcement. Bradley supported the initiative and portrayed himself as the environmental candidate, while Deukmejian opposed it. Since Bradley had no previous pro-environment track record, however, his new affiliation seemed opportunistic at best and posed problems of credibility. The debate over Proposition 65 somewhat eclipsed the gubernatorial campaign—part of the strategy of the Bradley supporters.

Under the Deukmejian administration, the aggressive toxics program put in place during the Brown governorship had been neglected. It was poorly staffed and slow to act on clean-up, and was criticized for poor recordkeeping and for allowing hazardous waste facilities to operate without permits. Governor Deukmejian had not made it one of his priorities. In 1985 (while Reagan was president) the Environmental Protection Agency (EPA) issued a report critical of the state's programs. Specifically, EPA criticized $28.6 million worth of contracts at three major California sites where it said competitive bidding procedures had not been followed. In February EPA, still dissatisfied, took back much of the authority it had delegated to California to conduct federal hazardous waste inspections and to perform other duties.[5] For the Reagan administration to have taken this step, given its anti-regulatory and pro–state implementation philosophy, meant that serious problems existed in California.

The neglect of the Deukmejian administration in an area that seemed to have high voter attention fueled the Bradley campaign. Bradley accused Deukmejian of protecting toxic waste companies in part because they had contributed more than $500,000 to his campaign. Bradley's advisors devised campaign strategy around Deukmejian's neglect of the problem of toxics, hoping that by linking Bradley's bid for governor to Proposition 65, its success would carry him into office and overcome his past lack of interest in environmental issues.

The major California environmental organizations, coauthors of the initiative, supported this strategy. The Environmental Defense Fund, the Natural Resources Defense Council, the Planning and Conservation League, and the Sierra Club all helped to engineer the whole approach. The initiative was uniformly condemned by the California Chamber of Commerce, which led the opposition and was only reluctantly supported by grass-roots environmental organizations because they felt the initiative set in place a cumbersome and ineffectual regulatory process and structure.

Proposition 65 passed, but Bradley was not elected. Bradley's strategists had not understood how the question of race would be subtly manipulated or recognized that the voting public would not automatically identify Proposition 65 with Bradley. Bradley's opponents portrayed him as a black, big-city mayor, implying that he was a liberal spender even though Bradley had not been such a mayor and his administration had done little over the years for the disenfranchised areas of the city, such as Watts. Bradley lost narrowly, the race factor seeming to have been the key issue, although he was also a poor campaigner. And though Proposition 65 did pass, environmentalists had put in place a structure of regulation that made the governor responsible for appointing committees of experts and special interests (following the Progressive form of the past) to hash out which chemicals would be regulated—that is, labeled as possibly carcinogenic. Written by the state's major environmental organizations, it nonetheless set up a process that was time-consuming and contentious, and allowed the law's intent to be circumvented. Agreement on the basics took months of acrimonious negotiation among interests. Proposition 65 did little to ban the use of carcinogenic chemicals. Its primary result was notices warning people that they might be exposed to harmful chemicals—posted at gas stations, for example, and published in newspapers—but Proposition 65 accomplished little else.

The Legacy of Fiscal Conservatism

Acting as though he had received an anti-environmentalist mandate with his victory over Bradley (despite the overwhelming passage of Proposition 65), reelected governor Deukmejian immediately acted to abolish the California Occupational Health and Safety Administration (Cal OSHA), put in place during the Brown administration. He justified the action by claiming it would save the state $8 million a year and that the federal government could do the job instead (though the conservative ideology of government during the Reagan administration emphasized devolving programs to states). Cal OSHA's jurisdiction included a wide variety of environmental responsibilities, such as disposal of toxic materials, monitoring of air quality inside industrial plants, and regulation of workplace chemicals used in manufacturing. The elimination of Cal OSHA was possible because in California the governor has line-item veto power of the budget. Even though a state budget is passed by the legislature after discussion and negotiation with the governor, the governor can still eliminate funding for programs after the budget has been passed. This gives the governor ultimate power over programs.

Deukmejian's approach to the Coastal Commission was similar, though less radical. The state's contribution to the commission's annual budget was reduced by nearly one-third, and the commission was forced to close its office in Eureka. The governor also ordered the shutdown of the Santa Barbara and Santa Cruz offices, claiming that any work in those areas could be handled by the two remaining offices in San Francisco and Long Beach. When the commission refused, finding money in the budget to keep the two offices open, Deukmejian decided the commission was overfunded and made a $1 million cut in its 1988–89 budget. The staff was cut by nearly half. Additional pressure came from the federal government, under Interior Secretary Donald Hodel, to promote off-shore oil and gas drilling, with Deukmejian's implicit support. The Commerce Department in 1988 published a report highly critical of the Coastal Commission, accusing it of mismanaging coastal resources. The report set forth a list of twenty conditions that would have to be met if federal funding were to continue and also launched a suit to force California to relax its environmental standards for off-shore oil operations. Inexplicably, the federal suit was dropped in mid-1988.[6]

The Coastal Commission was divided because of its appointment structure: Deukmejian appointees (usually aligned on the side of landowners and developers), the remaining conservationists, and a middle swing group. Nonetheless, despite these problems, it continued to muddle along to achieve its mandate. The commission published a coastal access guide, acquired more coastline (in 1972 there was a total of 263 miles of publicly owned coastline; by 1989, 447 miles), established 1,000 miles of public access ways, and maintained the visibility of the coastline by means of height restrictions for new construction.[7]

Governor Deukmejian emphasized management of the state, presiding over a deteriorating status quo, initiating little, vetoing much. A feeling of political paralysis was prevalent. As a result, Californians increasingly turned to the initiative process to resolve problems the state government was not addressing. This furthered the paralysis because so much of the budget was preallocated by the requirements of the initiatives.

Some of the reasons for the political gridlock in Sacramento at this time, according to Sacramento insiders, were these:

- A system of divided authority with a governor of one party and a legislature controlled by the other
- Major divisions among the ranks of both parties
- A legislature controlled by conservative Republican and liberal Democratic forces with an insufficient number of problem-solving centrists to forge a compromise and a governor who took hard lines on issues, furthering stalemate
- Millions of dollars required for legislative campaigns each year, giving special interests clout in the lawmaking process
- Concern about fund raising for the next campaign
- The initiative process increasingly in the hands of professional campaigners
- Initiatives sponsored by Paul Gann and Howard Jarvis that placed fiscal shackles on state and local government officials
- Growth warfare throughout California, with a proliferation of initiatives that created a see-saw effect where public officials were caught between developer persuasion (and the need to raise revenues) and voter backlash, resulting in rival forces winning control of city councils in alternate elections
- Lack of political leadership
- Local governments made up of haphazard, random government bodies, all fighting over the same dollars and contributing to a service delivery system that was more of a crazy quilt than a safety net.[8]

A State Still Haunted by the Politics of Growth

Declining federal aid, the fragmentation of government, the requirements of Proposition 13, and the lack of public accountability of local governments continued to drive a politics of frustration on the part of voters, as well as one of intense competition among local governments. Cities and counties found themselves pitted against each other in the competition for new tax-producing development. Although the race was often among neighboring cities, increasingly it became a competition between a city and the county where that city was located. State law gives cities several advantages in the revenue chase because redevelopment projects, annexations, and incorporations all can serve to transfer funds (both property and sales tax) from county to city coffers. As state and federal funds withered away, counties, still responsible for the implementation of many federal and state-mandated programs, took steps to block annexation and redevelopment. They began to become involved, to an unprecedented extent, in the urban development business in an attempt to achieve fiscal solvency. Counties are the administrative arm of the state; they operate their own programs and those mandated by Sacramento, programs that the state often does not fully finance. For example, trial courts are an important element in the state's judicial system, and they are operated by counties, which are required to fund the courts 63 percent from their own budgets. In 1999, thanks to the leadership of California Supreme Court justice Ronald M. George, the state will assume trial court budgets. The counties are also required to provide mental health services, maintain probation departments, and provide welfare for local constituents (general relief).

Counties were initially created by the state to implement such programs as health care delivery, welfare, and criminal justice, in a decentralized way. Implementation was devolved to the local level—in keeping with the idea of local control—but real power was retained at the state level, since counties had to implement state (and federal) programs or find themselves out of compliance and subject to budget cutbacks. Cities, however, are local entities created by an area's residents to serve municipal purposes, such as road maintenance, trash collection, and land-use regulation.

The financial pressure on counties opened the door for developers to play cities and counties against each other. For example, when the city of Davis, which had an urban limit line and an agricultural land-preservation policy in its general plan, rejected a big project by developer Frank Ramos, he simply went to talk with the officials in Yolo County. The county was happy to entertain his proposal for a development—adjacent to the city boundary. This fiscal competition, which Ramos exploited in order to develop his land, put at risk the entire county's policy of farmland preservation and the city's authority to maintain its general plan, undermining the already fragile structures of land-use planning.[9] The city of Davis caved in, and Ramos was authorized to build on land that had been zoned for agricultural preservation. This then opened the door for further land development in that pre-viously off-limits area.

Land-use planning, because of its fiscal vulnerability, is nearly helpless to guide development. Consequently, land-use development continues to be haphazard and to contribute to congestion, air pollution, and urban sprawl—the very factors that often lead to growth-control initiatives. The decline in state aid for counties and their own shrinking budgets have made counties play the land-development card in a way they had never had to previously.

Development Agreements

The proliferation of growth-control initiatives (and the fear thereof) led to an innovative approach on the part of developers and municipalities to se-cure the right to develop: "development agreements," in which a city and a developer enter into a long-term contract. The contract ensures the project will not be shut down by future slow-growth measures because it is a legally binding agreement on the part of the local jurisdiction that the land in ques-tion has been approved for development by a contract of long duration—re-gardless of the will of the public in the future. As of 1989 there were over 500 development agreements (DAs) in place throughout California. For large development projects, DAs have become nearly essential, especially for ten- to twenty-year projects that are built in several phases. Local govern-ments like the DAs, too, as they are able to gain more concessions that way than they could legally obtain through traditional regulatory review. Yet DAs only serve to exacerbate the feeling of frustration on the part of the public regarding local government's lack of responsiveness. Negotiations between city and developer are conducted largely behind closed doors so as to expedite planning. The public is allowed to intervene only once the com-plex plans and agreements have been drawn up. Once DAs are put in place, they are legally binding, giving the developer "vested rights" to the project that cannot be reversed, even by referendum, once thirty days have passed after approval.

One reason for the popularity of DAs comes from *Nollan v. California Coastal Commission,* a 1987 U.S. Supreme Court ruling that made it more dif-ficult for cities to impose fees on developers. The *Nollan* decision, not surpris-ingly, was part of a new round of defense for private property rights that came out of the Reagan administration. The ruling required local govern-ments to prove a "nexus," or direct connection, between the need for the fee and the development on which it is imposed. This was reinforced by Califor-nia's AB 1600, enacted in 1987, requiring a much closer nexus when impos-ing development fees. In addition, the fee revenue must be held in a trust fund, and the agency must draw up a plan to spend it. The money must be spent or committed in five years; if not, the local agency must make findings each year after that as to why the money is needed.[10] This has put additional pressure on local government to accommodate the development community, eroding some of local government's land-use authority.

In Orange County and Riverside County, DAs were rushed through ahead of two slow-growth citizen initiatives that would have made it more difficult to develop the lands in question. In both counties, advocates of slow growth had placed growth-control initiatives on the ballot in 1988. This caused the boards of supervisors to push through DAs before the election. The result was quick approval, and vested rights, for all 60,000 units proposed in Orange County and about 100,000 in Riverside County, despite clear opposition from citizens who wanted to slow growth.

In Orange County, because of the increased court scrutiny regarding the nexus between development exactions and the development, DAs have become the primary vehicle for obtaining development fees. The county extracts its fees and infrastructure through the development agreement—fees and infrastructure it would have attempted to obtain under the traditional process, but perhaps with less success because the scope of the proposed development would have probably been smaller. DAs permit counties to get more money from developers to offset the effects of development. Since Orange County had inadequate funds to pay for the arterial roads required by the new developments, nineteen developers agreed to provide the $235 million needed, in exchange for the vested right to build their projects. Though the vast majority of the funds actually came from bond issues, and not from the developers' pockets, the DAs guaranteed that the houses would be built and were a vital element in the successful marketing of the Orange County bonds on Wall Street.

Riverside County also has relied heavily on DAs. The Riverside growth-control initiative provided for a comprehensive growth-management approach to reduce traffic congestion, promote air quality, protect environmentally sensitive lands, ensure adequate public services and facilities, and "preserve and protect Riverside County's quality of life." The rate of increase in residential building permits in unincorporated areas was limited to the state's rate of growth in the previous year, which was lower than the county's rate (2.5 percent for the state, 5.7 percent for the county).[11] The intent of this growth-control initiative was circumvented by the board of supervisors' quick approval of development proposals.

Vested rights to develop gained through the DA procedure are immune to any future growth measure or change in board membership. In addition, DAs serve as "currency" because they bind land to a certain development future for an indefinite period of time. DAs themselves become marketable; many developers sell the projects before they are built, bringing in new owners who may want to change the approved plans, leading to renegotiation. This creates a lopsided situation, since the new owners may reopen negotiations, but the public has no ability to change the land-use designation either by vote or through the city council. The only option available would be to buy out the landowner—assuming that the landowner is willing to sell.

The Fiscal Crisis and Slow Growth versus Development

While DAs were being put in place in over 500 instances throughout the state, slow-growth initiatives were being placed on the ballot, and those initiatives fared well in the November 1989 election. At the same time, slow-growth candidates were elected to office in San Diego, Santa Barbara, San Luis Obispo, Gilroy, Moorpark, and other places. It seemed that while local government officials were busy trying to secure funding to keep their cities afloat by entering into DAs, local voters were going in the opposite direction, trying to put a stop to further development, at least in its current form. Yet the structure of local finance, especially with Proposition 13's huge property tax cut, required development to meet the needs of a growing population base that demanded more schools, more police, and services. Growth-control initiatives did not take into account the fiscal crisis of local municipalities. They concentrated on quality-of-life issues and were a response to increased congestion, the construction of mini-malls, and the rapid conversion of open space. This circle of dependence has been unresolvable by the ballot box and other traditional methods of political participation. Nor have the traditional methods of government finance through the development process proven to be an effective solution, because developers do not want to assume the burden of bailing out local governments without strong assurances they will be able to develop (hence the DAs). Once the bottom fell out of the California economy in the early 1990s, local governments had nowhere to turn for extra money. Land development came to a standstill. Local government budgets had to be reexamined and cut yet again.

Legislative Focus on Growth Control, Again

Some members of the legislature were not oblivious to the problems created by uncoordinated and essentially opportunistic growth. Hearings and studies had been commissioned by the legislature, and the local government committees of both the Assembly and Senate held formal hearings each year from 1987 through 1990. The continued success of ballot box planning spurred the California legislature to address growth management.

State Senator Marian Bergeson chaired the Senate Select Committee on Planning for California's Growth and the Senate Local Government Committee. Her select committee sponsored two conferences in the fall of 1987 to begin developing a consensus on a legislative program to provide state leadership in the growth-management field for 1989. The direction of her efforts, called the "new regionalism," was to develop ways for communities to "accept their regional responsibilities without direct state intervention."[12] Several other legislators, each with his or her own point of view about how to approach the problems caused by California's historical patterns of growth, also became involved. Senator Robert Presley, a Democrat from Riverside, had the Senate Office of Research develop a two-year urban growth policy project, to document the problems of urban growth and to increase public awareness and understanding of the issues. The project would also recommend legislation to reform the planning and development process to better achieve the state's policy objectives in transportation, housing, resource conservation, and economic development.[13]

The 1960s and 1970s had been rife with proposals to deal with the problem of growth. The difference with this new round was mostly the idea that regional coordination of growth and government could occur without "direct" state intervention. In reality, nearly all previous efforts had already used this approach of no direct state intervention. An example is housing: all cities were required to accept their "fair share" of low-income housing, simply by law, with no method of enforcement. The same approach also applied to the workings of the regional transportation planning agencies, LAFCOs, and many agencies with coordinating functions. They were always charged with promoting regional coordination, but were not given legal methods of enforcement, except for financial incentives when they were available. Sacramento had always been shy to intervene in what have traditionally been, in the United States, local government functions.

A growth-management consensus project was jointly launched by the two houses of the legislature. Frustrated with Governor Deukmejian's lack of interest, they introduced a wide range of bills in 1988–89 that were related to growth management. The bills addressed such issues as local revenue sharing (to reduce interjurisdiction competition for the sales tax), affordable housing, and strengthening of state and local planning procedures. None was successful. Again in 1990 several bills were introduced, but these also failed.

Wilson and Pandora's Box

Pete Wilson, ex-mayor of San Diego, was elected governor in 1990 after Deukmejian had served two terms. Wilson, who narrowly beat Dianne Feinstein, mayor of San Francisco, ran a centrist Republican campaign. Many environmentalists, while supporting Feinstein, remembered how Wilson had championed growth control in San Diego, and they were impressed when the new governor appointed Douglas Wheeler, an old-style conservationist, to head the Resources Agency. Wilson promised that one of the first items of business on his agenda would be to develop a statewide approach to managing growth.

The 1991 legislature gave promise of being more ready than any other to forge legislation on the management of growth. Preparing the terrain for the introduction of legislation, the Local Government Committee of the Senate Select Committee on Planning for California's Growth and the Assembly Local Government Committee held a two-day joint interim hearing. Just before the hearings in October, the Wilson administration, committed to producing its own growth-management proposal and eager to have its approach to the issue prevail, released a preliminary study put together by Wilson's appointed Council on Growth Management. The administration asked the legislature to hold off introducing bills until its own proposal was ready that coming January.

Wilson's council, charged with drawing up growth-management recommendations built upon a bottom-up approach (meaning no direct state intervention, but also no grass-roots political mobilization), consulted with many interest groups and held thirteen public hearings throughout the state. At the hearings, the director of the Governor's Office of Planning and Research, Richard Sybert, stated the governor's position that any growth-management plan would have to adhere to these principles:

- Protection of a strong economy
- Coordination and streamlining of the existing regional authorities
- The need for better, not more, government
- Maximum local flexibility in meeting growth-management goals
- A simplified and expedited development review and permitting process
- No increase in funding.[14]

The five bills developed by both Republicans and Democrats that were under consideration during the joint hearings had more precise goals but were unified by a common thread: the perceived need for a statewide planning effort to develop a clear, coordinated, long-term plan for the state's future. The bills, in different ways, also tried to improve local land-use coordination and cooperation among regional-level agencies. They all shied away from attempting to strengthen state and regional authority, however; the legislators had learned from previous attempts at growth management that cities and counties would ally with chambers of commerce in strong opposition to this approach. (These bills are summarized in the appendix.)

Wilson's Plan

Governor Wilson's long-awaited report, *Strategic Growth: Taking Charge of the Future, a Blueprint for California,* issued by the Growth Management Council, made a series of recommendations, though no concrete legislative proposals. It pointed to the need to manage and direct California's growth and change as a means to rebuild prosperity and infrastructure, create jobs, and stimulate both sustained and sustainable growth in the economy. To this end it advocated streamlining government at all levels ("reinventing government"). Implicit in the report was the assumption that voluntary state growth guidelines would be established to shape development. The state would use its resources to provide financial incentives to local governments (for instance, helping local government support a market for local debt) if they adopted the state's voluntary growth guidelines, developed by the Office of Planning and Research, but there would be no threat of punishment for failure to adopt the voluntary guidelines. Such problems as the lack of low-cost housing, noted in the report, would be addressed by reducing red tape and regulation. The Office of Planning and Research would play a significant role in reviewing local plans for consistency with the voluntary growth guidelines and would serve as a funnel for various forms of assistance.

The Office of Planning and Research was the linchpin in Wilson's plan. The office already had a great deal of power in the area of state planning and did not need any new powers to accomplish Wilson's plan, yet the Wilson administration did not act on this power by putting any of the recommendations into effect. No legislation was put forward.

The gist of the Wilson approach was to enhance the power of local government, while broadening the purview and strengthening the control of the state government, to draw local government more closely within the regulatory ambit of the state and to reduce the power of regional-level institutions. This was quite different from the legislative proposals, which mostly relied on regional-level institutions to coordinate growth. However, it was consistent with a conservative philosophy of government that tended to elevate the importance of local institutions because they are closer to the people, even though the proposed changes tended to remove decision making from local public scrutiny by reducing opportunities for intervention. These changes also made local governments far more dependent on state government for their fiscal stability and centralized decision making at the state level. (See the appendix for a detailed examination of Wilson's plan.)

Economic Decline and Growth Control

By the time the five growth-control bills came to be considered by the legislature, the state's economy had started to decline precipitously, and the control or management of growth seemed inappropriate. Once again, the management of growth in California was put aside. Yet an argument could be made that this was the very time for such a structure to be established. What better time to consider how the state ought to develop, where growth should occur, and how it should be managed? What better time to analyze the state's need for infrastructure and its role in creating conditions for healthy and sustainable economic growth? What better time to plan for resource protection and ecological diversity? What better time to reconsider the tax structure and its built-in inequities, and the unforeseen consequences of the passage of Proposition 13?

Actually, proposals had already been developed to address many of the state's pressing problems. Many of the more innovative ideas of the Brown administration of the 1970s resurfaced or were reinvented in the early 1990s. The era of limits had indeed come to California, but not out of choice on the part of its residents, nor in the form they might have preferred. While there prevailed a certain sense of unease about the obvious social and environmental problems arising from uncoordinated growth, the political climate had turned deeply partisan and bitter, so that no consensus on the causes of the problems of the state could be achieved. Instead, malign neglect settled in.

For example, a proposal to manage urban growth that had been successfully opposed by the real estate industry until late 1995 involved legislation, proposed by Democratic Assemblyman Dominic Cortese of San Jose, that would require cities to identify the source and availability of water before new urban development could be approved. This proposal followed on a similar idea put forth in Wilson's own strategic growth plan. Such a practice is standard in the far more humid regions east of the Mississippi. Supported by an alliance of farmers, environmentalists, and urban and rural water suppliers, the bill was defeated at first by the opposition of some of the state's most influential builders and developers, as well as the California Chamber of Commerce and the League of California Cities. They argued that the bill would cede local planning decisions to outside water districts with a hidden slow-growth agenda, even though historically water districts have generally tried to encourage growth, so they could expand as well. Opponents of the bill agreed that water and growth should be tied, but they argued that this should be done in a manner that kept zoning and general planning decisions solely inside city hall—once again defending the primacy of local control regardless of regional or statewide issues of resource management.

Cortese's bill responded to water-supply problems emerging in different parts of the state. For example, in El Dorado County near Sacramento, elected officials approved entire subdivisions without adequate water—a shortfall that could affect up to 50,000 average-sized households. In Madera County, north of the San Joaquin River, the state had to step in and impose severe water rationing in one large rural subdivision where the groundwater table had plummeted 10 feet a year over the past seven years and there was insufficient water available from other sources. In Contra Costa County, the board of supervisors had allowed an influential builder named Nathan Shapell (who had contributed more than $487,000 to California politicians over the past decade) to build 11,000 homes in the Doughtery Valley in December 1992. One month later the East Bay Municipal Utility District, which supplies water to Contra Costa and Alameda Counties, filed suit against the development, saying it did not have enough water to serve the proposed 30,000 additional residents.[15] Cortese's bill finally did pass later in the year.

By the mid-1990s, after decades of debate and reflection on the issue of growth in the state, there was no clear consensus on policy, no agreement on what growth meant, no shared perspective on the role of government. There was even sharp divergence on the possibility of any sort of common good at all.[16] Chambers of commerce, the development industry in general, and cities and counties all remained profoundly opposed to the concept of regional government and to state guidelines regarding local growth management. The local control over local land-use designations—although never directly threatened by any of the proposed growth-control measures—remained the primary concern for these jurisdictions.

Perhaps more seriously, all the discussion of and struggle over growth never yielded a serious dissection of the phenomenon itself. Growth is composed of various interacting and complex elements. These include population expansion, business growth, growth in traffic congestion, growth in commercial developments and housing construction. Often, all of these are lumped under the rubric of "growth," leading to general confusion and to imprecise or inappropriate policies and politics.

Breaches in the Hydraulic Society

Beginning in 1985 California entered another period of severe drought. The distribution of water, always a touchy subject, became even more contentious. Proposals for additional water development surfaced once again, including the Peripheral Canal, so roundly defeated by the voters in June 1982 (see chapter 5). Tensions around water distribution became acute, with urban interests pointing the finger at agriculture for taking the lion's share of the state's developed water. The urban interests claimed that this pattern of water distribution was outdated, based on agriculture's past economic preeminence, while California's economy was now mostly urban. Legislative representation had certainly shifted to urban centers, reflecting their demographic weight. The economic strength of the state had shifted too, with urban areas producing more of the state's wealth.

Environmental Concerns

Environmental interests had long been opposed to any further water development, as in the struggle against the Peripheral Canal. Now, they were ever more concerned with the effects of the drought on the state's ecosystems. With much of the available water developed, the drought left little behind to sustain natural systems. Water quality in the Bay-Delta area was continuing to decline dramatically as available fresh water was diverted for agricultural and urban uses. There was an alarming drop-off in the chinook salmon run and in Delta smelt. Striped bass were not faring well, either. Moreover, Delta water-quality standards did not meet the requirements of the Clean Water Act. As was the case with most federal laws, enforcement of Clean Water Act standards was delegated to the states, and in California it was the responsibility of the Water Quality Resources Control Board. The Wilson administration, like the Deukmejian administration before it, had not complied with the law, and the EPA threatened to come up with a plan if the administration did not comply. The drought conditions were also putting pressure on the remaining natural and artificially created Pacific flyways of the Central Valley. Even before the drought, riparian corridors were dying as urban water companies tapped streams and aquifers, leaving little or nothing behind.[17]

In response to continued pressure regarding Delta water quality, Wilson appointed a task force representing all the major interests—urban, rural, environmental, water—to develop a comprehensive water-supply program to meet projected needs to the year 2010 and Clean Water Act standards. Negotiations among all parties proceeded, but with great difficulty: for example, the Bay-Delta studies showing the ecological deterioration of the system were categorically rejected by agricultural interests. By February 1993 the Delta smelt were declared to be a threatened species by the federal Fish and Wildlife Service. Numbers of striped bass were said to have declined by 75 percent since the State Water Project had begun operation, and the numbers of winter-run salmon were down 90 percent. Because of the controversial nature of these claims and their implications for water policy, the

Wilson administration had not developed standards for the Bay-Delta estuary and thus could not calculate the amount of water necessary for the protection of those ecosystems.[18]

Loosening Agriculture's Stranglehold on Water

To end this long-standing impasse, whose origins preceded the Wilson administration, an alliance was reached between urban water interests and the major environmental organizations. Among the parties were, on one side, the Share the Water Coalition and the Western Urban Water Coalition, representing the interests of public and investor-owned water utilities of western cities, and, on the other, the Environmental Defense Fund. The alliance was specifically aimed at breaking agriculture's hold on water in the state. Several concerns were merged in the coalition: protection of the Delta, enhanced water deliveries for urban areas, and protection for other ecosystems. The coalition embarked on a strategy that would circumvent the stalemated negotiations over Delta water quality and would go far beyond merely assuring that the Delta would receive more water.

Creating Marketable Water Rights, or Privatizing Water

Proposals of "water transfers"—meaning water trades, water markets, water exchanges, or any other idea to save, create, or reallocate water by treating it as an economic good[19]—had been strongly advocated since the late 1970s by the Environmental Defense Fund, in particular by Tom Graff (who had been a member of Jerry Brown's transition team and had been involved in environmental politics since the early 1970s). Others in the liberal environmental intelligentsia, including researchers at Resources for the Future and the Conservation Foundation, both in Washington, D.C., also were persuaded that a market approach to environmental protection was more efficient and would yield better results than either command-and-control technologies (as in air or water pollution control) or bureaucratic regulation.

The concept that common property resources could be managed for the public good by the government had succumbed to the ever growing popularity of the free-market ideology so convincingly articulated by the Reagan administration's neoclassical economic analysis. There had been earlier advocates for bringing environmental values into the marketplace, but before the Reagan era, such an approach had not been strongly pushed because of a feeling that it was difficult to put prices on environmental values, such as clean air, clean water, or open space. There was also a feeling that air, water, and open space belonged to all and could not, or should not, become privately owned or controlled goods, subject to the decisions of individuals seeking to maximize personal gain.

But Tom Graff had long been interested in the application of market principles to preserve environmental quality. Seizing upon what seemed to be a window of opportunity because of the drought and increasing urban militancy regarding the allocation of water in the state, the Environmental Defense Fund (EDF) took an aggressive lead in forging an alliance with those powerful urban economic interests that found Graff's market-based approach to water compatible with their own. Graff set out to fundamentally change the management of water in the state.

As the main environmental player, Graff was the representative of the environmental community by fiat, in a state whose politics are organized by special interests. Further, alone among the interested parties, the EDF had conducted an in-depth analysis of the environmental water needs of the state's major water-dependent ecosystems—principally the San Francisco Bay-Delta and the Pacific flyway of the Central Valley. That it had used the state's own data to establish these water needs was significant because those data could not be disputed by the state or by other groups. Although the state had gathered data, it had not compiled its own information, out of reluctance to come to conclusions that might alienate Wilson's business supporters. Graff's conclusions pointed to dramatic ecosystem decline due to a lack of sufficient water.

Graff's astute strategy, combining strong data with a powerful coalition, put him in a position to establish many of the parameters of the Central Valley Project Improvement Act (Public Law 102-575), passed by Congress in October 1992. Graff's objective was to fundamentally change the federal government's management of the Central Valley Project to allow the sale of water by project contractors, outside the project area. Since the federal CVP is the largest developer, subsidizer, and transporter of water in the state—controlling 20 percent of the developed water supply in California (approximately 6 million acre-feet per year)—establishing water markets within this system could potentially lead to the redistribution of significant amounts of water, if there were buyers. Further, this change would also set a significant precedent for water management by other public agencies in the state and in the West, since the West's water is mostly federally developed.

Federally developed and subsidized water had always been subject to restrictions (mostly unenforced), including a prohibition on the sale and transfer of CVP water to non-CVP customers. Under these terms, the water contracted for by farmers was not theirs by right, it was only theirs to use by virtue of long-term renewable contracts (usually for thirty years). Farmers claimed that those contracts were essential to secure farm loans at favorable rates, since they served as assurance to lenders that the farmer would have a secure, long-term water supply. By establishing a market-based allocation system, the water that had previously been managed by the federal government as a common property resource became the private property right of the recipient and thus could be sold to other potential users during the period of the contract. The result was the privatization of a publicly developed, common property resource. Along with the right to sell water, however, came a revision of the long-term contract provision, reducing the term of contracts to twenty-five years and imposing an environmental review for renewal. This provision was strongly opposed by the farm community.

Forging the Central Valley Project Improvement Act

The approach conceived was a combination of environmental protection and market incentives. This involved preallocating a certain percentage of CVP water to environmental protection and then vesting CVP water contractors with property rights to the water they received and allowing them to sell their water on the free market, up to a certain percentage of the water district's allotment. Marketable water would be restricted to 20 percent of each water district's allotment from the CVP each year. In addition, it was proposed that an additional 100,000 acre-feet per year be made available for auction directly from the Bureau of Reclamation, the operator of the CVP.

The EDF analysis of the environmental needs for water in the state, based on state-generated studies, arrived at an estimate of 2.8 million to 3.6 million acre-feet necessary to achieve modest protection and restoration of the major streams and wetlands affected by the CVP and for the San Francisco Bay–Delta estuary. The total yearly delivery of the CVP averaged 6 million acre-feet. An amount of 2 million or 3 million acre-feet amounted to about 10 percent of the total consumptive water use in the entire state. EDF maintained that fish and wildlife water needs should come from agriculture, since it was the biggest water user in the state and was wasteful in its application of water and its choice of crops. These figures became the basis for the environmental mitigation set-aside waters of the Central Valley Project Improvement Act, as there were no competing analyses. By negotiation, the amount needed to achieve modest environmental protection and restoration eventually was reduced to 3–10 percent of the CVP water delivered (800,000 acre-feet at a minimum), depending on water availability. In drought years, water delivered for environmental protection would drop, in other years it could go to 10 percent.

At the congressional hearings in 1992, powerful arguments were presented in favor of allowing a market to be created for federally subsidized water. Carl Boronkay, general manager of southern California's Metropolitan Water District, claimed in his testimony that, on average, 1 acre-foot of water would produce 2,600 jobs, and in some specific industries as many as 17,000 jobs. Southern California uses 10 percent of the developed water of the state and contributes 50 percent to the state's economy. He explained MWD's concern that there would be growing water shortages for urban areas—on the order of 100,000 acre-feet a year in the foreseeable future—based on the population increase. He stated that the unreliability of water supplies, due to the effects of droughts in the state and the rigidity of water distribution, could deter businesses from coming to California, undermining confidence and investment in the California economy. This would reduce the state's competitiveness. Boronkay stated that, over time, the MWD wished to acquire about 10 percent of CVP water.[20]

Another powerful advocate for creating water markets was the Bay Area Economic Forum, a public/private partnership of the Association of Bay Area Governments (ABAG) and the Bay Area Council. The Bay Area Economic Forum had published *Using Water Better: A Market-based Approach to California's Water Crisis*, whose principal authors were Ronald H. Schmidt, senior economist for the Federal Reserve Bank of San Francisco, and Frederick Cannon, vice president and senior economist of Bank of America. In this publication the case for a market approach to water distribution was made very forcefully. According to this analysis, the free market would solve all the problematic issues around water allocation. As opposed to the current system—described as one where "centralized planners do not have sufficient knowledge to make wise choices about how to best allocate water"—a "decentralized market system allows actual users to decide how much to use, balancing the value of those uses against the value of potential uses by others. By taking into account these individual-specific needs, values and uses, a market leads to better allocations."[21] Water markets should make all water users better off. Farmers who did not want to sell their water would be under no obligation to do so. The model proposed for such a market would be similar to other utilities based on natural resources, such as oil, natural gas, or bulk electrical power. The MWD's approval, combined with the Bay Area Economic Forum's backing of water markets, brought very influential and very powerful urban-based support for the analysis put forward by Graff. Here were allied two of the most significant interests in the state: urban-based businesses and environmentalists. Congress could not help but be impressed by pro-market arguments.

Another Urban-Rural Connection

For the first time in California history farmers, the historic beneficiaries of the large water projects in the state, found their water supplies challenged. Clearly the balance of power in the state was shifting. But in whose interests?

The official position of the Wilson administration was that the federal government should transfer the Central Valley Project to the state. Douglas Wheeler, secretary of resources, testified to Congress in 1992 that in order to develop a comprehensive state water-supply program for the next twenty years, California had to include the CVP under its authority. This position was supported by the Bush administration's Department of Interior and Bureau of Reclamation. But something profound had changed. Even though large-scale agricultural interests had prevailed in Congress in the late 1980s in seeking removal of the acreage limitations attached to receiving CVP water, this time the arguments of agriculture did not seem to carry as much weight. This was so, despite the support of the Bush and Wilson administrations for the maintenance of the status quo. Congress was swayed by the new urban-environmental coalition, which argued that farmers did not have to sell their water if they did not want to; that free markets were better allocaters of resources than government bureaucrats; and that groundwater pumping was not to be regulated. Farmers could pump as much as they wanted, and sell CVP water. They could even sell the water they had pumped, if they could figure out how to do so.

A new political alignment had come about. Urban business interests, allied with major environmental organizations, had forged an unbeatable alliance and put forth a proposal that could not be easily ignored. The political power of the state seemed to have shifted.

But a look beyond the surface reveals another, associated change—a gradual shift of land use in the Central Valley from rural to urban. Urban land commands a far higher price per acre than farmland or rural land, and California has experienced an inexorable process of land conversion from rural to urban, a gradual disappearance of some of the state's richest and most productive agricultural lands. No strong mechanisms had been developed over the decades to protect agricultural lands, or to make their conversion less profitable, though some growth-management proposals had tried to address the issue. In the Central Valley the process seemed to take place even faster than elsewhere. Fresno, for example, nearly doubled in size and population in the 1980s.[22] This urbanization created a tremendous potential economic opportunity for agricultural landholders in the valley, especially those on the urban fringe and along the I-5 corridor. In the 1980s California had the highest growth rate in the nation in absolute numbers. "Using statistics on urbanization over the past fifteen years and projected population growth, it is estimated that between one and two million acres will be urbanized in California in the next decade to accommodate population growth." At the 1 million acre figure, 20 percent would be added to the existing urban land base, and most of the change would occur in the Central

Valley, the Sierra Foothills, and along the coast.[23] The California State Department of Finance has projected that the valley will receive an additional 1.2 million residents by 2010.

The eight-county Central Valley has far less regulatory organization and fewer cooperative agreements across county and city lines than other parts of the state, putting it at a disadvantage in dealing with these pressures. But local officials and community leaders are leery of the perceived erosion of local control that any multicounty agency or agreement might symbolize. Consequently there is no agency to take a wider point of view regarding the future course of urban development and agriculture in the region.[24]

Because urban sprawl typically costs more in government services than it generates in tax revenues, cities and counties in the Central Valley are likely to be operating in the "deep red by the year 2040," with as much as a 20 percent shortfall in revenues throughout those years. The American Farmland Trust released a study in 1995 projecting that from Bakersfield to Sacramento, the 300-mile span of Highway 99 would be an almost unbroken chain of smog-choked cities and suburbs covering more than 1 million acres of prime agricultural land and putting at risk an additional 2.5 million acres due to urban encroachment.[25] But the dominant view is the one expressed by Richard Lyon, a legislative lobbyist for the California Building Industry Association, in response to a 1995 analysis by the Bank of America on the negative effects of urban sprawl on the valley: "What's forgotten in all the hype are the jobs and tax base created by the construction industry." Currently the valley produces about 25 percent of the nation's table food, yet air pollution has already caused the reduction of many crop yields by 20–30 percent.

The introduction of marketable water rights signals the end of an era in California, even if that era was made up more of dreams than reality. It is the end of the possibility of a Central Valley that might have included family farms and small towns rich in services, retail outlets, and jobs. That vision of California was a chimera, but there were small islands on the east side of the Central Valley that showed it was possible. The Central Valley Project Improvement Act opened the door wide open to the valley's land uses being increasingly determined by large-scale property owners in the valley—the insurance companies, oil companies, and railroads. These are the interests that initially benefited from the largesse of the distribution of the public domain around the turn of the century, for they are the valley's largest farmers. These landholders are largely urban-based and quick to adapt to changing market conditions. Selling their water and converting their lands to urban uses are logical moves if they promise a profit. The eventual future of the Central Valley is urbanization. The Central Valley Project Improvement

Act in some ways represented the final erasure of any rural-urban dichotomy that might have existed, tying the regions together under a regime of deficit-financed urban growth.

Still, in California, visions burn eternal, and despite the overwhelming trends, the Natural Resources Defense Council, a nationwide environmental organization, sued the Bureau of Reclamation in the late 1980s to set aside the Reagan administration rule (the Reclamation Reform Act). The council's suit claimed that the rules were in violation of the National Environmental Policy Act, and that the Reagan administration allowed evasions of the subsidy limit. In 1991 the Reclamation Reform Act was set aside by court order, the judge agreeing with the Natural Resources Defense Council, and the Bureau of Reclamation was ordered to revisit the rules. The Reagan administration appealed. When President Clinton took office, his administration asked for time to put together new rules. These were promised in the spring of 1998, but as of this writing have not yet been promulgated.[26]

In one final, bizarre twist to the California water wars, the Texas-based Bass brothers, Sid and Lee, whose family's net worth is estimated at more than $3 billion, have been buying up some of the choicest farmland in the Imperial Valley. But they have no intention of farming their newly acquired $140 million acreage. Instead, under the 1992 legislation, they intend to sell their federal irrigation water from the Colorado River to San Diego for up to $400 an acre-foot—water they purchase at the federally subsidized price of $12 an acre-foot. The main opponent to this potential future water sale is the Metropolitan Water District, proponent of the 1992 act. For decades San Diego has been the MWD's biggest customer. After the last drought, claiming it was necessary to be prepared for future water shortages, the MWD built a mega-reservoir in Riverside County. San Diego is poised to choose between continuing with the MWD (and thus helping defray the cost of the new dam) and building a $1 billion pipeline to Imperial County for water from the Bass brothers.[27]

To complicate matters further, there are also two major agreements involving the transfer of Colorado River water to southern California. These concern the MWD and the Southern Nevada Water Authority, and the San Diego Water Authority and the Imperial Water District. In December 1995 the MWD board signed a memorandum of understanding with the Southern Nevada Water Authority—a group of purveyors serving the rapidly growing Las Vegas area—to share the cost of lining the All American Canal in the Imperial Valley. The All American Canal is an 82-mile, earth-lined channel that delivers Colorado River water to the Imperial Valley. Lining the canal is expected to increase its yield by 70,000 acre-feet a year, bringing its total water delivery to 300,000 acre-feet a year. The agreement would give the Nevada agency about 40 percent of all the water conserved by the project, enabling it to supply water to the booming Las Vegas area.

The San Diego County Water Authority signed a memorandum of understanding with the Imperial Irrigation District in September 1995 for an undetermined amount of water, up to 400,000 acre-feet. But the MWD deal with Nevada appears to have angered the Imperial Irrigation District, which claims that Nevada is not entitled to the water since it was intended to benefit users in southern California. This would give Imperial more water to sell. Currently San Diego is almost entirely dependent on the MWD and purchases nearly 25 percent of MWD's water, even though it is only entitled to 12 percent. San Diego fears water shortages in case of drought, since Los Angeles has a legal entitlement to be served before San Diego, so it is looking for additional sources of water. There is a price issue as well. MWD officials say they support the San Diego–Imperial Valley deal in principle, but they do not want to finance the cost of transporting water from the Imperial Valley to San Diego. Currently MWD's water costs San Diego from $25 to $75 an acre-foot. Imperial water would be far more costly, up to $400 an acre-foot—the same price the Bass brothers envisage charging for their water.[28] Water independence for San Diego will be a costly affair.

In any event, it appears that the Central Valley Project Improvement Act has set in motion an inexorable process of water sale to the highest bidders—growing urban areas. Further, it has created circumstances where the ownership of agricultural lands is potentially most valuable for its rights to federally subsidized irrigation water.

Forestry: Further Debates and Controversies

Despite the improved forest practice regulations passed in the early 1970s and the expansion of Redwood National Park, forest conditions in California and forest management, both public and private, continued to be of grave concern to the environmental community. Perhaps the most dramatic symbol of private forest management for environmentalists was the 1985 acquisition of Pacific Lumber by the Los Angeles–based Maxxam Group, Inc., under the leadership of Texan Charles Hurwitz. "By using high-interest junk bonds to acquire the company, Hurwitz' Maxxam Group, Inc., placed P.L. deeply into debt. The result was a decision to cut more and more of the bigger, older and more valuable trees."[29]

Pacific Lumber had been something of an anomaly among north coast lumber companies. It was 120 years old and had a tradition of conservation and paternalistic labor relations. Pacific Lumber was the only company that still had thousands of acres of uncut, old-growth redwood, including some ancient trees. The company had built a company town, Scotia, where it rented out small, nearly identical houses to its employees at a fraction of nearby rental costs. It had retained its mills, three of which milled only the thick, old-growth logs, continuing in the old, labor-intensive way. Founded in 1869, the company was taken over early on by Simon Murphy, a logging tycoon. The Murphys allowed their workers to stay rent-free in company housing during the Depression, and they had a long-standing relationship with the Save the Redwoods League, bequeathing redwood lands for a state park, now the Avenue of the Giants. Even in the early 1970s when the timber market was depressed, the Murphys put their workers on a four-day week rather than dismiss them. Their enlightened management included company doctors, company tuition funds of up to $8,000 a year for workers' children, and more. By the late 1970s the company was debt-free and cash-rich. Its timber worth was estimated at $1.4 billion. Clearly, this was an attractive candidate for a corporate takeover.[30]

Increased timber cutting by Pacific Lumber after the 1985 takeover by Maxxam had led the company to hire hundreds more mill workers and foresters. Modernizing mills in the north coast area had a negative effect on jobs in the area because the modern mills require less labor, but Pacific Lumber had retained a steady work force. If the company had continued to cut under the old management plan, there would have been sufficient old-growth trees to last forty-five to sixty years. Under the new regime, the company's holdings were estimated to offer only a ten- to fifteen-year supply of old-growth timber. This meant good but short-term employment for those additional hundreds of mill workers and foresters recently put on staff for the greatly accelerated harvest and milling schedule, and a shortened career for the old-time employees.

Before Hurwitz's buyout was final, he had claimed he would not change the company's forestry operations. He subsequently doubled the harvest rate and accelerated a clear-cutting practice that leveled thousands of acres of virgin redwood and Douglas fir, with the approval of the state Forestry Board, appointed by the governor. Soon the company was $754 million in debt even after draining $69 million from the employees' pension fund,[31] and the accelerated cut became critical to maintaining fiscal solvency. Selling a company's assets to pay off debt (either incurred in the purchase or from other previous company purchases) was the typical approach of takeovers financed by junk bonds (at which Hurwitz was a master) in the mid-1980s, one that led to the devastating nationwide savings and loan crisis.

Hurwitz's takeover of Pacific Lumber turned out to be quite controversial, causing numerous lawsuits by some former stockholders, who claimed they had been paid only a fraction of the company's worth. A timber cruise by knowledgeable foresters had not been performed in forty years, so the value of the company's approximately 200,000 acres was unknown. At the time of the sale, Pacific Lumber stock had traded for $25 a share. Hurwitz paid $40, but discontented former stockholders felt it should have sold for more than $60 a share, based on the timber assets, though their precise worth was unknown. Protests were to no avail.

Since then, a coalition of groups hoping to preserve the oldest and biggest redwoods on Hurwitz's land has been working to reach an agreement between the federal government and the state. Under this agreement several thousand acres of the Headwaters area in the remaining virgin forest would pass into the public domain. In exchange Hurwitz would receive valuable national forest land in northern California, as well as surplus military land with commercial real estate potential in Texas and elsewhere. Among Hurwitz's forest holdings there is a critical spread of 76,000 acres, habitat to the endangered marbled murrelet and possibly to northern spotted owls. The situation came to a head after the California Board of Forestry had permitted Pacific Lumber to log up to 10 percent of the "dead, dying or diseased trees" in this same area, in addition to allowing it to log in the area.

Hurwitz owes the federal government $1.6 billion for the government bailout of his Texas-based savings and loan, which collapsed in 1988. Federal regulators are suing Hurwitz for his alleged role in the failed thrift. At the same time, the federal government is offering Hurwitz a $380 million deal, including valuable federal timber and military lands, so that he will not log an ecologically irreplaceable portion of the ancient redwood forest. Environmental groups want Hurwitz to simply relinquish a large chunk of the land in exchange for his debt to the federal government, applying the debt-for-nature arrangements established for developing countries by the World Bank. They also doubt that Hurwitz will give up a sufficiently large chunk of the land for species habitat and ecosystem health through the negotiation process now under way.[32] Hurwitz himself is said to be willing to trade 7,500 acres of the unique old-growth Headwaters forest, which is estimated to cover 60,000 acres. He plans to harvest the remaining ancient redwoods of the forest within fifteen years.

In 1983 the state legislature, responding to complaints from the timber industry, took jurisdiction over logging permits away from counties, granting it to the Board of Forestry exclusively.

In the fall of 1998 the California legislature by a narrow margin approved AB 1986, funding the purchase of Maxxam's prized old-growth Headwaters Forest, acquiring the Headwaters Grove and Elkhead Springs Grove and two other areas. The bill specified changes in Maxxam's forest management, including "no cut" buffers along fish-bearing, year-round streams and non–fish-bearing streams; habitat protection for fifty years of set-aside areas for the endangered marbled murrelet; and some other changes in the company's required habitat conservation plan for its forests. The bill appropriated $245,500,000 for acquisition, administrative expenses, and economic assistance to Humboldt County—in addition to the $250,000,000 already appropriated by the federal government. Environmentalists felt that the acquisition area was far too narrowly defined and that it allowed the company to dictate price and terms. Although the arrangement is seen as better than nothing, Maxxam continues to hold large acreages of unprotected old-growth redwoods it intends to harvest.

Attempts to Improve Private Forest Practice by Initiative

The deteriorating condition of the north coast and Sierra Nevada forests under private ownership led environmentalists to resort to the initiative process. Republican governor Deukmejian's forestry board appointments were reliably pro-industry, and the state legislature was unwilling to update the Forest Practice Act of 1976. The act, like many other pieces of legislation, is implemented by an appointed board, a structure of governance put in place during the Progressive era. The governor appoints board members, and Governor Deukmejian appointed people favorably disposed to industry. Through the process of rule making, the board was able to gnaw at the edges of the 1976 act, giving timber companies more latitude in their cutting practices. Environmentalists were frustrated. They felt they had no other recourse than the initiative process. But rather than one initiative, several were put forward and qualified for the ballot, diluting the strength of the issue and the environmentalists' efforts.

The nonprofit Environmental Protection Information Center, under the leadership of Robert Sutherland, coauthored the "Forests Forever Initiative," a proposal that would have banned clear-cutting in all forests, prohibited the logging of nearly all old-growth timber, and authorized $742 million in general-obligation bonds to fund state purchase, over ten years, of specified ancient forests.[33] This initiative was heavily backed by Hal Arbit, a San Mateo investment broker who spent $5.1 million for the campaign. It was defeated by a vote of 52 percent to 48 percent.

A disgruntled Pacific Lumber employee wrote a proposal entitled "The Timber Bond Act of 1990," which would have authorized state purchase of Pacific Lumber Company to sell it back to employees in an employee stock ownership plan (ESOP). It would have also preserved several thousand acres of the company's old-growth forest. This initiative also failed.

Still another proposal, "The Environmental Protection Act of 1990," was also placed on the ballot, backed by Assemblyman Tom Hayden and other Democratic politicians and environmentalists. This bill was portrayed by its proponents as the most ambitious of all of the ballot initiatives. This initiative would have done the following:

· Established a $200 million fund to purchase stands of ancient redwood trees threatened by logging and allowed the state to use its power of eminent domain if owners refused to sell

· Established a one-year moratorium on the clear-cutting of old-growth redwoods

· Banned clear-cutting statewide

· Required developers to plant one tree for every 500 square feet of new development

· Phased out all agricultural pesticides known to cause cancer or birth defects

· Banned new oil drilling off the coast and set up a $500 million state cleanup fund for oil spills

· Created an elected environmental advocate with the power to sue to enforce the law.

This initiative was dubbed Big Green and was favored to pass until industrial interests mounted a fierce campaign of opposition, claiming such measures would wreak havoc on the state's economy. The initiative was further undercut as the state's economy began to feel the effects of budgets cuts in the defense industry and suffer from the global economic downturn. Recession had set in by the fall of 1990. The electorate's mood was changing, susceptible to the economic arguments.

In addition to attacking Big Green and the Forests Forever Initiative, the timber industry put its own initiative on the ballot, the "Global Warming and Clear-Cutting Reduction, Wildlife Protection and Reforestation Act of 1990." This act, sponsored by Californians for Sensible Environmental Protection, would have done the following:

· Kept the other two timber plans from taking effect if it got the most votes

· Allowed lifetime timber harvest plans for private forest lands rather than requiring the state to approve THPs for each year's proposed cutting

· Provided for $300 million in bonds for public and private forest rehabilitation projects

- Eliminated clear-cutting in some areas
- Authorized, but not directed or appropriated money for, the state's acquisition of 1,600 acres of old-growth timber.[34]

This initiative failed, too.

As these examples demonstrate, the initiative process was increasingly targeted as the vehicle for legislative change by interested parties in the state, since little leadership could be expected from the legislature or the governor's office. Environmental initiatives were only one area in which vested interests were active, but one of the most visible. By the mid-1990s, despite the expenditure of large sums of money by environmentalists and timber interests, no new legislation had been passed. Private forest practices were debated in courts of law and at the forestry board, but nothing was resolved.

Resourceful California

In 1991 attention turned to the Sierra Nevada mountains and the protection of the state's biodiversity. No doubt impressed by California's declining environmental quality and the political controversies surrounding environmental management, recently elected governor Wilson launched a new set of policies and approaches to meet these challenges. Called Resourceful California, the governor's program was introduced in the spring of 1991. It was described by the administration as an "unprecedented effort to improve the conservation of California's vast and complex biological diversity." The approach involved two main components. The first was an "unprecedented Memorandum of Understanding (MOU) on biological diversity between ten state and federal land managing agencies and the University of California."[35] This MOU created an executive council on biological diversity, chaired by the California secretary for resources and composed of the directors of the signatory agencies. The MOU, intended to promote cooperation and coordination in the development and implementation of biodiversity conservation, also created a structure whereby the executive council would promote locally derived solutions to regional resource problems and encourage the development of "bioregional councils" in each of the state's ten unique "bioregions." These smaller councils were then expected to encourage yet smaller groups, organized around watersheds or landscapes, which would form watershed or landscape associations to formulate local land-use plans.

The second component of Governor Wilson's Resourceful California plan was called the Natural Communities Conservation Planning program (NCCP). This state program, apart from the MOU, was designed to employ ecosystem planning to anticipate and prevent the controversies and grid-lock that often resulted from the listing of threatened or endangered birds or animals under the Endangered Species Act. California, by the 1990s, had lost more than 90 percent of its coastal wetlands and 98 percent of its cottonwood and willow riparian forest. The federal and state governments had listed more than 320 threatened or endangered plant and animal species in the state, most of which were at risk because of a lack of habitat. An additional 2,350 species were candidates for federal listing. The NCCP was designed to intervene early enough to protect an entire ecosystem or natural community and its interdependent species. It required the cooperation and collaboration of all involved parties, including landowners, conservationists, the scientific community, and government at all levels.

That fall Governor Wilson also convened the Sierra Summit, bringing together 150 people from government, industry, academia, and environmental groups in the lovely setting of Fallen Leaf Lake, near Lake Tahoe, to discuss the future of the "Range of Light." The Sierra Nevada mountains—430 miles long, encompassing eighteen counties, nine national forests, three national parks, and a half-dozen climatic zones—had been the subject of in-depth reporting by the *Sacramento Bee* that summer.[36] The eight-month study revealed a mountain range in poor health. Air pollution levels in Sequoia National Park were higher than those in Los Angeles; streams were polluted with toxic chemicals from abandoned mines; serious soil erosion threatened reforestation and stream health; and wildlife habitat, including trout streams and winter range for mule deer, had been destroyed by over-grazing, timber harvesting, and urbanization. Six of the counties in the Sierra were among the ten fastest growing counties in all of California.[37] The Wilson administration hoped that its two initiatives would be the vehicles for addressing such problems.

The Sierra Nevada Mountains: Urbanization and Endangered Species

John Muir had made the Sierras famous as one of the most beautiful mountain ranges in the world. Its beauty and unique qualities inspired California's early scientists. The Sierra Club was created in 1892 "to enlist the support and cooperation of the people and the government in preserving the forests and other natural features of the Sierra Nevada." The natural scientists of the time, aware of the extraordinary qualities of the mountain range, used it as the basis for several significant theories about the earth's evolution. These natural scientists were among the first to call for the preservation of the range, but their proposals were met with opposition from mining and timber interests, and in the end only 10 percent of the range was protected. This land is mostly in the higher elevations, where no economically important resources were locked out of the possibility of development. It was set aside based on the geological and other surveys done by the state to determine the state's resources so that they could be exploited by the private sector. Muir had written, "Our government is like a rich and foolish spendthrift who has inherited a magnificent estate in perfect order and then has left his fields and meadows, forests and parks to be sold and plundered and wasted."[38]

By 1992 Muir might not have recognized his "Range of Light," yet the perennial vision of a national park that would encompass virtually the entire mountain range and put its management under one jurisdiction was put forward at Governor Wilson's Sierra Summit. That proposal has not been mentioned again since the summit, though the Wilson administration's bioregional councils were put forward as an alternative measure at the time. Douglas Wheeler, secretary of resources, summed up the results of the summit: "The most important result of that meeting was the realization on the part of people that by sitting down, discussing these issues and identifying respective solutions, we can make real progress. The polarization of the past is not useful in terms of actually solving environmental issues. And, so, we've got a consensus now about the need to address these issues. No immediate solutions to all of them but a willingness to work on those solutions, which is new."[39]

What problems? What solutions? The problems of the Sierras are complex and substantial, and go far beyond local solutions. The need to address them is urgent. One of the most intractable problems facing the mountain range is that of air pollution, consisting of a mixture of ozone, sulfur dioxide, polycyclic aromatic hydrocarbons (PAHs), carbon monoxide, nitrogen oxide, particulates, and other chemicals. During the summer, west-facing canyons and foothills are immersed in the pollution that blows in from the Central Valley and the Bay area. The problem is worst in the southern part of the range, because of the increasing amount of air pollution in the San Joaquin Valley. This part of the state is second only to the Inland Empire (Riverside and San Bernardino Counties) in its rate of growth. Emissions from cars, trucks, power plants, tractors, and industries; pesticides; oil-pumping vapors; dust and dirt from agricultural activities: all combine to create a foglike layer of pollution. The valley is hemmed in by mountains on three sides, which restricts air flow and concentrates the poisons under the sun. Then in the evening the cloud of pollution rises, hour by hour, "effectively fumigating a large band of forest from Bakersfield to Lake Tahoe, including three National Parks."[40] The pollution obscures views: where once one could see 100 miles to the sea, the view now is only about 5 miles. Worse, the effects on fauna and flora are potentially disastrous.

Scientists worry that the forest ecosystem will be increasingly shaped by air pollution. Up and down the range, trees are dying in record numbers. In some areas, one of three trees is dead—up to 6 billion board feet of dead or dying timber. Ozone seems to be the primary culprit. Absorbed by pine needles, ozone starts a chemical chain reaction that starves the tree of nutrients. The needles begin to die, and that in turn cuts back on photosynthesis. Later the root growth is restricted, and the tree may die. The worst damage is closest to the San Joaquin Valley. In Sequoia National Park recorded ozone levels are about three times higher than in the valley. That means that at night, when trees begin opening their stomata (the tiny openings in the needles), they are pulling in a lot of gases and literally poisoning themselves.

All of the Jeffrey pines at the 6,000-foot level in Sequoia National Park are showing ozone damage. At Lake Tahoe ozone levels are also causing forest damage, even though they are not exceeding the state human health standard of 90 parts per billion. In Yosemite National Park nearly one-quarter of the pines sampled in 1987 had ozone damage.[41] What this means for the ability of the vegetation to regenerate is not yet certain, but seedlings are vulnerable to ozone. Should levels rise, there is a real possibility of substantial change in vegetation. Ozone damage also makes trees much weaker and thus more vulnerable to pests.

Certain animal species are also very susceptible to air pollution. Scientists now believe that air pollution is responsible for the disappearance of previously common amphibians, especially frogs. In the southern Sierras, the foothill yellow-legged frog, easily found streamside, has entirely disappeared from Sequoia National Park, and the mountain yellow-legged frog may be in trouble, too. This frog was previously found in virtually every fish-less pond in the high Sierras from Tahoe to the sequoias.[42] The continuing urbanization of the Central Valley, facilitated by the passage of the Central Valley Project Improvement Act, can only aggravate the problem.

In addition to creating air pollution, increased urbanization and human expansion into the foothills is also rapidly encroaching on wildlife habitat. Dams and reservoirs have created barriers for wildlife species associated with aquatic and riparian habitats; the bald eagle, peregrine falcon, and wolverine, among others, are listed as endangered species. The condor is extinct, the red fox increasingly rare, as are bighorn sheep. This list goes on, including fish, reptiles, amphibians, and plants. The great gray owl is almost gone because of overgrazing and logging on national forests. Only about fifty of the owls remain, about half of them in Yosemite National Park. Gray owls feed almost entirely in meadows, but when a meadow is grazed to the point where there is no cover, the owl's prey will leave. Throughout the Sierras, more than 2,000 miles of trout streams have been damaged by livestock grazing, water projects, and mining. The willow flycatcher has nearly vanished as its nesting grounds—streams and meadows—have been converted to other uses. Today only about 200 nesting pairs remain, all in the Sierras. This bird has been declared an endangered species. Of the thirty-four bird species that have been studied over the past 150 years in the Sierran region, eleven are declining. Fifty other animals are listed as endangered or threatened.

Since the nineteenth century the state has lost 99 percent of its valley grasslands and 94 percent of its interior wetlands. These lands, rich in fauna and flora, were mostly at lower elevations and were rapidly taken up during the disposal of the public lands. Over the past forty years about 800,000 acres of oak woodland have been cleared, nearly two-thirds of all the oak forest in California. The portions of the Sierra Nevada mountains that are now in the national park are the lands nobody wanted. The most critical and most diverse habitats remain in private ownership or are managed as part of the national forests, subject to logging, mineral exploration, and mining. Today, only 15 percent of the Sierras' oldest and biggest trees are left. These are stands of mostly pine and fir, believed to be the home of the healthiest mix of forest plants and animals that remain in the range.

In March 1991 the U.S. General Accounting Office criticized the U.S. Forest Service for putting higher priority on timber harvesting than wildlife, which received only 3–7 percent of Forest Service funding, compared with up to 37 percent for timber programs. Under the Reagan and Bush administrations, timber harvest quotas were greatly increased, while budgets for other activities (part of the multiple-use mandate of the national forests) were cut. The legislative mandate and imperatives from the President's Office for the National Forests have been for increased timber production, not preservation or the enhancement of wildlife. The GAO report, while perhaps accurate, was puzzling, since the Forest Service simply was following orders.

The U.S. Forest Service in the Sierras

The U.S. Forest Service manages 52 percent of the Sierras. During the Reagan and Bush administrations, between 1980 and 1989 the amount of wood cut in the Sierras on public and private land jumped 67 percent, from 959 million board-feet to 1.6 billion. The amount of timber harvested through clear-cuts in the 1980s rose to about 4,000 acres a year, from about 700 acres a year in the 1970s. Timber is the Forest Service's biggest single source of income—about 85 percent of its revenues in the Sierras. Without timber harvesting, the Forest Service budget would dwindle dramatically. Of the wood cut in the Sierras, 60 percent comes from the public lands, and county governments receive a portion of the income from those sales. Consequently, local communities and timber-dependent businesses rely on high timber harvest rates on Forest Service lands. This puts additional pressure on the Forest Service, beyond the quotas set by Congress and the administration. Thus, managing forests for their ecological importance cannot be the highest priority for the Forest Service. It is part of a circle of mutual dependency centered on providing timber for timber companies and generating sales to provide revenues for localities.

Forest Service management of its resource in the Sierras has come under heavy criticism. Clear-cuts have been poorly planned and prepared, seedlings planted after harvest are not taking, soil erosion is worsening, and the forest resource is declining. Before World War II the Forest Service was not obliged to sell its timber to private industry, and thus the resource was not under such intense pressure. Since then, the Forest Service has been gradually transformed into a government entity that helps private timber-processing companies stay in business. Because of this role, and because of the decline of easily accessible trees, timber is now harvested in increasingly marginal areas—those with steep slopes, where soil is unstable and subject to erosion. In addition, the Forest Service has increased the allowable amount of salvage logging by commercial timber companies, which now accounts for half the timber harvested in the Sierras.

Salvage logging is the removal of dead and dying timber. The idea behind this increase was to decrease the forest's vulnerability to fire by removing the most flammable materials, and also to find another wood product to sell. But salvage logging has had unanticipated consequences. It causes serious erosion and watershed damage when it is not carried out in a careful and knowledgeable way, and it significantly reduces wildlife habitat and biodiversity. Salvage logging in national forests received a boost in the summer of 1995, when President Clinton signed the Recessions Act containing the "salvage logging rider." In the summer of 1996 over 300 sales were being offered in California under the salvage logging rider (according to which a sale can go through even if it will lose money). The rider used a vastly expanded definition of salvage, including "associated trees." These do not have to be dead, fallen, or even damaged, simply "imminently susceptible to fire or insect attack." It essentially allows logging in remaining old-growth forests, and along wild and scenic rivers in sensitive riparian and roadless areas, with no restrictions based on slope or soil conditions.[43]

Throughout the United States a nearly century-old policy of fire suppression has been an integral part of Forest Service forest management. In the

Sierras, under natural conditions, fires occurred regularly every three to five years, clearing out the brush under the trees, leaving a sunny and open forest. Native Americans also burned the forest regularly. These were low-intensity surface fires that did little long-term damage to trees. Historical accounts of the Sierras describe a very different forest—groves of trees with little understory brush. Today, forests are thick with underbrush and dead material. This creates extremely hazardous fire conditions because fires that do burn become very hot, very intense, and hard to control. Fires become catastrophic, not only burning trees but killing them, thereby destroying the forest. But if there is no fire, the soil can become nearly sterile, as it is in the long-unburned sequoia groves today. The ash from fire revitalizes the soil and serves as the catalyst for seed germination for certain species. Fire suppression, an important aspect of modern silviculture as practiced by the Forest Service, is now being revised because of its detrimental effect on forest health. Accordingly, the Forest Service is developing and implementing control burn programs. Other taken-for-granted practices are also gradually being questioned, such as the ability of foresters to effectively replant after harvest—there are insufficient signs of successful forest regeneration in the Sierras.

The current reassessment of Forest Service silvicultural practices combines two elements. One is a rethinking of the role of the Forest Service in managing the nation's forests. This involves questioning the focus on forest products and economics as a measure of forest productivity and asking whether biodiversity preservation should not be a higher goal for the nation's forests, and hence for the Forest Service. The other element, not entirely separate, is the gradual realization that forest ecosystems are complex and interdependent and that Forest Service silvicultural practices, which encourage single-age monocultures that are easy to harvest and economically desirable, may not be sustainable. The forest reproduces when certain conditions of biodiversity exist, but it does poorly otherwise. The Sierras are a unique combination of Pacific Northwest, Mexico, Canadian, Arctic, and Great Basin desert. Plants and animals have evolved under these unique conditions of climate, rainfall, and location, each dependent on the others. Forest research, at least until recently, has been driven by the desire to increase timber production rather than to perpetuate biological diversity. Only recently has it become apparent that, at least in the Sierras, the two are inseparable.

Unanticipated consequences of Forest Service management continue to mount. One of the primary reasons why forests were set aside in the late nineteenth century was to maintain a healthy watershed so that water flows would remain intact, there would be good groundwater recharge and less flooding, and water quality would remain high. The Sierra Nevada mountains serve an essential role in California's water system, providing 6 out of every 10 gallons of the state's precious water resource. But poor harvesting techniques, clear-cutting, grazing, and lack of successful regeneration are threatening the quantity and quality of that water. "Damage to soil and streams is perhaps the most serious and overlooked problem in the Sierra Nevada, one that threatens the essence of the range and the lifeblood of California: mountain watersheds."[44] In the Plumas National Forest, 30 percent of the water is so fouled by erosion that it no longer meets state water-quality objectives. The Pacific Gas & Electric reservoir on Rock Creek, downstream from the Plumas National Forest, is filling up with mud and debris. Examples abound, but here too, paralleling the situation of wildlife management, only a small portion (2–3 percent) of the Forest Service budget is allocated to soil and watershed protection.

Logging roads, built by the Forest Service to facilitate harvesting by private timber companies, create damage. In many places the soil is shallow and subject to erosion. Because of the geology and climate of the mountains, once soil has been bared—by clear-cutting, road building, or the clearing of brush after a fire—there is a very high chance of its being eroded away by rain or baked dry by the sun, thus unable to sustain regrowth.

In all these ways, small and large, the Sierras are being steadily degraded, perhaps changed beyond recovery. Some of the problems can probably be addressed by improving the forest practices of the Forest Service, which are the object of severe criticism on the part of environmental organizations, and even of timber companies. This would require federal legislation. But many of the assaults on the mountains are caused by factors beyond Forest Service control—such as urbanization and air pollution—and these have not yet been fully identified, let alone addressed. Much of the mountains' threatened biodiversity is in the foothills, in the jurisdiction of counties and cities, beyond the Forest Service's domain. These are the grazing lands of the state's mule deer, of the great gray owl, of the willow flycatcher, of the foothill yellow-legged frog.

Island biogeography has shown that the degradation of lands in the periphery of ecosystems tends over time to erode the biological integrity of those other systems, slowly choking them. The fate of the federally managed Sierra Nevada mountains is bound up with the fate of the privately held surrounding foothills and the land uses in the great Central Valley. It cannot be treated in isolation. Yet Wilson's 1991 Sierra Summit did not broach the management of the lower elevations, or the relationship between further growth and automobile traffic in the Central Valley and the air pollution effects on the mountain forests. The Sierra Summit was asking the wrong questions. Debate and dialogue avoided the ever vexing issue of planning for growth and the delicate question of controlling private property development.

The Sierras are becoming an urban ecosystem, shaped by the forces of air pollution, recreation, and exploitation of resources for further urban development needs, like timber, water, and minerals. The forces causing the degradation of the mountains are artifacts of the cities, once again demonstrating the intertwined nature of urban and rural environments in California, and, indeed, the leading role cities have had in shaping the state's rural lands. Governor Wilson's watershed associations and bioregional councils would not go far in addressing this fundamental reality that is transforming nature in the state. Setting the whole mountain range aside as a giant park would not save the Sierras, it would merely be a first step.

The Grand Accord: More Timber Politics

A year after the Sierra Summit, Governor Wilson stood on the capitol steps, side by side with conservationists and timber company executives, to announce his endorsement of forestry reform legislation, dubbed the Grand Accord. The legislation followed on the heels of the defeat of Big Green and the Forests Forever Initiative, and further legal battles about private forest practice on the north coast. (The north coast battles had included lawsuits by environmentalists claiming timber companies violated the state's forest practice regulation, and countersuits by timber companies.) The Grand Accord was touted as the best possible solution. The California Board of Forestry had denied one THP in 1992, while approving 350,000 acres of cutting plans, plus another 250,000 acres approved to be cut under emergencies and exemptions. It denied one THP in 1993 as well. To environmentalists like Sharon Duggan, lawyer for the Environmental Protection Information Center (EPIC), this did not indicate any change in outlook on the part of the board or of the California Division of Forestry, despite Wilson's avowed concern about biodiversity conservation in the state.[45]

The Sierra Club had put together a reform of forest practice, called the Sierra Accord, in 1991. After incorporating changes initiated by the Wilderness Society and the Natural Resources Defense Council (to make it more palatable to the legislature), as well as changes defined by the legislature itself, the bill was passed by both the Assembly and the Senate. The Sierra Club, not entirely comfortable with the changes, took a neutral position, while grass-roots organizations, such as EPIC, felt it was grossly inadequate and fought the bill. The governor pocket-vetoed that bill, claiming that something better could be developed that would be more acceptable. The Grand Accord came out of this failed attempt.

Hal Arbit, the deep pockets of the Forests Forever Initiative, once again became involved, with the support of some disaffected Sierra Club members, the Natural Resources Defense Council, the Wilderness Society, the Audubon Society, and the California Planning and Conservation League. Negotiations with the Wilson administration led to this new piece of legislation, weaker than the revised Sierra Accord, but supported by the state's major environmental groups except the Sierra Club, which saw the bill as a sellout to industry. Grass-roots groups strongly opposed the Grand Accord. But the fiercest opposition came from the timber industry, especially coastal companies including Pacific Lumber and Simpson Timber. They hired some of Sacramento's most powerful lobbyists to canvass the legislature and the governor's office, and distributed books filled with photos of timber employees and their families.[46] The old "jobs versus trees" trade-off was resurrected, with timber industry lobbyists arguing that tighter forest practice would have a devastating effect on the local job base, despite the industry's own introduction of new mill technology, which had done more to reduce employment than any environmental protection measures.

The legislature failed to pass the Grand Accord, concerned about the state's high unemployment rate and susceptible to industry lobbyists' arguments. Moreover Wilson, at the last minute, did an about-face and refused to support his own bill. Meanwhile, not taking any chances that the bill, even in its weakened state, might pass, the timber industry had been assiduously working with the Board of Forestry. Industry lawyers obtained substantial modification of forest practice rules, gutting in advance the strongest regulations in the governor's forestry bill through administrative procedure. These new forestry rules were enacted as emergency rules, since the governor's forestry bill did not pass.[47] Ultimately the new rules were stopped by a court-ordered injunction, obtained by EPIC. The struggle continues, with lawsuit countered by lawsuit. Decades of controversy over private forest practice and Forest Service forest management remains unresolved, bogged down in a quagmire of special interests and conflicting scientific expertise and mandates, and subject to a volatile initiative process. What is certain is that the state's forest base continues to decline and, along with it, forest biodiversity.

Urban Struggles over Dwindling Biodiversity

In his concern to address the problem of loss of biodiversity in California, Governor Wilson went beyond the creation of bioregional councils—which did not figure in the forest management debates—to launch the Natural Communities Conservation Planning Program. This program, concerned with endangered species, was an attempt to accommodate development interests while attempting to comply with requirements of the federal Endangered Species Act. Naturally a rich repository of fauna and flora, California has led the nation in loss of biodiversity and in numbers of endangered or threatened species listings. Those listings have increasingly taken place on private property in rapidly urbanizing areas.

The Endangered Species Act

The federal Endangered Species Act (ESA) of 1973 provides for the protection of a species (plant or animal) if found to be endangered or threatened with extinction. "Congress took an especially strong regulatory approach to species preservation. In the 1960s the spiraling extinction rate of plant and animal species alarmed Congress." Congress concluded that the unknown but potentially valuable biological and ecological qualities of species made preservation imperative. The ESA prohibited actions threatening the existence of species. It formulated a process to protect the ecosystems in which endangered species and threatened species live. Congress hoped to elevate fish and wildlife concerns to a level that would, in the Supreme Court's words, "halt and reverse the trend toward species extinction, whatever the cost," and, in the words of Congress, preserve the "esthetic, ecological, educational, historical, recreational, and scientific values [species provide] to the nation and its people." Congress believed that scientific uncertainty about potentially unknown risks resulting from biological extinctions should be shifted toward preservation—that is, to risk preservation rather than disappearance.[48]

Determining whether a species is threatened or endangered is a complicated question, because it is difficult to ascertain the point at which a threatened species becomes endangered, and by then it may be too late to prevent its demise. Even if a species is designated as threatened, the Fish and Wildlife Service may consider economic factors in designating critical habitat. Although Congress hoped to protect species by conserving the ecosystems upon which endangered species and threatened species depend, it did not protect their habitat absolutely, as economic factors can be considered.

The framers of the Endangered Species Act could not have anticipated the degree to which it would be invoked in rapidly urbanizing areas. Because of the structure of land-use authority, it falls on local jurisdictions—cities and counties—to decide how land within their boundaries will be used. There is no requirement to coordinate their planning with neighboring jurisdictions, to take into account ecosystems that may cross their boundaries, or to proactively plan land uses to preserve lands for their environmental attributes, open space, or conservation. Local jurisdictions, through the tool of zoning, may plan as they see fit within the laws protecting private property in the United States. Thus, even if a local jurisdiction wishes to zone land for future open space, conservation, or nature preserve, it must generally purchase that land from the owner or establish a land-use designation that does not deprive the landowner of all economically viable use. If land is far enough outside the urban zone of influence, open-space zoning can be upheld, but as a city grows, this designation often becomes difficult to maintain because the landowner may claim he or she is being deprived of the land's economic value. In addition, the effects of Proposition 13 have made increased land development the primary source of additional local revenue, so there is a great deal of built-in pressure to zone land for economically viable uses.

The ESA requires species preservation measures through the development of habitat conservation plans (HCPs), which in urban contexts often means freezing development in an area large enough to provide habitat for the plant or animal to survive and reproduce. Given the pressures for development—fiscal, demographic, political—an endangered (or threatened) species designation can generate tremendous controversy. The NCCP was the Wilson administration's response to these concerns.

Natural Communities Conservation Planning

The NCCP program resulted specifically from the threat of a potential endangered species listing for the gnatcatcher, a small bird that lives in the dwindling coastal sage scrub ecosystem. A vice president of the Irvine Ranch Company met with the secretary of the state Resources Agency and outlined a plan that would "assure protection of adequate coastal sage scrub habitat, thereby making any listing of the gnat catcher and other coastal sage scrub-dependent species unnecessary" and would allow continued land development. In a 1991 letter to Douglas P. Wheeler, resources secretary, Vice President Monica Florian stated, "I believe there is a general consensus among major Southern California landowners and development interests to proceed with habitat conservation. . . . provided certain conditions are met." The letter went on to outline the conditions, including a delay or deferral of the state and federal listing processes. Florian also suggested that the governor appoint a scientific review board in the Department of Fish and Game to arbitrate the scientific evidence regarding the status of the gnatcatcher and the coastal sage ecosystem.[49] The Wilson administration adopted the Irvine Ranch Company proposals and put them forward as its own. It is worth noting that Don Bren, the chief executive officer of the Irvine Company, was a long-time supporter of Wilson and that Bren and his employees contributed more than $210,000 to Governor Wilson's reelection campaign.[50] Further, the Irvine Company (its holdings carved from an old Spanish land grant) controls about one-sixth of the total lands in Orange County and has been very influential in county politics. Developers and related businesses donated 42 percent of campaign funds collected by supervisors and board candidates for over a decade.[51]

The NCCP process claims to have as its aim the protection of wildlife and habitat before the landscape becomes so fragmented or degraded by development that the listing of individual species is required. Instead of saving small, unconnected parcels of habitat for just one species at a time, the NCCP process is supposed to bring together all the concerned parties—the landowners, the local jurisdictions, conservation interests, and agencies—to work cooperatively to develop plans that consider broad landscapes or "ecosystems" and the needs of many species. "Partners cooperate in the program development and, by mutual consent, crucial habitat areas are set aside and may not be developed. Partners work cooperatively to study and develop conservation plans for these 'reserve' areas. In exchange for setting aside land as wildlife habitat, the process fosters economic growth by allowing development in other areas."[52] The California Department of Fish and Game would be responsible for developing guidelines and coordinating the process at the state level. As the state's trustee for natural resource protection, it would approve plans ensuring that wildlife values are protected. The department's appointed commission would be responsible for determining whether a species qualified for protection under the state Endangered Species Act, guided by Wilson's appointed scientific review panel, and thus for setting state policy and directing the department's action.

In practice, the NCCP process has often allowed developers—through the voluntary participation process—to determine what lands they were willing to set aside for the preservation of potentially endangered or threatened species.

The Coastal Sage Scrub Ecosystem

The NCCP has so far been applied most fully on the coastal sage scrub ecosystem of southern California. More than 60 percent of the coastal sage scrub of that region has been urbanized, leaving barely 400,000 acres in all of Orange, Los Angeles, Riverside, San Bernardino, and San Diego Counties. Of this acreage, only 20,000 acres are suitable habitat for the gnatcatcher. Seventy-one percent of coastal sage scrub vegetation is found on private land, whose value, per acre, ranges from $4,000 to $200,000.[53] This plant community supports the California gnatcatcher and sixty-two other sensitive plant and animal species. The protection of the coastal sage scrub ecosystem was chosen as a pilot project because its potential (and probable) listing would have affected some of the largest landowner-development interests in the state and because the Irvine Ranch Company designed a process that it could accept.

Initially, in 1992, the California Fish and Game Commission (appointed by the governor) decided not to advance the gnatcatcher as an endangered species, despite the recommendations of both the director and the staff of the agency; the commission did not ask the opinion of the scientific review panel. A California court then ruled that the findings submitted by the commission on this issue were legally deficient and ordered the agency to prepare new findings. The commissioners appealed the ruling. In a parallel action, the building industry and the Orange County toll roads agencies filed a preemptive lawsuit against the U.S. Fish and Wildlife Service, reviewing the gnatcatcher's status and claiming that the service had unfairly withheld data about the bird's taxonomy. This delayed potential endangered species listing, and an additional 2,600 acres of coastal sage scrub ecosystem were lost in the interim.[54]

In 1993 Orange County developers and the toll road agencies drafted their own NCCP planning agreement with the concurrence of the Orange County government, excluding the other interested parties. The draft agreement demanded explicit assurances, in advance, that participating landowners would meet state and federal endangered species act requirements. This phase of the process is logically supposed to come later, after the planning is complete, rather than at the outset, before the land uses have been determined and agreed to. The plan also strictly limited the amount of time available for comment by the public and wildlife agencies, and stated that no new issues could be raised. Had this NCCP proposal been accepted by the state, it would have shredded the collaborative process, which the NCCP touted as its strength, because it enabled one party—the development community—to fully control the content and process of NCCP determination, thereby circumventing the NCCP's stated purpose. The draft agreement was not finalized.

On March 25, 1993, the California gnatcatcher was listed as threatened under the federal Endangered Species Act. This came after two full years of testimony, research, and activism on the part of a small, grass-roots organization called the Endangered Habitats League, with the help of the Audubon Society and the Natural Resources Defense Council. The Interior Department chose to list the bird as threatened rather than endangered, on the grounds that ongoing regional conservation planning efforts—that is, the NCCP program—had reduced the risk of extinction. In fact, interested parties in Orange County had found little on which they could agree, and developers there had tried to hijack the process. The habitat conservation plan still remained to be developed. Differences of opinion among all the "partners" about the necessary degree of habitat protection had been irreconcilable, so no plan had been put together, and it remained for the federal government to mediate.

Because the gnatcatcher was listed as threatened rather than endangered, the bird could be incidentally killed (taken), but only within the limits of specific standards determined under a special ESA "4(d) rule." The Fish and Wildlife Service specified that the scientific review panel of the state's NCCP (a panel appointed by the governor) was responsible for developing the standards guiding the special 4(d) rule—a good example of how the federal government delegates authority to states to implement federal laws. The scientific panel could thus decide how many birds could be killed. It was to develop the overall conservation plan for the gnatcatcher, subject to review by the Fish and Wildlife Service. The Building Industry Association and the Orange County toll roads agency challenged the listing of the gnatcatcher on procedural grounds, claiming that the Fish and Wildlife Service should have made available the raw taxonomic data used by its scientist in his paper delineating the southern range of the subspecies of gnatcatcher. Their position was first upheld by the court, vacating the listing, then the listing was allowed to be reinstated.

In a parallel development, less than three weeks before the decision on the gnatcatcher listing was announced, the Fish and Wildlife Service issued a finding of "no jeopardy" for the controversial Orange County toll road project, which cut through the heart of significant coastal sage habitat. The federal agency, under tremendous political pressure from the Republican-dominated 1995 Congress that wanted to eliminate the Endangered Species Act, caved in with regard to the NCCP process. Indeed, Secretary of the Interior Bruce Babbitt pointed to the NCCP process as an example of how the ESA could successfully be implemented, and he later proposed it in other situations. Yet, according to environmentalists, the Fish and Wildlife Service did not question the assumptions being put forth by the Irvine Ranch Company's hired scientists who developed the proposals for gnatcatcher habitat. Moreover, the agency accepted the toll road trajectory, despite its clear intrusion on prime gnatcatcher habitat, in order to avoid a greater challenge by development interests—a challenge to the Endangered Species Act itself.

The Wilson administration's position during this period was to claim that the NCCP would be sufficient to protect the coastal sage scrub ecosystem. The administration worked in close collaboration with the attorneys for the Orange County toll roads and the Building Industry Association. It submitted a court declaration describing the NCCP on behalf of those trying to remove the gnatcatcher listing, giving the judge the impression that the

NCCP could protect the bird without a listing. In addition, the administration attempted to modify the state Endangered Species Act by handing over authority to local agencies to determine the measures needed to save a listed species, using the NCCP as a "fundamental" justification for this shift.[55]

The NCCP process ultimately led to an NCCP plan for the coastal central portion of Orange County on Irvine Company lands, largely based on pre-existing open space, preserving about 37,000 acres in two major units. The NCCP lands, ironically, were the open-space lands set aside in exchange for the approval of the 1989 development agreements allowing the construction of 60,000 dwelling units. The NCCP process for the southern portion of the county stalled. Land in the south is largely owned by the Santa Margarita Company, which has no DAs securing growth; this may be one explanation for its reluctance to participate. The Orange County situation shows the power of large landed interests in the politics of the state and their ability to shape land-use regulation so as to preserve their ability to continue developing their real estate.

What the framers of the Endangered Species Act did not anticipate was the degree to which nature has become urbanized. The Endangered Species Act is in direct conflict with the land-use prerogatives of local government and the constitutional protection of private property rights. As long as it has been applied to public lands—for example, curbing the amount of trees cut on Forest Service lands—it has provoked grumbling and opposition among commercial interests. But in southern California, further application of the ESA means stopping development on private land where there are endangered species. What will happen if an endangered species is found on land that is legally bound by a DA? If an ESA designation is contested as a "taking without compensation," how will a property owner be reimbursed for that land? The protection of endangered species in southern California, and foreseeably in the Sierras, is likely to become increasingly heated and more complicated.

The NCCP process has also been applied with some success in San Diego County as a capstone to an ongoing process of ecosystem and open-space preservation, based on broad public involvement. Open-space preservation has been a value in San Diego County for two decades, and the NCCP provided a way of synthesizing efforts. In Riverside County, it has been introduced as an alternative after a disastrous series of initiatives aimed at preserving habitat for the Stevens' kangaroo rat. The NCCP process is also being applied in San Bernardino County, but it is unclear how it will fare in such a situation, where there are hundreds of landowners. Unfortunately, the NCCP process cannot resolve the deeply entrenched differences among competing interests; it needs a context of cooperation.

Like the Sierra Nevada mountains, the coastal sage scrub ecosystem has a precarious future. It may be protected, but even so it could become a vestige, a kind of nature museum or living artifact.

The California Spotted Owl

In another attempt to forestall the use of the Endangered Species Act in California, the Wilson administration initiated a process to study and coordinate policy for the California spotted owl, found in parts of southern California and the Sierras. As part of its strategy to force the federal and state governments to improve their forest practice, the Wilderness Society had threatened to start the process to list the California spotted owl, a relative of the northern spotted owl, as an endangered species. At the same time the Natural Resources Defense Council filed administrative appeals challenging Forest Service timber sales in the Sierras. The Forest Service had already designated the California spotted owl as a "sensitive species," meaning that any plans or projects for its habitat would have to be evaluated to determine their effect on the spotted owl. Yet there were few demographic or ecological studies specific to the California subspecies. Because of the lack of available information, the Forest Service instituted a new policy that called for specific consideration as to how individual projects would affect owl habitat, in relation to the habitat conservation measures generally required for known or probable sites of owl pairs or resident singles.[56]

In response, the state in 1991 established a joint steering committee consisting of representatives of the federal and state forestry and wildlife agencies, academics, and observers from county government, environmental groups, timber and forest products industries, and several other organizations. Agency representatives agreed to plan the implementation of conservation measures, especially those required if the subspecies were to be listed under the ESA. The charter for this project directed federal and state natural resource agencies to "work cooperatively . . . to assess local research, inventory and monitoring information for the . . . spotted owl . . . [and that as] more information becomes available . . . agencies will continue to work cooperatively to incorporate other species and habitat needs into a long-term ecosystem planning strategy for the Sierra and Southern California ecosystems."

The steering committee immediately created two specialized teams: the technical team to provide expertise in avian biology and ecology, and the policy implementation team to provide policy and economic analysis. Together, these teams were to provide a scientific and policy framework to guide agencies and policymakers with regard to the California spotted owl. The technical team completed its work in May 1992.

Owls, Mountains, and the Perception of Nature

The range of the California spotted owl in southern California includes the central Coast Range, the mountains ringing the Los Angeles Basin, and the ranges south toward the Mexican border. Little is known about owl demographics in the central Coast Range, and not much more is known about the owls in the rest of southern California. The technical team identified the southern California population as a *metapopulation,* a term used to describe any population that exists in a discontinuous fashion, with the possibility of exchange of individuals between the population groups.

The spotted owl metapopulation in southern California is distributed in a discontinuous manner across eleven major mountain ranges and mountain complexes, primarily within national forests. This metapopulation occupies several habitat "islands," surrounded by areas of unsuitable habitat consisting largely of desert, chaparral, and urban development. This discontinuous distribution reflects the effects of extensive human-induced habitat disturbance and fragmentation, as well as natural differences in vegetation, topography, and climate in the region.

The land between ranges has been subject to rapid urban and suburban development. As a result, individual southern California populations of the spotted owl may be isolated from each other, even where blocks of habitat are relatively close. Much development has taken place in the coastal plains and inland valleys, decimating riparian areas and oak woodlands that probably served as linkages between mountain ranges. In addition, the southern metapopulation may be isolated from the Sierra Nevada subpopulation due to the physical separation of these two areas by the Tehachapi Pass and its increased urbanization. Road building and traffic, activities detrimental to owl dispersal, have increased in this area.

Owl habitat was more extensive in the past than it is today in southern California. There are recorded owl spottings from the turn of the century at the mouth of the Santa Margarita River (in Orange County), a river once supporting a dense riparian vegetation. Such riparian corridors running from the mountain to the sea essentially no longer exist in the southern California region. Still, the technical team's study of owls in the state revealed that about 26 percent (547 sites) of the known owl sites in the state are found in southern California, though there may be others because substantial areas of potential habitat have not been surveyed.[57]

The number of owls is crucial to the survival of the population because the population is relatively small and unstable. If the smaller populations become increasingly isolated by reduction in size of their habitat islands or by barriers to dispersal, the likelihood of extinction increases. The evidence collected in southern California over five years of study showed an apparent decline in owl populations, especially in the San Bernardino Mountains, where the annual rate of decline was approximately 17 percent in the resident, territorial population during the study period. If the population in the San Bernardino Mountains were to collapse, this would probably result in the extinction of the entire population of spotted owls in southern California. In other words, "the spotted owl population in Southern California appears to be fragile."[58] This study was conducted during a period of drought, and the key population (for the entire metapopulation) in the San Bernardino Mountains might begin to rebound with more water. But clearly, survival conditions for the owls in southern California are not favorable overall. Several factors negatively affect the viability of owls in southern California: urban and dispersed residential expansion, groundwater extraction, wildfires, and increased recreational use of riparian areas. The primary reasons for this vulnerability are essentially urban-related. Land development greatly accelerated in the 1980s, destroying riparian corridors that might have been used for foraging and for dispersal among the different mountain ranges. Much of the riparian-hardwood zone of the foothills (where 32 percent of the owls live) is privately held and increasingly desirable for up-scale development, and little stands in the way of approvals. As the development noose around the national forests tightens, the habitat, foraging, dispersal, and potential habitat area of the owl diminishes, and the survival potential of the species decreases. The national forests in southern California are essentially islands in an urban sea.

In the Sierras the spotted owl population is distributed fairly evenly. Over 90 percent of the known owl sites are located in national forests, primarily in mixed conifer forests (82 percent). The owls prefer stands with large (that is, old) trees, with dense canopies and snags. The loss of suitable habitat in the Sierras is due to even-aged silvicultural practices, catastrophic fire, the decline of oak stands, and long-lasting impacts by miners and shepherds in the nineteenth century. The technical team estimated that the amount of suitable habitat would continue to decrease at a rate of 229,000 acres per decade under the existing land-management plans of the Forest Service for the Sierra national forests, which emphasized harvesting large-diameter trees.[59]

While the study of the spotted owl was prompted by concerns about the owls' viability in the Sierra Nevada mountains, it is the owl population in southern California that is most at risk from pressures of urbanization. The Forest Service finally developed an interim owl-protection policy in the Sierras, after an arduous process of negotiation and compromise between environmentalists and timber companies, whose point of view was supported by

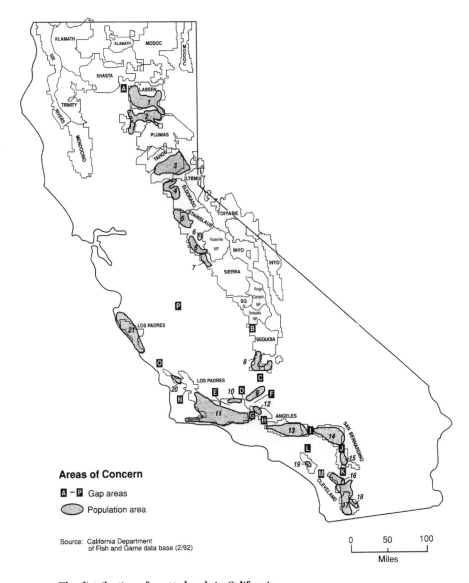

Areas of Concern

A – P Gap areas

Population area

Source: California Department
of Fish and Game data base (2/92)

0   50   100
Miles

The distribution of spotted owls in California

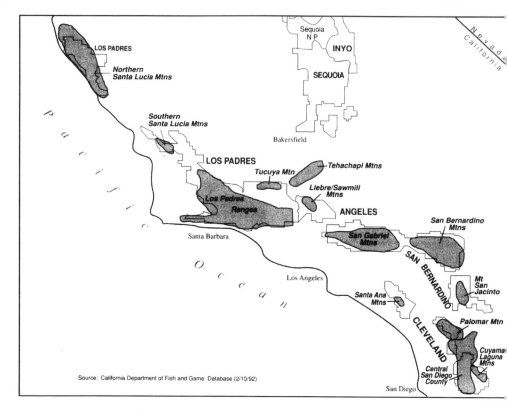

Spotted owl "island" populations in southern California

the Resources Agency and the Board of Forestry, but no change was proposed for southern California. For the Sierra Nevada mountains, the complex set of regulations was aimed at preserving large trees and dense forest canopies. The recommendations essentially meant less cutting of old-growth timber, a change of silvicultural practice to mixed-age forests, and the maintenance of felled trees so that owl prey would have a place to live. Like some other species, owls need old trees in dense forests that support high numbers of plants and animals; the owls therefore serve as a kind of indicator species, both in the Sierras and in southern California. The recommendations also addressed the significant fire hazards existing in major blocks of spotted owl habitat, the result of the accumulation of fuels during decades of fire-suppression policy. The salvage logging rider of 1995 has created conflicting management strategies for the Forest Service, which is charged both with preserving owl habitat and with implementing salvage logging, aimed at removing old and downed trees that are considered potential fire hazards.

The technical team's recommendations for the Sierras received close scrutiny and criticism from the timber industry in 1994, not only because they meant less cutting of timber, but also because they might require a change in management practices to achieve better owl protection on private forest lands. The struggles over the new Forest Service rules were couched in the well-worn terms of the "jobs versus trees" debate, the timber industry contending that such restrictions would have negative effects on the local economies. Environmentalists saw the plan as a positive step toward ecosystem preservation. Yet, once again, the effects on the mountain ecosystems of land use and urbanization in the surrounding rural counties were not raised.

For southern California the issues and dialogue were quite different. To begin with, because of scanty data the technical team was reluctant to develop specific preservation recommendations, as it had done for the Sierras. The policy implementation team was timid about its approach as well. Yet there was a general understanding that the southern California owl population, found to be in serious decline, was far more fragile than that of the Sierras.

Surprisingly, this situation aroused little interest in the environmental or scientific communities in southern California. Their apathy in this situation does raise questions about how nature is seen by environmental and scientific organizations in the state. Clearly, the large environmental groups have concentrated their attention on Forest Service management of the Pacific coast redwoods and the federal forests of the Sierra Nevada mountains, avoiding the issue of urbanization and to some extent softening their approach to private forest practice through their support of the failed Grand Accord. Since forest management in southern California is not oriented toward timber production, perhaps these organizations—the Natural Resources Defense Council, the Wilderness Society, and the Planning and Conservation League—felt less urgency about addressing the conditions of the mountains. If the southern California owl were declared endangered or threatened, what real difference would it make to forest management? Perhaps there would be a reduction in ski concessions, but probably little else. Or is their indifference due to an image, a vision of southern California, that excludes the possibility of beauty and nature, of grand, "pristine" scenery worth defending? Perhaps there has been an unconscious triage in which environmental values in southern California have been sacrificed to the advantage of the state's more scenic areas, a landscape equivalent of the "trophy species" preservation approach. Whatever the reason, this attitude is creating a hierarchy of values with respect to nature, creating boundaries and maps of inclusion and exclusion that run roughshod over fundamental linkages and interdependencies. It further raises questions about what nature is worth preserving, why, and how it is perceived—questions that are fundamental to the politics of environmental preservation and perhaps offer a key to understanding why urbanization policy and land use still remain off the table for the mainstream environmental organizations.

Local southern California environmental organizations are embattled, fighting species by species, development by development to preserve species immediately threatened—the gnatcatcher, the Stevens' kangaroo rat—that are in their backyards. Perhaps environmentalists are motivated to save the nature that contributes to their own daily quality of life and property values—an accusation often made by their opponents. Yet the reality in southern California is that these preservation struggles are taking place in a context where land is being purchased with a ten- to twenty-year development horizon, and development potential secured by DAs that are not always made fully public. By the time development has been scheduled, a challenge over a potentially endangered species is immensely complicated, as the gnatcatcher example illustrates. Protecting property values or protecting diversity? It is not so simple to draw the line. What is certain is that the process of continuing urbanization, opposed only in localistic, scattered preservation struggles, is tightening the noose around the southern California mountains. As a result of continuing urbanization, biodiversity throughout the southland is dwindling.

Air Pollution and Fire Suppression

Urbanization affects the mountains of southern California in similar ways and even more seriously than the mountains of the Sierra Nevada. Air pollution is critically attacking the vegetation, so that many species are simply not reproducing, meaning an end to the indigenous mix of flora. Nearly a century of fire suppression has created an extremely flammable and dense understory, suffocating certain species and preventing their reproduction, as well as creating conditions for catastrophic fire that would burn so intensely it would destroy the forest. Historically, fires burned regularly through southern California forests every five to ten years. Like their Sierra counterparts, these were low-intensity fires that cleared the underbrush. Now fires are far more intense and dangerous.

The Forest Service has begun to change its fire-management philosophy and strategy, recognizing the importance of regular burning. It has started to implement a program of regular controlled burning with the eventual aim of restoring the original forest canopy. In southern California, and also in some parts of the Sierras, however, the smog problem is so serious that local air quality management districts are strict about controlling the days when burning by the Forest Service is allowed. This creates a paradoxical situation: The forests in southern California are slowly dying because of the toxicity of the air and also because they cannot be burned at a rate sufficient to reduce the underbrush and restore them to a natural state because of the air pollution that fires produce. In addition, because of the increasing proximity of urban areas, controlled burns are becoming increasingly tricky to carry out. If a burn gets out of control, it might threaten houses (the Forest Service is liable for property damage), and the ashes and smoke from fires provoke complaints from neighboring residents even when the fire is fully controlled. This is in addition to the Forest Service's lack of funds for controlled burning. Most of its money is allocated to fighting fire—those huge conflagrations brought about by the previous lack of controlled burning over the decades. The forest and the Forest Service are caught by contradictory forces, creating increasingly difficult conditions for the survival of the forest.

It is difficult to see how the Wilson administration strategies for ecosystem management and the governor's proposals for growth management would effectively address any of the issues discussed here: the preservation of the gnatcatcher under the NCCP program, the management of the Sierra Nevada and private forests for increased biodiversity protection and enhancement, and the situation of the California spotted owl. These are only a few examples among many that could be used to illustrate the problems engendered by ineffectual land-use planning and lack of growth management in the state. All signs point to even more future conflicts, rather than less, because the fundamental structure of land-use controls has not been addressed—not by the Wilson administration, not by the legislature or local jurisdictions, not by special economic or environmental interests. This applies equally to the issues of biodiversity and of the quality of life in the urbanized parts of the state. The question of the management of growth underlies and connects the two, fundamentally and inextricably.

The Fruits of Fiscal Austerity and Economic Restructuring

The early 1990s were not an economically favorable period for the state. With the end of the Cold War the defense industry, an important part of the state's economy, declined rapidly, and hundreds of thousands of people were laid off, particularly in southern California. Corporate restructuring in other sectors consisted of trimming payrolls by reducing the numbers of employees. The slowing down of the economy meant that government revenues declined dramatically, both for the state and for most local jurisdictions. Development slowed, and thousands of square feet of office space stood empty. Real estate prices began to tumble. As a result, Governor Wilson faced the perennial choice: to raise taxes in order to increase state revenues and services, and to maintain the bail-out to the cities needed after the passage of Proposition 13, or else to cut the budget to reflect reduced revenues. As a strong Republican, the governor chose to cut the budget. He also reduced business taxes, believing that only in this way would the economic climate for business activity improve. In addition, environmental regulations came under scrutiny, since they were widely denounced by business as an obstacle to investment and economic activity.

In 1991, despite increases in the sales tax, liquor tax, vehicle registration fees, and college fees, Wilson cut monthly welfare grants for recipients of Aid to Families with Dependent Children—the state's largest welfare program—by 3 percent and permanently suspended automatic cost-of-living increases in health and welfare programs. The administration began a process to set counties on the road to financial independence from the state-mandated health and welfare programs. It also instituted pay cuts, mandatory unpaid furloughs, and in some cases layoffs of state workers.[60] After the 1991 budget, when Governor Wilson agreed to raise some taxes, he then undertook to regain the confidence of the business community by proposing to cut corporate taxes and curb environmental regulations. His Resourceful California proposals were part of this approach. Wilson also continued to raise the cost of higher education through tuition increases at the community colleges, state universities, and the University of California.

The 1991–92 budget also provided big business with a hefty tax break beginning in 1993. By the 1993–94 budget, things had become far worse. The state's economy had not rebounded, and its unemployment rate was one of the highest in the nation, hovering around 10 percent. The governor proposed to take $2.6 billion in property tax revenues from cities, counties, and special districts, in perpetuity, to help close an estimated budget gap of between $7.5 billion and $8.5 billion—twice the reduction in local funding that occurred in 1992. This was called the Educational Revenue Augmentation Fund, and it marked a fundamental financial redirection of local government finance. Wilson's approach to balancing the state's budget was unprecedented—never had a governor proposed to balance the state's budget by taking property taxes from local governments.

Local government property taxes, though greatly reduced since the passage of Proposition 13, have traditionally been the main revenue source for local government, designed to finance property-related services, especially to residential and nonretail development. Under the Educational Revenue Augmentation Fund, the cities' share of property taxes on a statewide basis was reduced to approximately 5–6 percent.[61] Counties absorbed 60 percent of the financial loss.

The structure of state government makes counties responsible for providing many services, of which jails and health and welfare are the most important. Now, counties found their budgets inadequate to meet the expenditures. For example, total criminal justice costs alone in Yolo County were around $16 million in 1990. Property tax revenue generated by the county government was only about $13 million. County libraries closed, especially in the small northern counties, and sheriff departments were cut. Such pressure is shaping cities' future development plans. For example, the city of Monrovia, in the Los Angeles basin, originally intended to accept a bid from Kodak to build a small manufacturing facility. City officials apparently abandoned the Kodak proposal and instead approved the construction of a Wal-Mart, primarily because the Wal-Mart facility offered better sales tax revenue potential for the city. The city turned away $20-an-hour jobs for part-time employment paying less than $10 an hour. For the economy in the area and for the workers, the Wal-Mart was far less advantageous, but the city was under pressure to increase tax revenues.[62]

Under these conditions cities and counties, as well as the state, could hardly increase social service expenditures for health, job training, housing, and critical infrastructure maintenance and development unless taxes were restructured and raised. This was not possible in the prevailing political climate created by the Reagan revolution, in which government spending was seen as part of the problem that needed fixing. Too much social welfare spending had created dependency. Government bureaucracies were inefficient, overstaffed, and unresponsive. The only solution was to create ever more favorable business conditions by reducing corporate taxes and eliminating red tape, such as permits and environmental regulations.

The erosion of city and county budgets was reflected in small and large ways: reduced hours of service, increased case loads for welfare and parole officers, closed libraries for children after school, less money for drug rehabilitation programs, less frequent trash collection. It was a gradual erosion of public services, which were not replaced. Local residents, resenting the deterioration of local services, attributed much of this to mismanagement and were thus susceptible to arguments for further budget cuts.

Los Angeles Erupts Again

In the spring of 1992 parts of Los Angeles erupted into flames. There was looting, death, and racially motivated violence. The city was gridlocked for three days, and the National Guard was brought in to bring order. Fear reigned for days, weeks, months.

The immediate trigger for the civil unrest was a surprising verdict in a well-publicized case of police brutality, the videotaped beating of a black man, Rodney King, by white policemen. The verdicts of not guilty revived a deep anger growing out of decades of neglect, poverty, and abuse. Analysts, politicians, and activists have all pointed to economic causes for the violence: persistent poverty and the widening income inequalities brought about by the economic restructuring.[63]

High damage occurred in neighborhoods like Watts that had historically been predominantly black, but were now at least half Latino in their population. Per-capita incomes were significantly lower in these areas, and unemployment higher. They had lower rates of home ownership, too. In fact, the damaged areas had roughly twice the poverty and unemployment rates, and half the per-capita income and home ownership levels of the rest of the city.[64]

For the large Latino community poverty stemmed less from unemployment than from low wages and obstacles to entrepreneurial efforts. Complicating the situation has been the lack of voting power and political representation for Latino residents. South-central, the historical heart of black Los Angeles, has become 45 percent Latino. Latinos make up 74.1 percent of the resident population in the Koreatown-Westlake neighborhoods, and over 44 percent of these people are of Central American origin, recent immigrants, most of whom are noncitizens. In south-central, over 75 percent of the Latinos are of Mexican origin, and 19 percent are Central American. Low rates of citizenship, language isolation, and poverty contribute to the alienation of the Latino community. Although they make up nearly 40 percent of the population in Los Angeles, Latinos constitute only 11.4 percent of registered voters and (until 1996) fewer than 10 percent of actual voters. In 1996 the number of Latino voters jumped to 15 percent.[65] Although this situation has been changing, with healthy increases in voter registration— and participation—it remains true that for many elected representatives there is often little incentive to do much for these residents, as they have no legitimate source of power and means to convey their wishes.

Disenfranchised Neighborhoods

The economic growth that graced Los Angeles in the 1980s did not include the poorest neighborhoods. Instead, they were the targets of budget cuts, while new suburbs were built and quickly incorporated (meeting approval from LAFCOs) to better control their own local land-use decisions. This process was facilitated by the Republican administration's fiscal policies, which systematically cut budgets for cities while continuing subsidies and programs for further suburban development. For example, funds to help build affordable or low-income housing greatly diminished. In Los Angeles alone there is a waiting list of over 90,000 families for housing vouchers (a housing subsidy), only 5,000 of which have been available each year. The

Los Angeles population has been increasing by an average of 26,000 house-holds per year, while an average of 15,000 housing units are built each year and 3,000 demolished, leaving a shortfall of 14,000 units a year.

The portion of personal income dedicated to mortgage payments in Los Angeles rose dramatically in the late 1970s and early 1980s as a function of the rapid appreciation of housing values and high interest rates. The portion of income devoted to rent also steadily increased, from a little over 20 percent in the early 1970s to approximately 30 percent in the late 1980s. Rents rose dramatically during this period.[66] At the same time, housing for high-income buyers continued to be built. There is no shortage of housing at the upper end, but there is little incentive for builders to provide housing in the city for middle- to low-income people, and land prices remain high in all neighborhoods. The skewed structure of incentives, combined with continued land conversion at the urban fringe, has continued to suck better paying jobs and better housing out of the city, furthering urban sprawl.

The politics of growth in California has been such that none of the growth has occurred in the neediest places. Cities and counties did not capture much of the prosperity because of the tax structure. The management of growth is nonexistent; policies are aimed to help disperse it rather than to target it to strengthen existing urban areas. City and county services had been in gradual decline since the passage of Proposition 13, but this new, speculation-driven prosperity bypassed their coffers or, as was the case for Los Angeles, was spent elsewhere.

Ironically, the Watts rebellion of 1965 had much the same causes as the rioting of spring 1992: frustration about neglect, lack of jobs, poor housing. Mayor Bradley's tenure had done little or nothing to ameliorate the economic conditions of the poorest neighborhoods of the city, which are also those where the most people of color live. It did, however, foster favorable conditions for the redevelopment of downtown Los Angeles into a dense maze of high-rise buildings, lining the pockets of major builders and real estate companies. At the same time, the most polluting and worst paying industries became concentrated in low-income neighborhoods.

Thus we can see how the lack of policy regarding growth in the state has allowed disinvestment in cities, contributing to urban poverty and violence, further alienating the middle class and business, and contributing to urban flight. This vicious circle has had extremely detrimental ecological consequences as well. These conditions were identified and understood as early as the 1960s, when Cry California put together its growth-management document.

Poor planning affects both the social and the environmental structures of the state. Social polarization and breakdown and environmental degradation are the results of the structures of investment whose effects span urban and rural landscapes.[67] The building boom of the 1980s in Los Angeles County coincided with the steady erosion of county planning staff, a result of Proposition 13 tax cuts. There was no money for land-use planning, no money to purchase open space or set-asides for fragile ecological areas. Instead, supervisors tended to "upzone" land in scenic areas, allowing developers to build more homes on the urban fringe than previous zoning had provided, guided by their philosophical opposition to public ownership of land and their desire for more tax revenues. Little was done to provide for less advantaged parts of the county. Unfortunately, residential development rarely pays for itself, only contributing to fiscal crisis. Although development pressure abated in the early 1990s due to the recession, the basic issues of how and where to build have remained unaddressed, as has the problem of the regional inequality of growth. Serious public discussion about these issues has not occurred, and lacks an appropriate forum.

Yet growth issues were important in Los Angeles of the 1980s. In 1986 Proposition U passed, essentially a downzoning ordinance for affluent neighborhoods on the west side of the city, which had been subject to great commercial intensification of land use with what seemed to be new shopping centers and mini-malls sprouting at every corner. At the same time, in the eastern part of the city where the poor lived, such new land uses as waste incinerators were being proposed. The juxtaposition of land uses on the east and west sides of town clearly illustrates the growth dynamics of the city that contributed to the 1992 uprising.

The San Francisco Bay Area

San Francisco, like the rest of the state, has experienced a significant increase in the number of its Hispanic and Asian residents over the last decade. Whites are no longer the numerical majority, constituting only 47 percent of the population. Asians make up 28 percent, Latinos 14 percent, and blacks 11 percent. At various times in the city's history the neighborhoods have been a powerful political force in opposing development and redevelopment plans. In 1987 neighborhoods elected Art Agnos mayor to represent their interests against further redevelopment and gentrification, but by 1991 they were dissatisfied and disappointed, feeling that the mayor and the city commissions did not give neighborhoods as much attention and accessibility to city hall as they had expected.

On the opposite side of the political spectrum, the business community's sentiments were even stronger. In 1991, "Jim Lazarus, vice president of the city's Chamber of Commerce, which has over 2300 members, said Agnos and the Board of Supervisors have left the business community high and dry to placate 'the city's far left wing.'"[68] Lazarus complained that in the last few years there had been little or no job growth and that political actions turned away businesses. Agnos faced the same issues as most big-city mayors—a budget crisis and greater demand and need for social services. The city, after pursuing redevelopment plans in the 1970s, faced a lack of affordable housing. High rents, despite rent control, forced many members of the city's middle class and working class, as well as many blacks, out of the city, creating a city of the affluent, immigrants, and elderly poor, according to Amos Brown, pastor of San Francisco's Third Baptist Church. Business interests opposed tax hikes, claiming the increases would hurt them and drive them out of the city, and neighborhood groups were unhappy because of the lack of response to the city's social problems. The homeless population soared to between 6,000 and 8,000 with shelter facilities for only about 4,000.[69] Homeless advocates were upset with Agnos's policy regarding the homeless, especially his enforcement of a law against "aggressive panhandling."[70] Mental health facilities, drug and alcohol treatment programs, job training services, and affordable housing were all inadequate.

In 1990 Frank Jordan, San Francisco's former police chief, was elected mayor with 70 percent of the vote. The large and visible homeless population was the main reason people voted for Jordan, who promised a get-tough plan of warrant checks and "workfare" for the homeless and for aggressive panhandlers. His strategy proved ineffectual in addressing the problem of homelessness in the city. Lack of affordable housing and employment opportunities are at the heart of the homeless problem in San Francisco, as elsewhere. Economic restructuring, suburban locations for new businesses, back-office operations, and the inability of cities to coordinate with the suburbs all contributed to San Francisco's social and economic problems— problems that transcend the ability of the mayor to solve. Jordan was defeated in his 1994 bid for reelection, and the long-time speaker of the state Assembly, Willie Brown, a black liberal, was overwhelmingly voted in.

The Desire for a Regional Government

The Bay area continued to host an enlightened elite, made up of environmentalists, business executives, and some academics, who persevered in a historical quest to establish a Bay area regional government to manage growth. The 1989 earthquake heightened awareness of the interrelation of the region's economy and infrastructure. In 1990 Bay Vision 2020 was formed as a public-private partnership, bringing together business, environmental, and transportation leaders. It was chaired by retired University of

California chancellor Ira Heyman. Nearly a century after Progressive mayor Phelan of San Francisco had promoted regional planning coordination, Bay Vision 2020 took up the struggle.[71]

According to a 1991 Bay area poll, 67 percent of area residents believed a comprehensive planning agency was needed to plan for and manage the region's growth. Support was strong across the region. The merger of separate regional agencies—the Bay Area Air Quality Management District, the Metropolitan Transportation Commission, and the Association of Bay Area Governments—was also favored and was a key recommendation of the Bay Vision 2020 commission. The poll further revealed that the public would favor merging the additional functions of Bay conservation and development, water quality, water supply, and landfill siting into such a body. Residents believed regional agencies should have significant powers in several areas, such as to offer localities financial incentives to make decisions consistent with regional needs (68 percent), and to resolve growth and development conflicts among local communities (68 percent). But a majority (54 percent) also felt that decisions on land use and zoning should be made at the local level rather than at the regional, state, or federal level.[72]

The public generally believed that "new housing should be built within existing communities before expanding to new areas, even if this means more people living on less land." Transportation was ranked as the most important problem facing the Bay area in every county except San Francisco, where homelessness was cited as the region's top problem.[73] With such strong support, Senator Rebecca Morgan, a Republican, introduced SB 797 (formulated by Bay Vision 2020), one of several growth-management bills introduced during the same period. Bay Vision 2020 proposed a board, of which 60 percent would be government representatives, chosen by a combination of the legislature, ABAG, and local governments. Together the board members would prepare a regional plan. The proposal would have created a fifty-seven-member commission, two-thirds of the members being elected officials from nine counties. The plan would have (1) set standards for meeting regional needs for affordable housing, open space, transit, water supply, and job creation; and (2) established criteria for siting unpopular land uses, such as airports and waste-disposal facilities. Once the plan was approved, cities, counties, and other relevant local government entities would have been required by law to bring their plans into conformity. The proposal sparked worries that the interests of small cities and outlying rural areas might be swallowed up by urban centers such as San Francisco. Senator Mike Thompson, a Democrat representing St. Helena, lobbied strongly against the bill, claiming it would create a "monster bureaucracy in which Napa and Sonoma counties would be underrepresented."[74] The more rural cities and counties around the Bay—Napa, Sonoma, and Solano Counties—adamantly opposed the idea of a regional government, fearing a loss of authority. Local officials claimed they felt left out of the process of planning and organizing the proposed embryo of a regional government. Such concerns led to the defeat of the bill.

Though the proposal was defeated, even the opposition did not raise many of the fundamental issues that are central to establishing regional government: Who would sign off on the regional plan, a governmental entity or the voters? Should the regional commission be appointed or elected? How should large-scale developments be modified and/or opposed? How should the issue of taxes and revenue sharing be handled? Although Bay Vision 2020 touted its consensus building and inclusiveness, the commission based its recommendations largely on the advice of a small Bay area elite: individuals representing government, academic, and community nonprofit groups. There was little room for the public at large to lend its input, even though public sentiment supported a regional approach.[75] Bay Vision 2020 failed to build a solid foundation of support among the public. This approach was similar to those in the past, and the reaction, too, was similar: Local jurisdictions felt vulnerable and feared losing their essential source of power, jurisdiction over local land uses. Yet it is just these local jurisdictions and their pressing financial needs that have paved the way for the tremendous growth all around the Bay area and have created a generally favorable public climate for better regional coordination of growth. Although proposals for regional government in the Bay area have been put forward over a seventy-year period, it is not likely that agreement will be forged in today's polarized political climate, despite public concern.

The Republican Legacy

Over a decade of Republican governorship in California did not bring the kinds of prosperity and streamlined government that had been promised at the outset. Governor Deukmejian was first and foremost an administrator, who believed the state should not play a role in developing policy and initiatives. He curbed state activities in land-use regulation and environmental protection. While he was governor, the state's economy remained strong overall and growth continued. The growth was manifested in accelerated land conversions from rural to urban uses, and in increased traffic congestion, densification, and increased retail uses. This pace of change and the tangible deterioration of people's quality of life led to an unprecedented number of growth-control initiatives, none of which was especially effective. At the same time, this pace of growth, fueled by speculative investments made possible by Reagan-era banking deregulation, bypassed large parts of the population and the older city cores, places like south-central Los Angeles. Rates of poverty increased at the same time the rich were getting richer.

Governor Wilson faced a much changed California economy and serious rates of unemployment, partly due to the downsizing of the defense industry and to investment changes in the global economy. California, for the first time since the Depression, was facing a deep economic recession. County budgets were strained by social needs, while the state budget ran a severe deficit. Wilson responded by instituting deep cutbacks, largely in social service programs and higher education. The polarization between rich and poor continued to grow.

The unbridled growth in the 1980s, and the failure to institute any planning for growth over the previous decades, also had environmental effects, seen in the number of endangered species listings and the heightened struggle over natural resource management in the state—forestry and water in particular. Wilson's strategy to meet the results of unmanaged urban and rural growth consisted of trying to remove regulatory obstacles and give the development community more voice in land-use decision making.

As for the urban consequences of unequal growth, the spring 1992 urban uprisings in Los Angeles amply demonstrated the depth of anger and despair of those neighborhoods. Predictably, the slow-growth movements of the city had little sensitivity to the connections between their struggles against further land transformation on the suburban edge, and the poverty and degraded environment experienced by those who lived in the older parts of the city. Governor Wilson, too, failed to address the interconnectedness of these processes, preferring to rely on private-sector initiative, which has shown little or no interest in facing the problems.

The legislature in the 1980s and early 1990s did not succeed in addressing the problems of growth and its unequal distribution. Instead, it fell into partisan bickering and symbolic posturing to win constituents' votes and campaign contributions. Its inaction was due to its organizational structure, a result of Progressive-era reforms, such as the initiative process. By the early 1990s the problems of the management of growth signaled in the 1960s—governmental, environmental, social, economic, and distributive—had grown to substantial proportions. And another factor now had to be taken into account that was not foreseen in an earlier period: the profound demographic shift in the state's population. Today, the population is young, majority nonwhite, and poor. Many people do not, or cannot, vote. Voters remain white, older, and more affluent. This poses serious challenges for the legitimacy of the entire structure of government.

The Jerry Brown administration had offered an era of limits based on a belief in human ingenuity and creativity, on a shared path of frugality toward a more harmonious relationship with the environment and greater social equality, as well as less government involvement. The era of limits of the 1990s, in contrast, was a result of conservative, anti-government ideology. This de facto era of limits has pitted interest groups against one another for an ever shrinking pie, as though civil society were a Hobbesian war of each against all. The principles of a competitive capitalist economic system have become internalized in the principles of governance, leading to malign neglect of the commonweal. Little effort is expended in trying to increase democratic participation and representation. The public sphere continues to shrink.

7 · CONCLUSION

Reconstructing California's Public Sphere

Politics is the activity by which humans choose and build their collective life together.   C. Douglas Lummis, *Radical Democracy* (1996)

CALIFORNIA, THE GOLDEN STATE, stands at a crossroads. Political change in the state has been driven by visions: visions of a cleaner government, visions of empowering the people directly, visions of eliminating politics from government. There have also been visions of preserving the redwoods, or the Sierra Nevada mountains and the transverse range in southern California; visions of peopling the Central Valley by establishing small farms, curbing urban sprawl, and improving the quality of life for all of its inhabitants. As Kevin Starr and others have pointed out, other visions too have played a role: visions of wealth and affluence, personal liberty, and the ability to indulge one's impulses. All these have been an important part of shaping the California of today and the possibilities for its future.

Over time the relationship between politics and policy, on the one hand, and representative, democratic government, on the other, has become fragile. The state's renowned landscape, its field of dreams, has been profoundly transformed. Well-intentioned reforms, coming from deeply felt frustration, have crippled the state legislature and paralyzed local governments. The process of government decision making now seems more remote in an era of "citizen" ballot initiatives aimed at remedying perceived problems. Voter alienation has increased, while polarization along lines of race, class, gender, and ideology has intensified. Many of the state's residents do not even participate in the formal political process of voting, because they lack money, feel it is useless, or lack legal status. Environmental degradation continues at an ever accelerating rate. Over the past decades, the issues confronting the state have been well known and well publicized, but solutions have proven elusive.

The preceding chapters have shown how problems, identified in the early twentieth century in incipient form, have not been solved and, in fact, have gotten worse. This is, in large part, because of the political structure of the state put in place during the Progressive period. Of course, the state's governance institutions have evolved, but the fundamental ideology of government shaping those institutions has been tenacious in its Progressive slant. Progressive ideology about human nature, the importance of technical knowledge, and the relationship of the political realm to the economic still dominates thought and public discourse, even if these notions do not fit today's realities and popular culture. This way of thinking is derived from liberal theory, inspired by the novel ideas of progress and individualism that emerged from the Enlightenment.[1] Among other principles, liberalism conceives of the individual as the building block of society, free and autonomous, whose activities are based on choice guided by utilitarian self-interest. Further, the individual is seen to operate within a framework of similar values that are assumed to be universal.[2] The outcomes of each freely choosing individual are assumed to be overall socially beneficial.

Progressives embraced many of the assumptions of liberal theory and made them the foundations of their political reforms. The Progressive period in many ways was the zenith of American liberalism. There was a belief that with sufficient scientific knowledge, social and other problems could be resolved; progress would be assured. With this faith, Progressives "universalized American experience . . . the nation exemplified the scientific laws of evolution. . . . [and would] carry mankind to new levels of rationality and productivity." In liberal thought, reason is seen as the liberating force in human history, and knowledge is unproblematic in the sense that "problems" in society can be resolved just as they can in science, from which liberal thought extrapolated freely. Thus, experts could be appointed to boards and commissions to come up with rational solutions for the government bureaucracy to implement.[3] Progressives placed the individual at the center of political discourse. They empowered the citizen with the referendum, initiative, and recall, dismantling political machines and other systems of mutual support. Progressivism involved creating the fiction of a universal individual and repressing difference, yet teaching people that they were free to pursue their individual ambitions and did not need to work with others to create a viable, representative democracy. Personal responsibility was removed by destroying accountability mechanisms, since it was now acceptable to pursue one's own interest—within the context of the law—in an individualistic manner. The notion that individuals might be embedded in, indeed shaped by, the society of which they are members—as bearers of history, culture, religion, and expectations—and thus inevitably socially conditioned, is not part of a liberal point of view. Contemporary American democracy has constructed a myth around the individual that is now encountering some difficulty as the society becomes increasingly diverse in its racial, ethnic, religious, and other orientations. Humans do not freely construct themselves in a vacuum. Society does not cohere if everyone is pursuing his or her own self-interest and there are no mechanisms to develop social solidarity.

We are witnessing the implosion of this national ideology at the end of the twentieth century, when the weight of diversity and social polarization has cracked liberal hegemony. The political structures put in place by Progressive reformers no longer correspond to the needs and aspirations of contemporary America, or much of the democratic West. If we are to arrive at policies and politics that can begin to address the issues facing the state, we need a democratic system that corresponds to today's social realities. At present democratic participation is largely limited to affluent, educated whites, reflecting not the state's demographics but rather the legacy of historical circumstances. Our democratic system resembles more a corporation in which citizens are treated as "shareholders in a company," who vote only in periodic elections of officials.[4]

State Political Gridlock

Public frustration with the seeming unresponsiveness of state and local government has resulted in the increasing use of the ballot initiative, a fragmented, issue-by-issue approach. The initiative is used by those well enough organized and with sufficient capital to conduct public outreach and advertising. Initiatives, aimed at fixing one particular problem or another, have created a "political nonstructure so complex, so subject to veto by political minorities, so incomprehensible to ordinary citizens and so subject to manipulation by special interest groups . . . that it bears less and less resemblance to what a civics textbook would describe as majority rule or representative government."[5] For the state's budget process, the result has been disastrous. Increment by increment, initiative by initiative, much of the state's budget has become preallocated, even before the legislative process begins, leaving smaller and smaller latitude to legislative discretion and decision making.[6] Certain issues are a priori off limits from legislative action. The state's elected representatives are unable to respond to changing public needs and desires even if they wanted to.

Budget decisions take on an especially nasty aspect because California has a constitutional requirement that allows no state budget or other appropriation to be approved without a two-thirds vote of the legislature. (California is one of only two states that have such a requirement.) The two-thirds majority requirement gives political minorities effective veto over state appropriations. Any group or coalition that can muster one-third of the votes has an effective veto power on all levels of government. So even when one party controls both houses of the legislature, it cannot shape the budget or determine state appropriations because of the power of the minority to block those initiatives. In addition, the governor has line-item veto power over the budget after it is passed. Elected representatives have little political power to represent the wishes of their electorate.

At the local level, matters are even more dire. Local governments continue to be responsible for their traditional functions, but after the passage of Proposition 13 and other tax-reducing initiatives, they have less and less money. Republican governors Deukmejian and especially Wilson, and state legislators, faced with reduced revenues and a predetermined budget mandate, turned to a twofold strategy: increase the state's share of local taxes while devolving more responsibilities onto localities, especially the counties. Under these conditions, cities and counties have been hard pressed to finance their traditional services and programs. They are no longer able to fill their former buffering role, creating innovative programs to respond to local needs and citizen requests. This strengthens the sense that there is no accountability in government and leads to even greater citizen alienation and anti-government sentiment. Despite renewed economic prosperity and higher state revenues, the changes implemented in lean times ensure that local budgets remain meager.

Other Initiative Effects: Term Limits and the Lobbyists

To add to a complicated situation, Proposition 140 was passed in 1990. This measure limits the terms of state Assembly members to six years and those of state senators to eight years, while also sharply cutting legislative staff. This has resulted in a continuous cycle of new legislators who have to learn the governmental process. With the budget process alone as complicated as it is, Assembly and Senate members will likely rely on the most informed sources they can surround themselves with—often a special-interest lobbyist whose full time job is to keep informed of government issues. Of course, even for lobbyists such turnover among legislators poses serious challenges and favors the larger, wealthier organizations. While the goal of the initiative was to break the back of incumbents, who were perceived as part of the problem of the ineffectiveness of the legislature, this initiative can do little to improve the legislature's responsiveness or effectiveness, as it does not address some of the structural factors limiting the legislature's abilities to set policy. By increasing reliance on lobbyists, it has reduced the professionalism of the legislature, built on years of accumulated experience and the assistance of knowledgeable staff. It has increased the polarization of the legislature, each candidate placing his or her own turf or special interest ahead of the general public good. It also means that legislators have less knowledge of their districts, because they will have less time to learn about them and meet constituents. For constituents, and especially grass-roots organizations, getting access is harder as well, since developing political skills at this level takes time and training. Groups that lack resources are at an ever greater disadvantage. Rapid turnover of committee chairs results in fewer staff developing expertise, and term limits combined with budget cuts means successive crops of poorly paid, inexperienced young staff.[7] Overall, the outlook for expanding democratic access, democratic process, and accountability does not seem promising.

Nearly 80 percent of the special interests with large lobbying operations in Sacramento are in the business sector. "Considering the wide disparity in strength between them, it is strange that many Californians persist in being more concerned about powerful parties than powerful interest groups. In a state that makes a virtue of nonpartisanship, political parties [continue to] labor under the negative image they obtained when they were dominated by the Southern Pacific [at the turn of the century]." In the eight decades since the weakening of parties by the Progressives, little attention has been given to the ever increasing power of special interests, other than a brief sense of outrage about the flamboyant Artie Samish in the 1940s. "Comparative research across several states in the Union demonstrates that weak parties exist in states with strong interest groups."[8]

When officeholders feel obligated to a broad coalition of party voters rather than to single-issue constituencies, they tend to be more accountable to the voting public. In the California electoral system, nonpartisan local offices, along with the constraints on preprimary endorsements by parties, have given interest groups far greater influence in the nomination of candidates to public office than citizens. "Given that the progressive reforms allow groups to play a major role in California politics, well-financed organizations (e.g. businesses) are ideally situated to take advantage of this opportunity to become the most powerful players in the state."[9] But party politics still seems to be targeted as the culprit in the state; in 1996 a ballot initiative was passed that reintroduced cross-filing for primary elections, allowing voters to choose a Democrat or Republican regardless of their own party affiliation.

Campaign Finances

The influence of moneyed special interests has only grown with budget constraints. Campaign costs drive legislators and other elected officials to search for campaign contributions. This creates a vicious circle of dependence between the individual politician and his or her contributors. Progressive reforms, aimed at reducing the power of political machines, bosses, and special interests in the political process of choosing candidates, have had perverse and counter-productive results. Election campaigns have become increasingly costly. In the 1994 state senatorial campaign, over $40 million was spent for a desultory voter turnout of little over 30 percent of eligible voters—largely white, affluent, educated, and conservative. Although the electorate did pass an initiative in 1996 aimed at reforming campaign finance, it is currently being challenged in court, with an uncertain outcome. In 1998 the gubernatorial election cost $49 million.

Today, the state's voting population does not reflect its demographics—a situation that raises fundamental questions about just whom elected politicians represent. Further, weak political parties have contributed to the politics of personality over the politics of substance. Campaigns are run on the basis of personalities, not issues, and thus there is no coherent program embodying a vision of the future that would unite the efforts of politicians in the same party. This situation was made poignantly evident in the fall 1994 election, when a politician was reported as "still searching for the right message" and having replaced three campaign managers. Steven Glazer, a senior advisor to Kathleen Brown, Governor Wilson's 1994 Democratic challenger for governor in California, put it this way: "Many candidates, their nerves clearly affected by a volatile electorate, cannot even seem to decide what they are trying to *sell* [my emphasis] in these all-important final days . . . we change our messages all the time, every day."[10] A sales pitch is surely a fragile basis for the future of democracy.

Democracy, Politics, and Citizenship: The Vital Chain

California has been transformed, not because of the power of the visions that have inspired its social movements and imagination, but because of demographic and economic changes. These changes have led to great social diversity and complexity, and an even greater estrangement of the people from their political system. Many eligible voters do not vote, and there are significant numbers of state residents who cannot legally participate. We have gone from machine politics to Progressive reforms, to a politics of personality and special interests that favors the affluent. The fundamentally elitist and undemocratic nature of the state's governance structures has created the conditions for the demise of democratic involvement and the impossibility of political debate about the public realm.

Progressives, seduced by the successes of the business model, created a political system to sustain the new age of business enterprise. They focused on physical infrastructure development and ways to make government work more efficiently. The success of the economy had as its effect the transformation of political categories and expectations into economic ones, integrating capitalist economic values and standards into politics and governance. Economic success became the measure of the success of politics, fostering a climate of growth and development regardless of social, cultural, environmental, and equity consequences. At the local level, "an alliance of public officials, businessmen, and bureaucrats effectively operates in most municipalities to channel expressed citizen interests into a system of land-use decisions constrained by the imperative to promote investment." This applies equally well at the state level, but through different mechanisms. These processes have created a situation in which only a small elite participates politically, undermining the legitimacy of democratic governance. Democracy as citizen action—participation in making collective decisions—occurs only at the margins. "Only such participation, moreover, can give persons a sense of active relation to social institutions and processes. . . . The virtues of citizenship are best cultivated through the exercise of citizenship." But this requires both the rebuilding of meaningful process, and the reconstitution of the citizen. It requires a commitment of time and effort.[11]

Democratic First Principles

American democracy is built on the fundamental principles of equality, justice, and liberty for all. These tenets are woven together in such a way that equality depends upon justice, justice upon liberty, and liberty on equality. This three-way interdependence has evolved historically and is in a constant process of interpretation, reevaluation, and adjustment. Citizenship is the key to the actualization of these principles as well as being dependent upon them for its existence.

The definition of a citizen has been of concern since the beginnings of democracy. "Since Greek times, both in philosophy and law, the concept of the person has been understood as the concept of someone who can take part in, or who can play a role in, social life, and hence exercise and respect its various rights and duties. Thus we say that a *person* is someone who can be a *citizen*, that is, a fully cooperating member of society over a complete life" (emphasis added).[12] Those who chose not to participate were termed "idiots"—private persons, separate from the polis. Citizens were, admittedly, a small, propertied elite, made up of Greek males. Others were not allowed to participate. Still, for the Greeks, personhood and citizen status were fundamentally linked. Women, slaves, and others were excluded from this category and the rights and obligations it entailed.

Over time, and most particularly during the Enlightenment, which provided the philosophical building blocks for contemporary liberal democracies, the notions of citizen and democratic society evolved. Since the eighteenth century, the conception of equality has expanded to include women, people who lack property, and nonwhites. The conception of society too has evolved to become the public sphere of interaction among all people. There are no longer reserved places for interaction among a select social class. Today, society can no longer be exclusionary; it is open and accessible.

But the United States inherited a distinction, popularized by Thomas Paine, between society and government. "Society," he wrote in *Common Sense*, "is produced by our wants, and government by our wickedness; the former promotes our happiness positively by uniting our affections, the latter negatively by restraining our vices." The Constitution has institutionalized that division by restricting the ambit of legislation while enlarging the constitutionally protected domain of free association—the sphere of society. This division has severely restricted the range of government power, as popular majorities are a priori constrained by the fundamental laws of the Constitution. This makes it impossible to achieve reform goals through direct legislation. "In the place of a politics of active involvement, the Constitution provided for the distant administration of national law." American ideology has increasingly fostered the disparagement of government and the dissociation of society from government.[13]

This distinction, which has dominated American politics, is one of the sources of contemporary political alienation. As the social realm has become increasingly complex and the center of change, the political realm has been left behind, relegated to a reactive role, incapable of absorbing and responding to social transformation. What is needed now is a fusion of the social and the political, so that the significant issues of the day can be dealt with democratically. As Alain Touraine has explained, democracy is not simply a goal, it is the institutional requirement for the creation of society by individual actors who may be different from one another, but who work together to create the public sphere. In this conception, it is not law (or the Constitution) that is the foundation of a democratic state, rather it is democracy itself that creates a state based on law. Touraine writes that democracy is more "work" than idea, and by that he means that it is the act of participation, and not the principles, that creates democracy. The members of a community must see themselves as equal partners in a cooperative political enterprise that is the creation of the society they live in. But for participation to occur, people must feel that they count, that their responsible public involvement is meaningful.[14]

Under slavery, for example, slaves could not participate in the construction of society. They were considered *socially* dead because they had no duties or obligations to the society, only to their owners; what protections they had were derived from decisions made by others. Slaves were not considered as persons at all. A democratic and political conception of a person involves full participation in society on the part of the individual.[15] Although we no longer have conditions of slavery, where entire categories of persons are under the life-and-death authority of others, today we are creating groups of people who are, for all intents and purposes, socially dead since they are de facto excluded from the public sphere. These are the people who do not participate politically, either because they do not or cannot vote. Such people, though not slaves, are socially and politically irrelevant, dispensable.

Democracy cannot work when the majority of its eligible voters are not participating, when others are not able to participate, and when the political structures themselves distance citizens from power so as to make their participation relatively meaningless. A democracy requires a participating citizenry, people who feel that they have a stake in society and that they make a difference, as well as a system whose institutions, practices, and conventions allow people to govern themselves. There is a vital need to reform the political system of representation to create structures that bring decision making closer to those affected by the decisions. The terrain of deliberation has to be vastly expanded so that people can engage in negotiations and discussion about decisions to be made, and so that social problems can be recognized as the expression and manifestation of social relations, which can be transformed by an elected government through democratic process rather than abandoned and considered the result of ineluctable economic factors. A person is a person only if he or she is a political being—that is, has the possibility of participating in the political community where the shape and type of society one lives in is determined through engagement in self-government.

The American notion of citizenship is that it is democratic because every citizen, regardless of cultural, social, economic, and biological differences, can equally claim the right to vote, speak, worship, acquire property and have it protected, and be assured of the elements of a fair trial.[16] This is the principle of individual equality. But it does not address the problem of equal representation and power. It does not address the process of democratic participation. If the process is such that there is not true public engagement, no genuine opportunity for people to become educated about issues and to engage in deliberation, then democracy is a shell, manipulated by the few who are insiders.[17]

Participation in California's democracy today is largely predictable by income. Candidates must have tremendous amounts of money to run for office, lobbyists gain access through contributions, and those who vote tend to be the more affluent citizens. Thus equality, the fundamental element of a democratic society, does not exist in the state; the current political system is what is usually known as a plutocracy.

Under conditions of inequality, equal justice is elusive. "If persons suffer material deprivation of basic needs for food, shelter, health care, and so on, then they cannot pursue lives of satisfying work, social participation, and expression."[18] Justice, essentially, is the quality of fairness. This conception of justice provides one of the fundamental elements of the cooperative virtues of a democratic society. Unless there is a climate of cooperation, of working together toward a public culture where each member of the society is an equal participant and where each member counts, then it is difficult, if not impossible, to maintain a legitimate and accountable system of democratic government.[19]

A viable democracy requires the building of tolerance, respect, and a sense of common belonging. It requires the creation of circumstances that develop the self-respect and self-esteem that are essential for individuals to be full members of society and to be able to accord the same respect and esteem to others. This cannot exist when whole categories of people are economically excluded, left to live on the street, or when the public sphere is left to be created through the "invisible hand" of each individual acting in his or her own self-interest. Acknowledgment that the fate of one part of the society affects the others, that there is a common public arena that each member of society is responsible to help maintain, is fundamental to citizenship. Thus the question of the distribution of wealth is an intrinsic part of democratic self-management.

In U.S. history there have been periods of political reform when attempts were made to enhance equality and formal representation. The Voting Rights Act of 1965 and anti-poverty programs of the 1960s and 1970s were intended to serve as instruments of political incorporation for black Americans. They have had limited success, since blacks are still proportionately underrepresented and have not achieved conditions of equity and justice. As Lani Guinier has written about blacks in America, just being able to elect a black representative does not ensure effective representation and policy responsiveness.[20] She describes the theory of black electoral success as fundamentally flawed. Successfully electing black representatives continues the pattern of the election of individuals who become models for equality without either mobilizing the black community or realizing the promised, community-based reforms that the Voting Rights Act was ostensibly intended to encourage. This approach—gerrymandering districts to enhance the possibility of electing a black representative—has been favored by the courts (this is now under increasing court scrutiny and challenge), but does not create meaningful enfranchisement. It ignores the concern with broadening the base of participation and fundamentally reforming the substance of the political process and decision making. Instead, it settles for an easily identifiable, uniformly enforceable proxy for the judicial inquiry into dilution jurisprudence: quantifiable results, which are used to demonstrate the capacity for racial bloc voting through the application of computer technology to precinct-by-precinct election results. This has resulted in the gerrymandered district, an extremely divisive and fundamentally unsatisfactory approach. It pits ethnically based groups against one another and does not result in improved representation. Electing a few black representatives does not make for political power. Exercising the vote, being a citizen, under the present formula carries with it no rewards.[21]

Likewise, grass-roots community movements that organize around specific issues and put pressure on local governments to change particular practices do not constitute successful models of a reinvigorated citizenship. "The experience of community seldom has any significant connections with the levers of power"; though gratifying for the people involved, and certainly making a marginal difference in people's daily lives, it does not lead to fundamental change.[22]

Questions arise about the structure of democratic representation as it presently exists in the United States and in California. This book has chronicled the legacy of Progressive-era reforms in California—the boards and commissions, special governments, nonpartisan elections at the local level, and other reforms. Many of these need to be reconsidered in the process of revitalizing democracy in the state, and even state political reform will need to be embedded in change at the federal level. There is no simple blueprint for change; instead, it will be a complex and painful process that puts the good of the commonweal above private interest, whether of the individual or of business. It requires common agreement that democratic processes are to be guided by the principles of equal liberty, justice, and "rough distributive equality."[23] Only from a position of relative economic security and equality can people participate equally and meaningfully in society.

Democracy must always be based in law; the rules of the game cannot change, and must protect basic civil, political, and economic rights—the structures that make possible a commonweal. But it must be a living process, not simply an idea. Given today's complex sociological terrain, democracy cannot be the tyranny of the majority, winner-take-all system traditional in American electoral politics. The commonweal is made up of the multitude of different peoples that make up society, and to be relevant, a democratic government must be one that most closely mirrors that diversity. "Having and exercising the opportunity to participate in making collective decisions that affect one's actions or the conditions of one's actions fosters the development of capacities for thinking about one's own needs in relation to the needs of others, taking an interest in the relation of others to social institutions. . . . Only such participation, moreover, can give persons a sense of active relation to social institutions and processes."[24] It must be recognized as well that democracy is a time-consuming, ongoing practice. It cannot be reduced to casting a vote in elections but must involve people meeting each other and talking, discussing, arguing about the issues at hand in a process of mutual education and recognition. Without dialogue and discussion, without the participation of people—their engagement with issues and with others—democracy remains an unpracticed skill, an unexercised muscle. And yes, it does require commitment on the part of people, but if people find they are engaged in something meaningful, then that commitment may grow. Such a democratic process requires institutions that allow participation in decision making beyond the mechanistic and polarizing public meeting, and that permit participants to be on a relatively equal footing.

What specific changes might foster a more democratic government? At the state level, they include the following suggestions, which, though neither easy to achieve nor sufficient in themselves, may provide a framework for further change:

- Removing the two-third majority requirement to pass a state budget
- Eliminating nonpartisan local elections to encourage the regeneration of parties at the local level, institutions that people could participate in forming and guiding
- Providing for proportional representation and fostering new parties to allow for greater political dialogue and better representation of the diversity and complexity in the state
- Establishing strict limits on campaign expenditures and requiring public funding of campaigns to equalize the playing field among parties and candidates, and between voters and special interests
- Eliminating appointed, interest-group-based boards and commissions to foster more open government
- Eliminating special districts and integrating their functions into other institutions of government
- Establishing tax-revenue distribution processes that equalize revenues among jurisdictions in regions to eliminate local competition for revenue-generating land uses
- Changing the structure of the taxation system in the state in order to more adequately reflect ability to pay

- Requiring land-use coordination on a regional scale
- Making growth through land development pay for itself
- Breaking up large jurisdictions (like Los Angeles County) into smaller units or electing more representatives so the ratio between the electorate and the representatives is such that people have access to their elected officials (this could be a stepped approach, a nesting of democratically elected councils)
- Creating regional governments that have power and are democratically accountable.

Concerning the last of these suggestions, following Young and others, regional governments should have the powers of legislation, regulation, and taxation. They should have significant power over land use and capital investment, and control over the design and administration of public services. To ensure democratic accountability, they could be made up of representatives from neighborhood assemblies or city councils, subject to a new system of proportional representation. These suggestions for reform would only begin to change the process of politics in the state and would be only a small step toward revitalizing democracy. The revitalization of democracy involves the revitalization of the role of the citizen.

Citizenship

Citizenship is not simply a legal status, it is a form of identity—our political identity—and a relationship to the overall civil society that carries with it rights and responsibilities. It is something constructed over time, not just an attribute given by virtue of birth or the passing of tests. It is, in some sense, an identity that has to be earned through the practice of democracy. Genuine citizenship requires an understanding that each person carries within him- or herself the fate and well-being of others and that each person's individual acts occur in the context of a larger society and have effects on that society. In this conception, society is not just made up of an amalgamation of individuals, it is the sphere in which our identities are created through interaction with others, and where we are recognized as individuals through that exchange and that recognition on the part of the other. This is possible only when society practices cooperation and tolerance. To the extent that people consider themselves primarily as individuals, free to act as they will, and no longer consider themselves as part of a greater public culture, they can only see their interests in opposition. The social sphere thus becomes polarized and alienating because the social process of creating a society through collective dialogue does not occur. As a result politics becomes a zero-sum game.

A democratic political system does not operate by the rules of the free market, where individual maximizing behavior is miraculously transformed into society by the free hand. A democratic political system requires participation based on the principles of liberty, equality, and justice. These cannot be derived from the marketplace, as they are aspects of human social relations and a result of human interaction; they require constant collective dialogue, commitment, compromise, respect, and agreements. Democracy is work—public, collective work. To be a citizen, to belong to a political community, requires a shared language of civil intercourse and shared ideas about the political principles of democracy.

This will require a change in the notion of citizenship. Today it is an empty vessel, an attributed status by virtue of birth or conversion, closer to a feudal-state social category than a democratic-state quality. This is partly because of the distancing of citizens from government, of the denigration of government that has occurred over the past decades, accompanied by a sense of government as other. In a democracy, government is not "it," it is "we," "us." For Americans and Californians to come back to that conception of government—democratic government—will require a revitalization of the concept and practice of being a citizen. It requires an active citizenry reclaiming the political sphere as theirs. Governmental decisions affect people's daily lives and should involve greater involvement by those very people.

In contemporary California, for democracy to be meaningful it must consider all people residing in the state as potential citizens. Global economic integration has brought with it global migration. Borders and frontiers are transcended by the free movement of money, goods, and people. This last element, however, is harder for nation-states to accept, so they do not acknowledge free trade at the human level. At this level, there are frontiers of inclusion or exclusion. However, in the age of globalization it is a bit paradoxical that money and goods can move freely, but not people. Hannah Arendt is said to have written that belonging to the world as a person no longer depends on family or blood ties, or nationality. In the contemporary era, people belong to the world, but only if they are political beings—that is, if they have the possibility of participating in the political community. If that potential does not exist, then one effectively does not exist as a person.[25] Currently, this situation applies to hundreds of thousands of California residents.

If the conception of citizenship is thus expanded, it would encompass all those who play a part in public culture, who participate socially and economically, and who, by virtue of that participation, also have a responsibility to society to engage in a constructive manner. This is predicated, however, on each person having a "fair index of primary goods"—that is, sufficient income to ensure dignity, choice, and a sense of being a full member of society. Homeless people, for example, have immense hurdles to overcome to engage responsibly in the public realm; at the most basic level, having no address, they cannot vote, and lacking money, they cannot give campaign contributions. A modern democracy cannot survive when there are entire categories of excluded people (the unemployed, the poor, people of color, legal and illegal residents) who, because they are different, don't count, and who can't count because they have no economic power.

Therefore the concept of citizen has to be renewed. A citizen is a person who fully participates in the process of self-governance that is democracy and who has the material basis to do so. This requires people to have an income and a sense of belonging to a society over the course of their life, the feeling that there is a public sphere of participation where their opinions count and their voice has meaning. It also requires that individuals have a sense of responsibility in their decision making because they are members of something larger than themselves. They are accountable for their actions. This sense of accountability can emerge only in a context of encountering others, of engaging responsibly and respectfully in dialogue about decisions that affect themselves and others, of entering into a process out of which emerges a political decision.

Just as individuals have responsibilities toward the social whole, they also have rights: the right to participate equally, the right to justice and to freedom, and the right to have their participation be meaningful. To the extent that people no longer consider themselves as part of a greater public culture, to the extent that they are isolated, self-contained, responsible only to themselves, democracy breaks down. Today, our liberal democratic system is characterized by voting, strategizing, elevating private interests, bargaining, exchanging, and being involved to only a very limited extent. It is a political system that is democratic only for the insiders who qualify largely on the basis of their affluence.

Just as the suggestions regarding possible directions for the reform of the present political system will not emerge full-blown and will have to proceed over time through trial and error, neither will a renewed citizen simply emerge. There needs to be a system of basic income support and a system of education for citizenship, instilling a sense of responsibility for one's actions and a commitment to the building blocks of democracy. This does not mean that there will be agreement, but that is the beauty of the political sphere—it serves as a forum for discussion among equals so that each feels that though his or her view may not have prevailed, he or she has been treated with dignity. Education for citizenship will need to involve learning to become political, to engage in creative and constructive dialogue regarding disagreements about how society is organized, and to come to a working arrangement based on respect. Education for citizenship will involve teaching people that they have a role and responsibility in formulating the conditions under which they live, guided by the commonly agreed-upon principles of democracy. And although these ideas may never be entirely fulfilled, they are the ideals toward which a democratic society must strive in order to maintain its credibility and its validity.

Democracy, Governance, and the Question of Growth

How does this discussion of democracy and citizenship relate to the substantive issues raised in this book, the questions of growth, environment, uneven development, the relationship of the urban and the rural, the urbanization of nature? When people cannot participate as full and significant citizens, when numbers of people are excluded, and when there is no real justice and equality or agreement on what constitutes a cooperative society, then the urgent, substantive issues of the state cannot possibly be attended to in a meaningful way. The question of the control of growth, for example, is reduced to a problem of technique, of regulation, of fine tuning, and of the definition of boundaries. Yet management of growth is fundamentally a political question, a social issue, not a question of technique, not a matter of drawing better boundaries. It involves fundamental questions about racial segregation, redlining, the affordability of housing, the relationship with nature, economic development and its location, private property rights versus public values. Without meaningful political discussion and participation by the state's citizens, the fundamental structuring process that is growth and its management cannot be addressed.

It is unlikely that any of the important issues facing California will be addressed unless there is fundamental political reform in the state. Political institutions need to be substantially revised, and a new conception of the citizen will have to be developed, along with a process of political education for citizenship at all levels over a substantial period of time.

The Progressives intervened at a time of crisis and formulated a vision for the transformation of California. It is time to do so again. The state has changed, and so should the visions.

The following summaries cover the main points of proposed legislation to control growth in California. They represent some of the most recent attempts to control growth without using the direct power of the state, so as to avoid opposition from local government and from business. For this reason, most of them use incentives rather than mandates. Reading them helps explain why growth control in California has been so hard to achieve. All were defeated, notwithstanding their limited scope.

1991 Growth Control Bills

Assembly Bill 3, sponsored by Assembly Speaker Willie Brown (D), created a State Growth Management Commission to guide the regional development and infrastructure agencies. It would have created seven regional development and infrastructure agencies combining the duties of councils of governments, regional transportation agencies, air quality management districts, and regional water quality control boards. It required a "State Conservation and Development Plan," adopted by the new State Growth Management Commission, to guide these decisions. This approach was reminiscent of proposals put forth in the 1970s by California Tomorrow, establishing a centralized agency to coordinate statewide land use.

Assembly Bill 76, sponsored by Sam Farr (D), created a State Planning Agency with functional departments and strengthened the current laws for regional planning districts. This agency would have replaced the Governor's Office of Planning and Research at the cabinet level and would have created a State Planning Advisory Council. The agency would have contained new state departments for environmental and plan review, permit assistance, environmental data, and mediation and conflict resolution. It also required that comprehensive regional plans be developed and that local general plans be consistent with the state and regional plans.

Senate Bill 929, put forward by Senator Robert Presley (D), called for the creation of a California Conservation and Development Commission. The commission would then adopt a long-range statewide plan, which regional planning agencies would have to take into account in developing a mandated regional plan to implement the state plan's policies. Subregional plans were to bring together currently fragmented programs for air quality, congestion management, LAFCO, open space, and public works. The intent of the bill was to try to reduce fiscal tensions among local agencies and promote managed growth.

Senate Bill 434, put forward by Senator Marian Bergeson (R), took another approach. She addressed growth as primarily an economic phenomenon and believed that public works financing was the best tool to influence growth and development decisions. Therefore SB 434 allowed local officials to voluntarily form "regional fiscal authorities" and raise public capital to build large-scale public works. To do so, an authority had to first adopt a "regional fiscal plan" that contained development boundaries, revenue-sharing agreements, and a revenue program. To guide these decisions, the Bergeson bill required the governor and the legislature to adopt a set of "California Growth Management Policies."

Senate Bill 797 was sponsored by Republican senator Rebecca Morgan, reflecting the work of a private group, Bay Vision 2020. It applied only to the San Francisco Bay area and created a San Francisco Bay Area Regional Commission, to replace three existing regional agencies. Morgan's bill, which was hardly innovative, showed the degree to which the idea of regional management of the Bay area continued to live on.

Governor Wilson's Strategic Growth Proposals

1. *Infrastructure.* State support for local and regional infrastructure was seen as necessary, but the state could not be a banker to local government. Instead it could act to reward jurisdictions that met state growth guidelines by helping to support the market for local debt. The California Housing Finance Authority could be expanded to become a general infrastructure agency, a state infrastructure bank that would provide 50-50 matching grants to local governments that qualified. In addition, all state infrastructure funds and mechanisms, whether loans or funds, would have to be used according to the voluntary state growth guidelines. This would include state-sanctioned infrastructure financing vehicles, such as developer fees, Mello-Roos districts, and others. Even water transfers would be contingent on the transferee meeting growth guidelines to ensure that water was used wisely.

This approach would have tightened state control over local finance, as the state would determine whether and how local jurisdictions complied with the state growth guidelines. At the same time, it made municipalities take on more debt rather than use state money for local and regional infrastructure. This is in accordance with the general Republican approach of giving local jurisdictions more responsibilities with no resources to carry them out.

2. *Housing.* The report targeted the problem of affordable housing and advocated better integration of planning and environmental review, permit streamlining, and greater state support of infrastructure (in the manner outlined above) as the means to promote more affordable housing. It advocated growth guidelines that included incentives for densification, "fair share" housing, better jobs/housing balance, and closer integration of transit and housing. The council suggested fiscal incentives for housing, such as reallocation of the local sales tax.

It is interesting to note that in this plan there is no mention of why low-cost, or affordable, housing has been scarce in California, other than the usual reasons, such as too much bureaucratic red tape. In fact, low-cost housing usually means lower profit margins for builders. As long as there was demand in the upper income level, there was no reason for builders to sacrifice a portion of their profit margin simply to satisfy the social need for this kind of housing. With little or no government subsidy available to fill the void, affordable housing was not being built fast enough to meet the need. Further, there was frequently intense local opposition to construction of low-cost housing, so that local jurisdictions were wary about encouraging its construction. The Wilson administration proposals did not address these fundamental obstacles.

3. *Integration and coordination of state planning.* This was the most important and best developed part of Wilson's strategic growth plan. It advocated making state planning simpler and more consistent. This would be achieved by having the Office of Planning and Research coordinate, at five-year planning intervals, an Integrated State Plan consisting of existing law that was largely uncoordinated but would become more coordinated through this process. The Integrated State Plan would include broad voluntary guidelines cast as performance standards for local and regional entities in various areas relevant to growth, such as resource identification and conservation, removal of barriers to housing, and the like. Land-use decisions, in the Wilson plan, were made by locally elected officials. The council recommended that the state focus its assistance on those local communities willing to grow responsibly. Thus consistency with the Integrated State Plan would become a condition or a competitive criterion for receiving future state infrastructure funding or loans, a condition for new use of infrastructure financing mechanisms, such as Mello-Roos and developer fees, and a condition for the receipt of any additional water transfers.

Such an approach—a structure of financial incentives to implement suggested policies—in practice would have uneven results because some communities would choose not to participate or would not have the technical capacities to do so. Potentially, this kind of approach would exacerbate inequalities among communities and regions rather than bring about better planned growth. Further, the Office of Planning and Research, under existing law, was already authorized to develop statewide growth management and land-use policies, as well as ensure the integration and consistency of planning criteria. The Strategic Growth Report merely reiterated the importance of the state to carry out its existing mandate (though carefully neglecting to mention that this was the case). When provided with the opportunity to link water availability with responsible growth in legislative session, the Wilson administration did not do so, thus calling into question the basis on which the growth management plan was put together.

4. *Local comprehensive plans.* The report suggested that the general plan (an obligatory city planning document) be reinforced and strengthened as the central tool for planning, and that it be renamed the Local Comprehensive Plan (LCP). The Office of Planning and Research would then issue new local plan guidelines, consistent with and inclusive of the voluntary state growth guidelines, which localities would use to

update the existing seven specific elements of a general plan. Each LCP would also specify methods of coordinating planning with the jurisdiction's neighbors and providing notification to them of the comprehensive plan process.

The Wilson report also proposed revising the role of the councils of governments in regional coordination. The report specifically ruled out any authority to devise regional plans and strategies for the councils of governments, but suggested they might prepare regional reports for submission to the Office of Planning and Research addressing the aggregate performance of local jurisdictions within the council area in meeting state growth management goals and standards, based on their LCPs. The new LCPs were put forward as providing much greater certainty for resource protection and development, as they would specify where development would occur, on what terms, and according to what criteria. Each LCP would also include a long-term capital facilities (infrastructure) and financing plan. In addition, the Wilson Commission recommended that challenges to the adequacy of an LCP should be made by administrative procedure to the local council of government, and then the Office of Planning and Research, and that challenges should be initiated by jurisdiction within the same council of governments, by any interested state department or agency, or by a qualified third party under traditional common law standing. The report stated that "subsequent court review after administrative remedies are exhausted should be subject to an abuse of discretion standard. Land use disputes generally, including disputes over the California Environmental Quality Act (CEQA), should be subject to formal mediation, and then to the same administrative and judicial review if necessary."

This approach to local comprehensive planning essentially tightened state government review of local plans, further disempowering the councils of government, except as review boards. Most significantly, the Wilson document proposed limiting the powers of citizens to intervene at the level of the courts. That is, citizens would have to challenge an LCP through an administrative appeal to a local council of government, made up of local municipalities and counties. Given the dynamics of local government, it seems highly unlikely that those representatives would look favorably upon the challenge of an LCP, since that would mean the possibility of setting the precedent for their own LCP to be challenged at a future date. The recommendations go further in suggesting that land-use disputes, including CEQA disputes, should be subject to formal mediation, without giving any details about how that mediation would take place or who would conduct it. Since the Wilson administration has been known for its hostility to CEQA, this approach seems to eviscerate the concept of legal challenge by the public. And for a governor who lauded local control over land-use planning, review of LCPs by the Office of Planning and Research seemed to centralize land-use power in a branch of government responsible directly to the governor, hence subject to political and ideological influence and change, depending on what party and what governor was in power.

5. *CEQA review.* The report recommended that the California Environmental Quality Act be revised to reduce uncertainty, improve assessment of cumulative environmental impacts, and reduce duplicative project-by-project review for routine

development. It suggested that environmental assessment and land-use planning be more closely integrated to improve both, with each jurisdiction preparing a Master Environmental Impact Review (Master EIR) consistent with the LCP. This Master EIR, along with clear criteria for routine development, including infill and smaller projects, would mean that project-specific environmental review could then be limited. Similarly, the report called for procedural changes in CEQA to tighten definitions and in the provision of lawyers' fees, shorter statutes of limitation, and limits on standards of review to discourage its use for delay.

CEQA reform proposals were a mixed bag, addressing some of the problems caused by poorly integrated land-use planning as well as proposing ways to limit CEQA review and curtail its use to challenge development.

6. *Single-issue permit / permit streamlining.* The goal of this proposal was to put into place a single land-use permit, cross-cutting agencies. The permit would be issued by the traditional local permitting authority, city or county, but mandatorily informed by integrated state and regional criteria.

7. *New and reformed councils of governments.* Councils of governments would be reexamined and revised to become the vehicles for streamlining the plethora of regional bodies that already exist, and to reduce and simplify the overall level of government and regulation. They would continue to serve as regional forums and information clearinghouses, but would continue to have no authority. They could not tax, would have no general land-use powers, and no operational duties beyond those they already perform.

Notes

Introduction

1. Theda Skocpol, *Protecting Soldiers and Mothers: The Political Origins of Social Policy in the United States* (Cambridge: Belknap Press of Harvard University Press, 1992; paperback ed., 1995), 39, 43.

2. Timothy Oakes, "Place and the Paradox of Modernity," *Annals of the Association of American Geographers* 87, no. 3 (1997): 509–31.

3. See John Logan and Harvey Molotch, *Urban Fortunes: The Political Economy of Place* (Berkeley: University of California Press, 1987).

4. C. Douglas Lummis, *Radical Democracy* (Ithaca: Cornell University Press, 1996), 91.

Chapter 1 · The Formative Years

1. Michael L. Smith, *Pacific Visions: California Scientists and the Environment 1850–1915* (New Haven: Yale University Press, 1987), 8.

2. Peter Nabokov and Robert Easton, *Native American Architecture* (New York: Oxford University Press, 1989), 287.

3. Kevin Starr, *Americans and the California Dream, 1850–1915* (New York: Oxford University Press, 1973), 66, 68.

4. Paul W. Gates, "California's Embattled Settlers" and "Pre–Henry George Land Warfare in California," both in *Land and Law in California: Essays on Land Policy* (Iowa: Iowa State University Press, 1991), 180, 185.

5. Samuel P. Hays, *The Response to Industrialization, 1855–1914* (Chicago: University of Chicago Press, 1957).

6. William Wycoff, *The Developer's Frontier: The Making of the Western New York Landscape* (New Haven: Yale University Press, 1988); John Mack Faragher, *Sugar Creek: Life on the Illinois Prairie* (New Haven: Yale University Press, 1986).

7. Carey McWilliams, *California: The Great Exception* (1949; reprint, Santa Barbara: Peregrine Smith, 1979), 95.

8. Gates, "Public Land Disposal in California," in *Land and Law,* 267–68.

9. *San Francisco Chronicle,* 10 May 1877, cited in Paul W. Gates, "Adjudication of Spanish-Mexican Land Claims in California" and "Public Land Disposal in California," both in Gates, *Land and Law,* 10, 250–71.

10. Henry George, *Our Land and Land Policy* (San Francisco, 1871), 14, 19.

11. Ibid., 338.

12. Edward J. Rose, *Henry George* (New York: Twayne, 1968).

13. Michael Williams, *Americans and Their Forests: A Historical Geography* (Cambridge: Cambridge University Press, 1989), 426.

14. Donald Pisani, *From the Family Farm to Agribusiness: The Irrigation Crusade in California and the West, 1850–1931* (Berkeley: University of California Press, 1984), 30–31.

15. C. A. Higgens, *A New Guide to the Pacific Coast: Santa Fe Route* (Chicago: Rand McNally, 1895), 240; cited in William L. Preston, *Vanishing Landscapes: Land and Life in the Tulare Lake Basin* (Berkeley: University of California Press, 1981), 138.

16. Smith, *Pacific Visions.*

17. Linnie Marsh Wolfe, *Son of the Wilderness: The Life of John Muir* (Madison: University of Wisconsin Press, 1978), 123–24.

18. Gerald Nash, *State Government and Economic Development: A History of Administrative Policies in California, 1849–1933* (Berkeley: University of California, Institute of Governmental Affairs, 1964), 195.

19. Ibid.

20. Douglas Strong, *Tahoe: An Environmental History* (Lincoln: University of Nebraska Press, 1984), offers a detailed and useful account of land-management politics in this part of the state.

21. Douglas Strong, "The Sierra Forest Reserve: The Movement to Preserve the San Joaquin Valley Watershed," *California Historical Society Quarterly* 46 (1967): 4.

22. Raymond C. Clar, *California Government and Forestry from Spanish Days until the Creation of the Department of Natural Resources* (Sacramento: California Department of Natural Resources, Division of Forestry, 1959), 87.

23. Strong, "Sierra Forest Reserve."

24. Sean L. Swezey and Robert F. Heizer, "Ritual Management of Salmonid Fish Resources in California," in *Before the Wilderness: Environmental Management by Native Californians,* compiled and edited by Thomas C. Blackburn and Kat Anderson (Menlo Park: Ballena Press, 1993).

25. Clar, *California Government and Forestry,* 114.

26. Arthur McEvoy, *The Fisherman's Problem: Ecology and Law in the California Fisheries, 1850–1980* (Cambridge: Cambridge University Press, 1986), 103.

27. Ibid., 114.

28. Nash, *State Government and Economic Development,* 201–6.

29. McEvoy, *Fisherman's Problem,* 66–72.

30. Richard J. Orsi, "*The Octopus* Reconsidered: The Southern Pacific and Agricultural Modernization in California, 1865–1915," *California Historical Quarterly* 5, no. 3 (1975): 197–220.

31. R. Hal Williams, *The Democratic Party and California Politics, 1880–1896* (Stanford: Stanford University Press, 1973), chap. 1: "California in the 1880s and 1890s: The Setting," 1–27.

32. Sucheng Chan, *This Bitter-sweet Soil: The Chinese in California Agriculture, 1860–1910* (1986; reprint, Berkeley: University of California Press, 1989).

33. Williams, *The Democratic Party*, 8.

34. There was also a national Workingman's Party, which dated from the 1840s and had its headquarters in New York City. William Deverell, *Railroad Crossing: Californians and the Railroad, 1850–1910* (Berkeley: University of California Press, 1994), 44.

35. Ibid.

36. Williams, *Democratic Party*, 21.

Chapter 2 · Reformers Ascend to Power

1. See, for example, Spencer Olin, *California's Prodigal Sons: Hiram Johnson and the Progressives, 1911–1917* (Berkeley: University of California Press, 1968); Kevin Starr, *Inventing the Dream: California through the Progressive Era* (New York: Oxford University Press, 1985); George E. Mowry, *The California Progressives* (Berkeley: University of California Press, 1951); and Daniel T. Rodgers, "In Search of Progressivism," *Reviews in American History* 10 (1982): 113–49.

2. Mowry, *California Progressives*, 22.

3. Starr, *Inventing the Dream.*

4. M. Christine Boyer, *Dreaming the Rational City: The Myth of American City Planning* (1983; paperback ed., Cambridge: MIT Press, 1986), 6.

5. John D. Buenker, *Urban Liberalism and Progressive Reform* (New York: W. W. Norton, 1973), 119.

6. Boyer, *Dreaming the Rational City*, 7.

7. Richard Hofstadter, *The Age of Reform* (New York: Vintage Books, 1955).

8. McWilliams, *California*, 196–97.

9. Ibid., 199–201.

10. My thanks to Gray Brechin for pointing this out.

11. Olin, *California's Prodigal Sons*, 11–12.

12. Frank Hichborn, *Story of the Legislature of 1911* (San Francisco: Press of the James H. Barry Co., 1911), 47.

13. Deverell, *Railroad Crossing.*

14. Buenker, *Urban Liberalism*, 5.

15. Jackson K. Putnam, "The Progressive Legacy in California: Fifty Years of Politics, 1917–1967," in *California Progressivism Revisited*, edited by William Deverell and Tom Sitton (Berkeley: University of California Press, 1994).

16. Tom Sitton, *John Randolph Haynes, California Progressive* (Stanford: Stanford University Press, 1992).

17. Richard B. Harvey, "California Politics: Historical Profile," in *California Politics and Policies*, edited by Eugene P. Dvorin and Arthur J. Misner (Reading, Mass.: Addison-Wesley, 1966), 15–17.

18. *Fresno Republican*, 23 March 1913. See Madelon Helfer Berkowitz, *Progressivism and the Anti-Japanese Agitation in California* (master's thesis, Stanford University, 1963).

19. Putnam, "Progressive Legacy," 249.

20. The Pacific Gas & Electric Company was quickly becoming northern California's primary power provider. It used its size and economic strength to monopolize access to and distribution of electricity and gas, and to eliminate small power companies.

21. Deverell, *Railroad Crossing,* 171.

22. Ibid., 239n.84.

23. Frank Hichborn, "Why the Corporations Win before the State Railroad Commission" (Santa Clara, Calif., 1926), 10–11.

24. Olin, *California's Prodigal Sons,* 67–69.

25. Putnam, "Progressive Legacy."

26. Hichborn, *Story of the Legislature,* xiv.

27. Gifford Pinchot, *Breaking New Ground* (New York: Harcourt, Brace, 1947), 355.

28. See Samuel P. Hays, *Conservation and the Gospel of Efficiency: The Progressive Conservation Movement 1890–1920* (Cambridge: Harvard University Press, 1959), for a critical account of the movement.

29. Pinchot, *Breaking New Ground,* 357.

30. Clar, *California Government and Forestry,* 330.

31. Williams, *Americans and Their Forests,* 196–97, 420.

32. Clar, *California Government and Forestry.*

33. Ibid.

34. William G. Robbins, *American Forestry: A History of National, State, and Private Cooperation* (Lincoln: University of Nebraska Press, 1985), 22–23.

35. Williams, *Americans and Their Forests,* 421.

36. Susan Schrepfer, *The Fight to Save the Redwoods: A History of Environmental Reform, 1917–1978* (Madison: University of Wisconsin Press, 1983). The following section is based on Schrepfer's analysis.

37. Anne F. Hyde, "William Kent: The Puzzle of Progressive Conservationists," in *California Progressivism Revisited,* 46.

38. Henry T. Lewis, "Patterns of Indian Burning in California: Ecology and Ethnohistory," in *Before the Wilderness,* 55–116.

39. Horace Marden Albright and Newton Bishop Drury, "Horace Marden Albright and Newton Bishop Drury, Comments on Conservation, 1900–1960," oral history interview by Amelia Fry (Regional Oral History Project, Bancroft Library, University of California, Berkeley, 1962), 12.

40. Schrepfer, *Fight to Save the Redwoods,* 70, 73.

41. Elsey Hurt, *California State Government: An Outline of Its Administrative Organization from 1850 to 1936* (Sacramento: Supervisor of Documents, 1936), 150.

42. Schrepfer, *Fight to Save the Redwoods,* 39.

43. Norris Hundley Jr., *The Great Thirst: Californians and Water, 1770s–1990s* (Berkeley: University of California Press, 1992), 237.

44. Pisani, *From the Family Farm to Agribusiness,* 269, 278–79.

45. The history and politics of water development in California are complex and

have received the attention of several authors of note, including Hundley, Sauder, Pisani, Walton, Worster, and Reisner.

46. Donald J. Pisani, *To Reclaim a Divided West: Water, Law, and Public Policy, 1848–1902* (Albuquerque: University of New Mexico Press, 1992), 287.

47. Hundley, *Great Thirst*, 237–38.

48. Robert A. Sauder, *The Lost Frontier: Water Diversion in the Growth and Destruction of Owens Valley Agriculture* (Tucson: University of Arizona Press, 1994), 107.

49. Ibid., 115.

50. McEvoy, *Fisherman's Problem*, 157, 91, 126, 133.

51. The best analysis of this philosophy remains that of Hays, *Conservation and the Gospel of Efficiency*.

52. Alfred Runte, *Yosemite, The Embattled Wilderness* (Lincoln: University of Nebraska Press, 1990), 54–56.

53. Ibid., 78; Hyde, "William Kent," 47.

54. Hyde, "William Kent," 49.

55. Boyer, *Dreaming the Rational City*, 61.

56. William Issel, "'Citizens outside the Government': Business and Urban Policy in San Francisco and Los Angeles, 1890–1932," *Pacific Historical Review* 57, no. 2 (1988): 138.

57. Ibid.

58. Ronald E. Blight, "Municipal Government 50 Years from Now," *California Outlook* 11 (21 October 1911): 11–12, cited in Robert M. Fogelson, *The Fragmented Metropolis: Los Angeles, 1850–1930* (Cambridge: Harvard University Press, 1967), 211.

59. San Francisco Chamber of Commerce, *Activities* 3 (1 June 1916): 3, cited in Issel, "Citizens outside the Government," 125.

60. Gray Brechin, "Termites," *Upriver, Downriver* (fall 1993): 18–21.

61. Fogelson, *Fragmented Metropolis*, 211.

62. Ibid., 192, 198.

63. George M. Day, "Races and Cultural Oases," *Sociology and Social Research* 18 (March–April 1934): 328, 335–39, cited in Fogelson, *Fragmented Metropolis*, 204.

64. Fogelson, *Fragmented Metropolis*, 207–8.

65. Deverell, *Railroad Crossing*, 121.

66. Issel, "Citizens outside the Government," 117–45.

67. Fogelson, *Fragmented Metropolis*, 131.

68. Tom Sitton, *John Randolph Haynes, California Progressive* (Stanford: Stanford University Press, 1992), 99.

69. Fred W. Viehe, "The First Recall: Los Angeles Urban Reform or Machine Politics?" *Southern California Quarterly* 70, no. 1 (1988): 2.

70. Fogelson, *Fragmented Metropolis*, 218.

71. This section is based on Steven P. Erie, "How the Urban West Was Won: The Local State and Economic Growth in Los Angeles, 1880–1932," *Urban Affairs Quarterly* 27, no. 4 (1992): 519–54.

72. Sauder, *The Lost Frontier*, 147.

73. Ibid., 115, 150.

74. Brechin, "Termites," 19–20.

75. Michael Kazin, *Barons of Labor: The San Francisco Building Trades and Union Power in the Progressive Era* (Urbana: University of Illinois Press, 1987).

76. Ibid, 40.

77. Ibid., 41, 45.

78. Kazin, *Barons of Labor,* 40–41.

79. Starr, *Americans and the California Dream,* 250–52.

80. Kazin, *Barons of Labor,* 120.

81. Starr, *Americans and the California Dream,* 292–93.

82. Issel, "Citizens outside the Government," 120.

83. Charles Wollenberg, *Golden Gate Metropolis: Perspectives on Bay Area History* (Berkeley: University of California, Institute of Governmental Affairs, 1985), 168–71.

84. James P. Walsh, "Abe Ruef Was No Boss: Machine Politics, Reform, and San Francisco," *California Historical Quarterly* 51, no. 1 (1972): 11.

85. Stephen Skowronek, *Building a New American State: The Expansion of National Administrative Capacities, 1877–1920* (Cambridge: Cambridge University Press, 1982), 249.

Chapter 3 · Transitional Interwar Years

1. Alan Wolfe, *The Limits of Legitimacy: Political Contradictions of Contemporary Capitalism* (New York: Free Press, 1977); Martin J. Sklar, *The Corporate Reconstruction of American Capitalism, 1890–1916: The Market, the Law and Politics* (New York: Cambridge University Press, 1988), 34.

2. Grant McConnell, *The Decline of Agrarian Democracy* (Berkeley: University of California Press, 1953).

3. This section is based on Robbins, *American Forestry.*

4. McConnell, *Decline of Agrarian Democracy.*

5. Elias W. Hawley, *The New Deal and the Problems of Monopoly: A Study in Economic Ambivalence* (Princeton: Princeton University Press, 1969), 6–8.

6. Issel, "Citizens outside the Government," 133–34, 137.

7. Gerald D. Nash, *A. P. Giannini and the Bank of America* (Norman: University of Oklahoma Press, 1992).

8. Robert Gottlieb and Irene Wolt, *Thinking Big: The Story of the Los Angeles Times, Its Publishers, and Their Influence on Southern California* (New York: G. P. Putnam's Sons, 1967).

9. Gates, *Land and Law,* 337.

10. Paul Taylor, "Migrants and California's Future," in *On the Ground in the Thirties* (Salt Lake City: Gibbs M. Smith, Peregrine Smith Books, 1983), 178.

11. Nash, *State Government and Economic Development,* 228.

12. Ellen Liebman, *California Farmland: A History of Large Agricultural Landholdings* (Totowa, N.J.: Rowman and Allanheld, 1983), chap. 3.

13. Ibid.

14. McConnell, *Decline of Agrarian Democracy.*

15. Rodolfo Acuña, *Occupied America: A History of Chicanos,* 3rd ed. (New York: Harper and Row, 1988), 179.

16. Taylor, "Migrants," 179.

17. Ibid., 182–83.

18. Ibid., 98.

19. Ibid., 180.

20. Paul Taylor, "What Shall We Do with Them?" in *On the Ground in the Thirties* (Salt Lake City: Gibbs M. Smith, Peregrine Smith Books, 1983), 203–4.

21. J. Donald Fisher, *A Historical Study of the Migrant in California* (1945; reprint, San Francisco: R&E Research Associates, 1973).

22. Ibid.

23. Ibid.

24. Timothy J. Lukes and Gary Y. Okihiro, *Japanese Legacy: Farming and Community Life in California's Santa Clara Valley*, Local History Studies 31 (Cupertino: California History Center, 1985).

25. Mary Montgomery and Marion Clawson, "History of Legislation and Policy Formation of the Central Valley Project" (Sacramento: U.S. Department of the Interior, Bureau of Reclamation, Region III, 1946), 21.

26. Walter Adams and Horace M. Gray, *Monopoly in America: The Government as Promoter* (New York: Macmillan, 1955), 46.

27. Arthur Desk Angel, "Political and Administrative Aspects of the Central Valley Project of California" (Ph.D. diss., University of California, Los Angeles, 1944), 207.

28. Ibid., 194, 192.

29. Erwin Cooper, *Aqueduct Empire: A Guide to Water in California: Its Turbulent History and Its Management Today* (Glendale: Arthur H. Clark Co., 1968), 163–66.

30. Angel, "Political and Administrative Aspects," 215–20.

31. Quoted in Montgomery and Clawson, "History of Legislation," 110.

32. Ibid., 115.

33. Cooper, *Aqueduct Empire*, 158.

34. Preston, *Vanishing Landscapes*.

35. William L. Kahrl, Marlyn L. Shelton, and William A. Bowen, *The California Water Atlas* (Sacramento: General Services Publication Division of the State of California, 1978), 61, 62.

36. Cooper, *Aqueduct Empire*, 168.

37. Skocpol, *Protecting Soldiers and Mothers*, 45.

38. Richard B. Harvey, *The Dynamics of California Government and Politics* (Belmont: Wadsworth, 1970), 80.

39. Ibid., 210–11.

40. This section is based on McWilliams, *California*, 199–201, 202, 205–6, and chap. 11.

41. Robert E. Burke, *Olson's New Deal for California* (Berkeley: University of California Press, 1953).

42. Constantine Panunzio, *Self-help Cooperatives in Los Angeles*, Publications of the University of California at Los Angeles in Social Sciences 8, no. 1 (Berkeley: University of California Press, 1939).

43. Ibid., 110.

44. Fisher, *Historical Study*, 53.

45. Burke, *Olson's New Deal*, 26.

46. Ibid., 219–220.

47. Williams, *Americans and Their Forests*, 461, 430.

48. William G. Robbins, *Lumberjacks and Legislators: Political Economy of the U.S. Lumber Industry, 1890–1941* (College Station: Texas A&M University Press, 1982).

49. W. S. Rosecrans, "Forestry by the People," n.d. (c. 1949), Sacramento State Library, 2.

50. T. F. Arvola, *Regulation of Logging in California, 1945–1975* (Sacramento: California Resources Agency, Department of Conservation, Division of Forestry, 1976), 12.

51. Rosecrans, "Forestry by the People," 7–8.

52. DeWitt Nelson, "Management of Natural Resources in California, 1925–1966," oral history interview by Amelia Fry (Forest History Society and Regional Oral History Project, Bancroft Library, University of California, 1976), 97–98.

53. Arvola, *Regulation of Logging*, 3–4.

54. Albright and Drury, "Comments on Conservation," 99.

55. Nash, *State Government and Economic Development*, 293.

56. Ibid., 304.

57. McEvoy, *Fisherman's Problem*, 176.

58. Ibid., 177.

59. Nash, *State Government and Economic Development*, 302, 182.

60. Ibid., 298. Much of this section is based on Nash's discussion.

61. McEvoy, *Fisherman's Problem*, 184.

62. This history is important to understanding urban form today. There are several excellent references; see Marc Weiss, *The Rise of the Community Builders* (New York: Columbia University Press, 1987); Mel Scott, *American City Planning since 1890* (Berkeley: University of California Press, 1969); Richard Walker and Michael Heiman, "Quiet Revolution for Whom?" *Annals of the Association of American Geographers* 71, no. 1 (1981): 67–83; Michael Heiman, *The Quiet Evolution: Power, Planning and Profits in New York State* (New York: Praeger, 1988); Kenneth Jackson, *Crabgrass Frontier: The Suburbanization of the United States* (New York: Oxford University Press, 1985).

63. Greg Hise, *Magnetic Los Angeles: Planning the Twentieth-century Metropolis* (Baltimore: Johns Hopkins University Press, 1997).

64. Weiss, *Rise of the Community Builders*, 1–3.

65. Hise, *Magnetic Los Angeles*.

66. Weiss, *Rise of the Community Builders*.

67. Jackson, *Crabgrass Frontier*, 202–6.

68. Scott, *American City Planning*, 209.

69. Hise, *Magnetic Los Angeles*, 11, citing McWilliams.

70. Californios are native Californians of Mexican descent.

71. Ricardo Romo, *East Los Angeles: History of a Barrio* (Austin: University of Texas Press, 1977).

72. George J. Sánchez, *Becoming Mexican-American: Ethnicity, Culture, and Identity in Chicano Los Angeles, 1900–1945* (New York: Oxford University Press, 1993).

73. Francisco E. Balderrama and Raymond Rodríguez, *Decade of Betrayal: Mexican Repatriation in the 1930s* (Albuquerque: University of New Mexico Press, 1995).

74. Charles Wollenberg, *Golden Gate Metropolis: Perspectives on Bay Area History* (Berkeley: University of California, Institute of Governmental Affairs, 1985).

75. Steve Scott, "Budget Dysfunction," *California Journal* 28, no. 9 (1997): 10.

76. Mansel G. Blackford, *The Politics of Business in California, 1890–1920* (Columbus: Ohio State University Press, 1977), 170.

Chapter 4 · The Problems and Politics of Growth

1. Joel Kotkin and Paul Grabowicz, *California Inc.* (New York: Rawson Wade, 1982), 9.

2. McWilliams, *California*, 233.

3. Cary McWilliams, "Look What's Happened to California," in *The Politics of California: A Book of Readings*, edited by David Farrelly and Ivan Hinderaker (New York: Ronald Press, 1951), 23.

4. James S. Fay, ed., and Ronald J. Boehm, pub., *California Almanac*, 6th ed. (Santa Barbara: Pacific Data Resources, 1993), 1.

5. Clayton Koppes, "Public Water, Private Land: Origins of the Acreage Limitation Controversy, 1933–1953," *Pacific Historical Review* 47 (November 1978): 617.

6. Ann A. Markusen, *Regions: The Economics and Politics of Territory* (Totowa, N.J.: Rowman and Littlefield, 1987).

7. Jackson, *Crabgrass Frontier*, 233.

8. Again, readers interested in the relationship between federal subsidies and the patterns of land-use development in the United States, and in California, should consult Weiss, *Rise of the Community Builders*; Scott, *American City Planning*; Jackson, *Crabgrass Frontier*; Walker and Heiman, "Quiet Revolution"; Heiman, *Quiet Evolution*.

9. Leo Katcher, *Earl Warren: A Political Biography* (New York: McGraw-Hill, 1967), 187–89.

10. Ibid., 196.

11. Ibid.

12. Governor's Commission on Metropolitan Area Problems, *Meeting Metropolitan Problems* (Sacramento, December 1960).

13. Stanley Scott and John C. Bollens, *Governing a Metropolitan Region: The San Francisco Bay Area* (Berkeley: University of California, Institute of Governmental Affairs, 1968).

14. Robert T. LeGates, *California Local Agency Formation Commissions* (Berkeley: University of California, Institute of Governmental Affairs, 1970), 17.

15. G. J. Miller, *Cities by Contract: The Politics of Municipal Incorporation* (Cambridge: MIT Press, 1981), 102–3.

16. Logan and Molotch, *Urban Fortunes*.

17. Robert Fellmeth, *Ralph Nader's Study Group Report on Land in California* (New York: Grossman, 1973).

18. Ned Eichler, *The Merchant Builders* (Cambridge: MIT Press, 1982).

19. Robert Fishman, *Bourgeois Utopias: The Rise and Fall of Suburbia* (New York: Basic Books, 1987).

20. Wollenberg, *Golden Gate Metropolis*, 258.

21. Ibid., 275.

22. Rice Odell, *The Saving of San Francisco Bay: A Report on Citizen Action and Regional Planning* (Washington, D.C.: Conservation Foundation, 1972).

23. BCDC membership: one member of the U.S. Army Corps of Engineers, Western Division; one member from the U.S. Dept. of Health, Education and Welfare, Western Division; one member from California Business and Transportation Department, San Francisco office; one member from the California Department of Finance, San Francisco office; one member from the California Resources Agency; one member from the California Lands Commission; one member from the San Francisco Bay Regional Water Quality Control Board. In addition, nine members drawn (one each) from the boards of supervisors of the San Francisco Bay area counties, appointed by the boards of supervisors in those counties; four city representatives appointed by the Association of Bay Area Governments from among the residents of bayside cities; seven representatives of the public residents of the San Francisco Bay area, whose appointments are subject to confirmation by the Senate (of these, five are appointed by the governor, one by the Committee on Rules of the Senate, and one by the Speaker of the Assembly). From the McAteer-Petris Act, amended in 1970, section 66620.

24. Alvin D. Sokolow, "The Williamson Act, 25 Years of Land Conservation" (Sacramento: Department of Conservation, December 1990).

25. Mary E. Handel and Alvin D. Sokolow, "Farmland and Open Space Preservation in the Four North Bay Counties" (Behavioral Sciences, Cooperative Extension, University of California, Davis, May 1994).

26. Bob Simmons, "The Freeway Establishment," *Cry California* 2, no. 2 (1968): 31.

27. Wollenberg, *Golden Gate Metropolis*, 268.

28. Curt Gentry, "Iron Heel on the California Coast" (1968), in *The New Book of California Tomorrow: Reflections and Projections from the Golden State*, edited by John Hart (Los Altos: William Kaufman, 1984).

29. Larry M. Dilsaver and William C. Tweed, *Challenge of the Big Trees of Sequoia and Kings Canyon National Parks* (Three Rivers: Sequoia Natural History Association, 1990), 281, 298–301.

30. S. E. Wood and Alfred Heller, *California Going, Going . . .* (Sacramento: California Tomorrow, 1962), 6.

31. Walker and Heiman, "Quiet Revolution."

32. See, most notably, Richard Babcock, *The Zoning Game* (Madison: University of Wisconsin Press, 1966). Babcock's work was commissioned by the American Society of Planning Officials and funded by the Ford Foundation.

33. Sidney Plotkin, *Keep Out: The Struggle for Land Use Control* (Berkeley: University of California Press, 1987), 152–61.

34. Walker and Heiman, "Quiet Revolution," 74.

35. The program was under the federal "701" assistance program of the Housing and Urban Development agency.

36. R. H. Banda, *Evaluation of the California State Planning System: The Impact of the 701 Comprehensive Planning Assistance Act on Planning in California* (San Francisco: U.S. Department of Housing and Urban Development, Region IX, Program Planning and Evaluation, April 1974).

37. Harvey Molotch, "Santa Barbara: Oil in the Velvet Playground," in *Eco-Catastrophe*, by the editors of *Ramparts* (San Francisco: Canfield Press, Harper and Row, 1970), 89.

38. William Fulton, *Guide to California Planning* (Point Arena: Solano Press, 1991), 116.

39. Charles H. Haar and M. A. Wolf, *Land-Use Planning: A Casebook on the Use, Misuse and Re-Use of Urban Land* (Boston: Little, Brown, 1989).

40. Alfred Heller, ed., *The California Tomorrow Plan* (Los Altos: William Kaufman, 1971).

41. Author's interview with Henry Vaux, professor emeritus of forestry, University of California, Berkeley, and chair of the California Board of Forestry, 1976–1983; interview conducted on 16 July 1984.

42. Diana Petty, "North Coast Dilemma: To Cut or to Conserve," *California Journal* 5, no. 10 (1975): 405–7.

43. Dudley J. Burton and Irvine Alpert, "The Decline of California's North Coast Redwood Region," *Policy Studies Journal* 10, no. 2 (1981): 272–85.

44. Schrepfer, *Fight to Save the Redwoods.*

45. Arvola, *Regulation of Logging.*

46. Ibid.

47. Vaux interview.

48. Arvola, *Regulation of Logging.*

49. Thomas Lundmark, "Regulation of Private Logging in California," *Ecology Law Quarterly* 5, no. 139 (1975): 139–88.

50. Ibid., 147.

51. Author's interview with John Nejedly, Walnut Creek, Calif., 15 January 1985.

52. Lundmark, "Regulation of Private Logging," 152.

53. Hundley, *Great Thirst*, 265–66.

54. Cooper, *Aqueduct Empire.*

55. Hundley, *Great Thirst*, 276.

56. Cooper, *Aqueduct Empire*, 201.

57. Hundley, *Great Thirst*; also Fellmeth, *Ralph Nader's Study Group*; and Liebman, *California Farmland*, 190.

58. Cooper, *Aqueduct Empire*, 201.

59. Hundley, *Great Thirst*, 290–93.

60. Walter R. Goldschmidt, *Small Business and the Community: A Study in the Central Valley of California of Effects of Scale Farm Operations*, report of the Senate Special Committee to Study Problems of American Small Business, 79th Cong., 2nd sess., 1946.

61. Fellmeth, *Ralph Nader's Study Group*, 45–53, 86–87.

62. Dean MacCannell, "The Effect of Agricultural Scale on Communities," and "Industrial Agriculture and the Degradation of Rural Communities in the United States Sunbelt," unpublished reports (c. 1986) given by MacCannell to the author. MacCannell was a professor at the University of California, Davis, and director of the Macrosocial Accounting Project, which conducted the research for these reports.

63. Fellmeth, *Ralph Nader's Study Group*, 167.

64. Ivan Hinderaker, "Politics of Reapportionment," in *California Politics and Policies*, 147.

65. This discussion is based on Hinderaker, "Politics of Reapportionment."

66. George Milias, "Interview with George Milias: Legislating for the Environment," *California Journal* 2, no. 11 (1970): 316.

67. "The Governor's State of the State," *California Journal* 2, no. 1 (1970): 8.

68. "Jurisdictional Disputes Slow Efforts to Give the State an Effective Role in Solid Waste Management," *California Journal* 3, no. 10 (1971): 284.

69. "Legislative Summary," *California Journal* 2, no. 8 (1970): 228–30.

Chapter 5 · Unfulfilled Visions

1. Donella H. Meadows, Dennis L. Meadows, Jorgen Randers, and William W. Behrens III, *The Limits to Growth: Our Common Future* (New York: New American Library, 1972), 29.

2. World Commission on Environment and Development, *Our Common Future* (Oxford: Oxford University Press, 1987).

3. E. F. Schumacher, *Small Is Beautiful* (New York: Harper Torchbooks, 1973), 47.

4. Ibid., 150.

5. John H. Mollenkopf, *The Contested City* (Princeton: Princeton University Press, 1983), 139.

6. This section is based on Mollenkopf, *Contested City*, 126, 128, 132–38.

7. "Coastal Zone Conservation," *California Journal* 3, no. 10 (1972): 311.

8. Michael L. Fisher, "California's Coastal Program," *Journal of the American Planning Association* 15 (summer 1985): 314–15.

9. Ibid.

10. "How the New Energy Act Should Work," *California Journal* 5, no. 7 (1974): 407–9.

11. Ibid.

12. *Cry California* (winter 1977–78).

13. California Department of Forestry, *California's Forest Resources: Preliminary Assessment* (Sacramento: Department of Natural Resources, 1979).

14. Ibid.

15. Dale A. Hudson, "*Sierra Club v. Department of the Interior:* The Fight to Save Redwood National Park," *Ecology Law Quarterly* 7 (1978): 781–859.

16. Stephanie Pincetl, "Roads Not Taken: The Environmental Policies and Politics of the Brown Administration, 1975–1983" (Ph.D. diss., University of California, Los Angeles, 1985).

17. Hundley, *Great Thirst*, 317.

18. Susan Sward, "Ecology Study OKs Plan for Key Canal Link," *Los Angeles Times*, 5 September 1974.

19. Philip Fradkin, "California Water War Boils Over Again," *Los Angeles Times*, 6 January 1975.

20. W. B. Rood and Bill Stall, "Who'll Get Water? U.S., State at Odds," *Los Angeles Times*, 3 October 1976.

21. Fradkin, "California Water War."

22. Richard Walker and Michael Storper, "The Expanding California Water System," reprint (San Francisco: Pacific Division, AAAS, 1982), 180.

23. Hundley, *Great Thirst*, 318.

24. W. B. Rood, "Brown's Water Bill Defeated in Senate," *Los Angeles Times*, 3 February 1978.

25. Michael Storper and Richard Walker, "The Price of Water: Surplus and Subsidy in the California State Water Project" (Berkeley: University of California, Institute of Governmental Affairs, 1984), 12.

26. Hundley, *Great Thirst*, 325.

27. National Land for People, "Intent of Reclamation: Bureaucrats Subvert Reclamation Intent" (Fresno, March 1979), 10–12.

28. Ibid., 17–18.

29. Bob Egelko, "Legislators Want Reins Placed on UC Spending," *Sacramento Bee*, 11 May 1977.

30. "Westland Biggies Scrap over Board Control, But SP Runs the Show . . . ," *People Food and Land: The Land for People Quarterly Journal* 2, nos. 3–4 (1981): 118–19.

31. Merrill R. Goodall and John D. Sullivan, "Water District Organization: Political Decision Systems," in *California Water Planning and Policy, Selected Issues*, edited by Ernest A. Engelbert (Berkeley: University of California, Institute of Governmental Affairs, Water Resources Center, June 1979), 207–25.

32. "Congress Gives West to Biggies," *People Food and Land: The Land for People Quarterly Journal* 3, no. 2 (1982): 35–36.

33. Stephen Johnson, Gerald Haslam, and Robert Dawson, *The Great Central Valley, California's Heartland* (Berkeley: University of California Press, 1993), 144.

34. National Land for People, "Is This a Railroad Station or a Farmhouse?" (Fresno, March 1978), 26.

35. Johnson et al., *Great Central Valley*.

36. "The Wrap-up: Reclamation, Death of an American Promise," *People Food and Land: The Land for People Quarterly Journal* 3, no. 3 (1985): 67.

37. Clarence Y. H. Lo, *Small Property versus Big Government: Social Origins of the Property Tax Revolt* (Berkeley: University of California Press, 1990), xii–xiii.

38. Ibid., xiii–xiv.

39. Ibid., 137–42.

40. This discussion is based on Lo, *Small Property*.

41. Ibid., 38.

42. Ibid., 39.

43. For a thorough discussion of the role of the "growth machine," see Logan and Molotch, *Urban Fortunes.*

44. Lo, *Small Property.*

45. Richard Edward DeLeon, *Left Coast City: Progressive Politics in San Francisco, 1975–1991* (Lawrence: University of Kansas Press, 1992), 42–43.

46. Edward W. Soja, *Postmodern Geographies: The Reassertion of Space in Critical Social Theory* (London: Verso, 1989), 208–9.

47. Mike Davis, "*Chinatown*, Revisited? The 'Internationalization' of Downtown Los Angeles," in *Sex, Death and God in LA*, edited by David Reid (New York: Pantheon, 1992), 25–27.

48. Harold Gilliam, "Beating Back the Bulldozers," *Saturday Review,* 23 September 1967, 67–68.

49. Governor's Office of Planning and Research, "An Urban Strategy for California" (Sacramento, February 1978), 4.

Chapter 6 · Years of Malign Neglect

1. Donald L. Barlett and James B. Steele, *America: What Went Wrong?* (Kansas City: Andrews and McMeel, 1992), 51–52.

2. Fulton, *Guide to California Planning,* 121.

3. Lillianne Chase, "Funny-money Classrooms," *Golden State Report* (September 1986): 33–35.

4. Michael Bowker, "Going for the Green," *Defenders* (March–April 1988): 18–20.

5. Ed Mendel, "The Politics of Toxics," *Golden State Report* (September 1986): 13–16.

6. Hal Rubin, "Combat Zone," *Golden State Report* (February 1989): 37–40.

7. Ibid.

8. California has about 6,000 units of local government—cities, counties, and special districts—all fighting for a declining tax base. Ed Salzman, "The Next California?" *Golden State Report* (December 1988): 15–20.

9. William Fulton, "City vs. County," *Golden State Report* (September 1989): 12.

10. Ibid.

11. "California Voters Lead Nation in Growth Management and Conservation Ballot," *Successful Communities: The Newsletter of Growth Management* 1, no. 1 (1988): 2.

12. Gary Jerome, Peter Detwiler, and Leslie McFadden, "Challenges and Opportunities," working paper for the New Regionalism Project of the California Senate Select Committee on Planning for California Growth, Senate Committee on Local Government, Senator Marian Bergeson, chair (Sacramento, 1988), 1, 4.

13. Elizabeth Kersten, Steve Sanders, and Diane Turner, "Does California Need a Policy to Manage Urban Growth?" report from the Senate Urban Growth Policy Project, Senate Office of Research (Sacramento, June 1989).

14. Richard P. Sybert, director, Governor's Office of Planning and Research, testimony to the Joint Interim Hearing, Senate Local Government Committee, Senate Select Committee on Planning for California's Growth, Assembly Local Government Committee, Sacramento, 31 October 1991.

15. Mark Arax and Virginia Ellis, "Developers Go to War over Water Bill," *Los Angeles Times*, 8 August 1994, A1, A14, A15.

16. Manuel Pastor Jr. and Dennis Zane, eds., "The California Dilemma" (Los Angeles: California Council for the Humanities, 1991).

17. Ponds were created for migrating birds, replacing the once vast wetlands that existed in the Central Valley, including Tulare Lake, which once covered 450,000 acres, and Buena Vista Lake. The artificial ponds are watered by drainage water from agricultural lands, helping to solve the serious problem of drainage that exists in the Central Valley. However, it was discovered that, in addition to pesticides and herbicides, some of these drainage ponds contain unusually high levels of selenium, a very toxic chemical found naturally in the Central Valley, and that as a result birds were suffering serious birth defects.

18. On December 15, 1994, an agreement was signed to meet Clean Water Act standards for the Sacramento Delta estuary and to provide reliable water supplies to farms and cities across the state. The final straw forcing agreement was a March 1994 warning by the investment evaluation firm of Standard & Poor's that unless measures were taken to end the Delta water dispute, the state's credit rating could suffer. The agreement guarantees 400,000 acre-feet a year for the Delta in normal years from the Central Valley Project and 1.1 million acre-feet in extreme drought years, in exchange for an agreement that no new species will be listed as threatened for at least three years. Frank Clifford, "Landmark Accord Reached on Use of Bay-Delta Water," *Los Angeles Times*, 16 December 1994, A1, A28.

19. Michael D. Rosen, "Conflict within Irrigation Districts May Limit Water Transfer Gains," *California Agriculture* 46, no. 6 (1992): 4.

20. U.S. Congress, House Committee on Natural Resources, *Legislative History, Miscellaneous Articles, and Background Information Related to Public Law 102-575 Reclamation Projects Authorization and Adjustment Act of 1992*, 103rd Cong., 1st sess. (November 1993), 282-317.

21. Bay Area Economic Forum, *Using Water Better: A Market-based Approach to California's Water Crisis* (San Francisco: Bay Area Economic Forum, October 1991), 1.

22. Arax and Ellis, "Developers Go to War"; Alvin D. Sokolow, "Everything Is Coming Up Houses," *California Journal* 21, no. 11 (1990): 535-37.

23. Deborah Jensen, Margaret S. Torn, and John Harte, *In Our Own Hands: A Strategy for Conserving California's Biological Diversity* (Berkeley: University of California Press, 1993), 95.

24. Mark Arax, "Sprawl Threatens Central Valley, Study Says," *Los Angeles Times*, 26 October 1995, A3, A20.

25. Rudy Platzek, "California's Most Important Choice: An Agricultural or Urban Central Valley," *California Planner* (November–December 1995): 8–9.

26. "Down on the Corporate Farm," *Amicus Journal* 19, no. 3 (1997): 8.

27. Mike Davis, "Imperial Pirates," *Los Angeles Weekly*, 23–29 February 1996, 11–12.

28. Morris Newman, "New Deals for Colorado River Water Called Landmark," *California Planning and Development Report* 11, no. 2 (1996): 1, 10.

29. Marie Gravelle, "Reaping the Redwoods," *Golden State Report* (March 1990): 27–30.

30. Jack Epstein, "Raiding the Redwoods," *California Business* (September 1987): 34–45.

31. Teresa Simons, "Epic Struggle over Redwoods," *California Journal* 11, no. 3 (1990): 151–54.

32. Frank Clifford, "Land Swap to Preserve Old Redwood Forest Takes Root," *Los Angeles Times*, 25 July 1996, A1, A24.

33. Gravelle, "Reaping the Redwoods."

34. Simons, "Epic Struggle," 154.

35. Douglas P. Wheeler, abstract of "Creating a State Strategy for Habitat Protection: The California Biodiversity Plan by the Resources Agency of California" (1991), in *Our Lands: New Strategies for Protecting the West, Blueprints for Action* (Sacramento: California State Resources Agency, 1993), 66.

36. Dan Blackburn, "Saving the Sierra, Master Plan for the Range of Light," *California Journal* 13, no. 2 (1992): 103–5.

37. Tom Knudson, "Majesty and Tragedy: The Sierra in Peril," *Sacramento Bee*, special report, June 1991. A compilation of four days of reporting on this issue.

38. Quoted in Blackburn, "Saving the Sierra," 103.

39. Ibid., 105.

40. Knudson, "Majesty and Tragedy," 4.

41. Ibid., 5.

42. Ibid., 7.

43. Katie Durbin, "The Timber Salvage Scam," *Amicus Journal* 17, no. 3 (1995): 29–31.

44. Knudson, "Majesty and Tragedy," 10. See also Frank Clifford, "Sierra on the Precipice," *Los Angeles Times*, 2 June 1996, A1, A22, A23.

45. Alexander Cockburn, "Serpent's Tooth: A Radical Confidence in Grassroots Activism: An Interview with Sharon Duggan," *Wild Forest Review* 1, no. 8 (1994): 8–12.

46. Pat Paquette, "The Environment and Jobs, Seeking Balance between Owls and People," *California Journal* 14, no. 2 (1993): 15–18.

47. Ibid., 16.

48. M. Bonnett and K. Zimmerman, "Politics and Preservation: The Endangered Species Act and the Northern Spotted Owl," *Ecology Law Quarterly* 18 (1991): 105–71.

49. Monica Florian, vice president, Irvine Company, letter to Douglas P. Wheeler, secretary of California Resources Agency, 2 April 1991, in files of Endangered Habitats League, Los Angeles.

50. James Sterngold, "Foiling the Best Laid Plans," *New York Times*, 17 September 1995, 3-1, 3-12.

51. Terry Timmons, *Structural Speculation as a Dynamic of Urban Growth: A Case Study of the Irvine Company*, Ph.D. diss. (Ann Arbor: University Microfilms International, 1993), 164.

52. Jeanne Clark, "NCCP—A New Approach to Saving Species," *Outdoor California* (March–April 1994): 4–9.

53. John F. O'Leary, "Coastal Sage Scrub: Threats and Current Status," *Fremontia* 23, no. 4 (1995): 27–31.

54. *Endangered Habitats League Newsletter* (January–February 1993), 4. Available by writing to 8424A Santa Monica Blvd., No. 592, Los Angeles, CA 90069.

55. This discussion of the NCCP process and the gnatcatcher is based on the newsletter of the Endangered Habitats League and the author's experience as a member of the policy implementation team for the evaluation of the socioeconomic impacts of preserving the California spotted owl for the state of California, 1992–94. See our report, *Conserving the California Spotted Owl: Impacts of Interim Policies and Implications for the Long Term,* report of the Policy Implementation Planning Team to the Steering Committee for the California Spotted Owl Assessment, report 33 (Davis: University of California, Wildland Resources Center, Division of Agriculture and Natural Resources, May 1994).

56. Ibid., 2.

57. Ibid., chap. 2.

58. Jared Verner, K. McKelvey, B. Noon, R. Gutierrez, G. Gould, and T. Beck, *The California Spotted Owl: A Technical Assessment of Its Current Status,* USDA Forest Service General Technical Report PSW-GTR-133 (Albany, Calif.: USDA Forest Service, Southwest Research Station, July 1992), 13–14.

59. Ibid., chap. 2, 7–8.

60. Steven A. Capps, "Wilson, Lawmakers Unleash Monster State Budget," *California Journal* 12, no. 9 (1991): 395–96.

61. "The League's Perspective on State Budget Policy," *Western City* (May 1993): 3, 22–23.

62. Mary Beth Barber, "Local Government Hits the Wall," *California Journal* 14, no. 8 (1993): 13–15.

63. Manuel Pastor Jr., "Latinos and the Los Angeles Uprising: The Economic Context" (Claremont: Tómas Rivera Center, 1993).

64. Ibid., 25.

65. Ibid., 51–52.

66. Mark Winogrond, "The Riots—One Year After," *California Planner* 4, no. 2 (1993): 1, 7; and Marc Huffman, "Los Angeles' Housing Crisis: A Fresh Perspective," *California Planner* 4, no. 2 (1993): 9, 12.

67. It is worth noting that shortly after the 1992 uprisings, the Bloods and the Crips, well-known and feared rival gangs, got together and wrote a list of demands to the city of Los Angeles. The demands included better pay for teachers, improved vermin control and trash pickup, cleaning and paving of alleys, a network of free health clinics, job training, more parks, and community policing by the gangs themselves.

68. Timothy Williams, "Open Season on Art Agnos," *California Journal* 22, no. 9 (1991): 405–9.

69. By 1996 San Francisco's homeless population was estimated at 12,000.

70. Williams, "Open Season."

71. San Francisco Planning and Urban Research Association, "Bay Vision 2020's Challenge: Politically Realistic Regional Planning," report 263 (San Francisco: San Francisco Planning and Urban Research Association, February 1990).

72. Bay Area Council, Inc., "Bay Area Poll, Solid Support for Regional Planning" (San Francisco: Bay Area Council, Inc. and KQED, Inc., November 1991).

73. Ibid.

74. Ken Hoover, "Bay Area Regional Government Plan Rejected," *San Francisco Chronicle*, 2 September 1992, A13.

75. Niels Erich, "Debating the Shape of the Table," *Citi Report* 12, no. 12 (1991).

Chapter 7 · Conclusion

1. I am using the term *liberalism* in its classical sense.

2. An important literature on liberalism has emerged in the past decade, revisiting its assumptions, analyzing its origins, and questioning its relevance today. The discussion in this chapter is inspired by some of this recent political theory, including works by Charles Taylor, Chantal Mouffe, Alan Wolfe, Jürgen Habermas, William Kymlicka, Iris Marion Young, Ronald Dworkin, Sheldon Wolin, Alain Touraine, Joyce Appleby, and John Rawls.

3. This section is inspired by Joyce Appleby, "Liberalism and Republicanism in the Historical Imagination: Introduction," in *Liberalism and Republicanism in the Historical Imagination* (Cambridge: Harvard University Press, 1992), 13 (quotation).

4. Ronald Dworkin, "The Curse of American Politics," *New York Review of Books* 43, no. 16 (1996).

5. Peter Schrag, "Why California Doesn't Work," *The Nation*, 12 October 1992, 390.

6. Proposition 13 in 1978 imposed restrictions on local government's ability to raise property taxes; Proposition 4 (1979) limited state government expenditures on a complex calculation of population increases and inflation; Proposition 111 (1990) restructured Proposition 4, allocating some funds to transportation and infrastructure repair; Proposition 98 (1988) required the state to appropriate at least 40 percent of its general fund revenues to schools, and so forth.

7. Elizabeth Capell, "The Rich Get Richer: Term Limits and Interest Groups in California," paper presented at the California Studies Association Conference, San Francisco, 1996.

8. Harmon L. Zeigler and Hendrick van Dalen, "Interest Groups in State Politics," in *Politics in the American State*, edited by Herbert Jacob and Kenneth N. Vines (Boston: Little, Brown, 1976), 94–95.

9. John H. Culver and John C. Syer, *Power and Politics in California* (New York: John Wiley and Sons, 1984), 89–90.

10. Richard L. Berke, "Political Notes: What Formula to Feed Voters?" *New York Times*, reprinted in *International Herald Tribune*, 5–6 November 1994, 3.

11. Iris Marion Young, *Justice and the Politics of Difference* (Princeton: Princeton University Press, 1990), 71, 92.

12. John Rawls, "Justice as Fairness: Political Not Metaphysical," *Philosophy and Public Affairs* 14, no. 3 (1985): 223–51.

13. Joyce Appleby, "The American Heritage—The Heirs and the Disinherited," in *Liberalism and Republicanism in the Historical Imagination.*

14. Alain Touraine, *Qu'est-ce que la Démocratie?* (Paris: Fayard, 1994).

15. Rawls, "Justice as Fairness," 244.

16. This section is informed by Sheldon Wolin, "What Revolutionary Action Means Today," in *Dimensions of Radical Democracy: Pluralism, Citizenship, Community,* edited by Chantal Mouffe (London: Verso, 1992), 240–53.

17. Charles Taylor has written about the necessity of developing processes in which there is room and time for such deliberation.

18. Young, *Justice and the Politics of Difference,* 91.

19. This section is inspired by John Rawls, "Justice as Fairness."

20. Lani Guinier, "The Triumph of Tokenism: The Voting Rights Act and the Theory of Black Electoral Success," *Michigan Law Review* 89 (March 1991): 1078–1154.

21. Guinier, "The Triumph of Tokenism," 1097.

22. Thomas Bender, *Community and Social Change in America* (Baltimore: Johns Hopkins University Press, 1978), 149.

23. Young, *Justice and the Politics of Difference,* 93; and Rawls, "Justice as Fairness."

24. Young, *Justice and the Politics of Difference,* 92.

25. Touraine, *Qu'est-ce que la Démocratie?* See also J. H. Carens, "Membership and Morality: Admission to Citizenship in Liberal Democratic States," in *Immigration and the Politics of Citizenship in Europe and North America,* edited by W. R. Brubaker (Lanham, Md.: German Marshall Fund of the United States, 1989).

Bibliography

Acuña, Rodolfo. *Occupied America: A History of Chicanos.* 3rd ed. New York: Harper and Row, 1988.

Adams, Walter, and Horace M. Gray. *Monopoly in America: The Government as Promoter.* New York: Macmillan, 1955.

Albright, Horace Marden, and Newton Bishop Drury. "Horace Marden Albright and Newton Bishop Drury, Comments on Conservation, 1900–1960." Oral history interview by Amelia Fry, Regional Oral History Project, Bancroft Library, University of California, Berkeley, 1962.

Andreano, Ralph. "The Structure of the California Petroleum Industry, 1865–1911." *Pacific Historical Review* 39, no. 2 (1970): 171–204.

Angel, Arthur Desk. "Political and Administrative Aspects of the Central Valley Project of California." Ph.D. diss., University of California, Los Angeles, 1944.

Appleby, Joyce. "Liberalism and Republicanism in the Historical Imagination: Introduction" and "The American Heritage—The Heirs and the Disinherited." In *Liberalism and Republicanism in the Historical Imagination.* Cambridge: Harvard University Press, 1992.

Arax, Mark. "Sprawl Threatens Central Valley, Study Says." *Los Angeles Times,* 26 October 1995, A3, A20.

Arax, Mark, and Virginia Ellis. "Developers Go to War over Water Bill." *Los Angeles Times,* 8 August 1994, A1, A14, A15.

Arvola, T. F. *Regulation of Logging in California, 1945–1975.* Sacramento: California Resources Agency, Department of Conservation, Division of Forestry, 1976.

Babcock, Richard. *The Zoning Game.* Madison: University of Wisconsin Press, 1966.

Balderrama, Francisco E., and Raymond Rodríguez. *Decade of Betrayal: Mexican Repatriation in the 1930s.* Albuquerque: University of New Mexico Press, 1995.

Banda, R. H. *Evaluation of the California State Planning System: The Impact of the 701 Comprehensive Planning Assistance Act on Planning in California.* San Francisco: U.S. Department of Housing and Urban Development, Region IX, Program Planning and Evaluation, April 1974.

Barber, Mary Beth. "Local Government Hits the Wall." *California Journal* 14, no. 8 (1993): 13–15.

Barlett, Donald L., and James B. Steele. *America: What Went Wrong?* Kansas City: Andrews and McMeel, 1992.

Bay Area Council, Inc. "Bay Area Poll, Solid Support for Regional Planning." San Francisco: Bay Area Council, Inc. and KQED, Inc., November 1991.

Bay Area Economic Forum. *Using Water Better: A Market-Based Approach to California's Water Crisis.* San Francisco: Bay Area Economic Forum, October 1991.

Bender, Thomas. *Community and Social Change in America.* Baltimore: Johns Hopkins University Press, 1978.

Berke, Richard L. "Political Notes: What Formula to Feed Voters?" *New York Times.* Reprinted in *International Herald Tribune,* 5–6 November 1994.

Berkowitz, Madelon Helfer. "Progressivism and the Anti-Japanese Agitation in California." Master's thesis, Stanford University, 1963.

Blackburn, Dan. "Saving the Sierra, Master Plan for the Range of Light." *California Journal* 13, no. 2 (1992): 103–5.

Blackford, Mansel G. *The Politics of Business in California, 1890–1920.* Columbus: Ohio State University Press, 1977.

Blight, Ronald E. "Municipal Government 50 Years from Now." *California Outlook* 11 (21 October 1911).

Bonnett, M., and K. Zimmerman. "Politics and Preservation: The Endangered Species Act and the Northern Spotted Owl." *Ecology Law Quarterly* 18 (1991): 105–71.

Bowker, Michael."Going for the Green." *Defenders* (March–April 1988): 18–20.

Boyer, M. Christine. *Dreaming the Rational City: The Myth of American City Planning.* Cambridge: MIT Press, 1983; paperback ed., 1986.

Brechin, Gray. "Termites." *Upriver, Downriver* (fall 1993).

Buenker, John D. *Urban Liberalism and Progressive Reform.* New York: W. W. Norton, 1973.

Burke, Robert E. *Olson's New Deal for California.* Berkeley: University of California Press, 1953.

Burton, Dudley J., and Irvine Alpert. "The Decline of California's North Coast Redwood Region." *Policy Studies Journal* 10, no. 2 (1981): 272–85.

California Department of Forestry. *California's Forest Resources: Preliminary Assessment.* Sacramento: Department of Natural Resources, 1979.

"California Voters Lead Nation in Growth Management and Conservation Ballot." *Successful Communities: The Newsletter of Growth Management* 1, no. 1 (1988): 2.

Capell, Elizabeth. "The Rich Get Richer: Term Limits and Interest Groups in California." Paper presented at California Studies Association Conference, San Francisco, 1996.

Capps, Steven A. "Revenue Increases." *California Journal* 12, no. 9 (1991): 398.

———. "Wilson, Lawmakers Unleash Monster State Budget." *California Journal* 12, no. 9 (1991): 395–96.

Carens, J. H. "Membership and Morality: Admission to Citizenship in Liberal Democratic States." In *Immigration and the Politics of Citizenship in Europe and North*

America, edited by W. R. Brubaker. Lanham, Md.: German Marshall Fund of the United States, 1989.

Chan, Sucheng. *This Bitter-sweet Soil: The Chinese in California Agriculture, 1860–1910.* Berkeley: University of California Press, 1989. Reprint of 1986 edition.

Chase, Lillianne. "Funny-money Classrooms." *Golden State Report* (September 1986): 33–35.

Choy, Philip P. "Golden Mountain of Lead: The Chinese Experience in California." *California Historical Quarterly* 50, no. 3 (1971): 267–76.

Clar, Raymond C. *California Government and Forestry from Spanish Days until the Creation of the Department of Natural Resources.* Sacramento: California Department of Natural Resources, Division of Forestry, 1959.

Clark, Jeanne. "NCCP—A New Approach to Saving Species." *Outdoor California* (March–April 1994): 4–9.

Clifford, Frank. "Landmark Accord Reached on Use of Bay-Delta Water." *Los Angeles Times,* 16 December 1994.

———. "Land Swap to Preserve Old Redwood Forest Takes Root." *Los Angeles Times,* 25 July 1996.

———. "Sierra on the Precipice." *Los Angeles Times,* 2 June 1996.

Cockburn, Alexander. "Serpent's Tooth: A Radical's Confidence in Grassroots Activism: An Interview with Sharon Duggan." *Wild Forest Review* 1, no. 8 (1994): 8–12.

"Congress Gives West to Biggies." *People Food and Land: The Land for People Quarterly Journal* 3, no. 2 (1982): 35–36.

Conserving the California Spotted Owl: Impacts of Interim Policies and Implications for the Long Term. Report of the Policy Implementation Planning Team to the Steering Committee for the California Spotted Owl Assessment. Report 33. Davis: University of California, Wildland Resources Center, Division of Agriculture and Natural Resources, May 1994.

Cooper, Erwin. *Aqueduct Empire: A Guide to Water in California: Its Turbulent History and Management Today.* Glendale: Arthur H. Clark Co., 1968.

Culver, John H., and John C. Syer. *Power and Politics in California.* New York: John Wiley and Sons, 1984.

Davis, Mike. "*Chinatown,* Revisited? The 'Internationalization' of Downtown Los Angeles." In *Sex, Death and God in LA,* edited by David Reid. New York: Pantheon, 1992.

———. "Imperial Pirates." *Los Angeles Weekly,* 23–29 February 1996.

DeLeon, Richard Edward. *Left Coast City: Progressive Politics in San Francisco, 1975–1991.* Lawrence: University of Kansas Press, 1992.

Deverell, William. "The Neglected Twin: California Democrats and the Progressive Bandwagon." In *California Progressivism Revisited,* edited by William Deverell and Tom Sitton. Berkeley: University of California Press, 1994.

———. *Railroad Crossing: Californians and the Railroad, 1850–1910.* Berkeley: University of California Press, 1994.

Deverell, William, and Tom Sitton, eds. *California Progressivism Revisited.* Berkeley: University of California Press, 1994.

Dilsaver, Larry M., and William C. Tweed. *Challenge of the Big Trees of Sequoia and Kings Canyon National Parks.* Three Rivers: Sequoia Natural History Association, 1990.

"Down on the Corporate Farm." *Amicus Journal* 19, no. 3 (1997): 8.

Durbin, Katie. "The Timber Salvage Scam." *Amicus Journal* 17, no. 3 (1995): 29–31.

Dworkin, Ronald. "The Curse of American Politics." *New York Review of Books* 43, no. 16 (1996): 19–24.

Egelko, Bob. "Legislators Want Reins Placed on U.C. Spending." *Sacramento Bee,* 11 May 1977.

Eichler, Ned. *The Merchant Builders.* Cambridge: MIT Press, 1982.

Endangered Habitats League Newsletter (January–February 1993).

Epstein, Jack. "Raiding the Redwoods."*California Business* (September 1987): 34–45.

Erich, Niels. "Debating the Shape of the Table." *Citi Report* 12, no. 12 (1991).

Erie, Steven P. "How the Urban West Was Won: The Local State and Economic Growth in Los Angeles, 1880–1932." *Urban Affairs Quarterly* 27, no. 4 (1992): 519–54.

Faragher, John Mack. *Sugar Creek: Life on the Illinois Prairie.* New Haven: Yale University Press, 1986.

Fay, James S., ed., and Ronald J. Boehm, pub. *California Almanac.* 6th ed. Santa Barbara: Pacific Data Resources, 1993.

Fellmeth, Robert. *Ralph Nader's Study Group on Land in California.* New York: Grossman, 1973.

Fisher, J. Donald. *A Historical Study of the Migrant in California.* 1945. Reprint. San Francisco: R&E Research Associates, 1973.

Fisher, Michael L. "California's Coastal Program." *Journal of the American Planning Association* 15 (summer 1985): 312–21.

Fishman, Robert. *Bourgeois Utopias: The Rise and Fall of Suburbia.* New York: Basic Books, 1987.

Florian, Monica, vice president, Irvine Company. Letter to Douglas P. Wheeler, secretary of the State Resources Agency, 2 April 1991. Photocopy in the files of the Endangered Habitats League, Los Angeles.

Fogelson, Robert M. *The Fragmented Metropolis: Los Angeles, 1850–1930.* Cambridge: Harvard University Press, 1967.

Fradkin, Philip. "California Water War Boils Over Again." *Los Angeles Times,* 6 January 1975.

Fulton, William. "City vs. County." *Golden State Report* (September 1989): 12.

———. *Guide to California Planning.* Point Arena: Solano Press, 1991.

Gates, Paul W. *Land and Law in California: Essays on Land Policy.* Iowa: Iowa State University Press, 1991.

Gentry, Curt. "Iron Heel on the California Coast." In *The New Book of California To-*

morrow: Reflections and Projections from the Golden State, edited by John Hart. Los Altos: William Kaufman, 1984.

George, Henry. *Our Land and Land Policy.* San Francisco, 1871.

Gilliam, Harold. "Beating Back the Bulldozers." *Saturday Review,* 23 September 1967, 67–74.

Goldschmidt, Walter R. *Small Business and the Community: A Study in the Central Valley of California of Effects of Scale Farm Operations.* Report of the U.S. Senate Special Committee to Study Problems of American Small Business. 79th Cong., 2nd sess., 1946.

Goodall, Merrill R., and John D. Sullivan. "Water District Organization: Political Decision Systems." In *California Water Planning and Policy, Selected Issues,* edited by Ernest A. Engelbert. Berkeley: University of California, Institute of Governmental Affairs, Water Resources Center, June 1979.

Gottlieb, Robert, and Irene Wolt. *Thinking Big: The Story of the Los Angeles Times, Its Publishers, and Their Influence on Southern California.* New York: George Putnam's Sons, 1967.

Governor's Commission on Metropolitan Area Problems. *Meeting Metropolitan Problems.* Sacramento, December 1960.

Governor's Office of Planning and Research. "An Urban Strategy for California." Sacramento, February 1978.

Gravelle, Marie. "Reaping the Redwoods." *Golden State Report* (March 1990): 27–30.

Guinier, Lani. "The Triumph of Tokenism: The Voting Rights Act and the Theory of Black Electoral Success." *Michigan Law Review* 89 (March 1991): 1078–1154.

Haar, Charles H., and M. A. Wolf. *Land-Use Planning: A Casebook on the Use, Misuse and Re-use of Urban Land.* Boston: Little, Brown, 1989.

Handel, Mary E., and Alvin D. Sokolow. "Farmland and Open Space Preservation in the Four North Bay Counties." Davis: Behavioral Sciences, Cooperative Extension, University of California, Davis, May 1994.

Harvey, Richard B. "California Politics: Historical Profile." In *California Politics and Policies,* edited by Eugene P. Dvorin and Arthur J. Misner. Reading, Mass.: Addison-Wesley, 1966.

———. *The Dynamics of California Government and Politics.* Belmont: Wadsworth: 1970.

Hawley, Elias W. *The New Deal and the Problems of Monopoly: A Study in Economic Ambivalence.* Princeton: Princeton University Press, 1969.

Hays, Samuel P. *Conservation and the Gospel of Efficiency: The Progressive Conservation Movement, 1890–1920.* Cambridge: Harvard University Press, 1959.

———. *The Response to Industrialization, 1855–1914.* Chicago: University of Chicago Press, 1957.

Heiman, Michael. *The Quiet Evolution: Power, Planning and Profits in New York State.* New York: Praeger, 1988.

Heller, Alfred, ed. *The California Tomorrow Plan.* Los Altos: William Kaufman, 1971.

Hichborn, Frank. *Story of the Legislature of 1911.* San Francisco: Press of the James H. Barry Co., 1911.

———. "Why the Corporations Win before the State Railroad Commission." Santa Clara, Calif., 1926. Pamphlet. Bancroft Library, Special Collections, University of California, Berkeley.

Higgens, C. A. *A New Guide to the Pacific Coast: Santa Fe Route.* Chicago: Rand McNally, 1895.

Hinderaker, Ivan. "Politics of Reapportionment." In *California Politics and Policies,* edited by Eugene P. Dvorin and Arthur J. Misner. Reading, Mass.: Addison-Wesley, 1966.

Hise, Greg. *Magnetic Los Angeles: Planning the Twentieth-century Metropolis.* Baltimore: Johns Hopkins University Press, 1997.

Hofstadter, Richard. *The Age of Reform.* New York: Vintage Books, 1955.

Hoover, Ken. "Bay Area Regional Government Plan Rejected." *San Francisco Chronicle,* 2 September 1992.

"How the New Energy Act Should Work." *California Journal* 5, no. 7 (1974): 239–40.

Hudson, Dale A. "*Sierra Club v. Department of the Interior:* The Fight to Save Redwood National Park." *Ecology Law Quarterly* 7 (1978): 781–859.

Huffman, Marc. "Los Angeles' Housing Crisis: A Fresh Perspective." *California Planner* 4, no. 2 (1993): 3.

Hundley, Norris, Jr. *The Great Thirst: Californians and Water, 1770s–1990s.* Berkeley: University of California Press, 1992.

Hurt, Elsey. *California State Government: An Outline of Its Administrative Organization from 1850 to 1936.* Sacramento: Supervisor of Documents, 1936.

Hyde, Anne F. "William Kent: The Puzzle of Progressive Conservationists." In *California Progressivism Revisited,* edited by William Deverell and Tom Sitton. Berkeley: University of California Press, 1994.

Issel, William. "'Citizens outside the Government': Business and Urban Policy in San Francisco and Los Angeles, 1890–1932." *Pacific Historical Review* 57, no. 2 (1988): 117–45.

Jackson, Kenneth. *Crabgrass Frontier: The Suburbanization of the United States.* New York: Oxford University Press, 1985.

Jensen, Deborah, Margaret S. Torn, and John Harte. *In Our Own Hands: A Strategy for Conserving California's Biological Diversity.* Berkeley: University of California Press, 1993.

Jerome, Gary, Peter Detwiler, and Leslie McFadden. "Challenges and Opportunities." Working paper for the New Regionalism Project of the California Senate Select Committee on Planning for California Growth, Senate Committee on Local Government, Senator Marian Bergeson, chair. Sacramento, 1988.

Johnson, Stephen, Gerald Haslam, and Robert Dawson. *The Great Central Valley, California's Heartland.* Berkeley: University of California Press, 1993.

"Jurisdictional Disputes Slow Efforts to Give the State an Effective Role in Solid Waste Management." *California Journal* 3, no. 10 (1971): 279, 284.

Kahrl, William L., Marlyn L. Shelton, and William A. Bowen. *The California Water Atlas.* Sacramento: General Services Publication Division of the State of California, 1978.

Katcher, Leo. *Earl Warren: A Political Biography.* New York: McGraw-Hill, 1967.

Kazin, Michael. *Barons of Labor: The San Francisco Building Trades and Union Power in the Progressive Era.* Urbana: University of Illinois Press, 1987.

Kersten, Elizabeth, Steve Sanders, and Diane Turner. *Does California Need a Policy to Manage Urban Growth?* Report from the Senate Urban Growth Policy Project, Senate Office of Research. Sacramento, June 1989.

Knudson, Tom. "Majesty and Tragedy: The Sierra in Peril." *Sacramento Bee,* special report, June 1991.

Koppes, Clayton. "Public Water, Private Land: Origins of the Acreage Limitation Controversy, 1933–1953." *Pacific Historical Review* 47 (November 1978): 607–36.

Kotkin, Joel, and Paul Grabowicz. *California Inc.* New York: Rawson Wade, 1982.

"The League's Perspective on State Budget Policy." *Western City* (May 1993): 3–4, 22–23.

LeGates, Robert T. *California Local Agency Formation Commissions.* Berkeley: University of California, Institute of Governmental Affairs, 1970.

"Legislative Summary." *California Journal* 2, no. 8 (8 August 1970): 228–30.

Lewis, Henry T. "Patterns of Indian Burning in California: Ecology and Ethnohistory." In *Before the Wilderness: Environmental Management by Native Californians,* compiled and edited by Thomas C. Blackburn and Kat Anderson. Menlo Park: Ballena Press, 1993.

Liebman, Ellen. *California Farmland: A History of Large Agricultural Landholdings.* Totowa, N.J.: Rowman and Allenheld, 1983.

Lo, Clarence Y. H. *Small Property versus Big Government: Social Origins of the Property Tax Revolt.* Berkeley: University of California Press, 1990.

Logan, John, and Harvey Molotch. *Urban Fortunes: The Political Economy of Place.* Berkeley: University of California Press, 1987.

Lukes, Timothy, and Gary Y. Okihiro. *Japanese Legacy: Farming and Community Life in California's Santa Clara Valley.* Local History Studies 31. Cupertino: California History Center, 1985.

Lummis, C. Douglas. *Radical Democracy.* Ithaca: Cornell University Press, 1996.

Lundmark, Thomas. "Regulation of Private Logging in California." *Ecology Law Quarterly* 5, no. 139 (1975): 139–88.

MacCannell, Dean. "The Effect of Agricultural Scale on Communities" and "Industrial Agriculture and the Degradation of Rural Communities in the United States Sunbelt." Unpublished reports on research conducted by Microsocial Accounting Project, University of California, Davis, n.d. (c. 1986).

Markusen, Ann A. *Regions: The Economics and Politics of Territory.* Totowa, N.J.: Rowman and Littlefield, 1987.

McConnell, Grant. *The Decline of Agrarian Democracy.* Berkeley: University of California Press, 1953.

McEvoy, Arthur. *The Fisherman's Problem: Ecology and Law in the California Fisheries, 1850–1980.* Cambridge: Cambridge University Press, 1986.

McWilliams, Carey. *California: The Great Exception.* 1949. Reprint. Santa Barbara: Peregrine Smith, 1979.

———. "Look What's Happened to California." In *The Politics of California: A Book of Readings,* edited by David Farrelly and Ivan Hinderaker. New York: Ronald Press, 1951.

Meadows, Donella H., Dennis L. Meadows, Jorgen Randers, and William W. Behrens III. *The Limits to Growth.* New York: New American Library, 1972.

Mendel, Ed. "The Politics of Toxics." *Golden State Report* (September 1986): 13–16.

Milias, George. "Interview with George Milias: Legislating for the Environment." *California Journal* 2, no. 11 (1970): 316–17.

Miller, G. J. *Cities by Contract: The Politics of Municipal Incorporation.* Cambridge: MIT Press, 1981.

Mollenkopf, John H. *The Contested City.* Princeton: Princeton University Press, 1983.

Molotch, Harvey. "Santa Barbara: Oil in the Velvet Playground." In *Eco-Catastrophe,* by the editors of *Ramparts.* San Francisco: Canfield Press, Harper and Row, 1970.

Montgomery, Mary, and Marion Clawson. "History of Legislation and Policy Formation of the Central Valley Project." Sacramento: U.S. Department of the Interior, Bureau of Reclamation, Region III, 1946.

Mowry, George E. *The California Progressives.* Berkeley: University of California Press, 1951.

Nabokov, Peter, and Robert Easton. *Native American Architecture.* New York: Oxford University Press, 1989.

Nash, Gerald. *A. P. Giannini and the Bank of America.* Norman: University of Oklahoma Press, 1992.

———. *State Government and Economic Development: A History of Administrative Policies in California, 1849–1933.* Berkeley: University of California, Institute of Governmental Affairs, 1964.

National Land for People. "Intent of Reclamation: Bureaucrats Subvert Reclamation Intent." Fresno, March 1979.

———. "Is This a Railroad Station or a Farmhouse?" Fresno, March 1978.

Nelson, DeWitt. "Management of Natural Resources in California 1925–1966." Oral history interview by Amelia Fry. Forest History Society and Regional Oral History Project, Bancroft Library, Berkeley, 1976.

Newman, Morris. "New Deals for Colorado River Water Called Landmark." *California Planning and Development Report* 11, no. 2 (1996): 1, 10.

Oakes, Timothy. "Place and the Paradox of Modernity." *Annals of the Association of American Geographers* 87, no. 3 (1997): 509–31.

Odell, Rice. *The Saving of San Francisco Bay: A Report on Citizen Action and Regional Planning.* Washington, D.C.: Conservation Foundation, 1972.

O'Leary, John. "Coastal Sage Scrub: Threats and Current Status." *Fremontia* 23, no. 4 (1995): 27–31.

Olin, Spencer C., Jr. *California Politics, 1846–1920: The Emerging Corporate State.* San Francisco: Boyd and Frazer, 1981.

———. *California's Prodigal Sons: Hiram Johnson and the Progressives, 1911–1917* (Berkeley: University of California Press, 1968).

Orsi, Richard J. "*The Octopus* Reconsidered: The Southern Pacific and Agricultural Modernization in California, 1865–1915." *California Historical Quarterly* 5, no. 3 (1975): 197–220.

Panunzio, Constantine. *Self-help Cooperatives in Los Angeles.* Publications of the University of California at Los Angeles in Social Sciences 8, no. 1. Berkeley: University of California Press, 1939.

Paquette, Pat. "The Environment and Jobs, Seeking Balance between Owls and People." *California Journal* 14, no. 2 (1993): 15–18.

Pastor, Manuel, Jr. "Latinos and the Los Angeles Uprising: The Economic Context." Claremont: Tómas Rivera Center, 1993.

Pastor, Manuel, Jr., and Dennis Zane, eds. "The California Dilemma." Los Angeles: California Council for the Humanities, 1991.

Petty, Diana. "North Coast Dilemma: To Cut or to Conserve." *California Journal* 5, no. 10 (1975): 405–7.

Pincetl, Stephanie. "The Regional Management of Growth in California: A History of Failure." *International Journal of Urban and Regional Research* 18, no. 2 (1994): 256–74.

———. "Roads Not Taken: The Environmental Policies and Politics of the Brown Administration, 1975–1983." Ph.D. diss., University of California, Los Angeles, 1985.

Pinchot, Gifford. *Breaking New Ground.* New York: Harcourt Brace, 1947.

Pisani, Donald. *From the Family Farm to Agribusiness: The Irrigation Crusade in California and the West, 1850–1931.* Berkeley: University of California Press, 1984.

———. *To Reclaim a Divided West: Water, Law, and Public Policy, 1848–1902.* Albuquerque: University of New Mexico Press, 1992.

Platzek, Rudy. "California's Most Important Choice: An Agricultural or Urban Central Valley." *California Planner* (November–December 1995): 8–9.

Plotkin, Sidney. *Keep Out: The Struggle for Land Use Control.* Berkeley: University of California Press, 1987.

Preston, William L. *Vanishing Landscapes: Land and Life in the Tulare Lake Basin.* Berkeley: University of California Press, 1981.

Putnam, Jackson K. "The Progressive Legacy in California: Fifty Years of Politics, 1917–1967." In *California Progressivism Revisited,* edited by William Deverell and Tom Sitton. Berkeley: University of California Press, 1994.

Rawls, John. "Justice as Fairness: Political Not Metaphysical." *Philosophy and Public Affairs* 14, no. 3 (1985): 223–51.

Robbins, William G. *American Forestry: A History of National, State, and Private Cooperation.* Lincoln: University of Nebraska Press, 1985.

————. *Lumberjacks and Legislators: Political Economy of the U.S. Lumber Industry, 1890–1941.* College Station: Texas A&M University Press, 1982.

Rodgers, Daniel T. "In Search of Progressivism." *Reviews in American History* 10 (1982): 113–49.

Romo, Ricardo. *East Los Angeles: History of a Barrio.* Austin: University of Texas Press, 1977.

Rood, W. B. "Brown's Water Bill Defeated in Senate." *Los Angeles Times,* 3 February 1978.

Rood, W. B., and Bill Stall. "Who'll Get Water? U.S., State at Odds." *Los Angeles Times,* 3 October 1976.

Rose, Edward J. *Henry George.* New York: Twayne, 1968.

Rosen, Michael D. "Conflict within Irrigation Districts May Limit Water Transfer Gains." *California Agriculture* 46, no. 6 (1992): 2.

Rubin, Hal. "Combat Zone." *Golden State Report* (February 1989): 37–40.

Runte, Alfred. *Yosemite, The Embattled Wilderness.* Lincoln: University of Nebraska Press, 1990.

Salzman, Ed. "The Next California?" *Golden State Report* (December 1988): 15–20.

Sánchez, George J. *Becoming Mexican-American: Ethnicity, Culture, and Identity in Chicano Los Angeles, 1900–1945.* New York: Oxford University Press, 1993.

San Francisco Chamber of Commerce. *Activities* 3 (1 June 1916).

San Francisco Planning and Urban Research Association. "Bay Vision 2020's Challenge: Politically Realistic Regional Planning." Report 263. San Francisco: San Francisco Planning and Urban Research Association, February 1990.

Sauder, Robert A. *The Lost Frontier: Water Diversion in the Growth and Destruction of Owens Valley Agriculture.* Tucson: University of Arizona Press, 1994.

Schrag, Peter. "Why California Doesn't Work." *The Nation,* 12 October 1992.

Schrepfer, Susan. *The Fight to Save the Redwoods: A History of Environmental Reform, 1917–1978.* Madison: University of Wisconsin Press, 1983.

Schumacher, E. F. *Small Is Beautiful.* New York: Harper Torchbooks, 1973.

Scott, Mel. *American City Planning since 1890.* Berkeley: University of California Press, 1969.

Scott, Stanley, and John C. Bollens. *Governing a Metropolitan Region: The San Francisco Bay Area.* Berkeley: University of California, Institute of Governmental Affairs, 1968.

Scott, Steve. "Budget Dysfunction," *California Journal* 28, no. 9 (1997): 8–11.

Simmons, Bob. "The Freeway Establishment." *Cry California* 2, no. 2 (1968). Reprinted in *The New Book of California Tomorrow: Reflections and Projections from the Golden State,* edited by John Hart. Los Altos: William Kaufman, 1984.

Simons, Teresa. "Epic Struggle over Redwoods." *California Journal* 11, no. 3 (1990): 151–56.

Sitton, Tom. *John Randolph Haynes, California Progressive.* Stanford: Stanford University Press, 1992.

Sklar, Martin J. *The Corporate Reconstruction of American Capitalism, 1890–1916: The Market, the Law and Politics.* New York: Cambridge University Press, 1988.

Skocpol, Theda. *Protecting Soldiers and Mothers: The Political Origins of Social Policy in the United States.* Cambridge: Belknap Press of Harvard University Press, 1995. First published 1992.

Skowronek, Stephen. *Building a New American State: The Expansion of National Administrative Capacities, 1877–1920.* Cambridge: Cambridge University Press, 1982.

Smith, Michael. *Pacific Visions: California Scientists and the Environment, 1850–1915.* New Haven: Yale University Press, 1987.

Soja, Edward W. *Postmodern Geographies: The Reassertion of Space in Critical Social Theory.* London: Verso, 1989.

Sokolow, Alvin D. "Everything Is Coming Up Houses." *California Journal* 21, no. 11 (1990): 535–37.

———. "The Williamson Act, 25 Years of Land Conservation." Sacramento: Department of Conservation, December 1990.

Starr, Kevin. *Americans and the California Dream, 1850–1915.* New York: Oxford University Press, 1973.

———. *Inventing the Dream: California through the Progressive Era.* New York: Oxford University Press, 1985.

Sterngold, James. "Foiling the Best Laid Plans." *New York Times,* 17 September 1995.

Storper, Michael, and Richard Walker. "The Price of Water: Surplus and Subsidy in the California State Water Project." Berkeley: University of California, Institute of Governmental Affairs, 1984.

Strong, Douglas. "The Sierra Forest Reserve: The Movement to Preserve the San Joaquin Valley Watershed." *California Historical Society Quarterly* 46 (1967): 3–17.

———. *Tahoe: An Environmental History.* Lincoln: University of Nebraska Press, 1984.

Sward, Susan. "Ecology Study OKs Plan for Key Canal Link." *Los Angeles Times,* 5 September 1974.

Swezey, Sean L., and Robert F. Heizer. "Ritual Management of Salmonid Fish Resources in California." In *Before the Wilderness: Environmental Management by Native Californians,* compiled and edited by Thomas C. Blackburn and Kat Anderson. Menlo Park: Ballena Press, 1993.

Taylor, Charles. *Philosophical Arguments.* Cambridge: Harvard University Press, 1997.

———. "The Politics of Recognition." In *Multiculturalism and "The Politics of Recognition,"* edited by Amy Gutman. Princeton: Princeton University Press, 1992.

Taylor, Paul. "Migrants and California's Future" and "What Shall We Do with Them?" In *On the Ground in the Thirties.* Salt Lake City: Gibbs M. Smith, Peregine Smith Books, 1983.

Timmons, Terry. *Structural Speculation as a Dynamic of Urban Growth: A Case Study of the Irvine Company.* Ph.D. diss. Ann Arbor, Mich.: University Microfilms International, 1993.

Touraine, Alain. *Qu'est-ce que la Démocratie?* Paris: Fayard, 1994.

U.S. Congress, House Committee on Natural Resources. *Legislative History, Miscellaneous Articles, and Background Information Related to Public Law 102-575, Reclamation Projects Authorization and Adjustment Act of 1992.* 103rd Cong., 1st sess., November 1993.

Verner, Jared, K. McKelvey, B. Noon. R. Gutierrez, G. Gould, and T. Beck. *The California Spotted Owl: A Technical Assessment of Its Current Status.* U.S. Department of Agriculture, Forest Service General Technical Report PSW-GTR-133. Albany, Calif.: USDA Forest Service, Southwest Research Station, July 1992.

Viehe, Fred W. "The First Recall: Los Angeles Urban Reform or Machine Politics?" *Southern California Quarterly* 70, no. 1 (1988): 1–28.

Walker, Richard, and Michael Heiman. "Quiet Revolution for Whom?" *Annals of the Association of American Geographers* 71, no. 1 (1981): 67–83.

Walker, Richard, and Michael Storper. "The Expanding California Water System." Reprint. San Francisco: Pacific Division, American Association for the Advancement of Science, 1982.

Walsh, James P. "Abe Ruef Was No Boss: Machine Politics, Reform and San Francisco." *California Historical Quarterly* 51, no. 1 (1972): 3–16.

Weiss, Marc. *The Rise of the Community Builders.* New York: Columbia University Press, 1987.

"Westland Biggies Scrap over Board Control, But SP Runs the Show . . ." *People Food and Land: The Land for People Quarterly Journal* 2, nos. 3–4 (1981): 118–19.

Wheeler, Douglas P. Abstract of "Creating a State Strategy for Habitat Protection: The California Biodiversity Plan by the Resources Agency of California." 1991. Reprinted in *Our Lands: New Strategies for Protecting the West, Blueprints for Action.* Sacramento: California State Resources Agency, 1993.

Williams, Michael. *Americans and Their Forests: A Historical Geography.* Cambridge: Cambridge University Press, 1989.

Williams, R. Hal. *The Democratic Party and California Politics, 1880–1896.* Stanford: Stanford University Press, 1973.

Williams, Timothy. "Open Season on Art Agnos." *California Journal* 22, no. 9 (1991): 405–9.

Winogrond, Mark. "The Riots—One Year After." *California Planner* 4, no. 2 (1993): 2.

Wolfe, Alan. *The Limits of Legitimacy: Political Contradictions of Contemporary Capitalism.* New York: Free Press, 1977.

Wolfe, Linnie Marsh. *Son of the Wilderness: The Life of John Muir.* Madison: University of Wisconsin Press, 1978.

Wolin, Sheldon. "What Revolutionary Action Means Today." In *Dimensions of Radical Democracy: Pluralism, Citizenship, Community,* edited by Chantal Mouffe. London: Verso, 1992.

Wollenberg, Charles. *Golden Gate Metropolis: Perspectives on Bay Area History.* Berkeley: University of California, Institute of Governmental Affairs, 1985.

Wood, S. E., and Alfred Heller. *California Going, Going . . .* Sacramento: California Tomorrow, 1962.

World Commission on Environment and Development. *Our Common Future.* Oxford:
Oxford University Press, 1987.

"The Wrap-up: Reclamation, Death of an American Promise." *People Food and Land:
The Land for People Quarterly Journal* 3, no. 3 (1985): 67.

Wycoff, William. *The Developer's Frontier: The Making of the Western New York Landscape.* New Haven: Yale University Press, 1988.

Young, Iris Marion. *Justice and the Politics of Difference.* Princeton: Princeton University Press, 1990.

Zeigler, Harmon L., and Hendrick van Dalen. "Interest Groups in State Politics." In
Politics in the American State, edited by Herbert Jacob and Kenneth N. Vines. Boston: Little, Brown, 1976.

Index

References to figures are printed in italic type.

AB 1600 (1987), 249–50

AB 1986 (1998), 267–68

accountability: citizenship and, 318; Local Agency Formation Commissions (LAFCOs) and, 143; of local government, 226

acreage limitation for farms, 90, 168–69, 217, 218–19, 220–21. *See also* Newlands Reclamation Act

activism: compared to citizenship, 314; Howard Jarvis, 224; National Land for People (NLP), 215–17; in 1970s, 236; People for Open Space (POS), 229–30; property tax revolt, 222–25; road-building plans, 148–49; San Joaquin Valley farmers, 213–15; Santa Monica Mountain preservation, 233–34; suburbanization process, 145–48; United Farm Workers, 176, 216, 217–18. *See also* environmentalism

African Americans, 133, 298, 313–14

Agnos, Art, 298, 299

Agricultural Adjustment Act (1933), 76

Agricultural Assessment Law (1957), 145

Agricultural Workers Industrial Union Local 111, 82

agriculture: on Central Valley Project and federal control, 89–90; on Central Valley Project Improvement Act, 262; corporate, 9, 77–78, 93–94, 96–97, 174, 177; family *vs.* corporate farm town, 176–78, 221–22; immigrant labor in, 79–85, 93, 217; land-grant colleges, 217–18; self-regulation of, 79; small farm ideal, vii–viii, 84–85, 89, 90; State Water Project and, 168–74; suburban expansion into prime land for, 147–48; water transfer and, 260, 265; water use by, 206, 209, 261. *See also* Central Valley Project

Aid to Families with Dependent Children, 294

air pollution, 184, 272–74, 292–93

Alameda County, 146

alienation, from political system, 186, 309–10, 311

All American Canal, 264

Alta California, 2

American Association for the Advancement of Science, 15

Anderson, John B. "Jack," 218

Andrus, Cecil, 211

annexation, 248

anti-urbanism, 192–93

Apartment House Association of Los Angeles County, 224, 225

apportionment, xvi, 96–99, 109, 180–82

Arbit, Hal, 268, 279

Arendt, Hannah, 317

Arvin, 176–77

Asian immigrants to San Francisco, 298

Associated Farmers, 83

ABOUT THE AUTHOR

STEPHANIE S. PINCETL is a native Californian who lived and worked a number of years in France. She received her Ph.D. degree in Urban Planning from the University of California at Los Angeles. She is a research associate professor of geography and coordinator of the Sustainable Cities Program at the University of Southern California. She serves on several environmental justice nonprofit boards in California and is a member of the Société d'Economie et de Science Sociales and a contributing correspondent to *Les Etudes Sociales.* Dr. Pincetl has received awards for her scholarly papers, two William Fulbright Scholarships, and a V. S. Ciriacy Wantrup postdoctoral research fellowship. She has been appointed by the Centre National de Recherche Scientifique as a research associate in urban and immigration studies.

Library of Congress Cataloging-in-Publication Data

Pincetl, Stephanie Sabine, 1952–

Transforming California : a political history of land use
and development / Stephanie S. Pincetl

p. cm.

Includes bibliographical references and index.

ISBN 0-8018-6110-1 (alk. paper)

1. Land use—California—History. 2. Land use—
Government policy—California—History. 3. Land use—
Environmental aspects—California—Planning—History.
4. Land use—Economic aspects—California—Planning—
History. 5. Cities and towns—Growth—California—
History. I. Title.

HD211.C2P56 1999

333.73'13'09794—dc21   99-11398

CIP